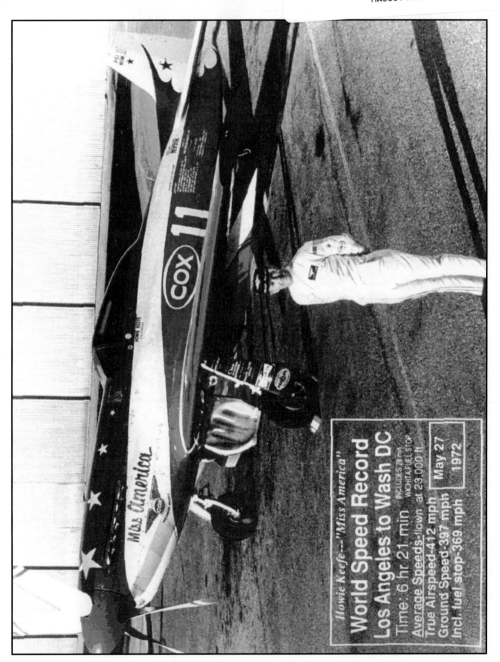

Howie Keefe—"Miss America"

World Speed Record
Los Angeles to Wash DC.

Time: 6 hr 21 min   INCLUDES 28 min.
WICHITA FUEL STOP

Average Speeds-flown at 23,000 ft.
True Airspeed-412 mph
Ground Speed-397 mph
Incl. fuel stop-369 mph

May 27
1972

The instrument panel of Miss America. *The top eyebrow panel has the clock to tell what lap I'm on. The cluster of seven small instruments at left (induction, coolant in/out, etc.) are for easy viewing during left turn pylon races such as Reno and Miami. The clockwise (right turn) courses such as Mojave and San Diego made it tougher to monitor these and still watch for pylons on my right.*

The Legendary P-51 Mustang "MISS AMERICA"

GALLOPING ON WINGS

With the P-51 Mustang

At Dulles Airport, Washington, DC after setting the speed record from Los Angeles in 6 hours, 21 minutes. Note exhaust airflow pattern.

The Legendary P-51 Mustang "MISS AMERICA"

GALLOPING ON WINGS

With the P-51 Mustang

Diary of an air race pilot

Howie Keefe

Cross-country races, navigation and IFR flying, pylon races at Reno, Mojave, San Diego, Miami and Cape May

Aviation Supplies & Academics, Inc.
Newcastle, Washington

Galloping on Wings with the P-51 Mustang
"Miss America"
by Howie Keefe

Aviation Supplies & Academics, Inc.
7005 132nd Place SE
Newcastle, Washington 98059
Website: www.asa2fly.com
Email: asa@asa2fly.com

Published 2007 by Aviation Supplies & Academics, Inc.
(First hardcover edition published by Prestige Group, 2001.)

Photography and illustration credits/acknowledgement: All photographs, illustrations, and articles are from the author's collection (unless otherwise indicated), and are either owned by the author or used by permission. Photo of Cleveland air race crash of 1946 on page 92, copyright Western Reserve Historical Society, Cleveland, Ohio, used by permission. Photo page 104 copyright Paul Neuman, used by permission. Some of the air race-related photography in this book comes from John Tegler's extensive collection (*Gentlemen, You Have a Race: A History of the Reno National Championship Air Races,* 1984) and is used by permission (as is the excerpt reprinted on page 295).

Cover photo © Buddy Childers, used by permission. Taken at California Air Races, Mojave, CA— Photographer in foreground is Bill Johnson. The wingtip looked so close in his viewfinder, he dove left. Next frame showed him parallel to the ground.

Printed in the United States of America
11   10   09   08   07   9   8   7   6   5   4   3   2   1

ASA-GAL-WINGS
ISBN   1-56027-643-6
            978-1-56027-643-2

Library of Congress Cataloging-in-Publication Data:

Keefe, Howie.
  Galloping on wings with the P-51 Mustang "Miss America" : diary of an air race pilot / by Howie Keefe.
        p. cm.
  ISBN-13: 978-1-56027-643-2 (pbk.)
  ISBN-10: 1-56027-643-6 (pbk.)
  1. Keefe, Howie. 2. Air pilots—United States—Biography. 3. Airplanes—Speed records. 4. Miss America (Airplane) 5. Air pilots, Military—United States—Biography. 6. Airplane racing—United States. I. Title.
  TL540.K423A3 2007
  797.5'2092—dc22
  [B]
                                    2007037943

Contents

Dedication

This book is dedicated to the two people who gave me the moral and financial support to have been able to race in the Unlimited Race plane class in part of three decades: 1960s, 1970s and 1980s.

Pete was a few years behind me at Hamilton College. I saw him at the airport while doing my aerobatic training in the Waco and gave him a ride. Twenty years later he offered me his plane to fly. He not only started me flying again, he served as navigator on cross-country races and was a loyal member of "Miss America's" crew.

H.S. "Pete" Hoyt
1923 – 2000

Mike, through his company Omni Aviation, gave me both moral and financial support. When I started racing, replacing a blown engine was $1,000. When I finished, they were about $40,000. Mike helped me re-place three. A great guy to have known. Always relaxed, always "up."

"Mike" Eisenstadt
1939 – 2001

Acknowledgements

Bob is the one P-51 Mustang pilot that all of us admire. He is truly the "pilot's pilot." His book *Forever Flying* is a great read for anyone in flying. His story is unique.

Bob checked me out in 1969 in his P-51 before I tried to fly mine solo. I sat in his back seat so I could be prepared for the loud roar of the engine and the landing attitude with the tail down (3 point). It was a ride I'll never forget! Bob Hoover was kind enough to write the following for this book:

Howie and his P-51 "Miss America" were always stand-outs at the many air shows we flew together—they were crowd pleasers. Howie catered to the kids at the shows, to have them sit in the cockpit to have their picture taken.

Many times when I was the pace plane starting a race, I'd look back over my shoulder at the echelon starting formation of the race planes and there was Howie in "Miss America" eagerly awaiting my release at the race start with my transmission of "Gentlemen, you have a race!" Howie always deserved the term "Gentleman" whether on or off the race course."

—R.A. "Bob" Hoover

The "pilot's pilot," Bob Hoover, with his vast experience flying P-51 Mustangs checked me out in the P-51 Mustang. It was something else! (1997 photo)

Bob shows his flying skill by landing on just one wheel! The crowd was always in awe of his flying feats.

My P-51 Checkout from Bob Hoover

We took off from LAX where the North American hangar was and went to the aerobatic area off Palos Verdes in the direction of Catalina Island. Bob did a slow roll. Never have I ridden through or even tried to do a slow roll with 0-G all through it. No sensation of leaving my seat. A barrel roll might do that but not a hold-your-nose-straight-ahead slow roll. I was in awe! Coming back to land at LAX, I looked forward to the 3-point landing which didn't happen. Instead he landed on just the left wheel, turned the plane off at the high-speed taxiway still on one wheel. When we got out he explained in his Southern gentleman accent, "I'm sorry about not doing the 3-point landing. I heard that the fellows in the tower gather together when I come in to see me do that. All day long they see just airliners. Giving them a little show breaks the monotony." I understood.

A special thanks to the volunteers who made it possible from 1969 to 1981:

Crew Chiefs
(from first to last)

Dick Tomasulo
Dave Zeuschel
Don Bartholomew
Bill Pitts
Skip Higginbotham
Jim Quinlan

Crew
(in random order)

Pete Hoyt
Jim Reid
Harry Quinlan
Don Reese
Ben Roberts
Brian Schooley
Ron Fleming
Bill Miller
Jack Corrick
Len Farmer
Ben Roberts
Bill Yoak
Bill Pruitt
Jerry O'Brien
Maurice O'Brien

Rich Horton
Steve Brown
Roger Vian
Randy Scoville
Hank Pohlman
Don Keefe
Dorrie Keefe
Mari Owens
Roger Davies
Tom Keefe
Sue Keefe
Mike Foster
Mike Cleary
Laura Cleary
Sue Pitts
Patrick O'Brien

Those who helped along the way:

(Listed in random order)

Clay Lacy—for accepting the presidency of the Unlimited Pilots Association
Don Hullet of Champion Spark Plug—for solving problems
Ben Garret of COX Manufacturing—for asking to sponsor "Miss America"
Bill Selzer, President of COX Manufacturing—for their sponsorship
Mike Smith—who rebuilt my scoop after I landed gear-up
Dan Macintyre, Navy Blue Angel—for getting me in the Chicago Air Show
Rodney Roetman—for donating aircraft painting
Don Dwiggins—for his articles
Verne Jobst, air boss at Oshkosh Air Show—for time slots
Starr Thompson, Oshkosh Air Show staff—for friendship
Pete Ross—for aid in getting spare parts
Dick Dobson—for building my prize-winning Glasair "Magic Carpet"
George Kiesel—for timely refueling at the Reno National Air Races
Bob Guilford—for advice on flying the P-51
Joe Hughes—for friendship on the air show circuit
Jim Raymond—for companionship with sponsor Omni Aviation
Dan Sabovitch, manager of Mojave Airport—for helping to bring races there
Don and Bill Whittington—for putting on the Miami Air Races
Art Scholl—for his contagious enthusiasm when COX sponsored us both
Thorton Audrain—a class act managing the Reno Air Races
Warren Lee—FAA supervisor of my early Reno Air Races, friend and advisor
Norm Winkle, LAX Center supervisor—for in-air favors
Laurie Lee Schafer—a "Miss America Pageant" queen who rooted for me
Marla Brubaker Pence—my secretary and parts shipper when far away
Herman "Fish" Salmon, Lockheed test pilot—for advice and counsel
Ken Rusnak, crew volunteer—for help developing my Sky Prints Atlas
Bill Kerchenfaut—for flight line advice on engines
Sil Petrancini, Trustee of Reno Air Races—for his can-do attitude
The Raumms: Mary, Jeannie and **Bob** of Aircraft Spark Plug—for top service
Richard and **Ursula Tracy**—for their support at the air races
Homer Groom—for drawing the first Sky Prints chart
Christa—for standing by me in good and bad times
Moya Lear—for her hospitality at the air races
Jim Reid—for working all night to repair my engine in my first Unlimited Race
John and **JoAnn Adler**—for friendship and great air race parties
Ted Thomas—for insuring me, and offering support and air racing advice
Phil Barber, Reno Gazette reporter—for his professional air race coverage

Ralph Payne

...and this "brain trust" of specialists:

Pete Law—fuel and ADI flow
Bruce Boland—dynamics
Bill Carter—headsets
John O'Crowley—radios
Ralph Payne—mechanical
Dave Zeuschel, Dwight
Thorne, Mike Nixon,
Jack Cochrane and
Bruce Goessling—engines

Pete Law

...those who brought "blue skies" to my flying:

Berk Baker
Suzanne Baker
John Mosby
George Sanders
Lorrie Blech
Jackie Herrington
Jack Leggat
Bill and Anne McNeely
Gerry Nelson
Dr. Robert Poole
Ralph Tisdale
Manny Hirschenhorn
Barry Schiff
Jean Johnson
Mike Barker
Jimmy Leeward
Jane Mikrut
June Allan
Robin NcNeill
Bob Newfield
Ben Schiewe
Pat Packard
Stan Brown
Margi Cellucci
Vance Stickell
Bill Sinkking
Pappy Boyington
Dick Sykes
Jim Modes
Cal Conroy
Condor Squadron
Bill Bennett
Mel Larson
Pat Brady

Bob McMilin
Henry Haffke
Jack Hovey
Sandy Bloom
Buddy Childers
Joy Childers
Bill Johnson
Paul Neuman
John Tegler
Steve Nelson
Susan Oliver
Ralph Pray
Joe Friedman
Wayne Turney
Tom Quinlan
Angelo Regina
Pete Regina
Alice Rand
Frank Sanders
Frank Tallman
Alan Hanks
Leo Volkmer
Paul Czendroi
Ed Zimmer
Max Conrad
Max Hoffman
Doug Etridge
Mary Hivley
Sandy Gale
Cliff Milton
E.B. Jeppesen
Fred Kohler
E. D. Wiener
Mike Norgat

Dale Nelsen
Bob Cummings
Robyn Astaire
Vicki Montgomery
Jim Wood
Suzanne Robinson
Marela Wagner
Eddie Smardan
Mike Purser
Bob Herendeen
Paul Merchant
LeRoy Berkebile
Monty Montgomery
Sandy Sanders
Walter Nielsen
Doug Cameron
Bob Schuler
Rick Schnepf
Glenn Mathews
Doris Mathews
Ron Thurber
Ron Golan
Michael O'Leary
Ed Schnepf
Gary Williams
Dave Jones
Lefty Gardner
Bob Cornwell
Donald Rumsfeld

...thanks guys and gals!

About the Author

Howie Keefe started his flying career in 1941 flying a Piper J-3 Cub on skis while in the Civilian Pilot Training (CPT) program. After graduation from Hamilton College, Clinton, New York, he received a commission from the Navy along with a pair of gold wings.

Being a prior civilian flight instructor, Howie taught aerobatic maneuvers to fledgling Navy flight cadets. Later, he moved on to multi-engine training, flying PBYs and P2V Neptunes for anti-sub patrol within the Bermuda triangle.

In 1950, Keefe retired from Squadron VPML-54, Glenview NAS, Chicago, Illinois, and went off to civilian life as Marketing Director for the Chicago *Tribune*. He was also a marketing instructor at Northwestern University in the Medill School of Journalism.

After military service, Howie's heart remained in the sky. He found a surplus North American P-51, had it highly modified by installing a new race engine, oversized propeller and clipping two feet off each wing. Howie Keefe flew his Mustang on to victory during the glory days of air racing. The famed "Miss America" became an icon within the racing circles and still races annually at the National Air Races at Reno.

Howie holds two records. The original speed record from Los Angeles to Washington, DC of 6 hours, 21 minutes, and the most consecutive number of unlimited pylon races—21 races.

Howie is now fully retired and spends his days writing flying memoirs. He resides in Florida with his wife, Midge.

COX made U-Controlled flying models of "Miss America" and Revell made a 1/32nd scale "snap-together" plastic model. It's pleasing to have men come up to me today and tell me how they enjoyed making or flying these models when they were kids many years ago.

Introduction

Howie Keefe
1,2,3,4

These pages make a "photo album" for this book…
In 13 years of air racing (1968–1980), these are the
pilots I still recall racing with me.

1 = Unlimited Pylon under 100 miles (Reno, New Jersey, Miami)
2 = Unlimited Pylon over 600 miles (Mojave, San Diego)
3 = Cross-Country Races (Milwaukee to Reno – 1969 and 1970)
4 = T-6 Races (Reno, St. Louis, Ft. Lauderdale, Cleveland)

Dick Minges–4

Ken Burnstine–1,3   Vic Baker–2,4   Burns Byrum–1,3   Rick Brickert–1   Doc Cummings–1,2   Bill Destanfani–1

Lefty Gardner–1   John Dilley–1   Sherm Cooper–1,2   John Crocker–1   Bud Fountain–1   Bob Guilford–1,2

Darryl Greenamyer–1,2   John Herlihy–1   Ben Hall–1,4   Max Hoffman–1   Dick Kestle–3   Steve Hinton–1

Skip Holm–1   Clay Klabo–1   Ormond Haydon-Baillie–1   Mike Loening–1   Clay Lacy & Snoopy–1,2

John Wright–1   Jim Maloney–1   Ed Snyder–4   Judy Wagner–3   Gary Levitz–1,2   Leroy Penhall–1,2

John Putnam–1   Bob Love–1,2   Jimmy Leeward–1   Howard Pardue–1   Jack Sliker–1,2,3   Dan Martin–1

E.D. Weiner–1,2   Dick Sykes–4   Mac McKinney–4   Bob Yancey–1   John Mosby–4   Leo Volkmer–2,4

Don Whittington–1   Paul Poberezny–1   Mira Slovak–1   Bill Whittington–1   Frank Sanders–1,2   Mike Smith–1

Vern Thorpe–1   Lyle Shelton–1,2   Wiley Sanders–1   Walt Ohlrich–1,2   Dennis Sanders–1   Roy MacClain–1

Jim Modes–1   Gene Akers–1,2   Bob Mitchem–1   Lloyd Hamilton–1,2   John Sandberg–1   Gunther Balz–1,2,3

Also: Chuck Doyle–1,3 • Ron Reynolds–1 • Mike Geren–2

They "Went West"—I Knew Them Well

In aviation, we tend to honor our fallen friends then surge on ahead. In these pages, I want to pause and remember them with this permanent record. These air race and air show pilots were all special. Though I lost them as friends and competitors, they "went west" where they liked to be — at the controls of a plane.

Dave Zeuschel
My Engine Man
Air Show

Harold Krier
Aerobatics

Ken Burnstine
Race Practice

Vic Baker
T-6 Race, NJ

Burns Byrum
Ferrying P-51

Sherm Cooper
Pitts Strut Broke

John Crocker
Mercy Flight

Don DeWalt
AT-6 Race, Reno

Bob Downey
Race Practice

Bill Falck
Racing

Bud Fountain
Unlimited–Mojave

Ken Brock
Tailwheel Broke

Charlie Hillard
Show Accident

Bob Hernedeen
Mountain Crash

Ormond
Haydon-Baillie
German Air Show

Max Hoffman
Personal Flying

Tom Kuchinsky
P-51 at Air Show

Dick Kestle
P-51 Crash

Mike Loening, Froze
After Forced Landing

Jim Maloney
Aerobatics

Paul Mantz, Filming
Flight of the Phoenix

Dick Minges
T-6 Race, NJ

Gary Levitz
Unlimited—Reno

Leroy Penhall
Twin, Mammoth Mt.

John Sandberg
One Flap Collapsed

H. "Fish" Salmon
4 Engine Ferry

Art Scholl
Filming "Top Gun"

Ed Snyder
T-6 Race, NJ

Jack Sliker
Bearcat—Fuel Out

Frank Tallman
Mountain Crash

"Skip" Volk	M.D. Washburn	Judy Wagner	Steve Wittman	John Wright	Frank Sanders
Aerobatics	T-6 Race—Reno	Twin, IFR Weather	Plane Failure	P-51 Aerobatics	Airshow Act

Not Pictured

Bill Fornoff—Bearcat Air Show Giff Foley—T-6 Show Aerobatics
Mike Geren—Unlimited Race Gordy McCollom—Wing Walker
Scotty McCrae—Glider-Show

John Trainor
IFR Weather

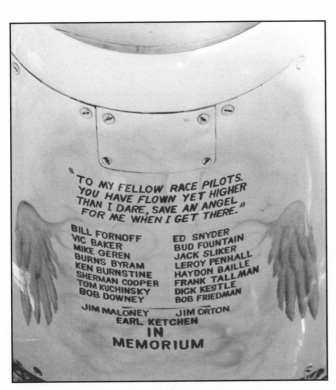

I lost a lot of friends who added a great deal to the exhibition and racing side of aviation, but there was no place their names were recorded so that I might honor their memory. My chin cowl became that place for me—and these pages expand on that by showing or listing those I knew in my years of racing.

Women's Air Racing

Women's Air Racing began with cross-country races like the famed Powder Puff Derby—then to pylon racing in the '60s in stock planes and Formula Ones, then to T-6s and even Unlimiteds.

1929 Women's Air Derby. Amelia Earhart is fourth from right. At far right, Pancho Barnes of the Happy Bottom Riding Club, the hangout for test pilots at Edwards Air Force base mentioned in books by Bob Hoover and Chuck Yeager.

Joan Alford
Formula One Racer

Women's Stock plane pylon racers, Ft. Lauderdale 1970. L–R Dorothy Julich, Judy Wagner, Mary Knapp, Edna White, Elaine (DuPont) Loening, Trina Jarish and Mara Culp. (John Tegler photo)

Bernie Stevenson
Formula One Racer

Colene Giglio – T-6

Erin Rheinschild
P-51 Mustang

With Susan Oliver at a book signing relating her transatlantic solo flight in her book "Odyssey."

Announcers Make the Show!

While I was racing and performing at air shows, these announcers kept the crowds alive with their dramatic voices creating an atmosphere of suspense and daring while narrating the show acts or races. Without their expert knowledge, few in the crowd would know what was happening. They and a good sound system are vital to any air event. These are some of the great announcers I enjoyed having on the mike 1968–1980.

The Reno Gang

Doug Cameron

Glenn Mathews

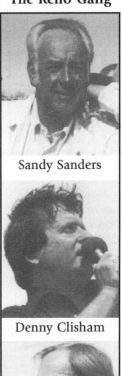

Sandy Sanders

Denny Clisham

Sandy Everest

Bob Singleton

John Tegler

Toby Towbridge

Bill Bordeleau

Roscoe Morton, a great one!
(not pictured)

...and many others at air shows all over the U.S. entertained the crowds.

Photographers!

Keep the Memories Alive!

I wish I had photos of all the photographers who devoted their careers to air show and air racing. These are a few of those who excelled during my time in the air.

Eric Everill

John Tegler

Jim Larsen

Jerry Howard

Dave Esler

Bill Johnson

Paul Neuman

Chuck Aro

My Youth was Filled with Aviation Heroes

I read his book "WE" over and over.

Meeting Roscoe Turner was awe-inspiring to me!

Max Conrad, the "Flying Grandfather" set amazing long distance records.

The great Jimmy Doolittle WAS aviation.

Few pictures were as pretty to me as this one of the Cleveland races in the 1930s.

I met "Wrong Way Corrigan" at the fete for Rutan's Voyager. He never admitted he meant to fly New York to Ireland July 17, 1938 vs. across the U.S. He was the "twinkling eye" tongue-in-the cheek of aviation.

Humor was rare in air racing, but what there was, helped relieve the tension we all felt.

The Air Racer as Seen by...

...other pilots.

...his crew chief.

...himself.

...the pylon judges.

...his wife.

Howie, I think we need to have a talk about your pylon technique.

Nick Jones amused us all with his annual award of his "Italian stiletto" to the unfortunate among us during that race week.

"I told you I was no Howie Keefe!"

AIRCRAFT MODELER Magazine Feb. 1974

My rubberband broke...

*In the Navy Reserve in 1946 following WWII at the Glenview Naval
Station north of Chicago. Although I was officially in the multi-
engine (land) Squadron VPML-54, I could check out an SNJ (AT-6)
like this one to keep up on aerobatic skills. We'd have exhausting dog
fights with the SNJs. The Navy wanted us to be as versatile as
possible by keeping our hands in all types of flight and navigation.*

Chapter 1

The Desire to Fly

As early as I can remember, my father would take us out to events in the areas north of Chicago. Events that were "flying-through-the-air" events. It was in the early 1930s. I was 10 years old in 1931. Dad was never one to take a chance himself, but he was an avid spectator. He passed away in 1966 never having been in an airplane—not even an airliner. But if there was something dramatic going on, he'd take us there.

I can recall Cary, Illinois about 40 miles northwest of Chicago where they had a giant ski jump. Dad would take us there and I'd marvel at the many foreign names of the ski jumpers. These men would fling themselves into the air and land smoothly a great distance below. It was amazing! Once it wasn't so good. I can still see him today. He was a Norwegian.

As Dad explained it, he was jumping in a strong crosswind. He lifted off the jump with his arms stroking forward. He was high above us. Then he started to drift to our left—to the side of the landing area where we were standing. I was standing there transfixed. To me these flying guys were super-human. Nothing could touch them. They were the Spiderman and the Superman that had not even been invented at that time. They could do anything.

Suddenly, he bent over as if in a crouch. He hit the downhill slope with a tremendous impact. Chunks of snow filled the air. He tumbled downhill with his skis flailing as he tumbled over and over. My young eyes could not believe this was happening! This God-to-me had become a mortal. He had literally flown off this high precipice, had taken flight and now he had crashed to the ground. How could this happen? My vocabulary did not have the designations of "super" such as super-heroes or super-persons, but if it did, he would have been one.

Boys at the age of 10 feel immortal. Anything we think we can do, we *can* do. Nothing can happen that could end our life. Maybe it would put us in bed a few days, but that was it. Make us a hero in school by having a cast on our arm so the girls could autograph it. Skiing was just starting to become big in the early 1930s, but 10-year-old boys didn't do it, so there were no ski injuries that you could wear as a badge to school. The stand-out hero was Tarzan. We saw his movies. We saw him swinging through the vines from tree to tree. Our neighborhood had trees. If Tarzan could do it, we could do it, too. Okay, we didn't have vines, but we had ropes. Just hang a few ropes in two trees and swing like Tarzan. If you didn't make the next rope, then grab the branch.

Problem was that we were not monkeys. Leaping for a branch just out of our grasp made you drop—and drop hard! If there was a pile of leaves below you, it wasn't so bad. But without that cushion, the fall hurt and many of us suffered broken bones. I think the modern science of orthopedics grew out of the "Tarzan era."

My dad took me to see the ski jumps at Cary, Illinois. I'd never seen man fly before and it fascinated me! Man flying like a bird—alone!

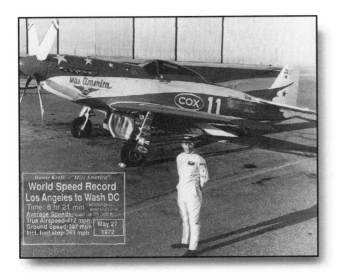

Howie Keefe—"Miss America"
World Speed Record
Los Angeles to Wash DC
Time: 6 hr 21 min
Average Speeds-flown at 23,000 ft
True Airspeed-412 mph
Ground Speed-397 mph   May 27
Incl. fuel stop-363 mph   1972

Between watching ski-jumping accidents and surviving my Tarzan years, I learned a great truth. Man was not born to fly. If you wanted to fly, you had better pay attention to a safe way to do it. Sometimes in later life I forgot that point, but still managed to survive.

Flying was simple back in the early 1930s. All planes had propellers. Some had cabins, but most seemed to have open cockpits. You could have your dad lift you up alongside the open cockpits to see the great number of instruments the pilot needed. Very impressive. Even the simple fluid compass mounted on top of the dashboard commanded authority. Cars didn't have a compass. Cars had roads. Trains had tracks. But a plane—that was different. They went all over the skies to exciting places. They needed a compass!

My Own Plane

One year at Christmas, I lucked out. I was 11 years old. A new toy came out. It was a 12-inch plane tethered to a pylon. An electric motor powered it. The neat part was that it had a joy stick and speed control. I could make it go up and down. Slow it down for a landing on the living room carpet. Then make it take off by adding power and pulling back on the joy stick. I could play with it for hours. Just plug it in to the wall socket. In those days you didn't need a trust fund to buy batteries that wore out after a few hours of play. My friends and I could do this all day long.

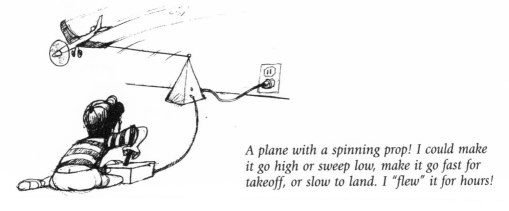

A plane with a spinning prop! I could make it go high or sweep low, make it go fast for takeoff, or slow to land. I "flew" it for hours!

The thought of getting into a real plane was about as remote a reality as it is for kids today to play with space ships and consider it a real possibility that they will ever sit in one, much less fly one. Flying an actual plane was just not available to average kids like me. Besides, my father was so conservative about risks that I'd never think of asking him to let me take a plane ride from a barnstormer of that era.

Attending My First Air Race

Curtiss–Wright Airport was a few miles west of Glencoe, Illinois where we lived. It was 20 miles northwest of Chicago. It later became the Glenview Naval Air Station. Dad took me out there for the Air Races. It was about 1932–1933. I was about 11 years old. What I saw happen at those races soured me not only on flying, but on air racing as well. Just before we arrived there, a small race plane had crashed into the powerlines at the south end of the field. Parts of the plane were still dangling from the power lines. It was announced that the pilot had been killed. This was not what I had dreamed what flying was nor what Lindy had done with his plane.

These planes were so small I felt I could lift one up by myself. These were the Formula One type racers of today, but they had open cockpits. At age 11, these cockpits were as low as my shoulder. I could look right into the cockpit and see the floorboards, the seat, the stick, the instruments, the rudder pedals, everything. But what I remember most to this day was that one of these planes had a St. Christopher medal attached above the instrument panel in plain view. Even though I was a Catholic and knew St. Christopher protected the traveler, these types of things belonged in our maid's room or in a church, not on the dashboard of a mighty race plane that courageous men flew. Okay, so a race plane hung in the wires a few blocks away and the pilot had been killed, but he wasn't really dead. He just died as they did in the movies of cowboys and Indians.

Then when one of my first heroes, Knute Rockne, the famed coach of Notre Dame, was killed in a passenger plane crash over the Midwest during a storm, the adventuresome world of flying started to take on a somber meaning to me. About that same time, President F.D. Roosevelt decreed that the Army Air Corp would carry the nation's airmail to link the country even closer. The results were a disaster!

Not the Army Air Corps, not anyone, nor any plane was suited to fly tight time schedules in almost any weather, day or night. The flight and navigational instruments were okay in marginal VFR (visual) weather, when the pilot had the say of go/no-go. But when pilots trained to dog fight were asked to do long cross-country flights in any kind of weather and on a schedule, the crashes were far greater than anyone had predicted. After the nation's hue and cry over the number of crashes, the numbers of pilots killed and the amount of mail lost, Roosevelt called off his order to have the Army Air Corp fly the mail. I remember a cartoon in the Chicago Daily News at the time that showed Roosevelt in an open cockpit plane making a U-turn in the air. The caption was, "It takes a good pilot to admit he's wrong."

The Movie
"All Quiet on the Western Front"

Flying was now a sobering thing to me. It still held a fascination, but one I would probably never realize in the real world I lived in. Go to high school. Study hard. Go to a good college. Have a profession. Get a good job. Raise a family. And, above all, be sensible.

Well, something changed all that for me. It was the movie "All Quiet on the Western Front" with Lew Ayers, a young German infantry soldier. It came out about 1931. Other movies like "Wings" with Buddy Rogers had made WWI seem glamorous. This movie, AQOWF, was the opposite. It showed guys getting legs blown off, living in mud, bombs falling everywhere.

You lived stuck in a trench, barbed wire tore at your body, machine gun fire mowing down soldier after soldier and bayonets stabbing each other in hand-to-hand combat. My aunt had taken me to see it at the State–Lake Theater in Chicago's downtown loop area. She thought any red-blooded American boy would enjoy this after having a tooth removed. I sat through the movie wide-eyed. I had never seen anything like this before. War movies had always been glamorous. In this, Lew Ayers was killed at the end reaching forward for a butterfly from his rifle position in a trench. Whoa!—this was a different take on war.

Eight Years Later—1940

In 1940, I was a junior at Hamilton College in upstate New York in Clinton just outside Utica. War was raging in Europe. We had "Bundles for Britain": food, clothing and money drives. Some dropped out of college to go to Canada to train for the Royal Air Force. To me these guys were like the adventuresome Lawrence of Arabia, Richard Halliburton and the famous race and air show pilot Roscoe Turner. There was no way I could break my station as a conservative student and toss away all the education I had been given and join these guys. I was going into the profession of law and that was it. Period.

Then a wonderful thing happened. A person from the War Department visited the campus. Of course, I was over 18 and had to be registered for the draft, so I was very interested in anything they said about what my status might be. Right now I had an educational deferment being in college full-time. He explained that the nation was short of pilots, that the government had a program that my college had in place to train pilots. My college would give us 3 semester credit points for taking the course. This sounded too good to be true!

At the time I had an English Lit course with a professor who giggled all the time and had odd theories like that the source of Shelly's "follow, follow" was from Christ. I really could not handle this vague thinking. My mind was too practical for it, maybe too immature. To be able to swap a course in flying for this was like being rescued from a semester of boredom.

Because I was only 19 and not yet 21, my father had to sign a permission statement saying that I could take the flight course. My father, the conservative take-no-chances person, was the key to my getting into the program. What luck. He probably wouldn't approve. All might be lost!

I had 30 days to get his signature on the application. All we had in those days was the mail. No FedEx or UPS. No faxes. Just the mail. Yes, there were Western Union telegrams, but not for forms and signatures. The mail took 5 days to get to Chicago and another 5 to 6 days to get back to college. There wasn't a lot of time for correspondence back and forth. In those days, long-distance telephone calls were for business and emergencies.

My letter had all the great arguments to get Dad to approve my application to take the flight program. This was only 9 years after I had seen the movie "All Quiet on the Western Front." Nine years today is yesterday to me. Then it was a different era. "It looks like war is sure to come, I don't want to be in the trenches, flying is the future, please sign and return it to me as soon as possible." Two weeks before the deadline to submit my application, I received it back signed, but with this note. "Please think this over for at least a week before you turn it in."

I must confess to my departed father that it took me only two seconds to "think it over." I ran through the snow across campus to the Dean's office with my signed application for the Civilian Pilot Training course. The magic, official, signed paper was done. It created my future more than any single event ever would. It led me into the world of flight!

Chapter 2

Free Flying from Uncle Sam

T he year was 1940 and it was winter in upstate New York in that famous snowbelt that picked up the moisture from Lake Erie. It stretched from the tip of Lake Erie through Buffalo, Rochester and Syracuse down to Utica where Hamilton College and the Utica airport were located.

Hamilton College sat on a hilltop above Clinton, NY about 40 miles southeast of Syracuse and 10 miles west of Utica, NY. The airport was about 5 miles to the right. It was tough academically, but I enjoyed its own golf course (top left) and the indoor hockey rink (top left building). At the time it was "men only."

As I reflect back on this government flying program—CPTP (Civilian Pilot Training Program)—I marvel at the vision and the simple way it was put together at a time when flying and aviation were pretty much a sport and exhibition-oriented. The idea of an air war in pre-Pearl Harbor days and a future need for pilots was not the hot button of the time. In fact, far too little has been said about this critical program to WWII and the development of aviation in the U.S.

The only full explanation I have seen of why and how it started was published by the Smithsonian Institution in its FLYER newsletter in the spring/summer edition of 2000, 61 years after it started! Written by Stanley D. Schneider, it's worth sharing:

"Even in these days of America's preeminence in air and space, few people can recall or have read about in their history books the Civilian Pilot Training Program (CPTP). It was the brainchild of Robert H. Hinckley in the late 1930s to teach American youth the fundamentals of flying.

"Hinckley was a Mormon born in Utah in 1891. He was nominated by then-President F. D. Roosevelt in 1938 to be one of the 5 members of the newly-created Civil Aeronautics Authority (CAA), now called the FAA. Hinckley believed that American youth not only should, but must, be introduced to the new air age by learning to fly and taking courses that would familiarize them with the emerging science of aeronautics. Soon after becoming a member of the CAA, he proposed a program that would give young people flight training through universities, colleges, local fixed-base operators, and flight schools certified by the CAA. The universities and colleges would provide ground instruction; the fixed-base operators and flying schools, the flight instruction. Hinckley believed his program would fulfill two national needs, stimulating private flying and providing a standing reserve of civilian pilots who could be called on in a wartime emergency.

"But before Hinckley's idea could take wings—and become a working government program—many obstacles had to be overcome. Not the least of these was industry's dislike of previous Administration aviation policies and programs, not to mention the concerns of the military about the directions, controls, and ultimate worth of the program. Many educators also raised questions. And, there were doubts in Congress, which would need to approve the funding. Debates in Congress covered many issues, but particularly contentious were the issues involving the military. Hinckley and his supporters had to assure Congress that the role of the CAA would not be to train military pilots, but only to establish a pool from which young people 'with the equivalent of primary training' could be drawn on now or in 'the time of emergency.' From there, the military could take them into advanced training. The hearings continued for several rounds, with sometimes bitter debates.

Senator Robert H. Hinckley (Utah)

"Finally, the legislation was approved and on June 27, 1939, President Roosevelt signed the CPTP Act. Debates continued over funding, however, and it was not until August of that year that the House and Senate agreed to appropriate $4 million, with a quota of 11,000 students.

"Even before its final funding was approved, a CPTP demonstration program was underway. Thirteen participating colleges and universities had been selected to start the program either because of their 'pioneering' work in aeronautical engineering or because they had flight training programs. Contractors bid for the flight training. The CAA selected approximately 330 students between the ages of 18 and 25 to take part in the initial phase of the program. Physical standards were developed based on military criteria, and a flight-training program was set up. Because of the success of the initial program, the pressures of the dangers abroad, and even some favorable publicity from Hollywood in the form of a movie '20,000 Men a Year,' the CPTP grew rapidly. By the end of 1939, it was training approximately 9,350 men and women at 435 colleges and universities throughout the country. It continued to expand and not just in the number of participants. The CAA contracted to train 60 students in so-called unconventional aircraft, which had built-in safety features. It also began a research program involving testing and training. This research was eventually to prove invaluable in establishing objective standards for predicting pilot success and measuring improvement and progress instruction.

"After the entry of the United States into World War II, the entire nature of the CPTP changed, reflected in a name change to the 'War Training Service.' Hinckley's idea of flight training to introduce American youth to the new air age gave way to the contingencies of war.

"All told, Robert Hinckley's accomplishment in launching and pursuing his vision of the CPTP made several contributions to this country. It provided young men and women of all backgrounds and race the opportunity to learn to fly. It also gave a scientific foundation to psychological testing and research into various aspects of pilot training and helped to bring instructional materials that would support the study of aeronautics into secondary schools. And, it did provide a pool of pilots that could be trained for the military. Many of these young people served with distinction in World War II.

"Perhaps CPTP's greatest success, however, was as a civilian pilot training program. Despite the criticism and budget cuts it suffered during its controversial period of July 1940 to June 1942, it trained more than 98,000 pilots. Largely as a result of the intensified CPTP, the number of licensed pilots in the U.S. increased from approximately 23,000 at the beginning of 1930 to 100,000 by the time of the attack on Pearl Harbor.

"By doing this, it helped develop a generation of Americans who would ensure the nation's leadership in ushering in today's great age of air and space. And all that makes the story of the CPTP a bit of history worth recalling."

I was a junior, had my Dad's permission to take flying lessons and my hockey coach gave me passes for practice. Everything was great. The snow wasn't a problem until I tried to land! Coming down on a snow-white landscape was a real challenge!

Up high, the snowscape was rather nice, but 10 feet above the ground it was this great white sea. Depth perception to an inexperienced student was tough. It was like "What can I look at! How can I tell how high up I am? Do I look straight down? Straight ahead? Out to the side and run into something?" The romance of flying was a lot less with such routine problems to face in the tough situation of trying to land a plane. Forget that the Piper Cub was coming in at only 40 miles an hour—it was 40 miles faster than I had ever been suspended 10 feet in the air with the end of the field of an unhealthy cornfield to think about too!

Slowly it began to dawn on me that the ski ruts on the runway area had some subtle shadows that could tell me where the ground was. Soon Jerry, my patient instructor in the front seat of the Cub, seemed to relax his grip on the stick, figuring I would not stall him 10 feet in the air with a landing gear breaking drop or do a plow job with the skis into the ground and perhaps an uncomfortable nose over?

Later, when landing the big PBY flying boats on glassy sea, the same problem returned but no ruts with shadows. I was then using the new polaroid glasses for flying which our squadron leader made us stop using. The value of polaroids was that they "saw through" surface glare, but that very surface glare is what we needed to let us see where the top of the water was to judge our height above it while landing. The polaroid advantage became a disadvantage! Even without them, a landing on smooth water required us to let down slowly and literally glide onto the water. This was okay in the open sea with no end to the runway, but here on land, the get-down area was rather limited.

The Piper J3 Cub probably trained more pilots than any other plane, except for possibly the Cessna 150. I soloed it on skis in upstate New York's snowbelt.

Every pilot remembers those first 6 or more hours before being allowed to solo. At that time, a minimum of 6 hours of dual instruction was required before you could solo and a minimum of 65 hours total before you could take your checkride to get that coveted private pilot license. After you solo, you get a Student License which gives you some bragging rights, but also the feeling that you are still in short pants when those you meet say, "You mean you can't even take someone up?"

With a private pilot license you could take up your girlfriend or a buddy. Fat chance that my parents, entrusting of me as they were, wouldn't go up with me. Dad never did in the 30 years I flew before he died in 1966, but he loved to watch planes as I explained. After Dad died, Mother, a more pliable soul, did take a memorable flight with me in my Navy fighter trainer (an SNJ or in the Air Force/Army Air Corp the AT-6 Texan) across Lake Michigan. I almost wound up in jail for doing a buzz job on our coastal house in South Haven, Michigan. The SNJ/AT-6 makes a tremendous amount of noise and as luck would have it, a retired Air Force colonel had, unbeknown to me, moved into the neighborhood.

When we landed, my mother marveled at the reception her son was getting at the local airport with three sheriff squad cars, lights flashing, following us down the inbound taxiway. In a procession of 5 family cars that had come out to meet us led by the 3 squad cars to the colonel's house, my mother must have thought she was in a parade! Thanks to a fast talking aunt who knew the colonel and the sheriff, I don't think mother ever thought it was anything but a nice reception for her son!

Back to 1940. In the first 6 hours, you had to learn to do nose-high stalls that left your stomach up somewhere while the plane's nose whipped toward the ground. When you stalled, faith in your flight instructor to get you back alive was the same as you would have in a brain surgeon. You had given up all thought of saving yourself and being on your own. Your macho stayed up there where your first stall started. Then the plane, out of flying speed, whipped its nose toward the ground like a hawk diving for its prey. Maybe you could force up a breath-holding heh-heh smile as the plane picked up speed and went back to level…and your stomach caught back up with your body. Nothing we have experienced on the ground prepares us for the sensation of that first stall. As pilots know, the stall is something like trying to go up a steep hill in a car in a high gear. Eventually you "stall."

In a plane, you do two types of stalls to get used to landing stalls and to warn you to avoid an accidental stall in a tight turn. Power-off stalls give you the feeling of stalling just before the wheels touch the ground. Power-on stalls add in the "torque-of-the-prop" element called the P-factor in which the turning of the prop tries to pull the plane to the left. You need to hold right rudder to keep the nose straight. After a day of stalls, I'd be a little woozy, but luckily never felt sick.

The Spins

Then the real thrill before soloing—the spins! If you trusted your instructor to get you through alive in your first stall, you saw him as God on top of a mountain if you lived through your first 3-turn spin!

It was one thing to get through the nose-high stall that started the spin and the plane's nose whipped toward the ground, but when the snow covered fields, the cows and the highway started swapping places as the plane twisted nose down toward that enemy—earth! Okay, so the spinning stopped and the nose of the plane slowly rose back up to level flight. Whew! Let's go home now!

The spin and its planned recovery of opposite rudder and forward stick was to show us how to get out of a jam if we ever did stall accidentally and found ourselves screwing a hole toward earth. In short, just keep breathing and do what you had learned from many practice spins that were to follow. Unfortunately I think, the Aircraft Owners and Pilots Association (AOPA) lobbied the FAA in the 1960s to take the spin requirement out of the flight training. They claimed that stalls alone to one side or the other would give the same training—and besides, the spin was keeping the more timid from wanting to learn to fly. AOPA's goal was naturally to get as many pilots in the air as possible. They would not even publish reviews on air show acts and certainly not have anything to do with publishing anything on air racing. Thankfully, AOPA's conservative attitude is changing today to include all the things pilots have to know about flying.

Some pilots who were not required to do spins have sought out flying schools that have Citabrias and other aerobatic light aircraft to have the chance to experience a spin and its method of recovery. It's smart to know how to recover and know what produces the spin in the first place and how it feels to be in one so there is no panic when it happens. I'll cover later on how a chance bit of advice from an aerobatic pilot saved my skin when I got into an inadvertent spin in my P-51.

The Solo

After the spins, you are hopefully ready to solo. If you can do the first 5 hours in a week rather then one hour per week, you don't have to relearn so much at the start of each lesson. The weather had been smiling on me and the third through the sixth hour were on successive days. I felt I had it, but the instructor is the person who says solo/no solo. After three or four landings, Jerry, my instructor, told me to taxi back to the hangar.

"Heck," I thought, "no solo today." He got out, pulled his chute out after him and said "Go back out there and solo it. You're not going to kill yourself." Again, every pilot knows that day he or she soloed. Unlike graduation from school where you know for sure the day you'll graduate, I don't think any pilot woke up the day they soloed and said, "Well, today I'm going to solo." It just doesn't work that way. There's the weather, your fitness that day, any incidents to other pilots that may have occurred that makes your instructor (who is the last word) think it's okay for you to solo. Every instructor has a tale of getting out of the plane and telling the student they can solo and have the student literally pull them back into the plane with the fright of seeing a charging lion on their face! "No, just a few more landings!" Naturally, no instructor is going to argue or plead with them any more than you would with your own child.

When the solo came that day, my reaction was the same as every pilot who ever soloed a small plane after the instructor got out. "Wow, it just leapt off the ground! I was flying before I realized it! Now there is no turning back! The plane's doing the flying! All I have to do is steer it!" With the instructor's weight out of the plane, it is amazing how the plane flies. It's like a butterfly with an engine. It climbs like a fighter jet and glides like a glider!

The solo always consists of staying in the traffic pattern around the field and making about two landings and takeoffs to give you the confidence that you can indeed fly—and fly alone. What a sensation! Maybe finally being able to ride your two-wheeler bike after your dad lets go of the seat and you're on your own is somewhat equal—your first drive alone in a car isn't. There's no balance, no coordination, no dealing with new forces on your body when you drive a car. In riding a bike and flying, there are.

Okay, so the instructor is out of the plane and you're coming in for your first solo landing. I remember him saying, "Okay, without my weight it won't 'sit down' as it has been doing…it will glide more—don't get nervous—there's plenty of runway—but don't hesitate to go around again if there is any doubt in your mind that you don't have enough runway." Again there are the tales of the instructors who say they have been practicing their duck shooting in case they had to shoot down a student who just kept going around the field because the plane floated the entire length without the instructors weight in it. It makes for a good tale! But it is a reality that every student faces on their first solo—and maybe more times again if you're not paying attention to the wind and the weather and the weight change of your plane with the reduced weight of gas burned after a long flight.

At a weight of 6 pounds per gallon, a long flight that burned 40 gallons is the equivalent of parachuting out a 240-pound passenger; that's a lot of weight to lose in the average plane. It can make the plane glide a lot farther in the calm air. Especially at the end of the day when the wind dies down and the pilot is tired after a long flight. No wind. Gas weight burned off. It's then when the runways get shorter because the glide gets longer. Hopefully, the little Flight Genie will whisper in your ear, "Full power! Go around. Try it again. Forget your pride!" That nice little Genie has saved my butt several times…even at air shows where thousands of pilots are watching and they know damn well that you did a go-around because you misjudged something—the wind, your speed, the runway length—something.

After the Solo

After the solo came more instruction like turns around objects on the ground to show how a steep bank is needed when downwind, and a shallow bank upwind to keep from drifting downwind. Figure 8s around two widely-spaced trees or barns. Fun. Easy to understand. But then the solo cross-country!

Solo Cross-Country

Leaving the airport area was like leaving the comfort of home to go to kindergarten. The airport was home. You could fly around it all day without any problem, but to venture away to places you've never flown over was a different thing. I studied maps of the Utica, New York area with my instructor. Drew a course line to and back from one of the several Emergency Landing Fields the CAA had in those days—usually a pasture the government rented from a local farmer. No sweat, just follow the line looking at the ground below. It crosses a road at one point, a railroad track at another point, a river bridge, a town on the right.

Off I went. To a destination only 50 miles away but might as well have been Africa. The training wheels were off. At the Piper J-3 Cub's speed of 80 mph on this calm winter day, my circular calculator showed it would take me about 38 minutes to get there, make 2 circles of the field (add about 3 minutes) and 38 minutes back for a total of 80 minutes or 1 hour 20 minutes away from home.

Got there fine. Found the field rimmed at its four corners with the red and white fenders used to mark the Emergency Fields and started to circle it. I was feeling pretty proud of myself. Maybe I'll just look around to see if the Red Baron is in this area and shoot him down. It must have been during this thought that I looked down and the emergency field had disappeared. It was there a minute ago! I've just been circling it. Where could it be? There were snow-covered fields everywhere I looked. Red barns everywhere. Where was I? I recall panic starting to set in. "No, no," I said to myself, "there has to be an explanation—and if you can't find the field, just head back to the airport."

The compass was wagging from side to side, but I had to get it settled down so I could find the 220° reading for the course back home. Yeah, but the course was from the field that I now had lost. Would 220° get me back to the airport? Hey, it's all I had to go by. Man, it was now getting cold in this unheated plane. We had to fly after school hours which meant the latter part of the day. In winter that meant colder. And I was getting colder and colder. I knew that my instructor Jerry was waiting for my return, so at least one person would know if I "never made it." As luck would have it, the late sun reflected off the Mohawk River. I could see it far away and knew my way home from there.

After I landed, Jerry came out to greet me. My time was only about 3 minutes different from what had been flight planned. He wasn't worried at all. And I was too proud to tell him how confused I had been and had lost my destination while circling it! Today, a student must land, and have a person at the airport to sign that they had been there. Maybe that's easier than losing a snow-covered cow pasture. I'll never know.

The Final Flight Check

The flight check in the Cub to get your coveted private pilot license was by a person you did not know; a very important (to me) CAA appointed flight inspector. We were still flying on skis and I had learned later that this inspector did not have much time on skis. I think that the fact I brought him back alive and could turn on skis with the proper bursts of power got me a pass on my flight check. I was now a private pilot with the license number 52072, which means that I was the 52nd thousand, 72nd pilot certified by the CAA (now FAA). This has bragging rights today, but to have been 3,000 sooner (under 50,000) would have been part of history and real bragging rights!

Advanced Flying at Last!

Back at Hamilton College in Clinton, New York as a senior the *fun* flying part of the Civilian Pilot Training Program started—AEROBATICS!

The White Scarf

Now, this is flying! Helmet—goggles—leather jacket—white scarf (the white scarf is perhaps the most impressive part of the outfit, especially when you looked at yourself in the mirror!). The pilots in the 1930's movie "Hell's Angels" wouldn't look like pilots without their white silk scarves—neither Clark Gable nor Buddy Rogers would have made it without their white scarves. It could be worn tightly around the neck to show real professionalism. Worn a little loosely gave the casual look. Mostly unwrapped and dangling meant that a mission in the air had been accomplished. Now just don't get airsick and mess it up!

The white scarf said "aviator."

The scarf served a great purpose for me. When flying inverted coming out of an Immelmann or on the bottom of a slow roll, gas would drip out of the top wing filler cap and coat my head. It really irritated my neck. We had to shave each evening before dinner at the fraternity. Shaving my neck after an afternoon of having gasoline wind-whipped into it was not a nice feeling. The white scarf could deal with it better than I could. Of course the goggles kept the gasoline from getting in the eyes—and the gas actually helped clean oil off the goggles.

When you're a student and doing aerobatics with a critical instructor, it seems that any little distraction is magnified. It's tough enough to get used to your body hanging on a single strap with gravity trying to pull you out of the plane without having to deal with gasoline in your face. It should be noted that where the instructor sat in the front cockpit, the gasoline went right over his head. Whether the instructor was in or out of the plane, the rear seat pilot got the spray. The scarf sure helped.

Aerobatics

The WACO was nice to fly. It had the power to get you off the ground, to pull you over the top of a loop and in case you messed up your landing approach and were coming in a little short, the power to pick the nose up over the hedgerow so you could settle softly on the grass field.

The aerobatic phase of learning to fly is not to teach you to be an aerobatic pilot. Its purpose is to teach you the controls and how they work when the plane is in various positions. Flying straight-and-level, the rudder turns the nose left or right with proper banking—like banking a bicycle when turning the handle bars. But when you are on your side as in a slow roll, the rudder then acts as the elevator and is used to raise or lower the nose. Aerobatics at high speeds, such as the Immelmann and the slow roll, teach you control pressures at speed, while stall types like the snap roll and the vertical reverse (cartwheel) let you experience the result of quick, forceful control movement at slower speeds.

The chandelle, as smooth a procedure as its name sounds, teaches control in both slow and fast flight. It is simply a climb to near stall and then a turn back with a shallow dive in the other direction, and a climb again and a turn back the other way. It's a mandatory sequence for a commercial pilot license. It shows the check pilot how you can keep directional control at different speeds without skidding or slipping.

The WACO UPF-7 was a dream machine for aerobatics. It's a revered classic today. This one had the FAA #NC30163 in 1942. I wonder if it has been restored and is flying today...

CUBAN EIGHT A maneuver in which the path of the plane forms a figure 8 lying on its side. It consists of a ¾ loop, a half-roll, another ¾ loop, and another half-roll.

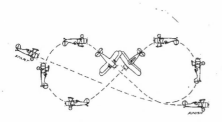

SLOW ROLL A 360° roll through the plane's longitudinal axis.

WING OVER A climbing turn followed by a diving turn and resulting in a 180° change of direction.

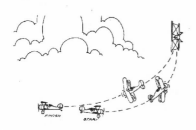

IMMELMANN An altitude-gaining maneuver in which the plane changes direction 180° — a half-loop followed by a half-roll. Named after World War I pilot Max Immelmann.

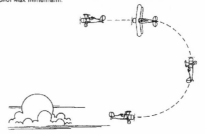

SPLIT S A descending maneuver consisting of a half-roll followed by the last half of a loop and resulting in a 180° change of direction.

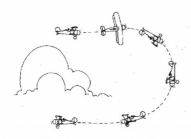

SNAP ROLL A horizontal power spin.

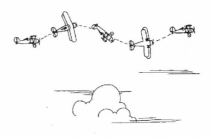

CHANDELLE A maximum climbing turn with a 180° change of direction.

LOOP A maneuver in which the airplane executes a circular path in a vertical plane.

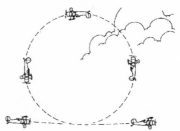

On to South Bend, Indiana
for Instrument and Flight Instructor Training

After graduating from Hamilton College in 1942 and having finished both the Primary Flight Course for a private pilot license and the secondary course for an aerobatic waiver, it was sit and wait for a call from the Navy to assign me to cadet training. The Navy Air Corps was taking a beating in the South Pacific and was short of instructors. The Army Air Corps used civilian flight instructors so they did not need to enlist, train and maintain them. With carrier flying the Navy's need, they felt that students needed to start off with such requirements as landing tailwheel first to catch the cable on the carrier— to take off nose high as you do off a carrier. Never were we allowed to raise our tail on take off.

While still waiting to be called up, I applied for more advanced training in the CPT program. I was sent to Bendix Field in South Bend to train at Stockert Aviation. The flying was free, but as civilians, we had to pay our own room and board.

The Stockert people were great. They arranged for 4 of us to rent a house together on Cleveland Avenue in a true mid-America town of South Bend. At the other end of town was the famed Notre Dame University where I taught a class in navigation to other aspiring pilots. We were now in the war with both feet. Just 7 months before, Japan had bombed Pearl Harbor and it seemed to fall upon the Navy and its Air Corps to make up for that act. I was proud to be enlisted in the Navy's flight cadet program, but at the same time was frustrated that I could not start Navy flight training.

A Dilemma!

A week before, Pan-Am (then Pan-American Grace Airways) sent me a telegram offering a job flying for them, saying the Navy would release me. My friend, Mike Watt, accepted and became one of Pan-Am's top captains for 35 years. This telegram was a follow-up to that one saying that the offer was in keeping with the war effort. Somehow, I still wanted to be a Navy pilot. It just seemed the thing to do with the war going against us as it was at the time.

A week later I received a Special Delivery letter from the Navy Air Corp addressed to "Ensign Howard M. Keefe, Jr. USNR"—Ensign? Ensign? My enlistment card said "Aviation Cadet." How could I be a Navy officer? But the orders were clear. Report to Naval Air Station at Pensacola in full uniform for the Navy Flight Instructor School. Somehow the Navy, at a time when there were no computers, had found out that the CAA had issued me a Flight Instructor Rating.

Now I was to learn to fly the "Navy way" and become an officer and a gentleman in the process! I almost flunked out!

Mike Watt and I were friends from sixth grade. He got the same telegram and went with Pan-Am. He conceived of Pan-Am's 1978 recordsetting round-the-world flight of 47 hours, 31 minutes on Pan-Am's 50th Anniversary. Mike also served as a vice-president of the Airline Pilot's Association (ALPA).

Captain Lyman G. "Mike" Watt, Pan-Am

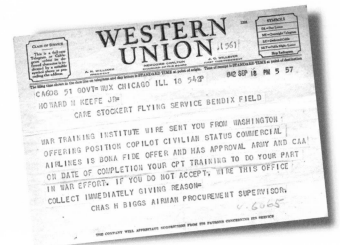

The Navy or the airlines? It was a tough decision, but the war in the Pacific was in trouble.

Chapter 3

Navy Flying
"What Could Be Better!"

B ut my orders to Pensacola specified that my appointment as an Ensign was temporary. I had to pass a physical in Chicago before I could report to Pensacola. No sweat. I had passed all the CAA flight physicals, did not have any abnormal conditions and my eyes were better than 20/20. What a shock to find I flunked the first Navy Air Corps physical!

My blood pressure was a low 102 (Navy minimum was 105) and my heart rate at rest was almost 90 instead of 72! The Navy used the Schneider test and you needed to get at least a 12 on it to be qualified—my score was a 9! Dr. Richburg, our family doctor, felt that low blood pressure was good—you'd live a long time. But the Navy had a different take on it. Low blood pressure meant you could "black out" more easily and take more time to recover. Later on I found out that as an old man of 23 versus the young tough-as-nails-cadets, I did "gray out" now and then as they pulled back on the stick to do their Immelmann maneuver of a loop with a slow roll to level flight on the top of the loop. If the wings were level when the "gray out" faded, they did a good job.

To me, no badge or medal is more coveted than the Navy's gold wings. Navy pilots were trained not only as pilots, but to serve as navigators (celestial too!), as bombers, as gunners, and in both water and land operations.

While low blood pressure was normal for me, the high heart rate was the product of smoking, little sleep and lack of exercise. In college, I played ice hockey and soccer. They kept me in shape. I had never really been away from athletics and didn't realize how fast you can go downhill lying around, late night dates and mostly junk food. It was a wake-up call!

The Navy's Schneider test was a comparison of your blood pressure and heart rate before, during, and after 30 climbs up and off a footstool. I could get my blood pressure up a few notches to 105 by tensing up my body, but when the corpsman kept trying to get a reading on the diastolic (bottom) rate, he said "I know you're alive because you're talking to me, but your pressure doesn't return—it just goes to zero." Oh no! My dream of becoming a Navy pilot was disappearing here on the seventh floor of a building in Chicago's downtown loop! — not even on a Naval Air Station! But they gave me a window. Report back in two days to take the Schneider test again.

Over at Dad's office he seemed at first relieved that his son would not have to go into that "unpredictable" world of flying, but then I pointed out that there were other worlds out there in wartime that made the life on a Navy carrier look plush. He agreed. He took me over to the trainer at the Chicago Athletic Club on Michigan Avenue.

I am sure the Swedish trainer looked at this scrawny 6-foot-tall, 150-pound, 21-year-old pampered juvenile delinquent with a few "ughs," if not disgust. Could he give a massage that could bring up my blood pressure and slow down my heart rate so I could pass the test? He tried. I had never been massaged (mauled) before. There wasn't any fat on my body to knead. He had to work with skin on bone. To see if this had done any good, Dad and I went to the family doctor, 20 miles north to our town of Glencoe, Illinois.

Nope. I was still low in the blood pressure department and fast on the heart beat after exercise. But the doc had a thought. Salt would raise the blood pressure and Phenobarbital would slow down the heart rate, which he kindly decreed was due to my "great excitement and concern" over the entire matter. So he gave me a prescription for the little Phenobarbital pill that worked its charm!

Back down in Chicago to retake the darn Schneider test, I felt like I was walking on air! The pills had certainly kicked in. Never had taken more than an aspirin before, but this felt more like a "bourbon-buzz" than medicine. As for the blood pressure, I had enough salt in me to be a stand-in for Lot's wife. The combo worked! Out of the 22 perfect score on the Schneider, I eked out the minimum passing score of 12. Eureka! This physical was over, but there was still one ahead at Pensacola, they told me.

The final hurdle in Chicago was a personal interview with a Naval officer. His evaluation of my character and general abilities from just talking to me was the final go/no-go step in the process. Here I got lucky. The Navy officer was the famous football all-American from the University of Chicago, Jay Berwanger. I sat speechless with awe in front of him. I did happen to mutter that Dad and many of my family had graduated from Chicago. That the famous Amos Alonzo Stagg, the football coach, was a hero of mine (I didn't mention "behind Knute Rockne").

One week I was a Seaman 2/c waiting to be called up as a flight cadet. The next week this was on my wall! I was amazed.

Berwanger was maybe only 24 himself at the time. He was clean-cut, soft of voice and had a strong face. Afterward he smiled, stuck out his hand and said "You'll make a fine Naval officer." During the 45-minute train ride back to Glencoe, I felt like I was living in a dream world!

In one week's time I had gone from deep despair that I had flunked out at being a Navy pilot to an elation never before known!

On to Pensacola

There it was on the check-in sheet of about 20 places we had to go. Along with the check-ins at the dog-tag station, the flight gear, etc., was the flight physical! Here we go again! I had changed my sleep and exercise habits, was watching the food I ate (plenty of red meat) and felt in better shape, but this physical might be a one-shot pass/go-home deal. We had 3 days to complete check-in. I waited until the last day to try the physical, thinking maybe somehow they would be so impressed with my check-in completed up to this point that it showed my determination to be a Navy pilot and maybe—just maybe—they'd overlook that dreaded Schneider test.

On the third day I had made sure that I had taken on as much salt as I could with the rationale that here I was in the heat of Pensacola and needed the salt tablets to survive. As for the Phenobarbital, I had plenty of that. What I needed, however, was a friend to come along with me while the pheno was doing its job of keeping my heart rate down and make sure I didn't leave any papers, etc., behind in my "happy" state. Another Navy-pilot-to-be, Jim Lewis of Coffeyville, Kansas, a can-do type of guy agreed to be my co-pilot for the day. He too had to take his physical.

I don't recall what my Schneider score was. All I heard was the corpsman say, "You passed, go have the doc check you out." Pensacola never looked so good as it did to me that night! Looking out at the sound from the Mustin Beach Officer's Club, with the ice in my 25¢ scotch high ball gently clinking against the glass, couldn't get any better! Jim's drinks were free. He thanked me.

Soon reality set in. We were officers, but not really. We were not permitted to wear the gold chinstrap that made our hats look so striking. We had not been through the officer training program, learned the chain of command and the endless set of regulations developed over the years of naval lore. It was as if we were going to be ship captains instead of pilots. To the Navy, a pilot could be a sub commander by just going to a different school. You spoke in "knots" not in "miles per hour." There was no difference whether you were in the air or on a ship. It began to make sense to me as we did our navigation problems. Finding our way back to a carrier which was on a 090° course (due east), doing 25 knots and you had been out 1½ hours flying 180° (due south) at 120 knots. Having it all in the same scale was rather handy to say the least.

Another thing I had not counted on was the drilling and marching! Hey, the Navy sailed—they didn't walk anywhere. I could dance, but this drilling, keeping step, keeping time with a straight back was very new to me. Five years of Boy Scouts hadn't even prepared me for this—especially at the awful hour of 6 a.m. or 0600 hours as they called it. We were awakened at 0530 and were supposed to be mustered in front of our barracks at 0600 with our beds made. Make a bed? What? Mothers did that. While we were out drilling, our beds and rooms (they were private rooms as

Getting all the shots at the same time in one arm for malaria, diptheria, tetanus, cholera and whatnot made for painful marching when trying to swing your arm.

befit our officer status) were inspected. Sheets and blankets had to be so taut that a quarter would bounce off them.

If I had not found a friendly Filipino seaman who would make my bed for a quarter a day, I might never have made it through the 6-week officer school routine! Not only making the bed and having to drill at an hour when only the milkman was out back home, it was the many shots! The shots in the upper left arm for malaria, diphtheria, tetanus, cholera and god-knows-what made swinging one's arm while marching a killer-pain ordeal. Our arms swelled up to twice their size. The word was that if the shots were painful, then all the more that you needed them to save you from a gripping death from one of these diseases. That thought did make it a little easier to tolerate, but oh, did it hurt!

When the 6 weeks were up and we were now officially Navy officers, we could put gold chinstraps on our hats and gain a little respect on the base. We got salutes and had to return them. Things were looking up—until…

Until we started flying! Instead of being able to show what a hot-shot aerobatic pilot I was, the course assumed we knew nothing about flying—and I almost started to believe it.

My problem was the N3N—the original "Yellow Peril." It wasn't a plane, it was a glider with a motor.

N3N "Yellow Perils" taxing out for beginner's Stage-A training—every one of them with an eager cadet at the controls. I'm probably one of them, even though I am an officer and an FAA Certified Flight Instructor! To me, these were gliders, not airplanes!

The N3N was great on floats. They added enough weight to help it set down. Every cadet at Annapolis, aviator or not, had to have 10 hours of instruction in the "Yellow Peril" on floats. One book referred to the cadets fearing this as much as emergency exit drills from a sinking sub. I would have liked to try it on floats, but I had to deal with the land-based version.

As in any basic flying, the instructor would suddenly pull back on the throttle when you least expected it and cry out, "Emergency landing!—engine's quit!—find and glide to a field and land!" I had done this to my own few civil students. No sweat. Except the N3N didn't want to land! We never did land

It was a proud moment when I was issued my Naval Aviator's ID in a small leather wallet case. I probably slept with it under my pillow the first week.

in these exercises. You'd just come in over the field about 20 feet in the air, and when it looked like you had made it, the instructor gunned the throttle and you went back up to do what you had been doing. I'd pick a field about a mile ahead upwind and when I got there, the plane was still 100 feet in the air. It simply would not slow down like the good ol' Waco. It just didn't make sense to pick a field 2 or 3 miles ahead! The most frustrating part is that I knew how to slip a plane to lose altitude by cross-control or to do sharp "S" turns to kill off altitude, but we were "new" pilots. You had to pretend you didn't know anything about flying except what you had learned in the last few hours. All I seemed to have learned was to be a glider pilot, but the Navy didn't have such a program. Only the Army Air Corps trained glider pilots.

My instructor tried to sympathize with me. But frustration with me was more like it. One day we flew in the afternoon and had a pretty good wind off the Gulf. That day I finally made a decent approach to a field and could have glided in with the wind helping hold the plane's glide to a more normal, for me, distance. So he put me up for the Stage A checkride with another instructor. I blew it! It was early morning. No wind. And the #$@*!! N3N would not stop gliding! We weren't allowed to pull the nose up to stall and of course, no slipping, "S" turns or anything but straight and level. I flunked my Stage A check! It was like having a college degree and then flunking an eighth-grade English test. I had 250 hours. I was a CAA Certified Flight Instructor and here I was about to be washed out of the Navy flight program. Passing the physical, enduring the drilling, solving my ineptitude in bed making—but now there was no seaman at 25¢ a pop to take my Stage A flight test for me.

The way the flight tests worked was that if you got a down-check, you had to fly two upchecks to pass on to the next phase. Yes, there was "squadron time" (more instruction) to make one last try, but that was it. Zippo. I'd lie awake trying to imagine fields ahead, the plane gliding nicely to them. Any positive thoughts I could drum up. Finally one thought hit me. I'd tell the check pilot my dilemma. He could read on my reports why I had gotten the down-check. I'd ask him if he'd let me get the feel of the plane first. Could we go to the aerobatic area and let me do a few? The strategy worked.

The check pilots checking us out in A Stage were mostly guys back from sea duty for a little spell from the war. They were bored being Stage A check pilots just doing stalls, takeoffs and landings. The idea of doing aerobatics appealed to them. Out in the aerobatic area, he gave me permission to do whatever I wanted. Only problem was that we had no way to talk to the instructor while in the air. He talked to us through the gosport tube that ran from his mouth bib to the openings in the ears of our helmets. The Navy felt that students learned faster if they could not talk back, ask a lot of questions and offer excuses. They were probably right, and as an instructor myself, it made sense. All he asked was to show him with hand signals what maneuver I was going to do so he could be ready for it—especially snap rolls.

With a gliding sled like the N3N, I thought it best not to try any sharp maneuvers like cartwheels, split-S's and snap rolls. I opted for the graceful ones like an Immelmann, loop and a 4-point slow roll. After about 5 maneuvers he said "Let's go home—you're okay." If he was looking in the mirror, he would have seen the widest grin I could make. It stayed there all the way back to the field.

Officer Instructor Class • Pensacola • November 1942
(top row, fourth head in from right) *We were all CAA Certified Flight Instructors who now had to learn to teach the Navy way of flying. We had to go through each flight stage from solo to formation just as if we were cadet "virgins" ourselves—and that included ground school of celestial navigation, Morse code at 20 wpm, signal flags, ship-profile recognition, navigating with just a plotting board (no visual charts over water) plus the regular subjects of weather, engines, aerodynamics, plane recognition, Navy rules and regs, water and shark survival, gunnery, bombing and student psychology. It was a full plate of studying and flying, crammed into a few months.*

That evening back at the rec room in the Bachelor Officer Quarters, he and my instructor, Hirsch, were playing pool. "Look, Keefe, we talked to the squadron commander. You're scheduled for your second checkride tomorrow and the check pilot has instructions to let you do some more aerobatics—it's ridiculous to make you guys do landings and not use the skills you know like slipping, etc. But we can't be seen at the practice area allowing anyone to do that stuff. Don't sweat it tomorrow." If I had thought about it, I would have gone over to the bar, rung the ship's bell to indicate I'd buy anyone in the house a drink.

I finally received my coveted Navy wings in March of 1943. That winter in Pensacola offered few good flying days. Rain, fog and low clouds seemed to be all there was. It had taken almost 4 months to get in enough flying hours to finish what should have been a 6-week period.

Each morning we got up at 0600 to catch the bus to the field at 0800. But breakfast was something I didn't want to miss! It was served to us by waiters who got to know just what we wanted. My order was always 2 eggs, very sunny-side up, bacon and pancakes. The coffee and orange juice were on the table. The only strange item was the milk. With no cows at sea, the Navy used what was called the "mechanical cow" which did a good job of blending milk powder with water to look and taste like milk. I love milk. It didn't take long for me to get to love Navy milk. It was served ice cold. But I looked forward to those morning breakfasts. If I happened to oversleep and miss breakfast, that bus ride to the coffee and donut table in the ready-room was the only out, and a sorry alternative it was. I rarely overslept.

In exchange for promising to instruct for at least a year to break the pilot backlog, it was indicated we could pretty well chose which branch of Naval aviation we wanted. Almost all of us wanted carrier duty and fighters. That was where the action was and of course, in the back of our minds, it was to be payback time for Pearl Harbor.

This official Naval Aviator document no doubt hangs on many walls. It recalls to me an interesting part of not only my life as I was maturing, but of all the many experiences flying in the Navy.

To Olathe, Kansas Naval Air Station
"Mid-America Navy"

I was sent to the Olathe Naval Air Station just outside of Kansas City. One thing about the Navy primary training bases was that they were mostly near a nice city like Chicago, Kansas City, Minneapolis, Seattle and Dallas. Not out in the middle of Texas where many of the Army Air Corps fields were.

Teaching Navy Cadets

New instructors in the squadron were naturally at the bottom of the pecking order. That meant you were given 5 "virgins" and had to teach them how to fly the "Navy way." These new cadets were as eager as ever to get flying. Because of the lack of instructors, cadets had been called up but then sent to "muscle" schools at various universities where the program was usually run by a tough football coach who would make sure that "his men" sent on to flight school were "tough guys." While I was waiting to be called up as a cadet, I had heard stories of having to play tackle football in just your shorts, among other rather strange activities. So these new cadets felt like they were in Shangri-La when they came aboard and would be flying.

My First Crash!

Stage A was always the landing, takeoff, stalls and emergency landing procedures. But it had a new wrinkle. Where in Pensacola they used the N3N for A Stage, here we used the Spartan (NP-1). Where the N3N was like a moth, the Spartan was like a lead sled! It had metal wingtips. We used to fly low over hayfields where they had wheat stacked in bundles and see if we could slice one in half with the wing. Not very smart. In fact, kinda dumb. If we missed deep into the wing due to a sudden crosswind gust, we'd have egg on our face and a busted plane. I tried it once. Fortunately there was a farmer in the middle of the field so I quickly pulled up and away.

My crash came into the third hour with one of my five students…and it was all my fault. We were practicing takeoffs and landings in one of the 10 grass practice fields. They were "touch and go" which meant the student landed, rolled about 25 yards, then put on full throttle for another go-around and another landing. The routine was to climb straight ahead to 400 feet on the altimeter, then make a climbing left 90° turn gaining another 200 to 600 feet and another 90° left turn climbing to 800 feet heading directly downwind.

The day before in hour 2, the wind had been fairly strong from due south and Cadet Earl was doing that pattern nicely. Today the wind had shifted to the southwest about 45°. However, on the narrow field he had to land due south. The plane had to be "crabbed" into the wind to keep it going straight down the field. He was starting his first left turn at 250 feet instead of 400 feet. I cautioned him to get to 400 feet first, but I also was strict about not "keeping your head in the cockpit." Just

ce at the instruments and quickly look out again for other planes, your drift
e, etc. Plus the fact that if they stuck their head in the cockpit after touching
__ m to adjust the elevator trim from back for the landing to neutral for takeoff, it
would cost them a carton of cigarettes. Even without tax on a Navy base, that was a
lot of money on a cadet's small stipend. I insisted they feel for the trim tab, not look
down in the cockpit for it while taking off.

I had seen a man in a Stinson Reliant crash and kill his family of four while
looking up at the trim tab on the ceiling that he had obviously forgotten to put back
into takeoff position. He had not done his checklist properly. As the plane passed
me, it zoomed up, stalled and crashed nose down on the field. The vision of it still
gives me the shudders.

So later I discovered that Cadet Earl had figured out during hour 2 how to not
look in the cockpit. He noted that he was at 400 feet when over a red barn. Turn
there and then at the road he'd be at 600 feet and down the road alongside the field
at the required 800 feet. But now at hour 3, it was a 45° crosswind—not on-the-nose
as it was yesterday. His first turn at 250 feet put him at only 450 feet crosswind and
650 feet instead of 800 feet downwind. After a few of these puzzling series and my
gradually-rising voice of desperation, I decided to cut the power in his downwind
turn and declare an emergency landing. We had only 500 feet.

He started a steep left turn back to the field. "I'll show him," I thought. "He'll
learn that he doesn't have enough altitude to get back into the wind much less make
the field." I sat there dumb and happy with my elbows resting on the top side of the
cockpit like I was waiting for the gas truck. He steepened his left turn as the wind
started blowing him sideways and pretty soon he pulled back more on stick and we
were in a spin at only 400 feet above the deck! In a spin in a plane that was a true
lead sled! It was underpowered and heavy. Its only saving grace was that it had a
landing gear built with gigantic oleo struts. It could be dropped in from 10 feet and
felt like you had landed in a feather bed. Whoosh! Great for teaching landings to
new pilots. Awful to get out of situations that required power.

I screamed, "I've got it! Let go! I've got it!" Finally he let go of the stick while I
applied full power hoping it would help. It did to some degree. It went from a nose-
down spin to a flat spin that wallowed around like a car slowly spinning on an icy
road. The wind seemed to have picked up and was drifting us sideways when we hit
in a cornfield. It all happened so fast—corn flying through the air—the plane tum-
bling wing over wing in a giant sideways cartwheel. When it stopped I still had full
power on trying to pull it out of the spin. The prop hadn't touched the ground, but
the wings, all four of them, were in a V-shape. I shut the engine off and looked in
the mirror. Cadet Earl was looking around in the same disbelief I felt. Thirty seconds
ago we were in the air and now we were upright on the ground with the dust and
corn settling down on top of us. I was just glad to see him move and that he was
alive.

There was no fire, no oil, but there was gas leaking from the top wing tank. Not
much, but in that dry corn area it got your attention quickly—get the hell out of the
plane! We both scrambled out and moved about 20 yards away in the swath through

the corn stalks that we had made. He was speechless and in a way, so was I. After asking him if he was okay, the first statement out of my mouth was "It was entirely my fault. This won't go on your record, cadet" He smiled lamely. It seemed that just being alive was all that he cared about at the moment.

Soon I had another worry. The planes circling overhead. With about 200 planes up each flight period, there were always many in your vicinity. Most had seen the crash, the dust and debris flying, and certainly could see this bright yellow plane with its large wings up like a resting butterfly. My fear was that two of them might collide and fall right on top of us! Yes, I worried about them, but naturally worried more about myself being right under them. I began waving them off as best I could— cross-arm waving, get-out-of-here waving—anything to shoo them away.

In about 10 minutes the farmer headed for us on his tractor. He said his wife had called the Navy base. Someone was coming out and that we should stay here and wait for the ambulance. Not try to move. Not try too move? The thought had occurred to me that I'd better run as far away as I could. What was going to happen to my flight career now? But then, I realized that I had a very viable witness, Cadet Earl, to whom I had expressed full responsibility. While we waited, I asked him why he had not climbed to 400 feet before making his turn. He explained to me about using the barn to turn instead of the altimeter.

A little later I saw a jeep coming toward us with an ambulance waiting at the roadside about a block away and two corpsmen (medics) running through the field.

It was my fault! I had let a cadet progress too far turning back into an emergency field — the plane, an underpowerd NP (Spartan), went into a flat-spin. This cartoon shows I was still adding full power to try to pull it out of the spin after we hit sideways. The wings took the shock of the crash. Now my worry was planes gawking overhead, colliding and falling on us.

In the jeep was our salty Operations Officer, Commander Faulkner, a cleaned up look-alike for Lee Marvin. I stood at attention next to Cadet Earl, saluted and mumbled that we were okay and that it was my fault. Cmdr. Faulkner walked over to the plane and looked it all over without saying a word. He came back to where I was standing in silence expecting to hear "Report to the brig, your flying career is over in the Navy." Instead he looked me square in the eye, offered his right hand and said, "Nice job, Ensign Keefe, we're trying to get rid of these damn planes—get in the jeep. Cadet Earl, go in the ambulance to get a check-up back at the base. Dismissed."

I had an image of Santa Claus, but Cmdr. Faulkner *was* Santa at that moment. Naturally, back at the base I was getting my 15 minutes of fame from the other instructors. I couldn't buy a drink that night. Hey, I'd only been on the base four weeks and already I was a legend. It could go to your head. But what went through my mind was how stupid I was to think that airplanes are like those bumper cars at the county fair—just horse them around—bump, and go at it again. With about 400 hours of flying time, I had started to mature. But I still had to get by that dangerous 500th hour when you feel you know most everything and then the 1,000th hour when you are sure you know everything!

Just Another Day at the Office

Today I almost fell out of the plane at 6,000 feet! I still get goose bumps when I think about it. I was giving a cadet a final checkride before he could go on to Corpus Christi or to Pensacola for advanced training. We had reports back from the fleet that pilots, especially dive bombers who had to make abrupt pull-ups, were going into inverted spins and didn't know how to recover. The illustration was in the Navy flight manual, but it was not in the syllabus to teach it to the cadets. So I decided that I would show it to those cadets I "final checked." The danger was that we did our aerobatics at 3,000 feet AGL and recover no lower than 2,000 feet. But the inverted spin could take as much as 2,000 feet to recover, more if it wasn't done right. Having cadets practice it could be a problem.

It was a cold, cold day in Kansas. Temperature was right at the minimum of 10° F for daytime operations (15° F for nighttime flying). I explained how to go into an inverted spin and recover. Go to 5,000 feet, do a half-snap roll, stop it on its back, push forward on the stick to stall it and kick right rudder—let it go three turns, pull back on the stick, push opposite rudder into a normal spin and then pop the stick forward to recover as you would from a normal spin.

"Got it?"

"Yes sir," came the reply.

"Okay, let's go fly."

The cold air gave us a good rate of climb. As he climbed through 4,000 feet, I felt a terrible burning sensation in my groin area.

In winter we wore heavy leather fleece-lined flying suits in the open cockpits plus heavy fleece-lined gloves (gauntlets), boots and face masks—and still I was cold!

The Stearman probably trained more WWII pilots in aerobatics than any other plane. We called it the N2S. I think it was the PT-13 in the Army Air Corps. Anyway, we all loved it if someone would crank the inertia starter.

I told him to keep climbing. That something was bothering me and I had to undo my seat belt. Finally getting my gauntlet off so I could stick my hand through the side opening into my right pocket, I felt the culprit. It was my Zippo cigarette lighter. I had just filled it that morning. The lower pressure at altitude as we climbed was causing it to leak. I pulled it out, stuck it in my knee pocket and, even as cold as it was, the air that came into my pocket was a welcome relief from the burning I felt in the entire groin area.

By the time I settled back down in the seat, we had climbed to 6,000 feet instead of just 5,000. Instead of doing a half-snap roll to enter the inverted spin, I told him to do a loop and stop on top. My reasoning was that we were in such thin air that stopping a snap roll upside down might be difficult. Besides, we had altitude to burn. He dove to get the 125 knots airspeed and then pulled back to start the loop. As the centrifugal force that keeps you in the seat at the start of the loop waned as we were about the 1 o'clock position of the loop (12 o'clock being the top where you are on your back), I felt myself starting to fall out of the cockpit! Damn! I had been so relieved to get rid of the burning sensation, I had forgotten to fasten my seat belt!

I grabbed the stick with both hands and still can't figure out how I held on to it with those big fleece-lined gloves. The next thing I knew, we were right-side up and I was standing on the seat! My seat-pack parachute was resting on my butt in front of the cadet's windshield. Okay, so I had a parachute. But the chutes we had were small, 24-foot diameter ones that dropped you fast. They were standard on fighters and other fleet planes so you didn't hang up there in the air any longer than needed to be shot at. And as for dropping you in the water, like jumping off a 2-story building wasn't going to kill you. But over that Kansas tundra with the ground harder than concrete and a heavy flight suit on, you'd come down like a rock…just broken legs if you were lucky.

I told the cadet to go back to the base. That he had an upcheck for sure. That I'd take him up again if he wanted and show him the inverted spin. I mentioned that if he had leveled off at 5,000 feet and had done the half-snap roll I said to do, I would have shot out of that cockpit like the seat was spring loaded (we didn't have ejection seats in those days, but that's what it would have looked like). I looked in the mirror. He was smiling and nodding. As I mentioned, the cadets had no way to talk to us. It was strictly a one-way communication in the air. In the pre- and post-flight it was two-way.

Back on deck we climbed out of the plane. I was still shaking from the thought of falling out which was compounded by my utter stupidity of not refastening my seat belt. Even though I had never unfastened a seat belt in a plane before and therefore did not have it in my memory bank to refasten it, I should have put it there when I unfastened it. It's sure there now! I said to the cadet, "I was hanging on the stick and we were upside-down. How ever did you roll the plane right-side up? His answer was, "I saw you coming out of the cockpit and heard you yell 'Get this bastard on its belly!'—and I pushed the stick sideways as hard as I could—we rolled out." Any kid that could fly like that was okay to be a Navy pilot!

Falling out of a plane haunted us…and I damn near did!

The French Connection

At one point, a platoon of French cadets arrived on base. France had been overrun by Germany, and England was getting pounded. My fitness report showed that I could speak a little French (I found out later just how little when we seemed to be headed for a crash!). I was assigned two "virgin" cadets. They had never flown. This was in addition to 3 U.S. cadets for our instructor load of 5 at a time. You didn't fly with all 5 everyday. After they passed their A Stage flight check, they were off on their own, practicing what you had taught them earlier, like slips and "S" turns to a 200-foot diameter circle, or aerobatics.

In a way, I was honored to have been assigned the French cadets. It was a distinction among your fellow instructors and it gave you a cosmopolitan feeling in the middle of mid-America. But the lack of two-way communication made teaching a chore. We had to get them to at least solo which meant through A Stage. There were only 4 of us who had French students, so we each not only had to teach them but also check each other's students. Our squadron's regular check-pilots couldn't speak French and seemed glad for this inability. They didn't want to authorize soloing a cadet they couldn't speak to.

The French cadets were eager to learn and very respectful. But somehow they had an unusual, almost generic, inability to keep their wings level while landing. It was the strangest thing. You could show them on the ground using a small model plane. Show it coming in with a wing down and say "Mais, non," then do it level and they nod eagerly "Oui, oui." Back in the air, sometimes the wings were level, but too many times one was low.

Night flight instruction with new cadets was not our favorite duty. In the winter in open cockpits, the temperature had to be at least 15° F. The wind chill factor at 110 mph must have been -50° F!

They could fly very well otherwise. They didn't fear the nose-high stalls or the sudden nose drops. Their recoveries were smooth. One of us, in desperation, wanted to see if maybe his student would pick up the down wing just before landing. No such luck. The wingtip slid along the gravel-covered landing mat. The repair guys didn't like us letting that happen. Refinishing wingtips was not their favorite pastime.

I had a theory about this problem. The cadets perhaps were used to riding bikes and motorcycles. Vehicles you could easily lean side-to-side on, not vehicles like cars and trucks that stayed on a level base. About an hour before I was to put my first French cadet up for solo-check, he was gone. They all were gone! Disappeared. This puzzled me until one day when I was ferrying a plane into the Naval Air Station at Grosse Ile near Detroit.

As I was on my downwind leg abeam of the field, I saw all the Stearmans neatly lined up on the flight line. They all had half-loop skids on the lower wingtip! The tips couldn't be damaged. This is where the French cadets had been sent. That it was the French name, *Grosse Ile*, must have felt more like back home to them than Olathe, Kansas.

What Now?

As my year of instructing was reaching an end and the thought of picking a future assignment in the Navy Air Corps approached, there was a major turn of events in carrier warfare. The Japanese had developed the "kamikaze" mentality of flying their planes into the ships on suicide missions. This was totally foreign to us. Sure, we heard that Japanese pilots would shoot at us not only while we floated down in parachutes and even when we were floating in the water. This was bizarre. In WWI there was a creed among pilots. If you were shot down, you were saluted and allowed to float to the ground and probably taken to the enemy's officer's club and toasted. Not with the Japanese. You were fair game in or out of your plane. At Pensacola they showed us how to catch a 50 mm bullet 3 feet under the water. At that depth it was like a lead sinker floating down. The point was that once in the water if you were being strafed, shed your life jacket and grab depth.

This business of being on a carrier that might not be there when you got back because some hot-head rammed her was not very appealing. I was almost 23 now. I was married and had a son. I've done what they asked me to do and now was given a choice. After looking at the many options from carrier to scout float plane aboard a cruiser to transport, the PBY flying boats caught my eye. Here was a "ship." My own ship. If I screwed up and got shot down, it was my own fate, not the result of some suicide idiot ramming my home airport in the ocean. Coming back, low on gas to an oil slick in the middle of the ocean wasn't something you could train for. Sure, you could ditch your plane alongside a destroyer (carriers always had those fast destroyers around them), but that ditching business wasn't a slam dunk.

Ditching a Plane

At Pensacola we had the "Dilbert Dunker" in the main pool. "Dilbert" in the Navy Air Corp was the ultimate screw-up cartoon character. We had to ditch in it, get out of our harness and swim 25 feet away and then tread water for 45 minutes using just our pants and other clothing for floatation gear. In the Dilbert Dunker, you were strapped in a cockpit with the canopy slid back (so you could get out) on a track at about a 75-degree angle to the water. Just before the cockpit hit the water, it was tripped so that your head entered the water in a violent arc in which your face was the first body impact with the water.

The point was to be in a plane that was ditching into the water, grabbed water, stopped suddenly and pitched you forward in a swift arc toward the water. If you didn't grab your nose to prevent water being jammed up your nose, you got a nasal douche that might affect your sinuses for years! Ditching a plane in the water became a thing to avoid, but it always seemed a better alternative to me than trees and shrubs on land. To this day, I'll take the water, especially a few yards offshore where it's deep enough so when the plane flips over on its back to be able drop out and walk ashore. Shallow water might trap you upside-down with no room to get out.

The reality of this was brought back to me nearly 50 years later when one of the friends I met on the air show circuit, Charlie Hillard, a very experienced aerobatic pilot, flipped over in his Sea Fury (British carrier plane WWII) at the EAA Sun N' Fun Fly-In at Lakeland, Florida. A brake had apparently locked up angling him on the runway. Normally, the tail is high enough to give you room to drop out of the cockpit, but Charlie's, being angled on the runway, sank into the soft sand alongside the runway. He suffocated before they could get him out. It was a freak, tragic accident that cost the life of a great guy and pilot. But it serves as a deadly lesson on the need for space in a flip-over.

Charlie Hillard

In the P-51, the ditching procedure is somewhat different than with the air-cooled engines on Navy planes that did not have an air scoop on the bottom. With a smooth bottom, a plane could be settled down nicely if the water wasn't too rough. Of course you never want to lower the gear in any plane. Nor flaps in a low-wing plane. They will act as fins to nose you down. Dump them as soon as you hit when ditching in the water. It may help slow you down, but it'll sure grab and flip you over rather violently. I'd almost say make it a belly (gear up) landing in any off-airport landing. A plowed field can be just as bad as water.

The scoop on the belly of the P-51 is nice on a smooth surface like concrete (I know! I did it by mistake as related later on). On rough terrain or water, the scoop will grab abruptly, flipping you head-over-head. The following rather strange maneuver will probably be the best way to land a P-51 off-airport. Slow it to near-stall just above the deck with full flap. Kick left rudder to cause left wing to grab first. This hopefully causes the plane to turn sideways, and cartwheels so the right wing grabs.

The Dilbert Dunker gave you a great nasal douche if you didn't hold your nose to keep water from being forced into your sinuses. Its purpose was to show us what a ditching in the water might produce. After coming to a rest upsidedown, we had to unbuckle, swim downward to escape the cockpit, then swim away and stay afloat for 45 minutes using only our pants and shirts as floatation gear. I felt sorry for those who didn't know how to swim. It was a struggle and a fear for them.

While the Army Air Corps may have practiced dropping in chutes on land, our entire focus was water. The main lesson was not to panic as the chute dropped over you. To calmly unbuckle, go deep in the water and swim away from under it. It was no easy task fully clothed plus your Mae West vest.

Now you're going backwards, the prop digs in like an anchor, the plane separates at the cockpit and you step or swim out! Sounds easy, doesn't it? To me it beats the alternative of a wild flip-over. I've executed this maneuver over and over in my mind so many times that I think I could do it in my sleep!

Of course, on land you could also hit an obstacle (tree, barn, haystack, etc.) with one wing to accomplish the spin around. In a real situation I think that this is what happened to the Red Baron P-51 at Reno in 1979. The pilot with a dead-stick put down the gear and flaps before being over the field, hit short, wing hit a rock pile, plane spun around, prop dug in, plane separated at the cockpit. Had it not hit first with the wing, I am sure the pilot would never have survived the impact as he luckily did.

Dave Higdon/Special to The Ledger

Charlie Hillard, an experienced aerobatic pilot, flipped over in his Sea Fury at the EAA Sun n' Fun Fly-In at Lakeland, Florida. A brake had apparently locked, angling his craft off the runway. His rudder sank into the soft sand alongside the runway. He suffocated before they could get him out. (Photo by Dave Higdon, The Ledger).

A P-51 went in landing off-field and didn't flip over when my engine man, the famous Dave Zeuschel, took off south from the Van Nuys airport. He was test hopping an engine modification. Just after takeoff the engine quit. "Quiet time" I call it because the P-51 engine is so loud in the cockpit, especially in takeoff power mode. When it stops, the silence is immediate and alarming.

It was in the fall just before the Reno Air Races. Dave wisely didn't try any turns back to the field. His gear and flaps were up. Straight ahead was a cornfield with dried stalks still standing. Dave, a good pilot, let it settle gently down into the standing corn. The stalks acted as a ground blanket as they were crushed in front of the plane, preventing the P-51's low-slung air scoop from digging in. The plane and prop had only minor damage as a result. His description of corn and stalks and dust flying through the air brought back memories of my flat-spin voyage into that Kansas cornfield. So I guess if you can find a field of tall corn stalks, head for it. That's what experience seems to say.

Chapter 4

I Choose PBYs

S ure, I could pick a fleet service I wanted after serving a year as an instructor, but the Naval Air Command with all of us "instant aviators" suddenly choosing advanced flying status, decided we really weren't pilots yet. I had instrument ratings, had checked out in advanced planes like the SNJ, the Twin-Beech, even the SBD Dive Bomber during my aerobatic instructor assignment.

The SNJ (AT-6) was our main instrument trainer. The student sat in the back with a black hood pulled over the inside of the cockpit. Climbs, glides and slow flight were at 120 mph, level cruise was 160 mph.

The "mechs" (mechanics) loved helping dock the PBYs in the hot Pensacola summers, as shown in this photo of a rare P3M. After a flight in that humidity, I envied them. Unlike single-engine prop planes, there was no cooling fan in front of you. Note the "meatball" in the insignia which was later eliminated because it was like the Japanese.

The nice thing about the Navy was that they had these advanced planes on the base and encouraged you to do cross-country training flights in them to hone your navigational skills and to fly heavier and greater horsepower.

My flight wing instructional schedule was 10 days on an a.m. schedule, 2 days rest then 10 days on the p.m. wing. I caught the night flying instruction duty once a month on the p.m. wing. If the temperature at half-an-hour before night takeoff was just above the 15° F minimum for open cockpit night flying, anyone would have been a hero if he could have figured a way to get it to drop to 14° F or lower! We couldn't figure out a way.

The a.m./p.m. wing schedule with 2 days off every 10 gave us what amounted to 3 days free time when going from the a.m. wing to the p.m. wing. You could sign out any available plane to start a cross-country in the afternoon of your last a.m. day and didn't have to be back until noon of the p.m. wing day. You were limited to 500 miles from base in case they had to go get a sick plane away from base. From Kansas City's central location, the 500-mile radius gave me a wide range of choices in a ring from Minneapolis to Chicago to Nashville to Dallas to Denver. My home was Chicago and even in a 100-mph-plus Stearman, I could make that in less than 5 hours each way and did it often.

You could always get a Stearman. The 5 SNJs, one twin Beech (SNBs—AAF's AT-11) and 3 Howards (DGAs) were usually available. But the rare fighter or dive-bomber went by rank which I rarely had. But I was low time in those, did not want to fly them on instruments, so usually checked them out for short distance one-day hops.

I assumed I'd be sent to a PBY squadron for water training but NAVPers, with maybe 200 worn out, aerobatic-weary, old (I was 23) flight instructors, they decided that none of us had any more qualifications than to just be aerobatic instructors. Even if we had formation experience, which we all had to teach our cadets, we had to take the cadet formation course. Although I had taught formation flying for a year and had an instrument rating, I had to go through the cadet formation flight and instrument training course.

Formation Flying

"It Takes Three to Tango!"

Formation training was in the SNV (BT-13) the "Vultee Vibrator." The tail section was plywood. They told us if you snap-rolled it, the rear section would probably depart in midair—I didn't try. I was an old man at 23. My only memory from this phase (and I can still vividly recall it) was at NAS Dallas on final check-out. We were checked out of formation stage in threes for a V-formation of 3 planes. The check pilot flew above and around us. There was no plane-to-plane communication. We took off singly and joined up on the person assigned to the lead plane. This particular day there was an RAF cadet going through the Navy syllabus.

The drill was to always think we were taking off from a carrier. Flaps down 20°, stick back for tail-low takeoff, full power, then release brakes. After takeoff, we retracted flaps (manually on the SNV). The gear was fixed. The lead plane made a wide arc left turn and we were to cut inside the arc and judge to meet him at a point we could match his position and speed for a join-up. I was the right wing man and was to be the first in position. When I got there I shot past him! Had to pull throttle all the way back to save face and slide back into a position 45° to his right. I was practically stalling to stay in position. Then I noticed the left wingman was having the same problem. He overshot the lead, was in a left turn with his nose high and wings wobbling near a stall.

Finally the lead, the RAF cadet, leveled out as he was supposed to do when we had joined up and flew straight. You are supposed to keep your eyes on the lead pilot for any hand signals he may give to show his next move. I could not figure out why I was almost stalling to stay in formation. Then I noticed that he had not retracted his flaps! No wonder we were nose high near stall trying to stay in formation with him. Meanwhile I could see the check pilot doing lazy eights around us checking our performance.

My God, I thought. Is this RAF cadet going to get me a down-check for my wings wobbling in this nursery school phase? When he'd look back at me smiling, I'd frantically do the "flaps up" rotating arm-fist signal. He just waved back, smiled and kept on with his flaps down! I couldn't believe it! His right arm was resting comfortably on the right side of the open cockpit canopy. He was even flying with his left hand. RAF style I wondered?

Back on the deck, I made up my mind to speak first and strongly to the check pilot, come what may. Fortunately, I started out with "you probably could not see this but we were trying to join up and fly on a plane with its flaps down"—then I looked at the cadet and said "you noticed that when you went to put your flaps down for a landing that were already down, didn't you?" The direct statement was meant to catch him by surprise and it did. He answered "Yes, they were down." Case closed. We passed. The other wingman just looked at me and shook his head.

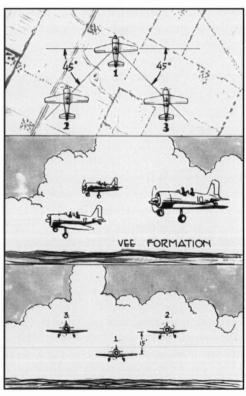

This illustration shows the necessary position of the aircraft while flying in the "VEE formation." This pattern was used by all branches of the military.

On reflection, maybe I should have put my flaps down too. It would let me carry higher power and more air over the tail to better control the plane. But then what if he suddenly retracted his flaps. I would have been left behind like a cottonball thrown out of the cockpit, never to catch up straight and level even at full power in an SNV. Sixty years later, I still think about it!

Instrument Flight Training
"Happy Under the Hood"

Now for the instrument part in the SNJ (AT-6). I already had an instrument rating so this was a snap. We were mixed in with cadets. The instrument instructors were used to the cadet level. We sat in the back seat with a black hood inside the canopy. We had two-way communication with the instructor. He told us the pattern to fly on instruments only such as a 360° turn to the right, then climb 500 feet on a heading of 090° to 2,000 feet, level off, turn to 270° and go down 500 feet to the starting altitude. The SNJ was a nice stable instrument platform. Flying it was easy. Having earned an instrument rating already, this was a walk in the park.

Twin-Engine Training
"A Bright Surprise"

Then came multi-engine training before the PBYs. Here again, I had been flying the SNB (AT-11) on my free time as an instructor back at Olathe NAS. Also the JRC (C-78) Bobcat—a Cessna with two giant Jacob engines compared to its size—and it developed carburetor ice quickly even on summer days if you throttled back and did not put on carburetor heat.

The SNB was a baby carriage with two engines, often referred to as "the Twin-Beech." It also had two tails like the B-24. I had understood that planes had two smaller tails instead of one large one so they would fit under the hangar doors. Made sense, so I never questioned it. But the SNB was a tail-dragger (it had a tailwheel versus a nosewheel). The tail height was lower than the prop clearance. It really did not need the lower twin tails to fit in a hangar.

Again, here I was in cadet training in a plane I had flown a fair amount. Put the gear up, feel the difference. Put the flaps down, feel the difference, cut one engine off, feel the difference. Determine which engine had failed because you had to hold rudder on the opposite side to keep the plane straight and level. The good engine pulled you toward the bad engine. Rudder on the good engine side compensated for that. Feathering engine drills, etc., that I had done many times.

But there was one notable memory from this phase. It was a night flight in Pensacola. There were isolated thunderstorms all around the area with a beautiful display of lightning everywhere. In Pensacola in the summer time, if you didn't fly at night in these conditions, you really couldn't get in much flying. It seemed there were always evening thunderstorms here and there. We flew two students per flight. The instructor sat in the right (co-pilot) seat and students in the left seat. I was first up, flew my hour of turns, mini-cross-country routes and then moved to a back seat while another student, a cadet, took the left seat for his turn.

Now, lightning is not supposed to strike a plane in the air because the plane isn't grounded. Same with a car, because it's on rubber tires and isn't grounded. Lightning seeks out grounded items like trees, metal towers, a person holding a golf club high while standing on wet ground, and hopefully lightning rods on buildings instead of the building itself. Well, there's one little item left out of this scenario. What if the lightning bolt is on its way to something on the ground and your plane happens to be in its path?

The cockpit lit up with every near bolt. No problem. Just adjust your eyes to the darkened cockpit again. Suddenly, the cockpit was a lot brighter! I mean a LOT brighter! From my rear seat, after my eyes got used to the dark again, I could not see any lights on the panel. The radio lights were out. I leaned forward to see the wingtip lights. Nothing. The instructor looked at the cadet. The cadet looked at the instructor. My rank was the same as the instructor—a Lt.(jg) (a 1st Lt. in Army and Marines). "What the hell was that?" the instructor called out as if he didn't know, but asked just hoping it wasn't what he thought it was—that we'd been hit by lightning.

The plane was flying okay. No apparent control damage. The instructor got out the flashlight and shined it around the cockpit. All seemed normal. Then he shined it out on the starboard wing. Whoa! There was a black spot about a foot in diameter near the wingtip. It looked like the aluminum had been fused. Back in the cockpit, the radios had that acid smell, but no smoke. But also no reception. He tried a couple of transmissions to the base tower at Cory Field about 20 miles away. No response.

The Beechcraft Twin Engine (SNB in the Navy, AT-11 in the Army) was the trainer all multi-engine pilots first flew. It's in use even today by parachute jump teams, as cargo carriers, small executive and personal planes. It is known as the Beech 18 in civilian life today. Many have a nose-wheel conversion vs. tail wheel, like regular airliners.

So here we were with fried radios. No running lights. No cockpit lights. No way to call the tower for landing sequence and no landing lights. No radar in those days. We were like a Stealth Bomber but wanted to be like a full lit dirigible. There were maybe 25 of us up there, all milling around in the dark except for flashes of lightning. The others had running lights, but we didn't!

The instructor was obviously concerned—and so was I. Just sitting there and letting fate take over is not in my vocabulary if there is anything I can do about it. So I calmly said to him, "Sir, I've been in this situation before (I hadn't). Would you mind if I took over?" He didn't grab me by the neck and fling me into the pilot seat, but it was something like that. He told the cadet to get in back and authorized me to take over. He pulled himself forward by clutching under the instrument panel and stared straight ahead.

The first thing I told him is that we would head straight north to get out of the area where all the other planes are which was northeast of the base. Then we'd head west to be northwest of the base over where the PBYs practiced, but they were out over water and we would be north of them over land. Then we'd head back toward base, but stay north of the incoming landing pattern of planes coming back from the east.

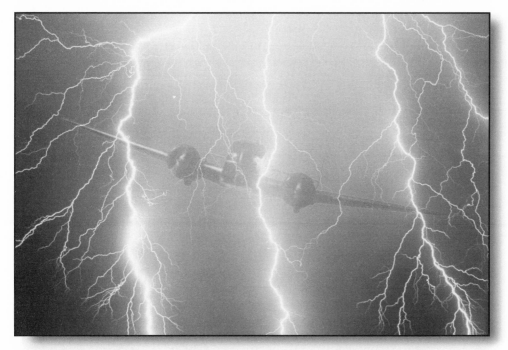

Lightning was a nightly occurrence in the Pensacola area during the summer time. I recall another officer's wife hiding under the bed during lightning. She was from the Seattle area and had never seen lightning before. As a mid-westerner, it was hard to believe there was a place in the U.S. without lightning. It bored a hole right through our wing.

Then we'd pick out a plane without another close behind him, tuck under him, land short hoping he'd land normally and we'd be on the deck able to see the plane ahead. If we got too close, I'd ground loop it to avoid running up his tail. Of course, then a plane might land on us.

He looked at me as if in disbelief, thought about it and then nodded okay.

I said, "It's your call, sir, okay?"

"Okay." he replied.

I found a plane approaching without a plane close behind. As he made his left turn to final, I tucked in under him about 50 yards behind. As he came over the field, his lights showed the runway ahead. When there, I cut power and made my first

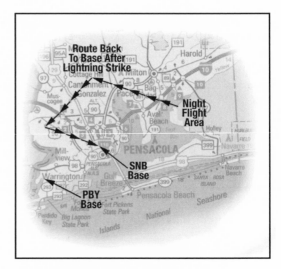

The route back after the lightning strike… at night, no radio, no lights…and with other planes to avoid.

and only tailwheel carrier-type landing in a twin. The plane in front was far down the runway. A quick turn off the runway gave us plenty of space for the plane behind who probably never saw us.

Out of the plane, we checked out the hole through the starboard wingtip. It was perfectly round with a 4-inch dark border all around. We walked to the hangar. The instructor didn't say a word to me, but the next day the squadron commander called me in and said the instructor had given me an unusually great write-up. "Good job, the plane is on view over at the A&R (Assembly and Repair) hangar." I wish I had thought of it as being a Kodak moment so I could have the pix today, but my thought was to put it as far behind me as I could.

Flying the PBY

Now here was a new experience! I hadn't done any flying like this before! Not only was it bigger and heavier than anything I had ever flown, but it took off and landed on water! This was surely now the Navy. It was Navy flying second only to carrier flying—and a far second it was. There is no way to explain to another pilot the sensation of flying a large flying boat compared to a ground-based plane. You don't need an airport. Seven-eighths of the world is covered by water. That's your airport. (Okay, so a bunch of it is at the North and South Poles in ice—there's still a lot more water than land). You can land on water, shut off the engines, drift and even fish as you drift along. The wings are so large, you bring your own shade with you if you drift onto a white sand beach.

The only screwy thing is taxiing downwind. Instead of putting in right rudder to turn right, you put in left rudder. Deflecting the rudder left presents a flat surface on the tail to the wind to blow the tail to the left so the plane turns right. Sort of like trying to do something while looking in a mirror. Only problem is if you do it wrong and discover it after the tail starts swinging the other way, especially in a strong following wind, you are in for a grounding or an embarrassing swing around—and there are plenty on board and at the dock ramp to witness your screw up!

Several things stand out during this training:

- The crew chief goes along even on student solo flights.
- Gassing it up requires one person on the high wing and one below holding the hose up.
- The way to land at night on the open ocean with no runway or telltale landing lights.
- Stalling it 20 feet in the air on a rough ocean. This is what I recall, 60 years later, as I write this.

Crew Chief is Always There!

If there is an unsung hero in the Navy flying, it's the Crew Chief on the PBYs used for training. He had to be in the plane even when we soloed for the first time! The way the PBY was configured (and I never really understood why) is that all the engine instruments were in a small tower in the center wing strut above the cockpit instead of in front of the pilot. It was somewhat like the larger planes that had an engineer and panel behind the pilots, but these were in 4-engine planes where there was a greater mass of engine instruments to display and monitor. The PBY had only two engines.

All the pilot had was a series of switches with lights that lit up a panel above in the Crew Chief's area. If we wanted a leaner mixture, we just flipped the mixture-lean switch and the Crew Chief adjusted it from his platform. He had a little window through which he could peer only straight ahead. All we had was a throttle and prop position control which was between pilot and co-pilot hanging out of the overhead. Our instrument panel had only the radio, plane attitude and basic navigation instruments. It seemed weird not to be able to scan for fuel flow, cylinder head temp, oil pressure, oil temp, etc.

Three students soloed on the same hop, so in a sense, we were risking our necks with each other. But the crew chiefs risked their necks day after day trapped in that small space with pilots on their first solo flights who might either drop the plane on the water from 50 feet in the air, or try to make a sub out of it with a nose-low landing, especially in rough seas.

Gassing Up After a Flight

I was an officer, but in the training phases I had to fly and do the same things the cadets did, including fly with them on an equal basis—no salutes, no "sirs." Naturally they respected me not only because I was an officer, but also because I wore the coveted Navy wings. After each flight when the PBY was put on a wheel-truck and winched or towed up the ramp to the gas pit area, one of the three of us had to climb on top of the wing which was plenty high off the ground. If there was a cadet among the three of us, we usually tried to con him into that duty because it required some agility not only to scramble up there, but to walk the slippery wing, grab the gas hose we held above our head for him and then unfasten the gas cap. The third person was at the gas pump waiting for the signal to turn it on, watch the person on the wing for the signal for a quick shut-off.

One time, (and it was the last time!) I was caught under a waterfall of gasoline. I was the person who handed up the hose, stood there keeping it slack above my head, while the guy on the wing stood watching to top it off. This day the cadet on the wing must have been staring out at the beautiful bay off Bronson Field about 15 miles west of Pensacola and didn't see the gurgle of the tank being topped off. I was looking straight up the hose at the trailing edge of the wing when this wall of gasoline cascaded down on me. I must have frozen with my eyes wide open, because the next sensation was that I was blinded and my eyes were stinging something fiercely.

I let go of the hose which came sliding off the wing spewing gasoline all over like an enraged dragon as it came down. I felt the heavy brass nozzle bounce off my shoulder thinking I'd been hit by a cannon ball, but the pain in my eyes was so great I didn't care. Then two or three guys grabbed me and helped me stagger to the nearby head where there was a large circular sink at which 8 people could wash from 8 sets of hot/cold water faucets. I half-laid down in it, they turned on the cold water. I fought to open my eyes so the gasoline could be douched out to relieve the sting. When I could stand up, I had to strip off my gasoline-soaked uniform and then go to the shower area to try to get the smell out of my hair and body. Fortunately I had taken off my poplin flight suit before gassing, so it was dry and could get me home with some clothing on. After that, I tried to always get the duty at the pump or even take the wing job. Never the hose guy again!

Night Landings On Water

This was a thrill! Our instructor this night was an experienced PBY Patrol Captain, Bill Normoyle, who had been in the famous Black Cat Squadron. This was a PBY squadron in the South Pacific noted for its night flights for both intelligence about Japanese movements, sea rescues of downed pilots and bothering the Japanese at their island bases. Their oft-told story is dropping coke bottles at night in the hours between 2 a.m. to 4 a.m. over the Japanese bases to keep them from getting any sleep. Now and then they'd drop a bomb. The coke bottles whistling through the air as they dropped made a sound somewhat like a bomb's whistle. On the ground, it was hard to tell the difference.

Bill regaled us with other tales of PBY lore. The one that fascinated me the most was how to land at night on a dark, smooth sea with no landing lights on for security reasons. Maybe to pick up a downed pilot near an island controlled by the Japanese. Our radios in those days were on the frequencies below the standard commercial radio frequencies of 500–1600 kc. We worked in the range below those from 200–400 kc. It could be transmitted over the curve of the earth for long distances if you had a long antenna which the PBY certainly had. I don't recall exactly how long, probably 50–75 yards of copper wire that we wound in and out on a fishing-reel-type spool. At the end of it was a white canvas cloth cone. When we unreeled it, the cone pulled it out behind the plane and kept it steady, not thrashing around. If we forgot to reel it back in on landing, the loss of the cone as it hit the water was a minor item to replace.

The neat trick Bill showed us that night was this (the crew chief up in the wing pylon must have been peering out at the black night in terror): Crank the antenna out as far as it would go. Figure the wind was blowing toward any land mass in the area, which it usually did. The PBY cruised at 120 knots (138 mph). Head into the wind using your compass. Go down to 200 feet on your altimeter (remember, it's dark and you can't see out or the horizon). Tune your radio to a static-free frequency. Retard the throttles to an airspeed that will give you a landing glide of 200 feet per minute down on the vertical speed indicator (about 80 mph). Listen intently on your earphones. When you hear static caused by the antenna cone hitting the water, pull back on the throttles, full back on the yoke and swoosh!—the hull settles into the water. Amazing!

This technique had to be the first Cat II instrument landing system ever developed! Of course, such a landing today is routine for airliners with air and ground-based equipment. But even the modern-equipped airliner of today can't do that on the open sea. This demonstration made the thought of flying PBYs even sweeter!

Rough Ocean Landings in a PBY

There is nothing in flying anything that prepares you for this. Stalling a shuddering giant plane "way up" in the air and letting it drop 20 feet (about 2 stories) into a raging sea! And on top of that, a raging sea that's not eager to have you there.

In normal sea landings, you look down at the wind streaks in the water which appear as long ribbons on the water surface. You know that the wind is blowing down those streaks, but without dropping a smoke flare you can't tell which way it's blowing. So you fly 90° across the streaks and note which way your plane drifts over the water either by observing something on the surface or by noting which rudder pedal you have to push to keep the crosswind heading (the wind is from the side of the rudder you push), then you land into the wind that way.

But in a rough sea, the waves tell you which way it's blowing. That problem of wind direction is easy. But you can't land into it. The high waves will turn you into a submarine fast. You have to land in the trough between the waves at least 45° to the wind. And you have to do it with virtually no forward flying speed which means a full stall, which means a heart-stopping 20-foot drop into the water—splat–smash!

The hull groans and you hope the rivets don't pop under the stress because then you'd be a submarine! Then you add full power and go up the first wave, pull off power and slide down its back at 45° like a surfer going the reverse way. In sailboat racing we call it "stepping into the wind" as you head upwind and then slide down the back of the wave. Taking off, you try to ride the top of a wave slightly downwind. Then when the suction breaks and the hull releases, turn into the wind holding on tightly to whatever talisman suits your mentality. As I said, there's nothing, absolutely no experience in aviation other than films of this being done that can prepare you for a rough-water landing in a PBY.

On Patrol

As officers with our wings, we were open to any flying duty even though we were in a cadet training syllabus. We liked being assigned to coastal patrol in Florida looking for German submarines. The U-boats were amazingly aggressive. They had even entered the harbor at New York and came up to periscope depth for a look around. The prevailing thought was that if you spotted one or its shadow in the water, to drop a few depth bombs in front of its course on either side. But I was cautious.

A friend of mine, Tom Alyward of Highland Park, Illinois, was flying a Vega Ventura in the early part of the war off the east coast. He spotted a U-boat, dropped a few depth charges, swung around to make another run. Instead of diving, the U-boat fully surfaced and shot him down on his run! He spent the rest of the war in a German prison camp. Of course the Germans wanted to rescue all the pilots they could because pilots had a great deal of information on how they hunted U-boats, etc.

As pilot-officers, we could fly along on sub-patrol for German U-boats operating off the coast of Florida. I never saw one, but every cloud shadow on the water was suspect if it didn't drift over the water. The U-boats even entered New York's harbor and came up to periscope depth. One had shelled the area above Santa Barbara, California.

In a turnabout situation, a U-boat is the only warship ever captured by the U.S. on the high seas. Admiral Dan Gallery, USN, did it. It is on view today in Chicago at the Museum of Science and Industry where you can tour it inside and out. So a U-boat is on display in the Midwest, far from the Atlantic Ocean they ruled for far too long.

Preparing for the Invasion of Japan

As I finished PBY qualifications, the lovable boats were being phased out in favor of land-based Navy bombers. We assumed it was to prepare for an invasion of the main islands of Japan. We had pretty much knocked them out of the South Pacific at the time. Of course, none of us knew what was going on in the planning. It was the summer of 1945. My classmate, Chuck Dumont of Mt. Pleasant, Michigan, had chosen carrier duty and was already at sea on an operational status.

To get more carriers as fast as possible, the Navy developed smaller, lighter, faster-to-build carriers called the Princeton class. Then to get even more carriers quickly, the famous Liberty Ships were developed and thrown together by the famous Henry Kaiser as troop and supply transports. They were converted into carriers, primarily for planes that were lighter and smaller like fighter planes. They weren't like the big, comfy carriers of the Essex class. Chuck once wrote that he looked forward to the day he could get off "this bucket of rust."

I was assigned to Jacksonville to fly the Navy's version of the 4-engine B-24 Liberator. It was called the PB4Y-2A, the "Privateer." It had a single tall tail instead of the twin tail of the B-24. The single tail gave it more stability and control at the slow landing speeds the Navy liked. The war had been over in Europe for more than a year, so the AAF traditional bombers were just about surplus. The idea of 4 engines on a land-based Navy plane was something new to us. We didn't have too many of them in the training unit during July 1945, so I was assigned to tow targets for the fighters out over the ocean. Not a pleasant task if the guy got flat behind the target and opened fire in desperation of getting his hits that he missed while coming in at 90° to the target. The thought of being shot down by "friendly fire" from the rear was not the highest priority on my volunteer list of duties!

Word was that we would stage somewhere in September 1945 for the assault on Japan. My fear was that the Navy usually drew the Aleutian Islands for duty because of the large expanse of open water up there. I didn't mind the over-water flying but, 1) it wasn't the nice warm waters of the South Pacific and, 2) the weather of rain and more importantly fog, the enemy of all pilots, was all too common.

Navy Flying After WWII

Though we were discharged from active duty after Japan officially surrendered, the expectation was that we would stay in the reserves and keep up our flying status. We "drilled" one weekend a month without pay. Each year we went on a "cruise" for 2 weeks. We were paid the enormous sum of $200 for the 2-week cruise. A real windfall when you were making only $65 a week. If you stayed in the reserve for 16 more years, 20 total (I'd be 46), you got retirement pay when you were 65. At age 65? I couldn't count that far ahead, but those 2-week cruises to Florida and other southern places were nice. They were on my vacation time. I was not in a financial position to take an away vacation with two kids anyway.

My home was in Highland Park, a suburb 25 miles north of Chicago. And just to the west was the Glenview Naval Air Station. So convenient. I joined the VPML-54 Squadron at Glenview. (V = Navy Fleet; P = Patrol; ML = Multi-Engine-Land). We had SNBs (S = Scout; N = Trainer; B = Beechcraft, the AT-11-twin-Beechs) 2 PV-2s (Vega Venturas), and several SNJs (AT-6). Somehow, I was assigned to be Squadron Leader for the SNBs for the weekend I was on duty. However, it was fun checking out the SNJs and take them up to dog fight with other pilots and do aerobatics. To compare my business life on Michigan Avenue selling advertising for the Chicago *Tribune* running parallel with military flying seemed strange. Here I was cavorting about the skies and tomorrow I'd be in a Brooks Brothers suit with wing-tipped cordovan shoes acting like a responsible person.

I had to check out pilots in the SNB so they could take them up solo. I still recall one checkout in particular. It was on a usual busy Sunday with planes all over the landing pattern. There were so many that we often used not only the runway going into the wind, but also the runway 45° to that if a crosswind was not too strong. Also, the chaps in the tower were also weekenders in the reserve. It was truly an amateur assemblage. One weekend a month, then back to our regular jobs. Naturally you were a little rusty not doing it every day.

My patrol squadron VPML-54 on a 2-week "cruise" staging out of the Naval Air Station at Opa-Locka, Florida in 1948. The mission was to learn to track the new snorkel subs the Russians (and we) had. A basketball-size breather floated on the surface to supply air. I'm above the arrow in the line of flight officers who are wearing ties in hot, humid Florida!

In the SNB you had a gear up/down light, but we also "grabbed a wheel." Each pilot pulled himself forward to look out of the side window to see that the wheel on his side was down. If it was, the reply was "got a wheel." If both pilots said that, all was fine. Go ahead and land. We did and he rolled out on final.

Just about as we were to touch down, the tower barked at us, "Go around, go around on one-eight!" (One-eight being the number of the runway that landed due south, 180°). I told him "full power and climb." I could see that we were on a collision course with another plane that was landing on the runway to our right that intersected our runway. The tower guys were doing their job.

As my student pulled up for another circle to land, I sat back in relief because these weekend things can get hairy. Just as we rolled out for final, the tower commanded "Pull up on one-eight. Pull up, your gear is not down!" How could that be, I wondered? I quickly reached over to the throttle quadrant and added full power for another go-around. I looked at him in disbelief and he looked at me. "Guess I instinctively put the gear up for the go-around without even thinking about it," he said. Made sense to me because that is the proper procedure. It's so drilled into our nervous system that it's almost an unconscious act—and later on I'll tell you how I bellied in "Miss America" in the same "psychological set."

Back on the ground I called the tower on the Ops Office phone. "Thanks guys, but how did you see that our gear was up that far out?" Answer: "An airliner was flying by on his way into Chicago and called us to tell us we had a plane coming in with its gear up." Whoever that airline captain was, I am indebted to him. But on second thought, I'm not. There is a saying that every pilot will land gear-up at some point—it's just a matter of when. As I look back, I wish it had been this time with the repair bill on the Navy rather than 30 years later with the repair bill out of my pocket with "Miss America"!

My Last Navy Flight
"An Air Force Plane Almost Did Me In"

This one still sends chills up my spine when I think about it. An officer who happened to be a co-pilot for United Airlines needed to have a cross-country checkout. I was assigned the duty of checking him out. The only twin available was an SNB. The route was to go to NAS Minneapolis, land, check-in, fly to Oshkosh, Wisconsin to pick up a flag officer at Oshkosh and take him back to NAS Glenview for a meeting with the base skipper the next day. Simple.

At NAS Minneapolis, we filed our departure flight plan for Oshkosh. The Operations Officer on duty had to approve it. "Show me your weight and balance form for the plane" he demanded. Immediately I could see that I was dealing with the enemy of all pilots "the regulations, authoritative jerk." Only two pilots in the plane? Weight and balance forms? Those were for heavily-loaded aircraft to make sure their weight was properly distributed so it wouldn't go nose-up or nose-down on takeoff. Not for routine missions with only a pilot and co-pilot aboard. I explained that at

NAS Glenview the forms were kept on file in the Ops Office, not carried on the plane and possibly lost.

Not to be denied, he picked up the phone and called the Ops Officer at NAS Glenview and proceeded to give him a bawling out in chapter and verse for not keeping the form on the plane. He finally settled for having a Western Union telegram sent to him by the NAS Glenview Ops Officer verifying that the weight and balance form was on file and okay for the plane. My problem was that in early March it was getting dark fast and I didn't know how to reach the officer I was to pick up in Oshkosh to tell him we'd be late. It was a civilian airport, not military on our com line. It didn't even have a tower.

I checked weather. Clear and cold all the way. Off we went into the darkness. I chose to fly left seat for this leg. About 5 miles from the airport we were suddenly in a swirling snowstorm. The weather check hadn't said anything about this. Must be something local, so I pressed on. Pretty soon it wasn't local. It was a full-blown snowstorm and it wasn't getting any thinner. I was not prepared for an instrument flight nor was the plane set up for IFR flight with a recent check of the instruments. There was no way to turn back to the airport. We didn't have enroute radar then. And I really didn't know where the hell I was. Suddenly, I saw the glow of the fire from the boiler of a train below. The airline co-pilot's eyes were getting larger all the time. I told him I was going to do a little Army IFR flying (I Follow Railroads) which is the way we used to tease Air Force pilots. I went down so we could read the names of the stations at the railroad stops to figure out where we were on the chart.

I finally saw a city name to spot our location. The artificial horizon instrument was working okay so I pulled up and headed due east figuring we had to fly out of this at some point. If weather had not told us about this, it could not cover too big an area.

At this point, let me explain what had happened as I reconstructed it later. Northeast of Minneapolis there was a large area of towns without weather reports. This storm

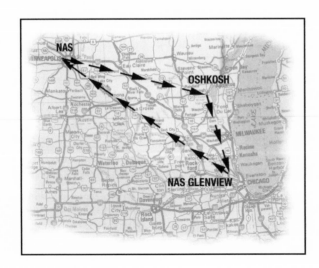

For us "weekend warriors" it was just another training flight in an SNB (AT-11), but it was my last Navy flight. It was a "hairy" one!

had developed in that area and suddenly engulfed the Minneapolis area, moving rapidly south. Shortly after we took off, a Northwest Airline's plane hit a tower north of Minneapolis and all were killed. What must have happened is that his altimeter read higher than he really was. Altimeters show altitude based on the air pressure. When you enter a low pressure (storm) area, the altimeter thinks you are higher and reads that way. We normally get altimeter adjustment settings from the tower, but the storm wasn't at the field yet, it was still northeast. The poor pilot in the NWA plane had no way of knowing he was lower than his altimeter said. Today, airlines also have radio altimeters that show their actual height above the ground and have warning horns when you get too low. A warning even sounds in the tower that has radar, and most do have it today. My logbook shows the date was March 10, 1950. I keep meaning to get a copy of the Minneapolis *Tribune* for March 12 to read about the airline crash, but it wouldn't have the details I sought. If they printed a weather map in the paper, it might. I would like to hear from anyone who might research this.

Suddenly, we were out of it. The view ahead was nothing but twinkling lights on the horizon. I had purposely headed north of Oshkosh so I'd know that it was to my right. Early on in cross-country flying you learn that when there is a destination that's on a river, railroad or highway, to aim to one side or the other so that when you get to that checkpoint you can follow it left or right to reach it. If you try to fly directly to your destination and you get to the river, etc., and don't see your destination, you don't know whether to turn right or left.

On this cold, clear moon-lit night, I could see the large glacier-formed Lake Winnebago in the distance. It was a big black hole rimmed with sparkling lights. Near its southwest base was Oshkosh and Fond du Lac was easily visible at the southern tip. Oshkosh's rotating beacon came into view and a landing was routine. On the ground, I kept the port engine running because the battery sounded weak when we started up back in Minneapolis. No way did I want to get stuck on a Sunday night in Oshkosh when I had to be at work the next day at the Chicago *Tribune*.

Naturally, our passenger had given up and gone home. We were about 2 hours late at this point. The airport attendant knew him and called to tell him we were there. He replied he'd be right back there. I must have waited half an hour with the engine running and burning up gas. Finally he came and strapped himself in the seat behind my co-pilot. He was a full commander. Scrambled eggs on his visor and all. He was lucky he wasn't a pilot, because he probably would have bailed out during what followed.

As we approached the bright lights of the Chicago area, I called the Navy tower at Glenview. No answer. I switched to another frequency. Still no answer. I switched to the emergency frequency. Still no answer, but the needle showed I was transmitting. Suddenly my hometown area looked strange. I had not flown at night in the area for some time. It was 1950, after the war, and it had grown far and wide along the lake and to the northwest. Surely I could find Waukegan Road and follow it to the base. Waukegan Road was out in the sticks. But not any more. I couldn't find it!

Okay then, head for Lake Michigan's shoreline, follow it south to our Point Oboe checkpoint we reported over, on the way in to land from the lake. Point Oboe was a large white temple with a lighted lace dome near the border of Wilmette and Evanston that could be seen far away. I knew that the Glenview Naval Air base was on a west-northwest heading from there. The problem was that I now had only about 20 minutes of gas left. I had a plan that if it got down to 10 minutes, I would ditch in the water off Oak Street Beach in Chicago near the Drake Hotel. Surely we'd be noticed and rescued—no sweat, really.

Over Point Oboe I gave another call to the tower. "If you read me, please flick the field lights on and off." In the mosaic pattern of lights ahead I saw a band flicker on and off! Wow! They heard me! I asked them to keep flicking them. They did. The commander was sitting peacefully in the rear seat enjoying the light show below. My United Airlines co-pilot was starting to hyperventilate. Me, I just tried to convince myself that this was nothing more than a game of "pinning the tail on the donkey." Suddenly on the downwind leg, the sky lit up above us. A plane with his landing lights on had dropped out of nowhere and missed us by about 10 feet!

I followed his red rotating beacon as he turned base in front of us and then upwind to land due east. We had about 10 minutes of gas left, probably not enough for a safe go-around with the required full power to climb out. I broadcast on the radio "What the hell was that? We're out of gas and have to land." Still no response. I was about a half mile behind him—not very far at 100 mph—so I dove for the first part of the runway, hit and must have bounced 20 feet in the air. My landing was like a basketball being dribbled down the court. Bounce, flair, bounce, flair. I couldn't take my eyes off the plane ahead in case I had to ground-loop to stop. Finally it settled down. The intruder had turned off the runway. I followed. By the time we got to the parking area, the Shore Patrol had the occupants of the other plane in custody.

They were Air Force pilots in a B-25 Mitchell bomber that had flown up from Kessler Air Force Base in the south for a personal stay in Chicago. The tower, it turns out, had told them to leave the pattern, they were not cleared to land, that there was a plane in distress (us). Their answer was, "We don't see anyone and we're already in the traffic pattern." I don't know what happened to them, but I know I kissed the ground and swore that was my last flight. The planes were poorly maintained. The military budget was low. This was not the way it used to be. I took a "pink card" retirement waiving claim to any future monies. As it turned out, my squadron was called to active duty for the Korean War, the first of two "Democrat wars" (the next was Vietnam). I had lucked out!

Chapter 5

Private Flying Episodes
Five Years of "Almosts" • 1960 through 1965

After retiring from the Navy in 1950, I felt flying was part of my youth. I was 30. Time to put the toys away. Be a responsible husband, father and employee.

Suddenly I was 40 and a strange thing happened, I was flying again! It was one of those weird chain of events that changed my future both in flying and business. I was living in Winnetka, Illinois a suburb north of Chicago. I was Marketing Director of the Chicago *Tribune*. I had a wife and 4 children. I was a good, common sense father and husband when the past came into the future.

*Peter Hoyt, myself and friends ready for a ski trip to
Michigan in Pete's 310 Cessna.*

Background for Return to Flying

While a senior in college taking the aerobatic stage of the CPT program at Hamilton College in the open cockpit Waco, I noticed a young sophomore at the airport now and then. He was paying for his own flying lessons. He had his own parachute, helmet, goggles and that all-important silk scarf that said he was a pilot—a *real* pilot!

He was paying the high rate of $25 an hour for what I was getting for free.

One day I asked if he'd like to go up with me. He responded yes, eagerly. I really wasn't supposed to take anyone for rides, but I had a private pilot license. As far as the CAA (now FAA) was concerned, I was legal to take someone up—it was just the rules of the CPT that you couldn't do it on training flights. The CAA required (and still does) that if you do aerobatics, all in the plane must have a parachute. He had one. So did I. What's more, he had a car there to make it possible.

The Utica airport had one grass runway. It went east and west. The hangars and flight office were in the center about 100 yards south of the runway in a cutout area. Tall cornfields blocked a view of the runway except for the middle one-third. I told him to drive his car to the east end (I'd be taking off going west), park it there on the road. Walk with his parachute the 100 yards through the cornfield to the start of the field and wait for me there. When I got there, run to the plane, throw your chute in the front seat, jump in and keep your head down while I took off passing midfield where the plane could be seen. Then I would land long, get out of the plane. Walk to the road. Stash your chute in the cornfield. Walk the half-mile back to your car. Get your chute and go home.

We had no way to talk while in the air. He could see me in the mirror. I'd do hand motions of what I was going to do next. The term in aviation is that "I wrung him out," and he loved it. The last I saw, he was entering the tall corn, looking back waving with a wide smile on his face. His name was Pete Hoyt.

Small World Opens Up a New World!

Fast forward 20 years. My father was opening a charge account at an Eddie Bauer-type of store in Winnetka, Illinois called "Trooping the Colour." This same Pete Hoyt owned the store. He had moved from the east coast area. I have the same name as my father and am a "junior." When Pete saw my father's name, he asked if he had a son who went to Hamilton College. Dad said he did. Pete asked where I was. Dad told him I was about three blocks away. Pete asked if I was still flying and Dad said I wasn't. Dad recalled him saying "Any person who could fly like the ride he gave me should never stop flying."

Then Pete called me, reminded me of the ride I had given him 20 years before, that he had been a B-17 "Flying Fortress" pilot in WWII with 35 bombing missions and had a Cessna 172 that I was welcome to fly...and that I should start to fly again. Me fly? Flying was part of my youth. It had been 10 years since I quit Navy flying. I protested that maintenance of planes after my last Navy flight concerned me. He assured me that planes today were like refrigerator motors—they go on and on (I found out later they don't!). Finally I said that I had not flown in 10 years, but if I could pass a flight instructor's flight test, I'd try it. The FAA inspector must have taken pity on this 40-year-old retread. He passed me. The fat was in the fire. I had to do some flying again.

Private Flying in the 1960s

I was like Rip Van Winkle awakening from his 20-year sleep. Everything seemed to have changed. It was a switch from AM to FM. The frequencies had switched from the aircraft (200–400 kc) band below the AM broadcast stations (500–1600 kc) to above (108–138 mc) the new FM band (90–108 mc). The enroute navigation "beams" and colored airways we had on the AM bands were now being replaced by new V-airways with FM freqs.

To me, sectional charts, the basic navigation charts issued by the government, were almost illegible with both the old beam routes in red and the new VORs in blue. To untangle this, I drew routes from Chicago to various places on the shirt boards that came from the laundry with my shirts. I had the routes to Kansas City to Miami to New York and airports in between. Next to me at my golf locker at Skokie Country Club was another private pilot, Ken Laird of the ad agency of Tatham and Laird. He wanted copies of my routes on the shirt boards. He made photostat copies of them at his company because Xerox machines had not yet been invented. He gave me extra copies for other pilot friends who wanted them.

Start a Business?

My father always spoke to me in short statements. "Don't die without going into business for yourself" was one of them. This I thought would be something I could do. As Marketing Director of the Chicago *Tribune* under the famous Pierre Martineau, and teaching a marketing course at the Medill School of Journalism at Northwestern University in Evanston, my mind was crammed full of ways to successfully research and market a product. I decided to try to develop and market the first Aviation Atlas ever produced. That was in 1962. By the year 2000 the Sky Prints Aviation Atlas, published annually, has since been used by an estimated 40,000 pilots for their cross-country navigation.

Now with an aviation business demanding that I keep flying, I sought out every opportunity I could. Fortunately, not only Pete Hoyt invited me to use his planes and fly with him, but Dean Clark, my wife's cousin, owned a Piper Comanche 250 N5274P for his business, but didn't know how to fly. So in exchange for the personal use of his plane, I flew him to various meetings and conventions in the Midwest associated with his grain-industry magazine *Grain and Feed*. He loved to have me follow the railroads to spot the gigantic grain elevators located alongside the rail tracks.

The Comanche 250 cruised at 175 mph and was a pleasure to fly.

Jeppesen was a pioneer in supplying charts and updates. In this photo taken in his den, he is showing me his famous "notebook" with airport data gathered when he flew for United Airlines in the 1930s. "Jep" encouraged me to develop my atlases.

In WWII, the military had "beam routes" in bound format. I yearned to have bound charts again, so I developed spiral-bound atlases for VFR, IFR and Topographic Charts. They have been well-received by pilots who fly cross-country in the U.S. You can get more information by calling 1-800-338-7221 or by visiting the website at www.airchart.com

This was a new world to me. Dean explained how they might blow up if the grain dust was too great, or how the grain would mold if it was put in the elevators damp. I really couldn't care less, but always tried to act interested. After all, this was the "bread-basket of America" that I was learning about. This entire area of farm-to-table is still not something I can really comprehend. Put raw metal into one end of a machine and have screws come out the other end was easier for me to understand.

A Night Pick-Up at Chicago O'Hare • July 8, 1960

It's hard to believe this happened. I can't even believe it today. Chicago O'Hare is the second busiest airport in the U.S. behind Atlanta, but back then O'Hare was a new airport. Chicago Midway Airport on the southside of Chicago was the main airline terminal for the area. O'Hare was out in the sticks. We used to hunt pheasants in the area while they were still building it. Then United Airlines, which was based in Chicago, switched their flights to O'Hare to jump start it. The rest is history. But pilots like to tell a story about those early days.

Because United Airlines had sole possession of the mighty O'Hare in the beginning, their pilots felt it was *their* airport. They had the right to everything. As other airlines came to use the field, United pilots felt they still had the priority they enjoyed as pioneers. This story is born from that.

Tower: "Continental Airlines, taxi into position and hold for takeoff."

CA to tower: "We can't. A United just taxied into takeoff position in front of us."

Tower: "Okay, United cleared for takeoff."

United transmitted as he started his takeoff roll, "How do you like them apples, Continental?"

When the United plane was halfway down the runway, the Continental pilot keyed (turned on) his mike and pressed the button to check the sound of the alarm in his cockpit which broadcast the alarm's sound in the United's headset and cockpit. Thinking it was their own warning, United stopped take off, applied the brakes and blew all their tires stopping just short of the runway end. Then transmitted without identification was, "And how do you like those apples, United?" This might have ended the one-upmanship at O'Hare. It is said that the Continental pilots were fined dearly for their act but that pilots from other airlines contributed to their fund.

On July 8, 1960 Chicago O'Hare was just another airport to me. Tower traffic was not much different than it was at most other airports. It was all prop planes. So what? It wasn't a big deal for me to fly there from Sky Harbor airport about 15 miles north in a Cessna 172 to pick up my brother-in-law, Norm Barker, who had come in on a commercial flight and fly him back to Sky Harbor. It was a "trick" flight—something to do.

What I remember are two things: 1) the approach and, 2) the taxi back for takeoff. The tower gave me this instruction, "Approach runway 36 and hold over it at 500 feet, 1 mile short in right-hand pattern." Hold over it in a right-hand pattern? One mile short? What kind of a landing clearance is that? What it was, was that with my little pip-squeak Cessna 172, I was trying to land with the airliners. After a few airliners had landed under me, the tower finally gave me permission to land. As I look back on that tower controller, he was one of the most creative I have ever heard. He well might have said to me "Get lost, little bug."

After I located Norm's flight and picked him up, it was back into the 172 for the flight back to Sky Harbor, 15 miles away. When I called Ground Control for taxi instructions, it was as long as the Declaration of Independence! I asked and it was given to me step-by-step. "Taxi to first left" when there, they said, "taxi to first right" and on and on. By the end, I think we had taxied almost halfway back to Sky Harbor! It was pitch black. I had no idea where I was. In the low Cessna 172, all the blue taxi lights blended in with the white runway lights. From the high cockpit of an airliner, it might make sense, but not in the low position a few feet above the ground in a Cessna 172.

We used to hunt pheasants with my well-trained Weimeraner named Kaira in the area where O'Hare was being built. Until that night, I had not realized how truly big O'Hare was. I was airborne at night in just the warm-up pad area. It was nice to hear the tower say, "Cleared for immediate 180 after takeoff to clear area…good-night, little one." That clearance saved me about an extra 10 miles if I had to go to the end of the runway and then circle all the way back to the Sky Harbor airport area just north-northwest of the Glenview Naval Air Station.

Crossing Over Lake Michigan in a Single Engine

Some of my family had a home in South Haven, Michigan which was about 90 miles directly across Lake Michigan, the north/south of the Great Lakes formed by glaciers many years ago. As a young boy visiting my grandparents there, I was always in awe of being able to see the Lindbergh Beacon rotating atop the Palmolive Building in Chicago. South Haven was a 2 to 3 hour drive from Chicago, but there, on a clear night, was a beacon all the way from Chicago. This is the kind of stuff that captures a young kid's mind. The moon and stars are too far away to comprehend, but I could stand in front of the Palmolive Building on North Michigan Avenue (later became known as the Playboy Building) and actually see the beacon atop it. I could relate to the whole beacon as I saw its momentary flash over 100 miles away…and then count the seconds until the next flash about 30 seconds later.

Now with a plane to fly and without the concern of a Navy Ops officer giving me a clearance, I could fly across the "the lake."

I'd carry several inflatable mattresses for rafts plus life preservers. The FAA had a special watch service called "Lake Crossing Service." Now that I think about it, it might have been better if such a service didn't exist. It seemed to encourage me to fly over the lake to save maybe 80 miles of flying, plus avoid the congested Chicago area. For the Lake Crossing Service, you filed a flight plan stating which VOR you were leaving to cross the lake and over which VOR you would report over on the other side. If you didn't report on the other side, the Coast Guard would immediately launch its Air–Sea Rescue unit.

My added caution was to get to 9,500 feet eastbound and the regulation 8,500 westbound. With the 172's glide ratio of about 10 to 1, in the case of total engine failure, I could glide 10 feet for every foot of altitude I had, so at 9,000 feet I could glide 90,000 feet over the earth or about 17 miles. At a descent of 300 feet per minute, I could be in a glide from 9,000 to 1,000 feet above the water before splash down (8,000 divided by 300) for 26 minutes—certainly enough time I reasoned for a rescue plane to reach the area after my initial mayday broadcast with radar knowing my position. I calculated the "point-of-no-return" (halfway across) at 45 miles.

I always tried to remain calm in front of my passengers, even citing those simple facts to bolster their assurance, but when I crossed the shoreline outbound, that point-of-no-return was my #1 checkpoint. I didn't want to have to stop and think whether to keep going or to turn around, if there was a problem. My little handheld E6-B computer was in constant use. I'd also suggest the passengers pass the time (about 45 minutes) looking for freighters going up and down the lake and to call out when and what o'clock bearing they were and to give a guess at about how far away they were. Then in my most authoritative ex-Navy pilot way, I would look to confirm their distance judgement with a, "Yeah, that's just about it." Acting that way raised my confidence level too! Of course, if anything went wrong, a splash-down next to a freighter would not be a bad idea.

As luck would have it, the only near-tragedy that I can recall occurring on one of the many over-the-lake flights was when I was with my two sisters, Sue and Patty, and my nature-loving son Chuck, about 10 years old. Everything was going fine with Chuck and Patty sitting in the backseat until Sue started to relax, started breathing again as she was getting used to the situation she was in and began looking around.

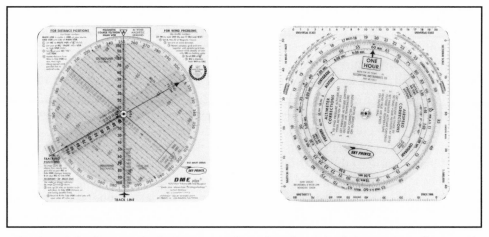

I developed the "DME Plus" plotter, an idea taken from the "plotting board" we used in the Navy. It used the intersection of two VOR radials to know when to report to radar that we were "20 miles out" when over the water with no landmarks and before DME was installed. On the back was a large, circular slide rule with aviation references. It won the "Aero Classic Award" in 1966 at Palm Springs.

We were at the eastbound altitude of 9,500 feet (you fly eastbound at odd altitudes, west at even, and add 500 feet if you are not on an instrument flight plan).

Patty asked my son, "Chuck, what do you have in that bag?"

It was a simple brown paper bag from a grocery store. He could have answered that it was something to eat and all would have been fine. But no, he had to tell her the truth.

Looking up at her smiling, he answered, "It's a rattlesnake I caught. You wanna see it?"

Wanna see it?!? Sue stopped breathing again! She lurched forward against her seat belt. Her eyes seemed frozen open. She was trying to mutter something like "I want out now—how do I get out?" Well, a 172 doesn't really have an aisle. As a matter of fact, it doesn't even have a partition between the front and rear seats. She started breathing again if you can call hyperventilating breathing. With my earphones on I didn't hear the exchange of words that had preceded her grabbing me by the shoulder and saying "Can't we go any faster? How soon before we land? Can I change places?" When I was filled in, I mustered up the sternest look I could, flashed a look over my shoulder at Chuck with a stern admonishment to "not open the bag…and you shouldn't do this." Turning back around, it was hard not to break out in a grin. I hope she doesn't read this part. Maybe I'll tear this page out of her copy of this book.

My First "All Hell Breaks Loose" at 9,500 feet!

On one clear "see-a-million-miles" Sunday, my fishing buddy, Nelson Hinde, and two of my sons were flying with me from Sky Harbor Airport north of Chicago to Wisconsin to fish at a trout farm. Nelson had outfitted the trout farm with a water self-oxygenation system he had patented. We were going to "fish-for-free" and as any father with sons knows, "guaranteed fish" and "fish for free" are beckoning calls.

We were cruising nicely at 9,500 feet headed slightly north–northeast when the engine sounded like a lawn mower cutting rocks. It was a loud banging sound with heavy vibration. Sure got my attention quickly. I throttled back from 2,400 to 1,000 RPM. The banging stopped, but we were losing airspeed. I applied power slowly. At 1,600 RPM the banging started again. My only thought was that it might be carburetor ice. Even on a summer day, ice can form in the throat of a carburetor with the drop of temperature in the air through the venturi throat. After a few minutes with the carb heat fully on, I advanced the throttle again. Banging again over 1,600 RPM. We were over Waukegan, Illinois, a fairly large city on the lake about 50 miles north of Chicago. I could see many airports below. I started a wide spiral glide down over the Waukegan airport.

All nontower airports at the time had only the one unicom (communication frequency) of 122.8. At my altitude transmitting on line-of-sight in that FM band, I could be heard by all airports within easily a 50-mile range. I broadcast my condition and was asking, because it was Sunday, if any of the airports in the Waukegan area had a mechanic on duty. None had. So I told the unicom at Waukegan that I was making an emergency landing and would they please advise the local traffic. They confirmed they would, but few unicoms have a view of the field and the traffic. It is a "heard and be heard" system among the planes themselves in the area. With all the altitude and a nice gliding plane, and having taught emergency landings to many students in the Navy, it was like setting up to drive into your own garage, until…!

Unbelievably, a plane was taxiing out and crossing the runway about 100 yards ahead of me. At 90 mph (I always carry extra speed in emergency situations), 100 yards is not very far. The plane slowly crossed the runway as if it were all alone in the area. I was able to just squeak by its tail. The landing plane always has the right-of-way. All pilots make a circle on the runway or clear the approach lane before taking off to make sure no plane is landing on that same runway. Problem, it turns out, this pilot had started his plane about 5 minutes after I broadcast my intentions, taxied out without calling unicom (not a violation, but not very smart) so he didn't know I was coming in on an emergency. He was headed for another runway so felt no need to check for landing traffic on the longer runway I was using. I made a mental note to check for landing traffic on any runway, not just the one that seemed best into the wind.

What was the problem? When Pete had encouraged me to start flying again, he answered my concern of "Oh, I don't know, Pete…planes' engines have to be checked every 25 hours…it's a real can of worms, this civilian flying."

He replied with the refrigerator motor comparison. "No, Howie, planes today are different. They're like refrigerator motors. They just go on and on. You don't need a 25-hour check anymore. Just an overall check every 12 months, an annual, and mine just had one." Oh? That seemed to make sense compared to the pre-war types I had flown. After all, it was 10 years since I stopped flying in 1950. This was 1960.

The VW Beetle was the great example of modern air-cooled engines and their reliability.

Well, electrically a plane engine is really two engines. It has two ignition systems with two magnetos. Each mag distributes a spark to one of the two spark plugs in each cylinder (cars have only one plug per cylinder). If one system fails, the other still gives firing power to the engine. Perhaps you have seen planes rev up the motor near their takeoff spot, hear the engine go a little slower, then fast again, then slow again, then fast again. The pilot is "checking the mags" by switching to the left mag, seeing if there is a drop over the recommended RPM, then back to both mags and then to the right mag, then back to both. When checking the mags at 1,500 RPM, a drop of over 150 RPM on one mag is usually a sign not to take off. Something might be wrong with a plug, the wiring or something else. It's a must-do check before take off for every standard cylinder (combustible) engine.

In this case what had happened is that the pre-greased felt with Vaseline-type grease that was sealed in one of the magnetos had dried out. The mag wasn't being properly lubricated. The copper distributing points had broken and the one mag was firing the cylinders at random while the other mag was doing its job. I didn't dare do an in-the-air mag check for fear the entire engine would shut down, because when mags fail they fail, they don't fire at random. To check them in-flight, I might lose even the 1,500 RPM I had to at least make the glide a little farther. On the ground, off the runway, I stopped and did a mag check at 1,500 RPM. Fine. Puzzled, I increased power to 1,700 RPM and all hell broke loose again. So I did a mag check at 1,700 and sure enough, it purred like a baby on one mag, but virtually quit on the other. If I were on a jungle airstrip with headhunters attacking, I would take off with only one mag working. But that's the only time I would. It's just not worth the risk.

I called to have someone pick us up and left the plane there. Two pilots flew up the next day to pick it up. One described to me what happened then. The pick-up pilot checked the mags at 1,500 RPM, it was fine, so he took off at where the runways intersected which gave him only about half the regular runway length instead of taxiing to the runway start. Too far down the runway to abort his takeoff, the pounding started. With only one person on board and without full tanks, the 1,500 RPM just kept him airborne enough to circle the field and land. He must have been a good pilot to coax it around just over the tree tops. They decided to leave it there until a mechanic could come and figure out the problem. I learned a great lesson from that. Mags can fail in a positive way too.

A Cessna 172 as a Deer Transport

In Illinois we didn't have the expanse of woods that Pennsylvania has or even Michigan. To hunt deer, we had to make friends with a farmer who probably wasn't too eager to have any more of his cows shot. Neither my brother nor I had ever hunted deer before. But a friend told me that you go out to the farm country about a month before season starts. You never just pull into a farm yard, jump out and ask "Can we hunt here?" The proper way to do it was to go up and talk about anything but hunting. Let him get to see "the cut of your jib" as the sailors say. Ask him how many milk cows he has, how much is planted in corn, wheat or soy beans. He knows darn well why you are there. And most farmers like to talk to someone about their farm, the weather they've had to deal with, the price of grain, etc.

In this case I was with my brother. It was a month before deer season would start. We had stopped at Merle Himerdinger's farm about 10 miles west of Freeport, Illinois. Merle, about 30, was a second generation on the farm. He had a happy face and a pleasant personality. We chatted, but I just couldn't bring myself to flat-out ask him if we could hunt the woods on his farm. In the distance I saw a hill with a mesa-like top on it. I asked him how long the top was. He guessed about half a mile. I asked if it was fairly smooth. "Yes," he replied, "It's a high-dry pasture."

"Would it be okay if I landed a plane on it?" I asked. His eyes lit up.

"Okay with me! Why?"

"Well," I replied kicking at a piece of hardened mud, "I'd sure like to do some deer hunting in this area and was wondering where I might land a plane."

That was it. Merle and I were instant friends He loved planes. But when opening day came, a cold front had come in with clouds near the ground. I called Merle and said I couldn't fly there that weekend. He told me to come anyway. He'd seen a lot of deer about a mile from his house. That's what I was hoping he would say. My brother Jim and I headed for our first deer hunt. In Illinois you can't hunt with rifles because the state is so populated. You were limited to using "slugs" fired from a 12-gauge shotgun. Instead of the small shot bee-bee pellets in a shotgun shell, the slug was a solid piece of lead. It could travel level for only about 100 yards. My brother and I were used to shooting pheasants at about 30 yards. Shooting a slug 100 yards seemed like massive fire power.

When we got there we probably looked like we had just exited from a Sears sporting goods store. Shotguns, shell belts, water-proof boots, stiff orange hats and vests. Merle was very cordial and said he'd walk us across the road and out to the edge of the forest. As we approached the forest line, a deer ran across our path about 75 yards away. I quickly raised my gun, looked at Merle who said "go ahead." I led the deer about 5 yards, fired and it fell. I was stunned. My first shot. A deer! Merle was amazed. "Never saw anyone take one that far away," he said shaking his head in disbelief.

In the Navy, every time we checked on a new base, we had to report to the range master and fire 50 rounds at clay pigeons crossing us from side-to-side. I had never fired anything more than a .22 rifle. The kick from a shotgun rattled my 150-pound skinny frame. No one had ever told me to plant the gun tightly to your shoulder. The more it kicked, the more I inched it away from my shoulder before pulling the trigger. The result was that the kick now became a pneumatic hammer. I was black and blue for weeks after checking on to each new base. But there was no way around it. You had to do it and have your score recorded on a report. This was elementary gunnery training for when you did get in a plane and had to understand "deflection shots" and the technique of leading your target before firing. After a few "check-ins" I got smart and slipped a large towel under my shirt. But it still hurt.

But it did teach me deflection shots—to lead and then pull the trigger.

I was hooked on deer hunting. The next weekend was cool and clear. I called Merle. He said he'd clear the cattle off the mesa if I wanted to land there…and just might he go for a ride? My brother couldn't go, so I went alone with Pete's 172. The thought that his insurance would be invalid if I landed at other than an approved airport didn't cross my mind, I am ashamed to say. It should have. So off I went. When I got there, Merle was sitting alongside the "runway" in his truck. A half-mile (2,500 plus feet) was ample distance to land a Cessna 172, especially on a surface with wheat stubble to slow down the landing roll. I taxied back to Merle's truck and beckoned him to hop aboard with his brother. Off that mesa, it was like taking off from an aircraft carrier. Just put down 20° of flap, get up to flying speed, experience a little drop off and you're flying. Voilà! We circled the farm, he pointed out where we were going to hunt that day, flew low over a neighbor's farm with Merle waving happily and then came back to land.

Merle and his brother had shotguns and the needed slugs. The strategy was to chase deer out of the woods into an open field about twice as wide and twice as long as a football field. They decided that I would be about halfway down the field while they would enter from the goal post area to the right. It would be too tricky for me to know the path from any other place around the field. Also we wouldn't be in each other's line of fire…and there weren't any cows in that field. So I took up my position while they went through the woods on the path around the open field. About 20 minutes later I heard a shout. "There goes one, Howie!" I looked up-field and sure enough there was a deer coming straight down the middle of the open field from right to left about 50 yards away. As it passed my point, I took aim, led it and bang—it dropped. I had hit it right in the neck. It died instantly from the impact of that large piece of lead.

Merle and his brother came running down the field on the same path as the deer had taken, shouting "You got it, you got it!" I went out to meet them. They looked at me in a rather weird way. "Where were you when you fired?" they asked. "Where you left me!" I replied. We dragged the deer to the fence line at the side of the field and dressed it down, removing all the internal organs. "Don't want to leave these in the open field," they remarked. I never asked or understood why.

When the deer had been dressed, they would go get their truck to haul it back to the plane. But before that, they wanted to see where I was standing when I fired. I led them to a place about 20 feet back from the fence line where they had left me. They looked around on the ground and there it was. The shell casing I had ejected from the shotgun preparing for a second shot. They needed to see that again a deer had been downed on a full deflection shot about 50 yards away. They were not used to this by "city folks." Suddenly all those painful rounds I fired in the Navy over 15 years ago seemed worth it all. I had the admiration of men of the soil.

For what followed, I wish I'd had a camera along. They took me back to the plane. The deer was about 180 pounds. We tucked it in the back seat and put a safety belt around its front legs and one around the back legs. Its face, with tongue hanging out, peered out the window behind me. I had burned a lot of gas getting there and flying them around, so decided I'd stop at Freeport to gas up. Landed, taxied up to the gas area and a line boy came out, brought his small ladder to reach the wing tank on top and circle the plane. When he caught sight of the deer with tongue hanging out peering out of the rear side window like a drunken slob, he dropped the ladder and backed off. I assured him it was dead, not to fear.

Back at Sky Harbor airport, I needed assistance to load it into my station wagon. When I got home, it was a neighborhood event. The kids brought everyone they could find to the backyard to see the deer strung up outside the kitchen window. My wife was not too pleased at the sight of a carcass hanging a few yards out her window. Only the children's enthusiasm kept her from insisting that I take it somewhere else. Next day I did. To a local butcher. We had "deerburger" meat in our freezer for many months.

Caught in Clear Ice

One thing Navy flying didn't prepare me for was icing.

Icing was not of great concern for water or carrier-based flying but units in the Aleutian Islands did have to confront icing. Of course I knew about it. That it was bad stuff. That there were two types of ice. The most common being rime ice, that foamy stuff looking somewhat like the ice that forms in old refrigerators. It forms on the leading edge of the wing and on prop blades, deforming the airflow over their surfaces. You can see it. Even watch it build up. Larger planes have flexible "boots" on the wing leading surface that either heat or flex in and out to break it off. The average private aircraft needs to go to a lower, warmer altitude below freezing before it will melt and break off. Solving it that way is a no-brainer.

The other icing is clear ice. This is the sneaky stuff. It coats the entire airplane. It happens in an instant and builds up from there. You get clear ice mostly from a temperature inversion where it is raining at warmer higher altitudes and you are in a colder lower altitude. Normally, air cools at the rate of 3.5° F each 1,000 feet you go up—it's called the adiabatic lapse rate. But not in clear ice conditions. When you wake up in the morning and see trees and telephone lines coated and drooping under the heavy weight of clear ice, ice that looks like icicles, that's what it's like. There was rain and warm air aloft that night compared to the below-freezing night air above the snow-covered ground. When the rain hit the colder surface, it froze. That's what almost did me in.

I was flying a Comanche 250 (N5274P) from north of the Chicago area to Washington, DC. It was March 18, 1961. Aboard was the plane's owner, Dean Clark, his wife and my 10-year-old son, Chuck. We had a full load of fuel for the flight of about 700 miles total, nearly 4 hours. With the tailwind, we could make it or choose to stop en route. Anyway, we were heavy. Though I had an old Navy instrument rating, I had not yet applied for a civilian instrument rating, so could not legally fly in the "soup." I was limited to VFR (visual flight rules) which meant I had to see the ground at all times and the ceiling could not be below 1,000 feet, nor visibility less than 1 mile. The ceiling was a comfortable 3,500 feet and visibility was a full 5 miles.

Upon take off north of Chicago, I asked for and received from Chicago area radar permission to fly south along the lake a mile off Chicago's lakefront, follow the curve at the bottom of the lake near Gary, Indiana and then, being out of Chicago's area, I didn't need a flight plan or permission from anyone until I got to the Washington, DC area. I could still do this in today's supposedly high air traffic world. But it wouldn't be too smart not to at least file a flight plan with the FAA.

Speaking of today's high air traffic that is ballyhooed so much by TV and newspapers, someone figured out that if all the planes flying today were flying above Kansas at the *same altitude* at the *same moment*, they would each have a full *square mile* to themselves! Crowded skies? Hardly. Back then there were about the same number of aircraft. I don't recall the term "crowded skies" ever being used.

We were flying at 2,500 feet at the south end of Lake Michigan when suddenly we were coated with clear ice. I could see out the side window, but the windshield was a solid coat of ice! Now, you can calm down your passengers in most situations, but not when they suddenly can't see out of the windshield. There's no calmly uttering "Heh-heh—well, whaddya know—no problem folks." I diverted all the cockpit warm air to the defroster on my side. A hole about the size of a half-dollar let me peer straight ahead. I could see the ice coating the cowling. They couldn't. But my son's "Hey Dad, look at all the ice on the wings, how come?" swiveled their heads to the still-clear side windows. There was no denying it. We were getting heavier by the minute with a coating of ice. Instead of trying to answer their questions, I grabbed the mike. We were still in Chicago's radar control area.

"Chicago control, this is Comanche 5274 Papa, over Gary area picking up a load of clear ice. Permission to divert back to Chicago Midway airport."

"Roger 74 Papa advise intentions." At this point another plane broke in with the transmission. "Control 669 King, I have some info for that plane that just called you over Gary."

"74 Papa, you copy?"

"Affirmative," I replied.

"Go ahead 9 King."

"74 Papa, I'm at 4,000 feet. It's warm up here. Rain but no ice. Climb up here and you'll be okay." Now, this got embarrassing. I couldn't legally climb "up there in the soup." He stated his altitude as 4,000 feet. That meant he probably was on instruments in this kind of weather. Planes cleared to fly on instruments (blind flying), fly at the cardinal altitudes (3,000 feet, 4,000 feet, 5,000 feet, etc). Non-cleared VFR planes fly at those altitudes plus 500 feet. That way there is 500 feet vertical separation.

"Thanks, 9 King, but we're so heavy now I don't want to risk trying to climb even higher." That was my face-saving out in front of my passengers. They didn't know I wasn't qualified to go up there. Their impression was that I was using good judgment. Control let me turn around and head for Chicago Midway airport about 15 miles behind me. The rain seemed to have stopped when I left the edge of Lake Michigan and with it the ice build-up. But the windshield was still solid ice except for my peep hole where the very ineffective defroster focused. Radar gave me steers (directions) to Midway, turned me over to the tower and let them know my plight.

Tower cleared me for a straight-in landing on the left runway heading southwest. I used the peep hole until I was about 20 feet above the ground where I had to pull the nose up slightly to land and lost view of the runway. The touchdown was made looking out the side window which is not too tough in itself, but keeping direction straight ahead down the runway after landing was a bit dicey with a few zig-zags. That Comanche did not have foot brakes and it was probably a good thing it didn't. It had what amounts to just an emergency brake in a car. Just pull and it applies brakes to both wheels at the same time. Had it had separate brakes for each wheel as most planes do, I might have hit just one and gone into an ugly wing-tip wipe-out ground loop that damages not only the plane which can be repaired, but your ego and reputation too, which can't be.

Fortunately, Chicago Midway was the Chicago airline terminal at the time with a choice of flights to Washington, DC. Dean Clark and his wife could get an airliner and make their convention in time. But I had another problem. It was Sunday. I had to be at work the next day and Chuck had to get to school. I didn't want to leave the plane at the costly Midway plane parking area. The ice had melted on the windshield. Using the plane's radio I was able to call the tower at Meigs Field, Chicago's lakefront airport. They said the rain had stopped.

From Meigs I could get a bus to the train station and a train home. Lying in bed that night, I reviewed it all to see if I could have done anything better. Yes, I could have. I could have just landed at Gary, Indiana below me and let my benefactor (he let me use the plane any time I wanted to) figure out how to get to Midway for an airline flight. I had stretched my luck, but not by much, I reasoned, so I could drop off to sleep.

The Bay of Pigs Experience

That Day Jack and Bobby Kennedy Lost Cuba—Thousands Died

About 3 weeks after my aborted flight to Washington, DC, I flew to Key Largo, Florida from Chicago to go bonefishing on April 10, 1961. Bonefishing is something you get hooked on and there is no cure. Especially if it's April in Florida after a hard winter in Chicago. You can be out on the "flats" all day and never even see a bonefish, no matter. The water is only 2 to 3 feet deep as far as you can see. You can be wading (which I like) or use a guide pole in a flat-bottom boat. There is peace all around you. It is a combination of hunting and fishing.

You see your prey in the shallow water either swimming by about 20 yards away or "tailing." Tailing is the most heart-stopping. The bonefish root the coral for shrimp and other crustaceans. They are silvery, prehistoric looking, powerful, not good to eat, easy-to-spook fish with a gravel-like tongue used to crush their prey. Maybe seeing a mermaid rise out of the water is a prettier sight, but to a bonefisherman who at one time hooked one, seeing the flashing of the fish's tail sparkling in the sunlight, it would be difficult to make the choice of which of the two to observe.

Hunting/fishing for bonefish on the flats of the Florida Keys is still a dream of mine. We release them after a photo is taken, to hopefully catch again. Also they're not good to eat.

You cast your live shrimp (pros might use a fly), see the fish approach it, feel a slight tug but know you can't strike because the hook won't penetrate its tough mouth. You wait an agonizing 10 seconds which seems like half an hour until it feels the hook and then starts its torpedo-like run which sets the hook. Right then you stop breathing, your heart probably stops too. Your rod is raised high above your head to reduce the drag as the bonefish heads for the deep water doing about 30 miles an hour! Your spinning reel is singing a high-pitched whine. You better have about 250 yards of line on your reel, because that first run is always about 200 yards before it stops.

Then a routine tug and rewind until it gets about 10 feet away and sees you again and zoom! Off it goes for at least another 100 yards. Probably 10 to 15 minutes have elapsed by this time. When he finally stops and you tug, reel it in, the fish is almost lifeless in the water but still looks powerful. It's easy to unhook from its bony mouth, but you never keep one. Just grab its tail and slowly pull it back and forth through the water to feed water through its gills. In about 3 minutes, it'll take off again.

So that's why I was in Florida this time in April. Along with me were two friends. At the end of the week there, the plan was to fly to the Bahamas. First to Freeport about 90 miles across the ocean to check for new bonefish flats and then about 100 miles south to Nassau to visit the city and tour.

On the morning of April 19, 1961, I was asleep in a motel on Key Largo when I was suddenly awakened by the loud, approaching sound of a powerful multi-engine plane. As the sound grew louder and louder, I was fully awake when it passed over-head. The guy couldn't have been more than 30 feet off the deck. Man, was he low. At 6:00 in the morning, I thought that guy is going to catch hell from the FAA. But then this was out in the Keys. He probably knew some girl in the area and was giving her an early morning heigh-ho. That's the dumb stuff pilots do to impress girls, women, ladies—any of them that isn't your mom. I went back to sleep until our agreed 8 a.m. wake-up. The others hadn't even heard it. They weren't pilots. They were not attuned to such sounds.

Later learned that it was the B-26 (WWII twin-engine bomber) that had bombed Havana and was sneaking under radar up the Keys to land unannounced at Miami International. He just flew in and landed. No tower contact at all!

The plan was to fly the 30 miles north to Miami International to pick up Reid Bronson, a retired dentist friend who lived in Coral Gables. With me were my friends from the Chicago area who came along to fish. Gerry Becker of Glencoe and John Saris of Evanston. At Miami, I'd file my Overseas Flight Plan at the FAA office and off we'd go. Not so fast as it turned out. I noticed that there were a lot of guys in brown uniforms walking around the ramp area. They were walking over and looking at the plane in more than a casual way. As I came back to the plane with my flight plan filed and a copy of it in my hand, two of them approached me.

Where was I going? Why was I going? What was I going to do? They seemed to accept everything until it came to the question of where do you and your passengers work. I mentioned Reid was a retired dentist in the area, John was a business broker in Chicago, I was with the Chicago *Tribune* and Gerry was with *Life* Magazine. With the mention of the last two, they became more than curious. "Newspaper? *Life*? I think we better have a talk inside. This way, please."

The four of us followed the leader with his partner walking behind us. After about 10 minutes of aimless interrogation on their part, the thought came to me that they thought we were on a "story" about Nassau and somehow that was taboo. When they asked to see our cameras, I was the only one who had one and it was a fit-in-the-palm-of-your-hand Kodak Brownie. They then asked if they could search the plane for any other cameras—or guns. There isn't much area to search in a Comanche 250. After they were finished, they said, "Okay, but don't go south of 135° (about 4:30 on a clock face) out of Miami."

"Why would we go so far south of our flight planned course?" I asked. "The course to Freeport is about 060° (2 o'clock)."

"Well, there are some fighter exercises in the area," was their reply.

It was an uneventful flight to Freeport. Didn't find any nice bonefish flats there. On to Nassau. Walk the straw market. See the sights and then start the 180 mile overwater flight back to Miami to get back down to Ocean Reef on the northern tip of Key Largo before dark. Ocean Reef airport not only did not have any runway lights, it

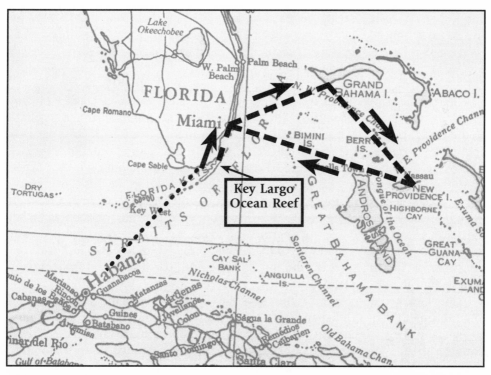

Although we filed an FAA flight plan for Freeport on Grand Bahama, the border patrol made sure we did not try to head toward Cuba where the Bay of Pigs was in progress. Who knew?

didn't even have that special green and white rotating beacon showing it was an airport. At the Nassau airport, their customs was a "maybe" situation. "Maybe" they'd just stamp your release and flight plan so you could go right away, or "maybe" they would act officious, call in someone else and question it. The deal was that there was no charge for crew, but a fairly good fee for each passenger. Their flight plan form had a listing on one side for crew and their assignments and on the other for the number of passengers.

It was a known ruse not to list any passengers to avoid their departure fee. I had written "none" on the passenger side and on the crew side listed H. Keefe, pilot; J. Saris, co-pilot (he had once called a tower for me for permission to land); G. Becker, navigator (he had a pencil and the map) and R. Bronson, engineer (an ex-dentist surely knows equipment).

"What's this? Four crew for a 5-passenger plane? Where are the passengers?" they asked.

"None" I replied, "We're on a training flight. We're training to fly passengers here sometime later on our larger planes." I guess they had never heard that one before and cleared us all through the customs' gate. No charge. I confess, I love avoiding taxes that do me no good. I'd gladly pay a reasonable landing fee, but to require airlines to be tax collectors for politicians is hard to swallow. The worst one I ever had to pay was upon leaving Australia back in 1982 on their own airline. Without any advance notice, Australia demanded $40 in U.S. funds for a "departure tax" as I was leaving! They would not accept credit cards or personal checks. Cash or Traveler's checks. Period. What if I had neither? I swore I'd never go back to Australia—or if I did, try to figure out how I could get listed as crew on the flight back out.

Upon landing at Miami to drop off Reid, the slow release at Nassau put my timing behind about half an hour. The sun had almost set when we landed. Twilight would last another half hour and then dark. No moon. I had to at least get near enough to the Ocean Reef airport so I could see it from the air in order to set-up for a landing. My landing lights would be enough during the landing itself. As I taxied up to the general aviation ramp, I told Reid to grab his things, say his "good-bye—it was a great day guys" now and then jump out when I stopped…that I was not going to shut down the engine. We didn't need to clear customs. As soon as he left the plane, I had Ground Control's permission to taxi to the runway. As I pulled away from the ramp I caught a glimpse in the corner of my eye of a brown uniform running after us. I didn't stop. If I did, I'd be there until dawn when I'd have enough light to find the Ocean Reef airport.

Later I learned from Reid that they took him into custody on the ruse that he had to go through the health department's screening because he was coming in from a foreign land. They wouldn't even let him go to the bathroom. He said he was almost doubled-up with the sensation of needing to pee. I had forgotten to tell them all to "hit the head" before we left. But Reid survived after extensive questioning which he did not understand at the time.

Not wanting to waste a minute of daylight, I didn't climb to altitude but hugged the deck all the way to Ocean Reef after takeoff. Maybe only 200 feet all the way over mostly water. Found the airport. Landed and taxied over to the old weathered Buick parked on the grass area where I had parked the plane. The marina owner where I rented the boat on Largo Sound, Dennis Mayo, lent me his old beat-up Buick for local travel. On the flights over the water, I had drilled the guys in the way we would abandon ship in case we had to go down in the water. The only door was on the right side. The person in that seat would open the door before we hit water to make sure it would not get wedged shut if the plane were twisted. He would exit with life vest in hand. Rear seats would go next with their life vests but first throw in my lap the life raft canister. I'd swim out last with the life raft. The Navy had taught me how to do this without getting panicky and swallowing a lot of water—and sea water is not nice to swallow.

It was now almost dark. When John opened the door to get out to the car next to us, the mosquitoes swarmed in like a snowstorm had hit us. I have never seen them so thick. "Close the door," I yelled. He did.

"Now look guys," I said. "The only way to do this is to leave the gear and fishing rods behind and do the ditching routine, but faster!" We scrambled into the car already filled with buzzing mosquitoes that had followed us in. I told them to wind down the windows while I sped out of there hoping the mosquitoes would be sucked out by the speed. I hit the runway doing over 75 mph. It worked. Most of the damn things were gone. We rolled up the windows.

Almost immediately I noticed a flashing red light in the rearview mirror. My first reaction was that it was a plane landing on the runway I was on and that it was his red rotating beacon I was seeing. I swerved off the runway and looked back. No, it wasn't a plane, it was a car and it was flashing its headlights as well. Ahead and to the right and to the left, I saw 2 other flashing red rotating beacons. They all converged in front of us at the end of the runway area. I knew it would be wise to stop where I was. Something was up.

What was "up" was us. They approached from both sides of our stopped car swinging strong flashlights ahead of their path. They almost blinded us when they shined them in the car. They demanded we get out. I pleaded that the mosquitoes were fierce here—could we get away from the area to be more inland. They were being tormented too and agreed.

"Follow my car," he demanded. The other 3 fell in trail behind us. About a mile down the road, he stopped, got out and came back to our car.

"Okay, out," he demanded.

Gerry and John had bought wide floppy straw hats in Nassau and had them on. After I thought about it, they both looked a little foreign in their fishing outfits and straw hats. I had on just a baseball cap and my old Navy khaki shirt with epaulets.

The interrogation started again. They wore brown uniforms. I started to speak, but he said he wanted to hear from Gerry and John.

As I learned later, they had staked out the parked car all day long, waiting for the owner's return. They were convinced that this had something to do with the Bay of Pigs. There was a tall concrete water tower near where we had parked. Border agents were atop it all day long on the lookout. With our rapid flight from the plane to the car to avoid the mosquitoes and then speeding off, they were sure we were what they were looking for—a plane that had bombed Cuba or had picked up Cubans.

When they realized that neither Gerry nor John nor I had Cuban accents, they agreed to follow us to the motel to check further. I told them to check the register as proof that we were all staying there. I still did not know what the problem was. We had not gone south of the course they had warned us about. When they checked the register, their suspicions flared anew. I had made the reservations directly by phone from Chicago and signed in all three of us upon arrival. No where were their signatures. They thought they surely had us until the motel owner's wife arrived on the scene and verified that all three of us were staying there, that she had cleaned our rooms herself and recognized us. The next morning, one of the squad cars was still there guarding our car. He must have been the low guy on their totem pole. We were to fly back to Chicago that day.

We hadn't seen a paper before leaving. I'd like to see again the headlines on a major paper on April 20, 1961 about the Bay of Pigs and what went on.

A Near IFR* Disaster!

Less than a month later, I was trying to get to New York for a meeting for the Chicago *Tribune*'s sales staff. I was the new Marketing Director scheduled to put on a presentation to our New York staff. We were allowed First Class airline fare on our expense account for any mode of travel we might choose. Some were afraid of flying and opted for the more expensive overnight train from Chicago to New York. For me with a free plane, the gas was cheaper. I could also take my wife, who loved being in New York. In my no-cost plane, she coming along was really free. Her light weight didn't mean I'd burn that much more gas. With 4 children, the cost of things was always a concern. When I flew other people, they all chipped in and paid for the gas so there was no cost to me.

We left Chicago for New York. The weather was marginal, but I had two days to get there. In Pennsylvania, the weather got nasty. Low clouds, low visibility. I still did not have my civil instrument rating to legally fly on instruments even though I could. I finally opted to land at Columbus, Ohio. Columbus was not exactly an airline stop in those days and I had to get to New York the next day. While my wife sat in the lounge, I was in the weather office reviewing all the options. Now it was dark and raining. She could see that. While talking to her about our options, I noticed a uniformed pilot walking into the terminal with his tell-tale brown case of airline charts.

I asked him what he was doing. He explained that he was "timed-out," meaning that he had flown all the hours the FAA allows an airline pilot to fly in one day. His charter plane was going on further west. That he wanted to get back to his home base in New York. My mind went into action. "You're IFR rated, right? You have approach plates to get into Allegheny Airport (Pittsburgh's main airport then)." It all worked out. He wanted to get to a major airline hub with flights to New York just as I wanted do to.

* IFR: Instrument Flight Rules (weather = low ceiling and/or visibility)

"How about you file an IFR flight plan to Pittsburgh using your license. I'll do the flying. You ride the right seat. You'll really be the pilot-in-command, but I'll do the flying for you because you're not qualified to fly the Comanche (it takes a pilot 5 solo takeoffs and landings in a different aircraft before they can carry passengers)." The plan was to get radar steers to Pittsburgh. Really a no-sweat operation, even at night, because it was only about 70 miles away—less than half an hour of flying.

Off we went into the dark night in a slight rain. My wife was not pleased with this part of the program. Sitting in the back seat for the first time, she had a lot of "but ifs." The presence of a uniformed pilot in the cockpit somewhat allayed her concerns. He was handling the mike, talking to radar, getting our "steers" to Pittsburgh. At Pittsburgh we were directed to make an ILS approach. He had the proper plate out and ready to show me. An ILS approach is the easiest approach to make. Just line up the cross hairs and it's like flying down the center of a large sewer pipe.

At the outer marker, I asked him to put the gear down. I saw him reach up and put the toggle switch down. With lights on, a long runway ahead, I pulled back on the throttle and started to lift up the nose for landing. Suddenly a loud noise filled the cockpit. It was the gear warning horn. The gear wasn't down! At times like that you don't stop to think. You give it full power and climb out of there then try to figure out what is going on. When I regained my wits as we climbed out, I saw the problem. The Comanche has 3 positions on the gear switch. Up, neutral and down. Most planes have just either up or down—no neutral in between. I had always treated neutral as a non-position. Full up after takeoff, full down for landing. To make it even more confusing, the light in the neutral position as a greenish yellow that could be mistaken for green (down) which is what my "co-pilot" thought. The runway was so long that I asked for and received permission from the tower to circle back within the field boundary. I didn't want to have to leave the traffic pattern, get put behind other incoming traffic and have to shoot another ILS approach. It might have been my first gear-up landing, but that was yet to come!

Up to a Twin Engine and an Instrument Rating!

Pete Hoyt, to whom this book is dedicated, had been a B-17 pilot in WWII with more than the required 25 missions. He had seen his share of planes shot down and limping home. Soon his single-engine Cessna 172 wasn't quite big enough for his family or fast enough—and he liked more than one engine, especially flying across Lake Michigan. His wife, Judy, had family in Benton Harbor. Again, avoiding the rapidly-growing air traffic in the Chicago area without needing to fly around the southern part of Lake Michigan, was a major consideration all of us north of Chicago had. The lake was nice to have, but at night the 90 miles of water was a little foreboding in a single engine.

Now with a twin-engine plane at my disposal, an instrument rating was really worth it. So I set about studying for the "mother of all exams—the instrument written test." In getting flight ratings, it's best to take your written exams first, then your flight test—it prepares you for the oral part of the flight test. I was 41 years old, and as those who have reached that age know, studying and cramming for tests doesn't seem as easy as it did 20 years ago. Today, there are excellent video aids to explain weather, flight rules, navigation, engine functions, aerodynamics, and best of all, the calculator. In 1962 everything was just the printed word, picture or diagram. Having a ground school session was well-advised.

In a way, my Navy training made it a little tougher because I had to unlearn a few things like the wind triangle—in the Navy we did it backwards on our "plotting-boards." In real life, the famous handheld E6-B computer was used and you pretty well had to use it to get the accurate answers the FAA's test required. I can honestly say that the instrument written flight test is the longest at one sitting that I have ever taken—in college, at Harvard Business School, anywhere. It was a 6-hour-long test. You could start at 9 a.m. but had to be finished by 4 p.m. with a supervised in-house lunch break. It covered everything that had any remote connection with instrument flight, even prescription drugs. My biggest bug-a-boo was drawing entry patterns for holding in a racetrack-like oval pattern.

We didn't have "holding patterns" of racetrack ovals back in the beam days. There was never that volume of traffic. When there was a conflict, there were 4 "legs" on every beam. We'd just pick an open one and do turn-rounds about 5 miles out until

Pete Hoyt (left) and I liked to ski the areas around Lake Michigan. His Cessna 310 made it an easy day journey out and back across the lake or deep into Wisconsin.

we were cleared in. But with the accuracy of VOR navigation today and the ability to have a spot (fix) anywhere at most any altitude, the holding pattern was born. The angle and direction you entered a holding pattern was different from each direction. For some reason, I had difficulty in figuring it out from diagrams. In the air, you were coming in from just one direction and the logical one was correct. So I recall getting only an 84 on the exam. You needed a 70 to pass. The actual flight test was no problem with all the Navy training I had. Even though it was 20 years ago, it's the old saying of "it's like riding a bicycle, you never forget how."

Brake Failure and Wild Ride Across Victor 68!

Pete's twin-engine plane was a Cessna 310 N5251A, about 10 years old. But "old" in an airplane is not like old in a car. Airplanes are well-maintained by law, inspected annually by a qualified FAA certified mechanic. But like in a car, older models may not have the newer equipment that experience develops. In this Cessna, it was the rather small brakes or "pucks." They'd heat up pretty fast under steady application.

Pete and I were flying back from his summer home on Cape Cod. We had spent part of the Thanksgiving weekend there buttoning it up for the winter. Chatham, Massachusetts at that time of the year was bucolic. Summer residents and tourists were gone. Clamming for cherrystone oysters was in season. Back at the house with a bucket of clams, pink cheeks, a roaring fire and a scotch was all I could ask for at the time. I had never had raw clams. Pete showed me how to open them with the wide, flat-blade knife. With a little cocktail sauce, the clam and the salty clam juice went down like heavy Jell-O. Delicious. I am hooked on them for life.

It was to be our last night there of male bonding, telling "war stories" and reliving some of our flights together. But the one we had the next day on November 25, 1962, we were still reliving 38 years later in December 2000 on the phone. I was in California and Pete was in Chatham, Massachusetts. He was in bed dying from prostate cancer. He could still chuckle about our experience. He died a few days later at 78. I'll always miss him.

After giving the house one final winter-check, we left the airport at Chatham on the elbow of Cape Cod. We had flown one of Pete's employees, Susie Whitemore, on the way out to Cape Cod, dropped her off for the weekend at Newport, Rhode Island and were flying to Newport to pick her up for the flight back to the Chicago area. The flight from Chatham to Newport was so short, we didn't need to get any gas for the 4-hour, 800-mile flight to Chicago. It was one of those clear fall days. No clouds. No headwinds. You could see for miles at 8,500 feet.

Susie had tucked herself up in the back seat and fell asleep. She had been on the party train since we dropped her off a few days before. We were estimating we'd arrive at Sky Harbor airport about 7 p.m. It would be dark, but it was our home airport. No tower and probably not even the local unicom would be monitored that late on Sunday afternoon. No problem. It was our home airport. We knew it well.

When Pete and I flew a long distance, we usually operated the way airline pilots do by trading legs. If you're on a flight, ask a crew member where the pilots are based. If it's a long flight, say Los Angeles to Chicago, and the pilots are based in Los Angeles, the odds are that the flight back to LA is being flown by the co-pilot. The Captain takes it out and the courtesy is that he lets the co-pilot fly it back, including the landing. If I'm on the return flight and it was a nice landing, I try to wave at the co-pilot on the way out and say "nice landing." Try it. You'll get a smile.

Pete, knowing I didn't fly it as much as he did, was often more generous than that. He'd let me do both the out and back legs. This time I was in the pilot's left seat. Over about mid-Michigan I started our let-down to save as much fuel as we could. Fuel costs money. With about 200 miles to go from 8,500 feet, a descent of 200 feet per minute was like driving down a long, gentle hill. It would take 40 minutes to get down to field elevation and we'd be doing about 225 mph at cruise power. As we started to cross Lake Michigan, you could easily see the lights on the far shore 90 miles away. There was the Northbrook VOR near Sky Harbor. Set the VOR receiver to it at about V-100 (Victor 100 airway) and just follow that compass heading. Piece of cake.

Pete called Sky Harbor's unicom to check on the wind direction and traffic. No answer. No other planes replied that they were in the Sky Harbor traffic pattern. Checking Waukegan, their winds were light and variable. So I set up for the approach landing due south which was a 2,800-foot runway versus the east/west one of 2,500 feet, even though the 2,500 feet landing west would have let me fly straight-in (and I am sure glad I chose the longer one!).

I was about to make a miscalculation. In the back seat was a little 100-pound girl. We had little luggage weight. The tanks were all low. There was little or no wind. It was night when you don't try to "put it on the numbers" i.e., land on the first part of the narrow runway. But at that low weight, we were like a motorized glider! I pulled all the power off and yet on we floated. It was like my A Stage checkride in

The Cessna 310 cruised at 200 mph. Pete's had a lounge-chair seat behind the pilot seat for an inflight "take ten," and a regular seat behind the co-pilot seat. It was great.

those floating N3Ns in the Navy. You want an anchor, a drag chute, anything to make it stop flying.

We touched down about halfway down the runway. Pete was leaning forward peering straight ahead out into the dark trying to see beyond the landing light beams. I immediately started to apply the brakes. They started to grab, then seemed to suddenly release.

I pressed on the brakes as hard as I could. Nothing seemed to be happening. Thinking I wasn't depressing them far enough and knowing that the twin Cessna toe brakes on the right side had an even greater throw, I called out to Pete "Hit 'em!" His back arched up almost as if he didn't have a seat belt on. He was putting all the pressure he could on his side. Still nothing.

Suddenly Pete reached down and hit the buss bar that cuts off all electricity in the plane. The engines went dead. The landing lights went out. We were still doing about 60 mph on the ground with the runway end lights coming up fast.

Without brakes, I couldn't ground loop it. Without lights, I couldn't see beyond the runway end lights. I quickly recalled that there was about a 5-foot-high sloping grass bank about 100 feet past the end of the runway. No buildings, and planes never parked there. I didn't want to hit that bank head-on and maybe crush the nosewheel. The plane had only a 15-degree steering ability on either side of dead center, but I kicked and held hard left rudder to use every bit of the 15 degrees that I could get. The plane approached the bank at a full 15-degree angle and rode up over the bank top and headed across the road.

The road was a major east/west 2-lane state route. Highway 68 was also called Dundee Road which connected the lake suburbs north of Chicago with the western rural areas like Dundee. About the middle of the road, I got the plane going straight across the road and was relieved to see no car lights coming from either direction. On a Sunday night of Thanksgiving weekend at 7 p.m., I was lucky. By the time we got across the road, the bank climbing and the turning had slowed us down to about 15 mph, but that was still enough to keep us going. I had no idea what was on the other side. No lights and no moon. It was pitch black. Then I saw a low barbed-wire fence which stopped us about 5 yards into the field. We got out. We were in a cemetery! The nosewheel was resting against a gravestone but both were okay. A quick scan of the scene and the plane with our flashlights showed there was no damage.

Pete came to his senses quicker than I did. He decided we had to get out of there. But how? The plane didn't have props you could reverse to back out. A 100-pound girl and the two of us couldn't push it back up that bank.

"Wait here," Pete said.

"Maybe Rip Fry and some of the guys are back in the lounge about halfway down the runway, a quarter of a mile away." While we were waiting beside the plane, Susie and I noted several cars whizzing by. One or two slowed down after passing us but then went on.

The next part of the story is what Susie's dad told me...and I still laugh at the sight and his expression. He was waiting to pick Susie up. Seeing us land but not taxi back, he got out of the car and came near the runway in time to see Pete running toward him, if running is a term that you could call what Pete does. Pete is strong, a good skier, but built like a fire plug. As he passed by still running, her dad called out, "Pete, I saw you land but where did you park?" Without breaking pace and doing a few loping sidesteps, Pete yelled back, "Across the road" and turned back to keep running toward the lounge. Susie's dad stood there bewildered. To Pete's dying day, I'd say to him, "Pete, where did you park?"—and we'd both laugh like little kids.

In about 15 minutes a car approached and stopped with its headlights shining on the plane sitting there like a cow stuck in a tree. Until the car's lights fully lit it and the area, the absurdity of where we were came into view. Out piled Pete, Rip Fry, Casey and two other guys. So there were 6 of us all together. Susie was back in the plane to keep warm. At only 100 pounds, we told her to stay there. The six of us were able to push it back up the shallow bank and on to the road. I got in, started the engines and taxied it sideways down the other bank so the props wouldn't get nosed down into the bank. Once on the other side, Pete jumped in and we taxied back through the end lights to his hangar near midfield. We pushed it in backwards, shut the hangar door and stepped outside to look around.

We could hear the sirens of two squad cars. One coming from each direction down the highway with red lights flashing. They stopped at the spot where we had been. Their spotlights scanned the entire area. Pete and I wondered if they would see the plane's wheel tracks up the bank. Without brakes and the hard ground at time of the year, there weren't any tracks. We checked the next day.

Pete dropped me off at my house about 9 p.m. I asked him to come in and we'd talk it over. Up to that time, it was "let's get out of here." My house in Winnetka was on the way to his on the other side of town. He could call his wife, Judy, and tell her he was on his way. Judy was one of those wives that every pilot should have. Her attitude was always, "Just go have fun, boys."

In the house, we sat in my dining room. He was at one end of the long Early American farm table we had and I was at the other end.

We each had a bottle of scotch and a glass.

After Pete had poured his and taken a sip, he looked at me with a half-smile and half-challenging look and said, "Keefe, admit you were scared."

I answered, "Look, Pete, let's review the situation, we were…" He cut me off in mid-sentence.

"Keefe, damn it, admit you were scared—don't act so relaxed." He poured another drink, then another. His normally ruddy complexion was getting even ruddier. Each time he demanded my admission he would pound the side of his fist on the table for emphasis. His bottle would pop up with each blow. My 6-year-old daughter, Dorrie's room was above the dining room. To this day she remembers being awakened from her school-night sleep to hear what was going on down below. She liked Pete as everyone did. She knew we weren't fighting because we were laughing too, especially at the absurdity of it all. It could have been serious.

"Pete, look. What did we learn tonight?" The question got his attention. For the moment he put his demand aside.

"Well, I thought when you yelled 'hit 'em' that you meant the bar that shuts off all switches."

"No, I meant the brakes," I replied calmly.

"Keefe, admit you were scared!"

"Wel-l-l-l," I slowly replied "it was interesting—speeding down the runway with no brakes, no lights and no engines to use to spin around, but I kinda recalled that bank at the end, I really didn't have time to be scared." He just stared at me shaking his head slowly from side-to-side with that "what-am-I-going-to-do-with-you" look on his face.

We did sort it out, mostly that night. I had not considered our light weight and no wind. But the recall of winding up in a cemetery and the squad cars responding to a startled motorist's call but finding nothing got us giggling…with the help of a few scotches, of course.

The airlines and the military work hard on phrases of communication between pilots in emergency situations. A classic one was in a United cockpit coming into Denver one night. Seeing construction equipment on the runway ahead, the captain landing the plane called for "takeoff power!" The co-pilot retarded the throttles, thinking he meant "take – off – the – power." The captain meant to add full power as needed for takeoff. They slammed into the equipment. Most airline pilots can cite a litany of ambiguous commands and requests that could spell trouble if misunderstood when immediate action is needed. "Hit 'em" was ours.

Major interstate roads are designated with an "I." Those running mostly north and south are odd numbers (I-1, I-15, I-23) and those going east and west are even numbers (I-10, I-40). The airways generally follow that same pattern of east–west being even, and north-south being odd numbers. Low-altitude airways have the letter "V" in front of the number. In communication, we refer to them as Victor airways and say "on Victor 10, crossing Victor 23" for example. To start the recall of our crossing the road, as we did many times over the next 38 years, Pete's lead-in was, "Do you remember the night we crossed Victor 68?" 68 being the highway number for Dundee Road. We'd both break out in a smile. If a good pair of curious ears was nearby, I'd say "Tell 'em the story, Pete." His eyes would light up and you would think he was telling the story of Captain Ahab stalking Moby Dick. Pete was a master storyteller. He had adjective and adverb combinations I never thought of using. The "cow in a tree" was one of his to describe a ridiculous situation. Again, I'll miss him.

Influences Along the Way

I was a normal family man at 47 when I began racing: wife Rosemary, sons Chuck, Don, and Tom, and daughter Dorrie; Pacific Palisades, California 1967.

Hamilton College's hockey rink attracted me because I loved ice hockey.

Favorite uncle, Tom Keelin, Aide to CO NAS Glenview, pulled strings to let me get carrier-qualified on the Sable, a mini-carrier, in Lake Michigan.

Dad and I in Ensign garb in 1942, 14 years after WWI. His uniform still fit him!

Mom and Dad in front of a 1937 Lincoln Zephyr. Dad never would fly in a plane, even with me, but he took me to air races and ski jumps—and signed the form to let me take CPT in college.

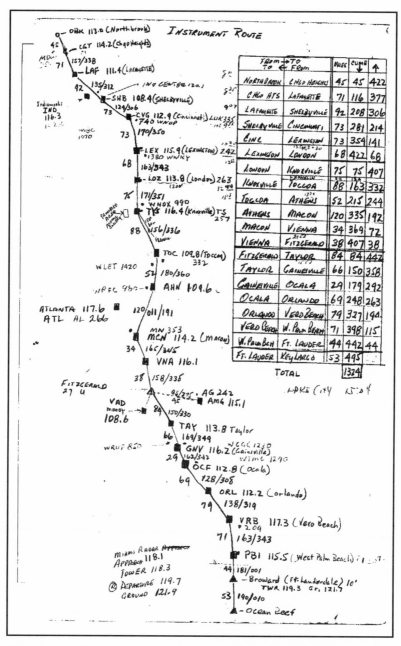

When the VOR airways were added to the Sectional Charts in the 1950s, the beam airways were still on the charts. The clutter was so great, you could barely read the frequencies. This is a chart on a shirt board from Chicago to Key Largo. The Sky Prints charts grew out of these. I had one for routes from Chicago to New York, Washington, DC, etc. Friends wanted copies and the Sky Prints Atlas was born.

Popular Race Planes

"Bearcat"—Navy F8F Fighter

Sport Bi-Plane

"Corsair"—Navy and Marine Fighter

P-38 "Lightning"

P-51 "Mustang"

AT-6/SNJ "Texan"

Formula One Racer

"Sea Fury"—Royal Navy Fighter

Chapter 6

Air Racing Starts
Buying My First Plane — A Navy SNJ (AT-6)

When you are nearing age 50, your kids don't pay much attention to you. Everything is now routine. You see life as pretty humdrum. You are open to new ideas, new thoughts. That's the way I was in the spring of 1968. I was sitting in my new home in Pacific Palisades, California on the ocean near Los Angeles. The Chicago *Tribune* had fired me for publishing something myself, but the *Tribune*'s wonderful Wallie Kurz arranged to have me join the newspaper industry's Bureau of Advertising which transferred me to Los Angeles in 1965. In this Shangri-La, I was bored!

At age 46 in 1967 I bought a "toy," my first real plane, for only $2,500 (they were selling close to $100,000 in 2001!). It was an SNJ-5 (AT-6) that I flew in the Navy. The start of a second childhood!

Glancing through the LA *Times* classified section, I looked at the "Aircraft" classification. I don't know why I did it that day. I rarely had before. There was an ad that stood out. It said, "SNJ for $2,500." An SNJ? That's a Navy plane! If it had said an AT-6, the Army designation, I might have passed it by. But an SNJ…that was part of my youth. And only $2,500? I could put it in my backyard and let my kids and the neighbor kids sit in it, move the controls and enjoy. No one had anything like that for the kids.

I called the number and met the owner, Walter Neilsen, at the Torrance airport. He was being forced to sell for business reasons. I flew back seat out to the aerobatic area over the ocean. It had been 18 years since I had been in an aerobatic plane. It was like getting back on a bicycle again. You never forget. Slow rolls, snap rolls, Immelmanns, the works. Youth had returned! I bought it on the spot. But I felt sorry for him having to sell it. I told him he could buy it back for what I paid plus what I might put into it. He never took me up on that offer. Little did I realize how this impulse purchase of a war surplus plane would change my life forever!

Flying Friends for Fun

I based the SNJ at Santa Monica Airport. It was only a few miles from my house in Pacific Palisades. Man, it was fun to fly. The real fun was that I could take my friends up. I wasn't able to do that with Navy planes. Included in the purchase of the plane were two seat-pack parachutes. Not only were they needed to sit on in the military-style bucket seats into which they fitted, but the FAA required them when doing aerobatics—and they had to be freshly repacked by a licensed parachute rigger every 60 days. That 60-day rule stemmed from the days the chutes were made of cotton. Today's nylon chutes could easily go 6 months to a year if stored properly, but FAA rules are tough to change.

With our home on a bluff overlooking the ocean, it was a treat to be able to put on an air show for the neighbors. Out over the ocean was away from people. Over water, you're allowed fly as low as 200 feet. Over land it's 500 feet, and over populated areas the minimum is 1,000 feet—but you need to be able to glide to an open area if your engine quits. My open area would be the beach below. I never did more than about 10 minutes of aerobatics—a few slow rolls and a snap-roll. That was it. There's always sure to be someone who doesn't understand the rules, who might call the FAA to complain saying I was "too low and endangering people." Plus the fact that the SNJ did make a lot of noise.

Keeping peace with the FAA is always a good idea.

My First Air Race

Okay, so I was entering my second childhood. Why not?

Reno, Nevada is about 500 miles north of Los Angeles, but talk in LA about the National Air Races up in Reno made it seem that they were just next door. The LA area was a hot bed of air-racing talk, planes and pilots, especially around the Van Nuys airport in the San Fernando Valley just across the mountains. A Civil Air Patrol search-and-rescue outfit called the Condor Squadron was based at Van Nuys. It was made up of about eight AT-6/SNJ planes owned and flown by mostly ex-military pilots.

The Reno Air Races, called the National Air Races, began in 1964 by Bill Stead. It had been 15 years since air racing in America had been abruptly halted following the crash at the Cleveland Air Races of Bill Odum flying a P-51 Mustang. The story I heard was that Odum was a distance-race pilot, but did not have much experience in closed-course racing around pylons. During a race, he saw that he was cutting inside a pylon, quickly applied right aileron and rudder until clear, and then quickly applied opposite aileron and rudder causing the plane to do a vertical reverse. He lost control and half-spun into a home near the race course killing two women inside the home. Up to that time, while racers had crashed, no people on the ground had ever been killed before.

Courtesy of Western Reserve Historical Society

Post-WWII air racing came to an abrupt end in 1949 when Bill Odum, an inexperienced pylon race course pilot, snap rolled his P-51 with a sharp right turn to avoid cutting a pylon, then a sharp left turn at the Cleveland Air Races. Two women were killed in the house he hit. For 15 years there was no Unlimited Air Racing until Reno started in 1964.

I flew my SNJ to Reno to see the races in 1967. The Condor Squadron from Van Nuys was there putting on a demonstration race to have the AT-6 considered as a race class the following year. That year there were just 3 types of race classes—the Unlimiteds, the Sport Bi-planes and the Formula Ones, a small traditional type of race plane somewhat like I had seen in 1932 at the air races near Chicago.

The AT-6/SNJ demo race pleased the crowd. They were big, 600-hp engines and noisy as hell with their small-diameter props at high RPM breaking the speed of sound. Also, the races were close. They had to be stock aircraft, no modifications, which holds true today. It was almost impossible to pass one another by speed alone because they were all so close in performance ability. They asked me to join their group next year if its class was added to the race program. It was.

First AT-6 National Air Races • 1968
"First Race...Last Place...but Safe"

As I look back on it, the relaxed way I prepared the plane and myself for the race would never get you very far today. The pilots flying in the Condor Squadron were experienced formation pilots. At air shows, they often flew in formation. Formation was part of their weekly flying. Plus most of them had experienced low-level pylon racing together the year before. Though I knew formation flying, they were a lot better at it than I was. That was nice to know, because it was sometimes almost wingtip-to-wingtip around the pylon turns. You don't need a guy with a jerky, unsteady stick hand in those close situations.

The AT-6s at that time, and up until about the 1990s, raced on the same course designed for the Bi-planes and the Formula Ones. The AT-6 had a gigantic wingspan of 42 feet, wider than even most Unlimited Racers. But the Unlimited race course was too long for planes doing only 200 mph. It was designed to be rounded in less than two minutes by planes doing over 350 mph. The 200 mph speed of the AT-6s was in the speed range of the Bi-plane and Formula One classes. After several midair collisions, a wider race course was designed for the AT-6.

Pete Hoyt came out from the east to crew for me. It was a nice relaxing time on the ramp and in the pits. The almost indestructible, 600-hp Pratt & Whitney engine in the AT-6 rarely gave any problems. Just feed it gas which it loved!

My plane carried the FAA numbers of N9060Z, but I coveted the No. 11 as my race number. It was the race number on the GB Racer of the 1930s. I had drawn it many times in my math book in school. Jimmy Doolittle used to race it. It was snub-nosed and looked like it was all engine with a little tail on it. It was a race plane that *looked* like a race plane.

Amazingly, I was the fastest qualifier at 179.7 mph! Pete and I had only given the wings a pretty good wax job and I purposely didn't carry any more gas than I thought I'd need for the one-lap qualifying run to save on weight. Then in my Heat Race, I came in second with an average speed over 6 laps of 177.04 mph. But something troubled me. The course was really too small for those large 42-foot-wingspan planes. In spite of the good flying ability of the others, I just did not feel comfortable in those tight turns that close together, especially at the first pylon where all 6 of us seemed to be at the same time following a race-horse start on the ground.

I sought out the advice of a Western Airlines captain, Howard Terrell, who raced bi-planes. They also did a race-horse start with planes that were fairly equal. His advice was to climb immediately toward the first pylon to get out of the pack and then use that higher altitude to dive back down passing the others in the straightaway. In the finals on Sunday, because of my low qualifying time, I had the pole position on the ramp. The other 5 planes were to the right of me. I would be the closest on the angle to the first pylon.

The starter gave the signal to rev up our engines. It would be one minute until the start flag would come down, signaling we could start to race. With my stick tucked back as far as it would go into my stomach to keep the tail down, my toes full pressure on the brakes and the throttle almost all the way forward, my plane shuddered like it was flying in a violent wind. The flag came down and when I released the brakes, the plane literally leapt into the air. Out of the corner of my eye, I could see that I was well ahead of the others on the initial start. I climbed straight for the No. 1 pylon and leveled off at about 200 feet. Fine so far. No other planes were around me. **Fact:** I couldn't *see* any other planes! Where were they? Where did they go? With

L to R: *Walter Morrison, Chuck Rei, Dick Sykes (Squadron Leader), Vic Baker (my attorney), Ray Marsh, Nick La Rosa. The Condor Squadron at Van Nuys provided the first T-6 races at the National Air Races. They were well-trained, many were WWII pilots and knew how to fly formation. Their Reno demo race in 1967 thrilled the crowd and T-6 racing became an instant hit.*

the giant AT-6 wing, I couldn't see that they were all under me. What I knew was that I wasn't turning at the first pylon until I knew where all 5 were. And I certainly wasn't going to dive on them either until I saw all five. I wanted to finish my first race in one piece.

One, two, three of them rounded the pylon below me, then the fourth and a little later the fifth. I dove trying to catch them, but the planes were all so equal, all I could do was to get in trail. On that short straight-away there wasn't time to pass. In the turns, you had to almost stay in a wing-man formation position flying farther around the pylon in the outside position to keep the planes below you in sight. The result was that I finished last, sixth place, in the finals. But glory was to come.

I was never comfortable in T-6 tight formation racing. They had a whopping 42-foot wingspan. On the short-oval pylon course designed for bi-planes and Formula Ones, it was much too crowded for me. In three separate races, 7 were killed in midair collisions. Less than 2 midairs in all other race classes. Reno now has a larger course for the T-6 race. We'll see.

ABC's *Wide World of Sports* was filming the races in their first year of doing so. I wasn't really aware of what they were doing. The *Wide World of Sports* was fairly new in the 1960s, as was network TV. One day my kids came running home from school all excited. "Dad! My friends saw you on TV! You're a race pilot. Your name was on the screen and it showed your plane racing." They repeated their programs at later dates and the children and I had a chance to see it. I was no longer, at age 48, just a plain-vanilla old dad to them. I was cool (although I don't think that saying was invented then—that was even before hip). Unfortunately VCRs weren't invented yet. Neither were video cameras. I do have some grainy 8-mm movie film that, when copied onto a video tape, looks like it happened just after the American Revolution. I was told that ABC stores their film and for a price I could get a copy, but I never tried. Last place doesn't warrant the effort.

The Laid Back Atmosphere of Air Racing

As a little kid, even a race plane starting up with puffs of smoke and that roaring, no-muffler backfiring sound was enough to send chills up and down my spine. These were real machines and the pilots were real men. They had helmets. They wore goggles. They had that all-impressive white silk scarf wrapped loosely around their necks. And, of course, they had leather jackets.

What I saw at Reno may have looked like that to a 10-year-old, but to a 48-year-old, they seemed far too human. Cut-off shorts, T-shirts with sayings on them, surplus jumpsuits, fashion-styled sunglasses. Where was Roscoe Turner in his military riding pants and puttees? His trimmed mustache? His look as if he were above all mortals? What I saw were "dressed-down" pilots. Pilots who seemed to think that their P-51 Mustangs were all that they needed to project a flamboyant image. Either that or it was almost as if they didn't want to stand out among the other pilots. Plane crews looked like roving car mechanics in all manners of dress. No crews had look-a-like uniforms to admire.

Back home I thought about this a lot. I had 3 sons and one daughter. She was the youngest. Three hits and a "miss" I would say when asked what children I had. She was the apple of all our eyes. My sons were always watching popular TV programs of the day. As I noticed them watching an episode of "The Man from Uncle" it struck me that current TV fare featured situations with a behind-the-scenes father-figure that either aided them as in "Get Smart" with Maxwell Smart, "Charlie's Angels" and even 007 with not only his futuristic cars and devices, but in the movie "Goldfinger" being rescued at the last minute by an outside father-figure. Also it took 500 people to put astronauts on the moon.

While I was growing up, one person was not only the doer but also the father figure. Lindbergh flew the ocean alone. Knute Rockne coached Notre Dame alone. Admiral Byrd discovered the South Pole as a leader. Even John L. Lewis, head of the CIO union, (as much as I detest most unions) stared down the government. Huey Long snuck by Congress a low bridge over the Mississippi River at Baton Rouge so no large ships could sail north of there and had to use Baton Rouge as a port of

Probably every kid in the 1930s drew the famous G-B (Granville Brothers) racer in his math book. I know I did. It was raced by the famous Jimmy Doolittle who led the B-25 raid on Japan. I was delighted to learn that the race number of 11 was still available when I started. Number 11 was on my T-6 and on "Miss America."

transfer. Houdini escaped unaided from total captivity. Barney Oldfield drove recklessly on the race tracks. Gar Wood set speed-boat records. Walter Hagen played superb golf. Tilden was the tennis star as was Helen Wills Moody. My youth had role models that did things by themselves. Maybe a committee was involved but I never knew it. My youth had individuals as role models, not groups and certainly not behind-the-scenes father-figures.

Between the laid-back atmosphere of the Unlimited Air racing group and what I saw as the lack of role models and excitement for youth like my 3 sons, I had in the back of my mind a desire to create something of what I had as a youngster.

I Find "Miss America"

While strolling around Santa Monica airport, I saw a P-51 Mustang in a hangar. I had seen others a few year before in 1967 at the airport for the high price of $14,000. But this was painted red/white/blue. It was $25,000. I had recently sold my *Sky Prints Aviation Atlas* business to John Mosby in St. Louis and had some extra cash.

The plane was gorgeous. It glimmered in the rays of sunlight coming through the hangar doors. It was majestic in every sense. It looked proud. Above everything around it. A thoroughbred. I couldn't take my eyes off it. This was insane to think of owing a P-51 Mustang. To own a P-51 Mustang was like owning the Eiffel Tower, the Brooklyn Bridge, even the Taj Mahal. Plus the fact I had never flown anything that "hot" before. We didn't have sleek engines like that in the Navy except our battleship and cruiser-based float planes—and those could barely climb above 4,000 feet. Ours were big round noses, not the sleek in-line engine of the P-51 Mustang. But I had to have it. This would be the image I could project to kids. I'd name it "Miss America." The name had always fascinated me ever since I saw a picture as a young boy of Gar Wood's race boat with the "Miss America" name when he set speed records on the river near Detroit.

Getting possession of the plane was strange. The owner asked and received a fairly good down payment. I had to wait a few weeks to raise the balance. It had a rear seat already installed. I asked him if he would take me up for a ride. I had never flown in a Mustang. He used some excuse not to. I asked him if he'd taxi me around in it so I could hear and feel it on the ground. He seemed to not have time. I asked him if he would just show me how to start it and then could I just taxi it around the airport to get the feel of it on the ground. Again, I got a "No."

I was mentioning this strange attitude to someone else and his question was, "You know why, don't you?" I didn't. This is what I was told. I don't know if it is true, but it would explain at least the fact that he wouldn't give me a ride before I paid the full amount and also not offer to check me out.

The story I was told goes like this. He and another Mustang pilot were at the Van Nuys airport in the San Fernando Valley just north across the mountains from Santa Monica and the city of Los Angeles. They had asked the tower for a formation takeoff which really was a simultaneous takeoff because they were on parallel runways about 100 yards apart taking off to the south. The other P-51 was on the left runway, which was short. When cleared for takeoff, the other P-51 on the short runway gave it full power compared to the normal gradual power it's best to use on such a powerful engine. As the other P-51 pulled quickly ahead, more power was added to stay up with him. Looking 100 yards to the left while adding full power to a P-51 does not

It was "Love at First Sight" in 1968 when I saw a red-white-blue Mustang for sale for $25,000. I had to have it to fill my desire to give kids a positive image. I named it "Miss America" after Gar Wood's famous race boat that I followed in the 1930s.

give you the best presentation of what a P-51 is doing. According to this witness, the plane started to veer toward the left edge of the runway. Then it was up on just its left wheel heading off the runway to the left when more power was applied. (Note to non-pilots: props turn clockwise as you sit in the cockpit and that whirling force makes the plane turn left. The greater the power and prop size, the greater this force.) Just getting airborne as the plane left the runway in a left direction, its wing was about 5 feet off the ground heading even more left. As it crossed the runway where the other P-51 had departed, it was now headed across the path to the rear of the departed plane. Suddenly the wings leveled, possibly as the prop wash of the other plane hit the lower wing. It then flew straight ahead between two hangars and climbed out. They say he flew it back to Santa Monica airport, put a "For Sale" sign on it and never flew it again.

The P-51 Mustang's Killer Reputation

Many stories, even at Santa Monica airport, told of how a pilot landing a P-51 suddenly rolled over to the left on his back and crashed, inverted nose down. What I learned later explained to me why this probably happened. To me, landing a P-51 was like pushing a baby carriage up the front walk. It was hard to believe anything could cause the P-51 to flip over on its back in the hands of even a low-time pilot.

The military version of the P-51 had a special feature installed called the Symonds regulator. Its purpose was to keep the throttle at a fixed setting of about 42" MP while the pilot was in a dog fight that might range from 30,000 feet down to 15,000 feet and back up again. The pilot did not have to concern himself with retarding and advancing the throttle as he changed altitude, (pressure changes 1 inch per thousand feet) just fly the plane. The Symonds regulator would keep his manifold pressure at the proper setting of 42" no matter what his altitude. Now comes the problem.

With the regulator in control of the throttle, there would naturally be a slight delay while the regulator did its calculations. A pilot coming in for a landing would see that he is coming in a little short and adds power. Nothing happens, so he adds more power, then more power. Suddenly the regulator kicks in and a strong surge of power comes from the engine. The torque of the powerful engine rolls the plane on its back before the unsuspecting pilot can react to the sudden power surge. With a 10,000-pound plane at slow speeds and the 2,000-pound engine doing its thing rolling it, few pilots would be able to keep it flying level and recover. Probably none did. The P-51 earned its killer reputation from that and one other factor, its short-elevator surface which I conclude was the cause of five P-51 crashes I know about. The sixth was a low-altitude loop, a very dangerous maneuver in any high-performance aircraft—it has caused several crashes at the Paris Air Show by experienced pilots as well as the Air Force's Thunderbirds flying into the ground in formation. The speed you build up on the back side of a loop in a high-performance aircraft is awesome. Many either go straight-in or mush into the ground trying to pull out.

The narrow elevator surfaces on the P-51 were built for speed, not for slow speed maneuvering as were the elevators on carrier-based aircraft. I had "Miss America's"

CG (center of gravity) moved even slightly ahead of maximum to keep the nose slightly heavy for going around pylons—an aft CG is an invitation to disaster in pylon racing. When I flew it in a slow mode like in traffic pattern turns for landing, I always flew with the nose slightly lower in low-altitude turns to avoid any possible stall from another plane's prop wash, a sudden gust of wind or my needing to pull back pressure on the stick to avoid another plane. Pilots know what I'm talking about. A nose-high, slow-speed turn in a steep bank can turn you into an angel pretty fast in any plane. In a 60° bank, your stall speed is over 60% higher than in level flight—a big increase when you're looking for traffic and take your eyes off the airspeed indicator.

While I'm on the subject of stalls and the P-51's narrow elevators, let me relate how I almost "bought the farm" (pilot jargon for crashing). I was in Santa Barbara, California for an airshow. I was there a day early and a locally-based pilot with a P-51, I think Les Grant was his name, and I decided to do a little dog fighting over the mountains north of the Santa Barbara airport. I lost sight of him and pulled up fast looking back over my shoulder when I was suddenly in a cloud. I totally lost my

In 1970 this picture appeared on the cover of FLYING magazine's Air Racing edition. It was the reason COX model planes sponsored me—a most fortunate event. It ensured the future of "Miss America."

spatial orientation while in a high-speed climbing left turn. I must have pulled back on the stick too much at the top of a Chandelle-type climb. The plane was spinning. As I came out of the cloud in a left spin, I saw the green hillside rushing up. I chopped the throttle, gritted my teeth, added rudder into the spin with back stick to make the spin go faster, then released left rudder, and popped forward stick. The plane stopped its spin and I pulled out about 500 feet above the slope of the mountain. If an aerobatic pilot had not told me what you should do, and I had not programmed that into my reaction mode, "Miss America" and I would be imbedded in that hillside.

The P-51, with its narrow elevator surface, needs downward speed and at least 4,000 feet to recover from a spin. If you try the normal recovery of opposite rudder to the spin to stop it, then pop the stick, you'll need at least 6,000 feet and maybe that won't even be enough. What will happen if you try a normal spin recovery is that the nose will come up in the second turn of the spin as if the spin is going to stop, it will wallow through that turn and then start a vicious nose-down spin, pick up downward speed and there won't be enough speed to recover. The reason to first make the spin accelerate is to build up enough speed so the P-51's skinny elevators can be effective. With the ground rushing up, it's a reflex action that must be programmed into your brain. It's not something you have the time to sit and discuss with yourself. You need speed to get out of a spin in any high-performance aircraft.

I have suggested to anyone building a P-51 three-quarter scale, or even a large size to be flown for recreational use, to double the width of the elevator surface or their planes will have a high-crash-rate—especially at low altitude turns in traffic patterns by pilots with low time in high-performance aircraft.

I Solo the P-51 • May 20, 1969

This was a Red Letter day for me in my flying career. Bob Hoover had just given me a P-51 check-out sitting in the rear seat of his P-51 about a week earlier which I relate in the front of this book along with his picture. Now I had to bite the bullet and face the reality of flying a P-51 Mustang by myself. If you're flying your own plane you think about two things a) your neck and, b) the cost of what you might lose. The military pilot thought about "a" but never about "b." I thought more about "b." Who the hell was going to pay for the damage or the replacement if I screwed up? I had some money, but not as much as it would cost to replace a plane and pay for all the damage I might do to something else. No insurance company would cover an inexperienced guy taking off in a P-51 for the first time.

The FAA rules were that, as an inexperienced pilot, I was allowed to take off from a regular airport in a plane like a P-51. In order to return, I had to make 5 takeoffs and landings at an airport far away from the congested, residential area of Santa Monica. I planned to fly to the Mojave Airport in the desert about 100 miles north of LA to do my 5 landings. It had long runways with no houses in the area. I later learned that my planned takeoff from Santa Monica airport had become a "must see" event. Here was an inexperienced P-51 pilot taking one off for the first time. Maybe the bets were that I'd let it roll on its back halfway down the runway. It didn't.

At the run-up ramp I checked the mags, maybe even wishing that one mag would be faulty so I'd have to abort the takeoff and taxi back in for another day to think this thing over. But, no, they checked out perfectly. The engine purred. What a wonderful sound! It was like "Come on, I want to go!" The tower cleared me to taxi into position for takeoff. Okay, this was the moment of truth. There was a 5,000-foot runway ahead of me. Almost a mile of concrete. But I thought that might not be enough. So I lowered the P-51's gigantic flaps to 20°, put the toes of my shoes on the brakes and revved up the engine to 36" MP. Then I released the brakes, held a strong right rudder as Hoover had told me to do, and suddenly I was off the ground! The P-51 was trying to fly! It startled me. I added more power and started to climb almost as if it was being lifted from above. I was flying! I was in a P-51 and I was flying! Never before

Lloyd Stearman, designer of the bi-plane many military pilots first trained with during WWII.

had I felt such power. Power that literally lifted me off the ground and wanted to propel me into space. It was awesome! I'll never forget the sensation of that takeoff. My first encounter with high horsepower in over 25 years.

I was told later that those who had come to the airport to witness this first-timer taking off in a P-51 Mustang had never seen a P-51 leave the ground so fast. The word was, "Oh, he was a Navy pilot. That's the way they take off from carriers." Not only was my carrier takeoff a "touch 'n' go" with an SNJ, but I had no intentions on that first P-51 takeoff of trying to pretend I was taking off from a carrier. I just wanted to be airborne by the end of that 5,000-foot runway. One said it looked like I was off the ground in only 150 feet!

In 1962 with "Babe" Meigs, on a field named for him on Chicago's lakefront, looking at the first edition of my Sky Prints Aviation Atlas.

Meeting two of the greats in aviation in 1997. Lee Atwood, Mr. P-51 at North American, and Tony LeVier, Lockheed's P-38 test pilot and race pilot who is in Aviation's Hall of Fame. Both great guys.

Flying out to the Mojave Airport, I was amazed at the heavy pressure required to move the ailerons by moving the stick from side-to-side. The high speed, 250 mph of the Mustang in just normal cruise, made the high-speed airflow over the wing surface a force I had never felt before. To deflect a control surface into that force required more than the marshmallow pressure other planes needed. When the throttle was retarded and the plane slowed to about 175 mph, the pressure was more like what I was used to.

The Mojave Airport in 1969 had gigantic runways but very little traffic. It was ideal to use for my needs: to practice landings and takeoffs in a high-performance aircraft. I was determined to make the landings 3-points instead of just coming in level, landing on the two wheels and then letting the tail down at the end of the runway. That was okay, but it would take longer runways. Setting it down on all three wheels with the nose high would let you land on shorter runways. As I floated over the runway on my first landing with a little power still on, the plane settled down on the runway like a butterfly landing on a leaf. With 45° flaps down and a little power in a nose-high 3-point landing position, it touched down so softly I didn't realize I was actually rolling along the ground. Then it suddenly started to lurch to the right. I tapped the left brake and it straightened with a downward-movement feeling. The next landings felt the same way—settling down, then a lurch to one side.

In describing this to an experienced pilot, he explained it as follows. The P-51 has a long oleo strut, a telescoping landing gear that settles under pressure. On that long runway at Mojave, I was able to set the plane down so softly that, as the speed dropped and the weight of the plane was put on the oleo strut, it retracted on one side before the other side retracted. With one wheel strut shorter than the other, the plane veered toward the shorter, more collapsed strut. Tapping the opposite brake put weight on the other strut to collapse it too. From then on, landing the P-51 with its wide landing gear was a piece of cake, especially after I clipped the wingtips that were designed to take it to 40,000 feet (almost 5 miles up). The clipped wingtips made it settle down without floating as much.

*The Staggerwing Beech was **the** rich sportsman's plane in the '30s! It was Naval Air Station base CO's private plane during WWII. As Aide-to-CO, I was checked out in case I had to pick it up or ferry it to my skipper. Tough duty, but somebody, etc.*

Courtesy Paul Neuman

Bob Hoover conducting a pilots' meeting prior to a race. It was important that we all knew his route so we could join up in formation on him for the race start, and where he was going to release us on the course for the race start. Left to right: *Len Tanner, myself, Ormond Haydon-Baillie, Clay Lacy, Bob Hoover, Leroy Penhall and Gunther Balz.*

Chapter 7

Me-109s and P-51s
Encounter at High Altitude

I mentioned clipping the wings on Miss America for more speed and why they were as long as they were. Let me insert at this point a story I read about the first encounter a P-51 Squadron had with the Messerschmitts. As I recall, it was over the Mediterranean. The method they used to attack allied planes was to use their ability to fly high, up to 38,000 feet, and then coming out of the sun, dive through the enemy formation below. Erich Hartmann, the all-time ace of any country with 352 victories, describes this strategy in the book *The Blond Knight of Germany*. Rarely would they try to engage in a dog fight. It was dive through a formation, firing constantly, then use the speed built up in the dive to hightail it out of there back to base.

The story I heard of P-51s meeting a *Schwarm* of Me-109s, is that the Me-109s could fly much higher than our P-47 Thunderbolts and P-38 Lightnings, but the major duty of our fighters was to protect the bombers that could not get much above 23,000 feet with heavy loads. In flying cover for the bombers, our fighters did not need to go much above 25,000 feet. However, the Me-109s diving on them from higher altitudes made it necessary for a fighter of ours to go even higher than the Me-109 whose ceiling was about 38,000 feet.

As the story goes, a *Schwarm* of Me-109s spotted a P-51 formation coming at them. The Me-109s always had the height advantage and felt they must be higher than the oncoming P-51s. Besides, as pilots know, it's hard to judge the height of an oncoming plane a few miles away. As the P-51s approached, the Me-109s sought to engage them. As they came closer and closer, the Me-109s tried to climb to meet the P-51s. The result was that the tight Me-109 formation started to stall and as they did, they crashed into each other, falling and spinning out of the sky. What few were left were easily bettered because of the P-51s higher altitude and maneuverability. When I set the speed record from Los Angeles to Washington, DC at 23,000 feet with the clipped wings, I could move the stick from side-to-side with no effect because my ailerons had been shortened, too. At that altitude, the plane had to be kept level or turned ever so slightly with just the rudder—somewhat like turning a bike with your hands off the handlebars by leaning from side to side. It's a strange feeling, especially in a Mustang with the usually heavy force required to deflect the ailerons at low-altitude cruise speed.

Erich Hartmann, WWII German Ace of Aces

I met Erich when he was a celebrity guest at a P-51 tournament sponsored by Leo Volkmer in Alton, Illinois across the river from St. Louis. It was May 1971. Five years later, Christa and I visited Erich and his wife Ursula at their home north of Stuttgart, Germany in the hamlet of Weil-im-Schoenbuch. It happened to be his birthday party and he invited us to join in. As before, he was most gracious, modest and unassuming with the soft characteristics of a pensive little boy. He held a high-ranking officer's position in the revitalized German Air Force. But now he was retired and was into private flying at the time. He remarked to me in his excellent English, "Howie, it's all over for us. Private flying is dead in Germany. All the airspace is restricted to military and commercial flying, there is no enjoyment. You can't go anywhere."

After WWI, the armistice decreed that Germany must give up military flying and also, what little private flying there was, was also curtailed. As a result, gliders gained wide use throughout Germany after WWI. Every decent hill seemed to have a way to launch a glider. When I was there in 1976, I saw their gliders in operation. Erich took me out to a field near his house. There they were. About 5 gliders on the ground and two or three soaring in the vicinity. His outstretched arm swept from left to right over the area of about 100 square yards.

"This is really all we have…and even these are not allowed to soar very high." It was about 1,000 feet maximum as I recall. The gliders were being launched into the air by gasoline-powered winches. A long cable wrapped around a drum was pulled out about 50 yards. It was hooked on to the nose of the glider. When ready, the clutch on the winch engine was engaged, pulling the glider about 25 mph over the ground until it would lift gracefully into the air. Then the cable detached and fell to the ground. There are many stories about how good the Germans are at gliding. Finding the air currents and updrafts, knowing just what the wind will do was second nature to those who were drawn to the sport. It was from this experience base that Germany was able to assemble its Luftwaffe for WWII. In our many talks, Erich confirmed that the Luftwaffe strategy of WWII was to avoid dog fighting as much as possible. One reason was that their planes did not have the gas capacity to sustain long high-powered flight.

Before the P-51s, no plane of ours had the range to escort the bombers all the way to their targets in Germany. Therefore, the Luftwaffe really didn't have to engage our fighters very often. They could wait until our bomber escorts, like the P-47 Thunderbolts, nicknamed the "Jug," had to turn back. Then the Me-109s were able to attack our bombers at will. Things changed when the P-51s came on the scene with wing-mounted gas tanks that could be dropped clear of the plane when in combat.

A young Erich Hartmann, "The ace of aces" and his bride-to-be, Ursula Paetsch on June 14, 1943. After the war, the famed pilot was later captured by the Russians and spent $10^1/_2$ lonely years in a Soviet prison camp.

But as Erich explained to me, he was on the Eastern front attacking mostly Russian formations, often made up of the U.S.-made P-39 Airacobras and P-38 Lightnings that Russia had obtained through the allies "Lend-Lease" program. He said he might make as many as 4 sorties in one day. Climb high with his group, spot a formation below and dive, shooting all the way through the formation before it had time to break and engage them. He'd go back to base, land, refuel, rearm and was off again. One time, when he bailed out, an American Mustang had him in its sights as he floated down. He felt his end was near, but as did the Germans, the Americans felt that shooting a pilot in his parachute was not fighting, it was murder. The American pilot, Erich said, waved as he flew by.

Unfortunately, Erich Hartmann was "captured" after the war was over by the Russians instead of by the Brits or us. The Russians forced him to spend almost 11 years at hard labor as a penalty for shooting down so many Russian planes. Imagine that! It was in the modern times of 1955 before he was released as a prisoner of a war that had ended in 1945! I understand the title of his book in Russian or German is *Get Hartmann from the Skies* instead of *The Blond Knight of Germany*. In spite of many people and organizations wanting Erich to visit the United States again and be paid handsomely for signing art and photos, he was concerned about leaving the health-care facilities of Germany because of his bad heart. People even offered me $5,000 if I could entice him to come back to America to appear at air shows. No fighter pilot in history had

Erich Hartmann, getting the "Blue Max" from Hitler. Erich was soft-spoken and very intelligent. It was a pleasure visiting with him and Ursula in 1976 at his home in Germany.

ever had over 80 victories—and I predict none ever will match Erich's 352. As much as I would have loved to greet Erich back here, I didn't try. In 1993 when Erich was 71, he died of a heart attack at his home in Germany. He could have made a small fortune touring the U.S. air shows in the 1980s. I liked him.

Racing a T-6 and P-51 in the 1969 National Air Races

In September 1969, I not only had the P-51 but also the AT-6/SNJ that I had raced the year before. I was elected head of the T-6 race class to formalize their rules. They must be stock without any alterations. The only exception was that if any model of a T-6 had a desired feature, you could modify yours with that feature. The two major ones were the small tailwheel (not the big one the P-51 had) and the more stream-lined canopy of the AT-G. Of course, the Harvard AT-6 which is what the Canadian Air Force flew, had a long exhaust pipe on the right side that served as a cockpit heater in the cold Canadian air. You could have that long stack not only removed, but you could go to the even smaller exhaust stack of other models. But that was it. No setting the prop governor to go faster and no doming of the cylinder heads to increase the compression ratio. The real mods were to get the weight down, as many did, but still have the rear seat, basic instruments, etc. They went faster as each pound was shed. I never got to that level of T-6 competition.

After racing both the P-51 and the T-6 at Reno in 1969 at the age of 48, I decided that coming at a pylon at 200 mph in the T-6 and 30 minutes later coming at that same pylon at double the speed of 400 mph required too much adjustment to be competitive. Just flying it was not the problem. The problem was that at 200 mph, you started your turn about 50 yards before the pylon, but at 400 mph, it was 50 yards sooner at 100 yards. What if I started the P-51 turn at 50 yards? I'd be way beyond the pylon. But what if I started the T-6 turn twice as far from where I'd start the P-51? I'd either cut inside the pylon or have the dangerous maneuver of flipping back over into a right bank, possibly into another plane, or hit the pylon as one T-6 plane did, losing his wing and spinning in upside down. I wasn't enjoying racing both types in the same race event.

The Joy of Early T-6 Racing

Reno was the only site of Unlimited Racing in 1969–70. There just weren't any places large enough to have the fast unlimited racers. Their courses required a lot of real estate. The FAA rules were that the crowd had to be about a mile from the closest high-speed pylon turn. This is where the plane's belly faced the crowd in a turn and could flip, as did Bill Odum at the 1949 Cleveland Air Races, crashing into a house and killing two people. The T-6s needed only a one-half mile and much smaller courses. As a result, T-6 races started in places other than Reno, and I went into all of them. Sadly, they did not repeat again, but they were sure fun, low-cost racing. You weren't running your engine to the breaking point and could fly home relaxed.

The Amazing 18 Months of T-6 Air Racing • 1968–1970!

September 1968—Reno • February 1969—Ft. Lauderdale
• August 1969—St. Louis and Cleveland • September 1970—Reno
• April 1970—Ft. Lauderdale

I explained my first T-6 race at Reno in 1968. This is what followed.

Ft. Lauderdale T-6 Races • February 1969
"Racing in the Sun...and Rain"

After the crowd-pleasing initial T-6 races at Reno in 1968, John Tegler (later known as the famous author of the air racing classic *Gentlemen, You Have a Race!*), staged a T-6 race in Ft. Lauderdale, Florida. It was unique in that the race course went around the Bendix industrial plant just north of the Ft. Lauderdale Executive airport. It made sense that the safest spot on an air race course was actually in the middle of the race course oval. Problems were most likely to occur on the turns where the planes were pulling high-G loads and debris would fly outward from the course, never inward. Even so, the FAA mandated that the plant be vacant, which was the case on weekends anyway.

Getting to Florida from the west coast was a long 16-hour flight sitting on a parachute pack in the slow 160-mph T-6. It took me two days. In a T-6, it always seemed that flying from one end of Texas (El Paso) to Arkansas was a day-long flight in itself. If Texas wanted to make private-plane pilots feel better (and motorists too), they would divide Texas into 3 states—West Texas, Central Texas and East Texas, just to make us feel we're making some progress over the earth, especially when flying west into a 30-mph headwind.

Florida can't be beat for air racing. Its flat terrain, soft climate in the late winter and gentle winds make it a great air-racing venue. Part of my job as head of the T-6 class was to check out the new pilots and instruct them in the rules of air racing. Although I was one of a few west coast pilots who had ever raced, I was no expert with only several heat races and a final race under my belt. No one that I recall came from the Condor Squadron at Van Nuys. That was the most experienced group of T-6 pilots in the U.S. at the time and perhaps still is today. Under their long-time leader, Richard (Dick) Sykes, they maintained not only proficiency but a semi-military organized discipline that kept the "hot dog" pilot attitude out of their flying.

My first "virgin check out" in a T-6 was for my friend John Mosby. I had purchased a T-6 for John and flown it out there for him. In 1967 John bought my chart company, *Sky Prints Aviation Atlas*, but we had known each other for over 5 years before that. John was an experienced pilot, but did not have military flying experience nor any time in the irascible T-6. I have always stated that the two toughest planes to land that I have flown are the cabin plane, the Howard DGA (the NH-1 in the Navy) and the T-6, especially the T-6 compared to the Navy SNJ.

The Howard DGA (designated by Howard, its builder, to stand for Damn Good Airplane, which it was) had a narrow landing gear and handled like a loosely-jointed truck as it settled down with the almost 400 pounds overload we had in the instrument trainer version. I always stopped breathing at touchdown and then inhaled deeply when I knew I had control of it on roll out.

The T-6/SNJ was much the same. Its gear wasn't as narrow as a Spit-Fire or an Me-109, but it was a bigger mass plane. The irony of it was that the Navy SNJ version had a tailwheel that could be locked in position straight-ahead to help maintain directional control on both takeoff and landing, important for use in training on carrier decks. The Army Air Corps and Canadian version had a free-swiveling tailwheel. Upon landing, those versions might take off in any direction. When it started across the runway, it took more than a tap on the brake pedal to get it straightened out down the runway. Landing a T-6 was always filled with anticipation. There was always the chance of a strong ground loop if you were late on the toe brake. If it got headed more than 45 degrees off the runway centerline, the chances were that you either started to apply brake on the wrong side, a strong crosswind was causing you to weather-vane or you figured out too late what was happening. A ground loop was often the outcome to avoid going off the runway into a ditch. The ground loop of spinning around and having a wingtip scrape the runway was the better choice, but a most humbling one. I fear to even mention the third choice of nosing over. It's like avoiding the saying "shanked it" in golf.

John Mosby, in spite of his lack of experience, was eager to learn to fly his new toy. The attitude was that if cadets in WWII flew these things with less time than I have, I too should be able to fly one. The only airport in the area that I could find without much traffic was Boca Raton just north of Ft. Lauderdale and had one east–west runway. Because of the sea breeze off the ocean, the landings were usually to the east. At the end of the runway was a golf course providing an overrun if needed. I made a few landings from the back seat to give John the sense of attitude and then told him to take over. When you're in the back seat of a T-6, every little change of direction on the ground at landing seems magnified. John was doing a good job, but

John Mosby from St. Louis was born to love aviation. He bought my Sky Prints Atlas business in 1967. Later I introduced him to T-6 air racing. He rose to become Class Champion at Reno. We had, and still have, a "big brother/little brother" relationship.

I was getting too mother-hen-like. Too much "use brake…use rudder, not aileron to pick up a wing…come in with wings level…" and so on. I was on his case on every landing.

Finally John begged, "Look, I've got it. I understand. Let me do some by myself." Well, it was his plane. I had a Flight Instructor Rating. I was legal to solo him, so I got out and stood on the walkway about halfway down the runway in front of the FBO's office. Standing there as I walked up was a chap that I had noticed watching us land and take off.

"Are you an instructor?" he asked in a challenging way.

Before I could answer, he said "Are you crazy? Are you going to let him solo?" I nodded and answered that he'd be alright. Let's watch.

John taxied back to the end of the runway, did an engine run-up to check mags, made a circle to clear the approach lane to make sure no other plane was landing, lined it up down the runway and gave it power. Off he went. Made the left turn out to come back in for his landing, which I watched. It was a "controlled landing." The plane never veered totally off the runway, but there weren't many parts of it that were missed. When it started to go left, John hit the right brake. When it started to go right, John hit the left brake. With each side-to-side dance step, a wing would come up and the other wing would go down to about 6 inches off the ground. It was a masterful dance and a good act at any air show. Then John saw the end of the runway coming up fast and swung the plane to one side for a grand swing-around stop that looked like it was planned instead of being half-of-a-ground-loop. As he taxied back by us for another takeoff, John waved and smiled with a "there, I did it" look on his face.

I recall the observer saying, "Do you realize your liability here? There are hangars within 100 feet of the runway." I shrugged my shoulders. John came around again for another landing. He greased it in, rolled out straight and did two more nice ones. I nodded at the observer, walked out to the runway to signal John that I'd get back in. In the coming years, John went on to not only be the class champion of the T-6 race group, but held the record for the fastest qualifying speeds in a T-6.

Back at the races in Ft. Lauderdale, I checked the other new race pilots for their logbook time in a T-6. Over 50 hours was good enough. Then I checked their planes for visual compliance with the class rules. To check that they had not increased governor limit on the prop, I had a neat little device that model airplane builders use to check RPMs on their engines. It would give a readout of the RPM speed of the turning prop.

At the qualifying runs, I qualified No. 1 with a speed of 185.8. I'd finally gone through the 180 wall. After winning my heat race, the new pilots were catching on to the technique of air racing—staying tight on the turns, holding a constant altitude and finding an altitude not too low or too high to match the best turn radius with the wingtip on the pylon. By the time the finals came, I was lucky to even get the third place I did.

Several things happened at that race that I still vividly recall. One was the rain that began suddenly. I don't think I had ever seen a downpour like that. A black cloud appeared and then WHAM! We ran to our planes to close the cockpits, but the rain was so intense, I stayed inside the closed cockpit to ride out the storm. Hail started bouncing off the metal wings. All large surfaces on the T-6 were metal except the big elevators in back. I wondered if they were standing up under the barrage of hailstones which Southern California planes aren't exposed to very often. Then one of the most amazing sights I had ever seen appeared before me. A P-51 Mustang came streaking out of nowhere down the runway and landed in the violent rain! Incredible! How could it be? You could barely see across the runway much less find it in a fast plane.

With all the running around checking other pilots, etc., I had not known that John Tegler had scheduled a cross-country race for P-51s from Frederick, Maryland terminating in Ft. Lauderdale as part of the air race program. All the other pilots had landed at other places, but not this fellow. I wish I could recall who it was. I spoke to him admiringly that evening, eager to discover how he had managed to land in that storm. What he explained to me was a trick I used later when I lost my compass in the soup over the Rockies.

He explained that he was in contact with the radar approach facility in the Ft. Lauderdale area when he arrived and asked for radar steers 500 feet over the airport that would take him down the longer west runway. When radar told him he was headed down the runway, he set his directional gyro at 0° (i.e., 360°), dropped his

In the cockpit of "Miss Sky Prints." Navy pilots of the 1950s will recognize the gold helmet of the Navy Air Corp. They remind me of old leather football helmets.

landing gear, made a standard-rate left turn to 270° on the gyro, flew for 30 seconds, then a turn to 180° on the gyro which put him downwind. Flew that heading for one minute then turned to 090° for 30 seconds and then back to 0°, put down full flaps, went down to 200 feet and there was the runway in front of him to land. I still say, *Incredible!*

Another memorable event at that race was when "Mac" McKinney of Johnstown, Pennsylvania came in with his landing gear still up. In the excitement after his first race, he had forgotten to put it down. Those standing by the end of the runway watched as he approached from the east and could see that his gear wasn't down. When he was about 100 yards from touchdown, about 5 people started waving their hands in all sorts of directions. Some were crossing their arms above their heads as if to say "Don't land!" Others were doing the "tossing a baby in the air" motion, telling him to "Go up! Go up!" One ran out on the runway almost in the plane's path waving his arms frantically above his head. As Mac passed the multi-waving crowd, he waved back thinking it was a good-ol'-boy welcome. A few seconds later, he said he realized what they were trying to tell him. About 20 of us ran out to the plane that looked like a duck sitting on water in the middle of the runway. We gradually coaxed one wing up, put our backs under it, then others did the same with the other side. As it rose, the wheels dropped and it was pushed clear of the landing runway. He was the butt of many jokes that night like "Mac, what does this signal mean?" as the questioner rocked his overlapped arms back and forth as if cradling a baby. But, as always, Mac was good-natured about it. His deep jaw wrinkled as he smiled and shook his partially-bowed head.

My race trophy was given to me by the famous retired Eastern Airline pilot, Dick Merrill. Most knew of him by the fact that he had married the movie star, Toby Wing. To me, he was a friend of Eddie Rickenbacher, WWI ace and founder of Eastern Airlines. Even at age 70, Dick Merrill, though shorter than I had imagined him, had the bearing of a military officer, did not need glasses and had eyes so clear and blue you'd think you were looking into the eyes of a baby. And he was such a class act and ever smiling.

St. Louis Air Races • August 8, 1969
"Crowd Too Big — A Dinged Prop"

T-6 air racing was on a roll! In this month of August, one was scheduled in St. Louis at the Spirit of St. Louis airport in Chesterfield about 30 miles west of St. Louis for the Formula One and T-6 Class, and then over Labor Day at Cleveland. It was like my getting two for one—just one of those long flights back east. I could leave my plane in St. Louis, fly airline round trip to Los Angeles, come back and fly the short hop to Cleveland. It chewed up a lot of my vacation time, but I was living on a cloud! As it turned out, I made a boo-boo and had to leave it in St. Louis anyway. But more about that later.

The races were sponsored by the County Sheriff's Department for their pension fund. What a great combo! They could deal with the FAA and they sold so much advertising in their race program that it looked like a bible. The program was so thick and they were a no-cost traffic control for the entire area to say nothing of all the free press promoting it. The race was financed before the first paying customer walked through the gate. This looked like a Golden Goose to us, especially after the tight financial situation at Ft. Lauderdale. But the great success of the race was the undoing of the St. Louis Air Races!

The crowd that descended on the air race site was massive! There were only a few minor roads coming into the airport area and it was reported that the traffic was backed up for 5 miles. Drivers were seething. Finally, they stopped trying to collect for admission as the cars came in and opened the gates so everyone got in free. There was a feeble attempt by the harried ticket-takers to collect as people streamed across the hayfields from their cars.

We were asked to delay the start of the races to accommodate those arriving late. The great success had turned into a promotional nightmare for the sheriff's department because no one had anticipated the size of the crowd.

To start the races, we were still using a ground race-horse start verses a formation air start. The runways were only wide enough to permit two abreast. We started using two runways that went off about 30 degrees from each other. I was lined up in the crotch on the left runway on the right side. The starter was standing in the crotch with his two flags on 3-foot poles. He put up the red flag when it was 5 minutes to the start. At 4 minutes, he would put that down and hold up the green flag. When the green flag came down, you were released to start the race.

When the green flag went up, it was time to start revving up the engines. I could see the starter and his flag in my vision just to the right of the nose of the plane and still be able to check my instruments. I was watching my RPM gauge come up to max and was checking the oil pressure gauge when I suddenly saw the green flag go down out of the corner of my eye. It had been only about 30 seconds since it went up instead of 60 seconds, but thinking it was a start I released the brakes at full throttle. As I started to roll, I saw the starter flailing on the ground trying to get up. He had stumbled in the high grass and fallen sideways, dropping the flag as he went. It wasn't a start! Instead of continuing, I hit the brakes. The tail came up, the nose dipped, then the 300-pound tail came down with a thump, but I hadn't crossed the start line. Baron Leo Volkmer was in the plane to my right. He could see that I was preparing to start while the starter again raised the green flag high. He transmitted on the race frequency, "Howie, I saw chunks of concrete fly when your nose went down. You may have damaged your prop."

When the green flag went down to start the race, I stayed there. I wanted so much to race, but my conservative flying nature kicked in and I aborted, taxied back to the pits and shut down the engine to check the damage. Sure enough, about 6 inches of each prop tip was curled out, a sign that the prop has struck while engine power was on. If you come in with a free-whirling prop in a dead-stick landing, the tips will be bent backwards. Actually, I could have safely taken off and flown it, which I would have done if Baron had not alerted me. If there were enough blade left to get me off the ground, I could have made it back, but as for racing, it would not have been worth the chance.

The amazing thing is that there was no damage to the engine. To have a prop hit at that RPM might easily twist the crankshaft, but it was such a momentary hit (I hadn't even realized it) and that Pratt & Whitney engine was so massive, I was lucky. So my plan to leave the plane in St. Louis to pick it up two weeks later caused me little trouble, except to my pocketbook. I think it was all of $600, big bucks at that time to buy and have a new prop installed. If the Spirit of St. Louis airport had an eight-lane highway going into it, I think there would still be air racing there today.

The Cleveland Air Races • August/September 1969
"Respect for the Early Days of Air Racing"

The name Cleveland and "air racing" went together like "hot-fudge sundae." Before and after WWII, Cleveland was air racing. As I explained earlier, the crash of a P-51 into a house that killed two people in 1949 brought an end to Cleveland Air Racing and to air racing itself. But now two things had changed. Cleveland had a lakefront airport without any buildings around it and racing now could be held without the Unlimiteds. The T-6s, Formula Ones and Bi-planes were joined by the women's stock-plane racing group—Bonanzas, Piper Comanches and other fast, low-wing planes women had flown in the Powder Puff Derby.

The women's stock-plane races were a good crowd-pleaser. But it was the start of "feminism" in the U.S. and Gloria Steinem somehow got into the act. She, learning of women's races, as the story goes, and looking for publicity for herself and her movement, rattled public officials enough to question why the "men only" races were being held on airports that were federally funded. That women should be allowed to race in those "men only" races, too.

Yes, there was "discrimination," but air racing did not have the specific physical qualifications that the Army, Navy, fire and police departments had to point to. It was just assumed that the endurance, sweat of cramped cockpits, the danger and power to handle the control forces at high speeds were not conducive to women. There really wasn't an out-and-out ruling that I knew of against women racing around pylons in any of the classes. It was like women's tennis and golf were for women. But Gloria Steinem's crusade spelled the death-knell for women's stock-plane pylon racing.

The stock-plane pylon racing program died out because men, angered by Gloria Steinem's intrusion, decided to reverse the point and enter the women's races. I think Darryl Greenamyer, a constant winner in Reno's Unlimited races, was the spearhead. He applied to enter the Women's Stock-plane races. Once men started to fly in them, the unique glamour was gone. As I heard it, he even tried to enter the Powder Puff Derby and actually showed up to fly in it, but was rebuffed because this was not a race at one airport. It was a cross-country race across the U.S. hosted by various nonpublic companies and organizations en route. Now, most women realize more and more that Steinem's "feminism" stole from them rather than gave them more privileges they really did not want in the first place.

My SNJ making a landing at Cleveland, Ohio. I carried the number eleven on both the T-6 and the P-51 Miss America.

Racing at a lakefront airport had a lot of advantages. No hills to give you a deceptive horizon. Like the Florida terrain, there was a flat horizon around most of the course. The trouble was that when you rounded the first set of pylons and turned out toward the lake, there was often no horizon at all! Between the water and the sky was a hazy fog-like area. I guess it's somewhat like photosynthesis when the air is picking up its moisture from the water via radiant energy of the sun. There was nothing to focus on. A pilot needs some sort of horizon unless he's flying solely on his instruments. But there is no way to race around pylons without your eyes out of the cockpit.

My method was to focus on the shoreline as I went into the turn at the first pylon, glance at my altimeter and vertical speed indicator while picking up the second pylon. Once I spotted the third pylon, I'd look hard left to pick up the gigantic Cleveland lakefront football/baseball stadium just west of the airport. In that way, I could keep my spatial orientation. We lost a very experienced Formula One racer over the lake, Bill Falck. No one that I know saw him go down. He just didn't come back around on one of the laps. He must have hit the water on the back stretch, possibly losing his spatial orientation coming around the third pylon before the back straight-away. As far as I know, neither Bill nor his plane were ever found. Strange.

Reno T-6 Air Race • September 1969
"Two Too Different Race Planes"

This was my second T-6 race at Reno. I also had the P-51 this time. As I mentioned, if felt strange racing the fast Unlimited P-51 Mustang and the slower T-6 at the same site on the same day. The T-6 required virtually no care, but the P-51 required more care than a high-maintenance woman plus an experienced crew. Maybe racing Bi-planes and Formula Ones with T-6s would not be such a contrast, but Unlimiteds were to me.

In the finals of the T-6 races after racing the P-51, I discovered halfway around the course that I had left the carburetor heat in the ON position. That took about 20% of the engine performance away. With so much to think about and checking in the P-51, the T-6 had become too casual for me. And that's not good. Even in a car. It would be my last race trying to mix two levels of race planes. My mind had room for only one at that level of my experience. Maybe after 8 years of racing P-51s the edginess would wear off and I could give equal attention to both. Maybe a ski jumper could also do grand slalom downhill racing in the same day, or a speed swimmer could also concentrate on high-diving in the same meet. I think both might be risking their necks if their timing went awry. I felt mine had.

Second Florida T-6 Race • April 1970 • My Last T-6 Race
"Los Angeles to Florida at only 160 mph"

There was another T-6 race in Ft. Lauderdale the following year that John Tegler again organized. In spite of the 16-hour-long flight from Los Angeles, I had to be there. The September before when I had my P-51, I had raced it in the Transcontinental Air Race and at Reno's National Air Races, but T-6 racing and the many great friends I had come to know in it were like "family." Also, I had another carrot. Bill Ross in Chicago offered to buy "Miss Sky Prints" for $4,000. I could take it to Florida, race it and then drop it off in Chicago and head home with a profit of 100% over the $2,000 I had paid for it. What a deal! Today, that plane would bring over $100,000, maybe $120,000, but who knew then?

By 1970, T-6 racers were coming out of the woodwork! ABC's *Wide World of Sports* TV coverage of the 1969 T-6 races lit a fire in every corner of America. Anyone who had a T-6 showed up at the races. The Reno National Air Races were amazed when over twenty T-6s applied for race credentials to enter the 1970 races, Reno's only second official T-6 race. In the second Florida races in 1970, my neophyte racer the year before, John Mosby, was the top qualifier. I had moved down now to 13th position. But my focus was really on Unlimited Racing now.

Flying out to the 1970 Florida races, a tousle-haired, young blond chap, Jim Reid, flew with me. Jim was a pilot in his own right. He was originally from Florida in the Merritt Island area. Jim had magically appeared at the Daytona Auto Races in 1963. He found me the slower Cessna single-engine 170 rather than the twin-310 I had, so my friend could shoot aerial movies of the Daytona 500 in 1963. In 1969, Jim suddenly appeared in the pits at Reno while my crew chief was brooding over how he could replace a torched valve by himself in my first Unlimited race. Jim jumped up on the ladder beside Dick, rolled up his sleeves and said "Let's do it." They worked all night and I was able to qualify the next day.

So now I had the opportunity to partially repay Jim's favors by flying him cross-country from Los Angeles to Florida. Here is the story of how we met, as Jim Reid tells it.

"My dad lived in Florida. My first view of Howie was in the door of a motel in Daytona Beach. I had been directed to go there to pick Howie up, take him to the airport and check him out in a friend's Cessna 170. I tooted the horn outside his motel room, the door opened and there was this guy standing in the doorway with a towel wrapped around his waist brushing his teeth. He gestured he'd be right out. On the way to the airport, he explained that the twin-engine Cessna 310 he had flown his friends there in to shoot movies of the Daytona 500 race, was too fast to make the turns on the oval track and still get good shots of the race.

Once Howie got in the plane and handled the controls I could tell that he had been in a plane before. He seemed like a surgeon walking into an operating room. Everything was checked and we were on our way. A few landings and he had perfect control of the plane. I gave him the keys and told him where to leave it when he was through. That was 1963. The next time I saw him was in 1969 on the ramp at the Reno Air Races. His P-51 Mustang "Miss America" was sick. I had some experience with the Rolls Royce Merlin engine and offered to help. We worked all night to get it well again. At dawn, it purred like a happy baby.

Now I had a chance to both fly again with Howie and to get a free ride back to Florida to see my family and friends. Howie let me fly it from the back seat. It was a good feeling. The first night we stayed in Midland, Texas. The next day he wanted to make Florida, but a massive rainstorm settled in over Mississippi. We were flying VFR (not on instruments) up to that point without any contact with a radar controller. Howie figured he'd head for Meridian, Mississippi where they had an Air Force base and probably good radar facilities. While I listened on my ear phones, Howie contacted the radar control, explained he was in a rain storm and needed radar steers to the airport. In those days there were no transponders. Radar identification was made by you making a series of turns as directed by radar so they could tell if the target they had was you. After several turns one way then the other, then again, they announced "Radar contact, turn left for a heading to the airport." Howie didn't turn. He paused for a moment. Then he said to Radar Control "Don't you mean turn right instead of left?" With all the turning we had done, I lost track of where we were headed. Suddenly, the radar controller came back with "Correction, turn right." It was dark now and the rain was coming down in sheets. It was nice to know there was a pilot up there in front who knew what he was doing—and was so calm about it all...so professional."

Jim Reid again proved valuable to my air-racing career when he brought me together with my future sponsor, the genial Mike Eisenstadt, owner of Omni Aviation, an aviation insurance company.

Chapter 8

Flying and Racing the Mustang
Thirteen Years of Magic 1969–1981

I often think of the question that many probably do, "Would I like to relive a part of my life?" It's tempting for me to single out the 13 years of flying and racing "Miss America." However, upon reviewing all those years with the ups and downs of owning, flying and racing, I would not choose those years. The reason I would not? The unpredictable would disappear. If I knew I was going to blow an engine, get lost in the soup over the Rockies or enjoy being on stage at an air show, the thrills and chills it gave me would not be there.

Jim Reid and Pete Hoyt shake hands with joy after the engine tests okay after their all-night work replacing my torched valve. Reno 1969, my first Unlimited Pylon Race.

I'd rather relive being on the bonefish flats around the Florida Keys or skiing down a slope with new powder where the sheer joy of being there is a wonderful memory that's devoid of the surprises of dealing with a high horsepower machine that wants to bite you if you let it. It's best to leave the chills behind, but let me share them with you now.

My First Transcontinental Air Race • September 1969
"Baby Bottle Gas Tanks Give Thrills"

It was from Milwaukee, Wisconsin to Reno, Nevada the week before the National Air Races at Reno. It was 1,667 miles long. If there is one thing I do enjoy, it's flying with a purpose. I never was one to just go out to an airport, take a plane up, fly around and come back. To me it was like taking a car out of the garage, just driving around then coming back home. But secretly I do envy those who enjoy going for a "$100 hamburger" at some away airport, sitting, chatting then flying back home. Those pilots get a dimension out of flying that I never really had.

The race was my first cross-country air race so I didn't know what to expect. There were tales and stories about past cross-country races. In one race, how E.D. Weiner had flown his wet-wing Mustang (the entire wing was a gas tank) nonstop flying out of sight below and to the rear of Mike Carroll in his long-range Sea Fury (a British Navy carrier plane). When Mike dove to cross the finish line, Weiner gave it full power and shot out underneath Mike to cross the finish line first. That happened to me in the race from Milwaukee to Alton, Illinois near St. Louis which I'll cover later.

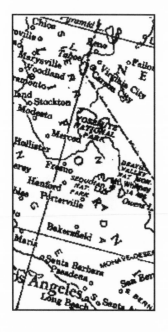

One thing I did want for this first transcon race was for Pete Hoyt to come along. Pete was always a can-do guy, a former B-17 pilot in WWII and great in the moral support department. I had gotten the P-51 just six months earlier and needed all of the moral support I could get. It had a nice rear seat already installed. Pete had his own business and could get away. If we had to stop somewhere en route because of engine problems, Pete would be there with me to help sort things out so I didn't have to worry.

The P-51, with its main tanks of 184 gallons (92 in each wing) had about a 600-mile range. But this was an almost 1,700 mile race—and at higher, race-power

After racing the engine hard, the 500 mile flight from Reno back to Los Angeles over mountainous areas kept my attention all the way until touchdown.

settings, I had gas for maybe a safe 500 miles. I needed at least 850 miles worth of gas to make it to a halfway gas stop. And with the last leg over the Rockies with few gas stop choices, I had better have enough gas to make Reno. Brainstorming the problem came in handy. While Marketing Director of the Chicago *Tribune*, I had the portfolio of being the expert on the use of brainstorming. It was the discipline of trying to solve problems by letting my mind wander over many crazy thoughts without making any judgment as each one came to mind. Then, later let the judgment kick in.

While going through the brainstorm routine, my mind hit on the baby bottles my kids used. They collapsed as the milk was taken out so air inside was reduced. Light bulb goes on! Design collapsible tanks to put in the ammunition bay of each wing. Using polyvinyl thin, rubber-like material, it gave me 42 gallons in each wing for a total of 84 more gallons. With the regular tanks of 184 gallons, that would be a total of 268 gallons. At 60 gallons per hour (a gallon of gas a minute), that would give me a $2\,^1/_2$ hours (160 gallon burn) max. If I saw gas was going to be short, I could reduce power to make it.

To test the tanks en route from Los Angeles to Milwaukee, I filled them up at a stop in Las Vegas. Gas prices in Nevada were lower because of their lower taxes—and

when you're throwing gas into an engine from buckets, you tend to think about price. I sure did. As I was climbing out of Las Vegas heading for the Milwaukee area with full main tanks and full wing bladders, I saw to my horror gas streaming out of the left wing area. It's okay when you are sitting in your easy chair and thinking about it, but heading over the Rockies and seeing gas streaming out of your wing gets a little disconcerting.

I immediately keyed my mike and called back to Las Vegas radar. I didn't want to declare an emergency which would have meant a lot of paperwork and

The right side of the cockpit included electrical equipment and oxygen controls. Top right is the emergency canopy release. Radios are on the right. Lower left: start switches, prime, lights, pitot heat, strobe, etc. Gear up/down lights are just left of the stick grip.

explanations, but I sure wanted to hear a human voice and to let someone know that in case I became a human fireball (a very real thought to me at the time), I was alive at that time. Never had I experienced gas streaming from a wing. Okay, it was from the outer area of the wing and not near the P-51's six exhaust stacks on the left side (round engine planes usually have one exhaust stack on the right side of the plane out of which all cylinders exhaust—inline engines like the P-51, Spitfire, etc., have an exhaust for each cylinder—six on each side for the 12 cylinder P-51 Rolls Royce engine). To me, anything east of Las Vegas was the Rocky Mountains and those are something that are very hostile to aircraft. Las Vegas radar came back with the reply that they had me in radar contact and that there was an airport just miles ahead at St. George, Utah.

St. George? I had never heard of the town, had no idea of how long the runway was. A grass strip? A large field? If I had been a Mormon I would have known that St. George is one of the thriving Mormon communities of Utah, just across the border from Nevada. It turned out to be a nice airport and in future years I always kept it in mind. But I didn't need it this time. The gas streaming out had stopped. Apparently there was some air trapped in that bladder that I had not squeezed out when filling it at Las Vegas. As I climbed higher and the air pressure got lower, that pocket

The left side of the cockpit had all the controls that affected flight so you could keep your right hand on the stick. From L to R are: (low) flaps, landing gear, nose up/down, (mid) aileron and rudder trim. Throttle, mixture and prop are in the quadrant at the top right. Make sure you have the rudder trim set at 6 degrees right rudder at take-off. The torque at full throttle will pull the nose left.

The instruments were in a compact area that I could see at a glance, but later in life, the Varilux variable lenses with 12 focal lengths were ideal to see instruments both close and far. The ram air eye-ball (top center) brought air into the hot cockpit.

of air expanded, forcing gas out of the vent of the tanks. Putting vents on these tanks like they are on normal tanks was not the thing to do. They are supposed to collapse, not be vented. I closed off the vents. In the race, Pete and I had the engine quit over Aspen. But more about that later.

Upon arriving at Mitchell Field in Milwaukee where we were to start the race, I was surprised to see Paul Poberezny himself on the ground directing me to a hangar. Paul founded the Experimental Aircraft Association virtually single-handed, yet here he was out on the taxiway like a normal line boy directing traffic. He sure loved airplanes and all phases of them. It showed in his eyes and in his unbounded enthusiasm.

That night, all the racers were at the same motel. We eyed each other as both new friends and as challengers. The big "secret" was how and where we were going to refuel on the 1,700 mile route to Reno. No one would tell or even talk about their refueling plans so Pete took on the role of undercover investigator trying to find out. I had made arrangements to refuel at Denver's Jeffco Airport, just northwest of the city where there was a Phillips gas outlet. I had met the owner a few weeks before and he was rather excited to have his operation be part of the race strategy. As my first race, trying to find out what the others were planning to do was more of a learning experience than anything that could change what I had planned. I suppose Pete and I were looking for some wild plan like someone was going to have in-air refueling along the way.

The way we took off from Milwaukee was by lot. But it really didn't make any difference, because you were clocked from the time your wheels left the ground to the time you crossed the finish line at Reno. If you took off 5 minutes before another plane, you had to beat him by more than 5 minutes to place ahead of him. It was all by elapsed time. Being first or last off the field didn't really matter. What did matter is the runway you were assigned. The field had two runways intersecting in the middle of the field. At that point, 4 airplanes could take off at the same time in 4 different directions from the middle of the field. Visualize an X with planes at the center headed in 4 different directions to the ends of the X. That's the way we did it. Those taking off away from the course made a high climb and then a climbing turn back over the field like homing pigeons getting their bearings. It added maybe less than a minute to the route, but we did finish closely time-wise.

With Pete in the back seat, he also had an oxygen mask on for the planned altitude to Denver of 16,500 feet. The one thing that I had not calculated was the volume and duration of oxygen for the two of us. I did not plan on getting an oxygen refill for the flight. I was a rookie at this high-altitude flying. I had calculated the gas and the oil consumption but not the oxygen. Heading out of Denver after refueling, we were over Pete's familiar territory. He had a house in Aspen and we were over Glenwood Springs a few miles north of Aspen. Pete was feeling comfortable with the flight at that point until suddenly the engine quit. As I mentioned before, it was called "quiet time" when a P-51's engine stops—and when it stops, it stops suddenly. From its roar to totally quiet is that eerie feeling of being suspended in space. You have no control. The engine is so powerful, it becomes your heartbeat, your breathing, your life. Without its roar, you're nothing.

I realized that I was using gas from the left wing bladder tank. In the fast refueling stop, I had not worried about getting all the trapped air out of the unvented bladder tanks that I had added in the ammo bays. As we started to dive toward the ground to pick up speed, I switched the tanks to the regular mains. Miraculously, the free-spinning prop acted like a car in third gear and turned over the engine. This made it start up and fire again. Whew! Over the Rockies is no place to lose an engine. Pete knew where we were. Hostile country for any plane without an engine, especially a P-51.

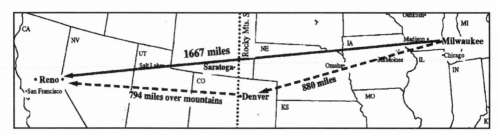

The Transcontinental Air Races were 1,667 miles direct from Milwaukee to Reno. I couldn't fly more than 1,000 miles nonstop at race power. Denver was a logical refuel stop, but Saratoga, Wyoming was right on course. However, Saratoga didn't have an instrument approach if the weather was bad.

I think this is what caused the oxygen drain to start.

After a few minutes of getting my wits back together and confirming course headings from there to Reno with Pete, I glanced at the oxygen level gauge. We had only $1^{1}/_{2}$ hours left between the two of us for a $2^{1}/_{2}$ hour flight! And the rest of the flight was over the Rockies. No way could you go down to low altitudes like you could over the Midwest. Pete, whose lungs were bigger than mine, was really sucking in the oxygen after that engine-out over the Rockies. It seemed the gauge was going down like a stopwatch hand. I told him about the problem and the only way out that I could think of was for each of us to go off oxygen for 5 minutes at a time. In other words, to ration what we had left. And if he saw me dozing off, to start pounding on my back to wake up and go back on the oxygen.

The rationing worked. When I was off oxygen, I kept my left hand up in the air gently waving it from side-to-side to show him I was alert. If my hand stopped, he was to reach forward and pound on my back. He never had to. The gauge showed the rapid oxygen drain had stopped and we could make it to Reno on our rationing system.

Somehow during all the confusion, I had gotten south of my course by about 50 miles. I was flying over checkpoints and VORs (radio navigation stations) quite south of my course. I was losing time. I called radar to give me a heading to Reno which they did. Then I asked them if they saw any other targets in the area heading for Reno. They had one about 50 miles north of me where I should have been at about the same speed of 350 mph. At that speed it had to be one of us. Airlines would be higher and faster and all other planes would be doing no more than 250 mph. Who the hell was it? Could I get ahead of him? Nearing Reno, I contacted their radar center, told them I was in a race and would they tell me what fast planes they had on their scope, where they were and how fast they were going? The answer I got amazed me!

"Sorry, you're in a race. I can't give you that information." What? The FAA has decided they can't give out info because it's a race? Later I related this to Warren Lee, the FAA supervisor for the race. Incensed, he got the transmission tapes of my request and gave that radar controller a good dressing down for attempting to officiate in a cross-country race instead of doing his job.

It's always amazing to me how close the finishes are over nearly a 1,700-mile course with all except the fastest needing to stop for gas on the way.

Here is the finish of the race as described by John Tegler in his classic book *Gentlemen, You have a Race!*

> *"Slicker flashed across the finish line first in his Mustang…less than 2 minutes later, Kestle crossed the finish line in his Cavalier version of the Mustang and was declared the winner because he had taken off $2^{1}/_{2}$ minutes after Sliker…5 hours, 19 minutes elapsed time…(then those who had to stop for gas) 28 minutes later, Tom Kuchinsky crossed the finish line in his Mustang and over the next 12 minutes came three more Mustangs flown by Burns Byrum, Chuck Doyle and Howie Keefe. Behind Keefe were the Bearcats of Gunther Balz and Walt Ohlrich…Dick Thomas in a Corsair and Judy Wagner in her E33C Bonanza that had been fitted with long-range gas tanks in the cockpit so she could fly nonstop."*

My First Unlimited Pylon Race

"High Adrenaline Plus Low Experience — Poof!"

The parties and hospitality by Harold's Club, sponsor of the cross-country race, was worth the race itself. Everybody was happy. Then the reality of hard-core pylon racing set in. Although I had raced in the T-6 class, when it came time to race the Unlimiteds,

the tummy started to get tight and those butterflies started to set in. In the T-6 race it was all strategy. No one blew an engine. No pieces came off their planes due to the high speed.

In the Unlimited, you needed high-test 145 octane gas, water injection, cooling bars and above all, a crew. If you raced in stock condition, which many did and I mostly did this first year, it wasn't too stressful. Even so, making arrangements for the crew's quarters, finding sources for rags, oil, spark plugs, etc., took a lot of time and attention. In your rookie year, you have to do a little begging to get Champion to give you those $20 spark plugs—the 12-cylinder Rolls Royce engine needs 24 of them—and to get 10 gallons of 70-weight oil from Pennzoil. They are needs you can't even buy at normal stores. They are items with specs for racing at high power. In the case of the plugs, you needed one type for cross-country and normal flight, one type for the exhaust plugs (high-temp), and another type for the intake side (med-temp). You had to have oxygen (a race requirement) so the fumes in the cockpit at high-power settings and heat ranges would not get to you. Then there were gallons of coolant and distilled water for the Mustang's all-important cooling system—something the Bearcats, AT-6s and other "round-nosed" engine crews didn't have to worry about. In short, there were logistics. In my rookie year, each need caught me by surprise and unprepared. This was not T-6 racing! It seemed like I was always playing catch-up.

Maybe I can blame my befuddlement and oversight in my first Unlimited race on this harried state of so many things to think about all at once. After 1970, when the cross-country races were no longer offered, I had time to go to Reno early to get all the supplies and needs organized. Plus, Pete Hoyt got there a few days earlier than I did to get a spot in the pits reserved. My choice of a pit spot was at the farthest end from the ramp so the plane could be easily viewed from the spectator walkway. But more importantly so that photographers could get a clear shot of "Miss America" and therefore,

hopefully, get her in more articles and magazines as publicity for the sponsors. Also, the sun tended to be behind the photographer, making it more enticing for him/her to take a photo.

The other school of thought in picking a pit spot were the pilots or sponsors who wanted the advantages of an end spot on the opposite end of a line bordering on the ramp. The ramp is where all the action of plane run-ups, gassing, engine testing, etc., takes place. Also a ramp-side pit is the best area to watch the races from the pits. Your pit can be a seating area for sponsor's friends inside the roped-off areas. You don't need the high viewing platform atop trailers to see the races. Another advantage is that the plane can be pushed outside the pit area to the ramp area without having to wait for a line tug to come by and hook up. Back where I prefer, you need a wing-walker on both wingtips to warn people to get out of the way as the plane is being towed through a rather congested narrow aisle. However, I saw this "parade" as a bit of showmanship and those of the crew who did the wing-walking readily volunteered. This procession was beneath seasoned crew chiefs, but was reserved for those

A view of the pit area looking toward the race course. At top are people with pit passes standing at the limit line. Beyond, planes are gassed, engines are run-up for high-power tests and planes return from racing.

who had helped degrease, wax, polish or otherwise tend to the plane's cosmetic needs so they could enjoy a moment on display as you'd hear the crowd murmur, "Oh, here comes Miss America."

I made sure I was never in this display. I wanted those unpaid volunteers to have the limelight. Someone should be in the cockpit, of course, to be able to brake and to set the parking brake once the tug unhooked its tow-bar. That had to be someone trained in the way to do all that, but also get in and out of the cockpit without disturbing the oxygen hose, parachute and instrument settings, etc. A really salty crew chief like Jim Quinlan wouldn't even stoop to that role of display, but then he had an ample stable of crew who were not only qualified to manage the cockpit, but also to start the engine for a check and a pre-race warm-up. My crew chiefs who were pilots, though not qualified to actually fly the P-51, could handle the start-up, mag check run-up, and any taxiing to the gas pits, etc. A special place in this entire process was always reserved for my friend Pete Hoyt. He stood on the wing alongside and slightly behind the person in the cockpit to act both as a topside lookout and a majestic figure to round-out the scene, waving ever so nonchalantly to someone who might call out his name. Sometimes, this procession went so far out into and down the ramp that I found myself asking people if they saw the plane and where it was. Of course, I was not too put-out by having to walk in front of the crowd and do a little of my own preening. When you're in your 50s and can't sing, dance, act, or play the piano, and are bald, it's nice to be noticed.

An Unlimited Rookie Pilot's Experience

I don't recall reading anything written by Unlimited race pilots about their experiences. Perhaps they are too busy fixing and caring for their planes to have the time to write, or are too busy working to earn enough money to maintain a $50,000 a year habit. Now that I don't have that overhead and do have the time, and no Unlimited pilot has written such a book, is one of the reasons I am writing one. However, I did come across an excellent piece written by a rookie Unlimited race pilot after his first race. It's an all-inclusive account of what happens and can happen in today's world of Unlimited Air Racing. My only variation to his actions are:

1. I would not put my gear down until I was on a short final because you never know what will happen, so you'll need that extra drag-free distance.

2. Not think of landing on the first part of the runway so you can "stop at the middle" ...I'd "land at the middle and stop at the end." I favor the old saying of "you're always going slower if you crash at the end of the landing than at the beginning of the runway." But here is a rookie telling a story I could not tell. After 13 years and the record of 21 consecutive Unlimited air races, it's hard to recall the first year minor yet colorful details. His wide-eyed freshness of a rookie year is a pleasure to read.

"An Unlimited Rookie's Review"

by Vlado Lenoch, Pilot-Owner of the P-51 Mustang "Moonbeam"

Months prior to Reno took some preparation. To a stock Mustang I made the following alterations and additions: Added were, a water injection system, spray bars for the radiator to add cooling to both the water cooling the engine and the oil radiator, both in the scoop under the belly. To the airframe I clipped the wingtips, modified the dorsal fin and increased horizontal tail incidence, a longer coolant door and smaller canopy. Also the engine was retuned. If you want to be competitive, these modifications are necessary.

On arrival at Reno on the Sunday before the final races the following Sunday, the briefings began as well as on-site airframe and engine mods. The briefings were for all pilots to review and reinforce race and emergency procedures. To the race pilot these briefings were to prove valuable, especially for a rookie like me. In the heat and passion of flying on the race course at high power settings, you need to have in your mind preplanned emergency procedures. There's no time to stop and think. Vlado Lenoch wrote a rare insight into a rookie's experience with Unlimited air racing.

For example, if my engine blows, what do I do? Where do I go? How do I fly the airplane? All of these situations have been experienced by race pilots over the years. By sharing with us what they did, we'd have a better understanding what we should do in an emergency when we have one or what we should do when we hear another pilot call a "Mayday." Did I say Mayday? Yes, this is one airport where a Mayday is a daily event!

After the briefings, the rookie pilots were assigned to a check pilot for flight checks. The entire check flight from "start engines" to shut-down in the chocks at the end was done in a race scenario. My race number, Race 51, was used on all radio calls instead of the N number used everywhere else. My group of 3 rookies taxied out in race order, took off in trail, as is done in a regular race and formed on the check pilot's wing in an echelon formation. We spread out for the air check of doing a slow roll and a short flight inverted. Then it was down onto the race course.

The race pilots talk about the course somewhat reverently. No one is allowed on the course without permission from the race course boss in the race control tower. The check pilot took us around the course for a few laps for a look-around. Then we would practice passing the check pilot individually. Then on his call when we were in front of him, he would call us to pull up and off the course to simulate an engine failure to a dead-stick landing. When I passed my check flight, I was cleared to go on the race course to do 10 laps on my own. Once I finished the 10 laps in good form, I was considered a qualified race pilot. Qualified, but inexperienced!

That check flight on the first day would take the entire day to accomplish. The following days consisted of going out on the course for practice, doing engine power checks and get speed qualified. There are qualifying spots for only 24 planes in the Unlimited class and there were 45 Unlimited planes entered. The race course had to accommodate all race classes. It was open to the Unlimiteds twice a day for 90 minutes each time. The smaller race planes were favored by getting the earlier times before the winds got strong. The Unlimiteds were last in each set.

My first solo runs were to check the engine power available. With water for the spray bars active and 145 octane fuel, it was time to see how it would go. After a few warm-up laps, I pushed the throttle to the fire wall. To get this power not only took throttle movement but a bit of courage! I had never gone above 55 inches of manifold pressure before. Now I was going to push my darling little Merlin up past that. I had the confidence that it would work. All my "consultants" had told me that the Merlin could easily go up to 80 inches as it was a strong mechanical engine design. But to do that required some preparation. First, the engine needed higher octane fuel than the 100LL normally used. At Reno, 145 octane is available for racing as well as 5 grades higher with additives.

This high-octane fuel would get me through the 55 to 75 inches of manifold pressure range. As the power in the Merlin goes up into the 80 inch area, another problem arises, that of high induction manifold temperature. Like low octane gas, these high induction temperatures can also cause engine blowing detonation. The way to solve this is by the use of a water injection system with a 50/50 mix of distilled water and methanol sprayed into the induction manifold to cool the induction temperature. At much higher power settings and temperatures, the stock after-cooler system in the Mustang becomes ineffective in the 120 to 140 inch settings the super-fast racers use.

The first time I got the engine up to 77 inches, I ran a few laps to get the feel of this high-power setting. It took some personal conviction to run at this fabulous power setting! To get this power, the prop governor was reset from 3,000 RPM to 3,200 RPM. At this power setting, the wind did howl and the wind noise was more intense even inside the canopy (or was it my heavy breathing?!) But the Merlin did run remarkably smooth. The smoothness was very comforting in spite of the maelstrom outside the canopy.

On the course, a race pilot is required to make a radio call to request the "timers," in order to obtain a race course qualifying time. This qualifying time sorts out the top 24 fastest planes that will be permitted to enter the races that start on a Thursday and end on Sunday. With little traffic, these qualifying times are the fastest times you will record. During a race, if you are not in the lead, the prop wash and turbulence from the other planes will slow you down as well as you may need to fly a wider course around pylons in traffic.

My third qualifying lap at 77 inches produced a surprise. While rounding the far pylon on the course, my engine began to sputter. Immediately, I thought my darling Rolls Royce Merlin engine was detonating. Low, out on the far side of the course, I decided not to try playing mechanic by trying to diagnose what was wrong. So, I immediately radioed "Mayday" and pulled up to the center of the course. This action was almost automatic because this procedure was discussed repeatedly at pilot briefings. Turn in toward the center of the course and pulling up to get as much altitude as you could would almost assure you of being able to reach one of the three runways on the airport. My engine had sputtered at Pylon 4 which is headed away from the airport, therefore I could not see any of the runways behind me. But as I gained altitude in the center of the course, I could pick out the airport in the desert glare and sage brush. With 363 mph airspeed when the engine coughed, I could easily pull up to 3,500 feet above the course, then the problem was how to come down to the intended point of landing.

As I went up, I did pull the windmilling prop back to high-pitch to reduce drag as much as possible. Next as the airspeed dropped, I did put the gear down as I did have the airport assured. But now to fine tune the approach, I needed to use a combination of flaps and prop pitch as a brake to keep it on the right glide path to runway 8. That combination again as discussed many times in pilot briefings did work out beautifully with touch down on the end of the runway and a roll-out to the center taxiway. Oh yes, the problem...too much water being injected into the engine making the induction temperature too cool for the power setting. In other words, the flame in the engine was being dowsed by too much water being injected into it. Pete Law stepped in, thankfully, to adjust the water nozzles.

Monday, Tuesday and Wednesday are the same intense routine each day. Each morning, pilots must attend the briefing. The FAA has almost no involvement in these. Each class self-regulates itself to promote safety and improve safety in this unique sport. Obviously, no FAA employee has the experience to regulate or dictate operational issues in this race situation. Thus, though they were present at the briefings, the FAA did very little in any of the briefings. Each pilot is judged and regulated by his/her peer group in all the race classes.

While the pilots are briefing, the aircraft crews are cleaning, inspecting and servicing your aircraft. This takes a lot of intense effort. The aircraft must be gone over fully twice a day for each of the twice daily 90-minute time slots allowed for qualifying and/or practice. The right fuel load, engine oil, water for the spray bars and injection unit were some of the items that needed tending before every takeoff. If it were not for the pit crews, the aircraft could absolutely not fly. There is just too much to do and coordinate.

Qualifying ends on Wednesday and on Thursday the races start. Based on each pilot's qualifying speeds, they are placed in heat races. Also based on qualifying times, the final cut was made to be race eligible. Of the 45 that did not make the cut of 24, those 21 planes could stay in the pits for the *duration, but could not fly. Each day of the races, there were 3 Unlimited races of 8 planes each race. The 8 slowest qualifiers flew the first heat and the fastest 8 in the final heat of the day at about 4 p.m.*

Based on my qualifying speed. I was seeded in the Silver heat (middle 8 fastest) on Thursday. Thereafter, I flew in the slower Bronze heat based on my speed the prior day. The pace plane produced a smoke trail making it easier to locate it and join up on it in formation. The pace plane would take off and the racers would follow in trail. It headed first to the west side of the valley then fly the group to the south side of the valley where its final turn to the left would start to dive the group down onto the race course. The race entry was always very exciting as the crowd reacted with an air of anxiety and anticipation. To see a group of racers descending down onto the race course with their engines wound up to high power was a thrilling sight and even a more thrilling sound if all 8 were Mustang engines.

When the pace plane radioed to us those stirring words, "Gentlemen, you have a race," each pilot's eyes shifted from the line abreast formation to the race course that lay ahead. All motors powered up to accelerate to race speed. The heavier Sea Furies tended to nose over more to use their heavier weight to gain more airspeed. The Mustangs and other aircraft throttled up to enter the course directly near Pylon 3. All racers already had their race systems, spray bars and water injection systems turned on prior to being released by the pace plane.

Diving on the course involves subtle techniques. The flight path chosen must minimize G-loading to avoid induced drag and its resultant speed loss. This requires a flight path around the pylons with a smooth entry and exit. Once the power is up and all systems are working well, all the pilot must do is to fly this perfect flight path around the course. But a few aviation gremlins jump in to mess up this perfect equation. There is ground turbulence, heat thermals, and, oh yes, wake and vortex turbulence from the other planes. All this reduces your speed and can force you to fly a wider course to avoid traffic. There isn't much one can do about the atmospheric problems, but as far as traffic goes, one can simply add more power to get ahead of everyone else (easy to say!).

At the Reno race course, the pylons are flown with 2.5 to 3.5 G-loads on the meter. The turns are flown at high speeds and thus are sustained for a long duration. With upwards of 10 laps per race, the race becomes physically grueling, even though it lasts for only 10–13 minutes. I finished the races without any technical problems though improvements could be made to get more power and less drag. My main goal was to complete my first race with "all systems go." In this, I was successful.

Technically, the shortened wings did work, increasing speeds by about 20 mph. The short tips did increase the turn radius at each pylon. As long as the high power could be maintained, I could remain competitive. Also, the radiator spray bars were essential in keeping the coolant and oil temperatures in

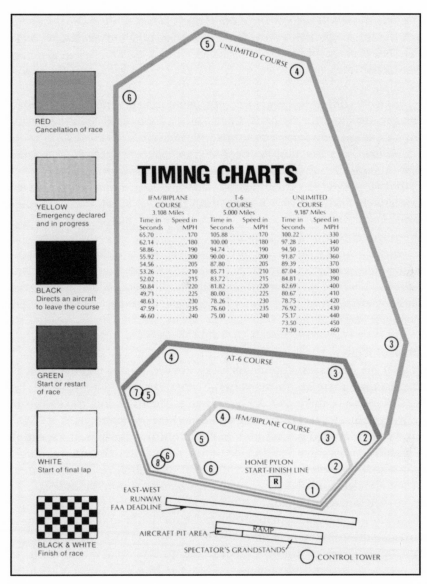

RED
Cancellation of race

YELLOW
Emergency declared
and in progress

BLACK
Directs an aircraft
to leave the course

GREEN
Start or restart
of race

WHITE
Start of final lap

BLACK & WHITE
Finish of race

TIMING CHARTS

IFM/BIPLANE COURSE 3.108 Miles		T-6 COURSE 5.000 Miles		UNLIMITED COURSE 9.187 Miles	
Time in Seconds	Speed in MPH	Time in Seconds	Speed in MPH	Time in Seconds	Speed in MPH
65.70	170	105.88	170	100.22	330
62.14	180	100.00	180	97.28	340
58.86	190	94.74	190	94.50	350
55.92	200	90.00	200	91.87	360
54.56	205	87.80	205	89.39	370
53.26	210	85.71	210	87.04	380
52.02	215	83.72	215	84.81	390
50.84	220	81.82	220	82.69	400
49.71	225	80.00	225	80.67	410
48.63	230	78.26	230	78.75	420
47.59	235	76.60	235	76.92	430
46.60	240	75.00	240	75.17	440
				73.50	450
				71.90	460

UNLIMITED COURSE

AT-6 COURSE

IFM/BIPLANE COURSE

HOME PYLON
START-FINISH LINE

R

EAST-WEST
RUNWAY
FAA DEADLINE

AIRCRAFT PIT AREA

RAMP

SPECTATOR'S GRANDSTANDS

CONTROL TOWER

The Reno Unlimited course keeps evolving over the years due mainly to new homes being built. Until 1970, it was an oval like the AT-6 course. The 3 pylons at each end were easy to spot with only 2 turns per lap. Pylon cuts were rare. The asymmetric (I called it the cross-country course) is hard to pick up pylons when flying low. I understand that problem is being addressed. Races were limited to 100 miles—10 lap maximum. I blew my first engine on the ninth lap at pylon 6.

*the green, as well as keeping the coolant doors closed in their low-drag posi-
tion. The water injection system worked in preventing any detonation problems. Though the engines were not always operating at the threshold temperature
where water injection was needed, it was assuring to know that the system
was in place.*

*Just as exciting as the final races on Sunday, were the crosswind landings.
With my aileron authority limited by also being shortened with the shorter
wing-tips, it was a bit of work to keep a wing down into the wind during flare
and roll-out. Later that day, the Gold race winner, Strega, would experience
heavy damage from a gust that ballooned the Mustang on landing.*

*The races were an amazing assortment of men and machinery. The ca-
maraderie on the ramp was just amazing to me as a newcomer. Anytime
anyone had a problem or lacked a part, every other pilot or their crew was
glad to loan a part or lend a hand.*

*Last year's air races are history. The results of the Gold Race are docu-
mented in most aviation magazines in the U.S. and abroad. These published
results don't even begin to express the sweat, excitement and satisfaction that
goes into participating in an Unlimited air race. I'll be back to renew and to
enjoy these racing thrills."*

His enthusiasm, now that I recall after reading his story, was somewhat what I experienced after my first races. But he was lucky not having any real mechanical problems the first time out. I wasn't. Many of the experts he used, I used as well. Pete Law
and Mike Nixon were sharp guys 25 years before. Their learning curve probably had
many advances in 25 years of solving Unlimited racers' problems.

In my first Unlimited pylon race I qualified ninth at the amazing speed (to me)
of 340 mph. Today, you have to do at least 300 mph even to be allowed to be in the
races, no matter how many planes are entered. In qualifying, I torched an exhaust
valve. The diameter of a valve in a Rolls Royce Merlin engine is a little larger than a
half-dollar. My torched one looked like a small pizza with a piece cut out. My poor
crew chief, Dick Tomasulo, with no experienced mechanic to help him, stood on the
ladder with a forlorn look on his face. There was no one with enough experience to
help him. I didn't even know how to change the spark plugs at that time. He had that
droopy dog face anyway. It drooped even more as he gazed down at the uncowled
engine. Even worse, it was at the end of the race day. Unlimiteds are always the last
ones to have a time slot. The sun was getting low, the desert air was starting to chill
and I didn't have a hangar to use. In my usual stoic attitude, I felt that "Okay, so I
can't race tomorrow, Thursday in the first heat races. At least I've been to Reno and
qualified." Then out of nowhere, Sir Galahad rode up on his horse!

Sir Galahad was a tousle-haired blonde chap by the name of Jim Reid. Jim was
the fellow at the Daytona 500 races who I met back in 1963. He got me the Cessna
to be able to have the camera man shoot movies of the car races around the Daytona
oval track. That was 6 years before and I hadn't seen him since. He asked what the
problem was. When told, he jumped up on the ladder and said to my crew chief,

"Okay then, let's fix it." With just basic tools, they worked all night to take out the bad valve and insert the new one. This included the tricky operation of lifting off the cam shaft that operates the 24 valves without letting it rotate even 1 degree so it goes back in the identical position. All I could do was get them all the pizza and coke they wanted, but if they did get it fixed, I had to get some sleep to be able to make the 8 a.m. pilot briefing and be ready to race at 10 a.m. Jim and I still talk about that night. I am forever indebted to him for his leadership on that ladder…and for some more things to come.

In reviewing my logbook on that race week, it reads, "had second place in the heat race but wound up in fourth place. During the race, my engine quit. I ran a 90-gallon tank dry in about 12 minutes because I had neglected to switch tanks." I had no idea that that much gas could be used at the high-powered race speeds, plus the gas I used to take off and join up on the pace plane. It took me too many seconds, perhaps 10 seconds, to figure out what had happened and to switch tanks. I did have the sense not to try an air restart with full power on or to pull back power quickly and get a backfire that would blow the carburetor out of service by warping the butterfly valve. I had heard about that happening. But going along for 10 seconds with no power and then a low power restart from the windmilling prop and getting back up to power and race speed was too much to regain my second-place position.

In those days, we had only enough entries for 18 planes to qualify. Everyone who showed up got to race if they just ran a qualifying lap. The heat races were only 6 planes. In the late seventies, the prediction was that Unlimited racing as we knew it would disappear. There would not be enough planes or engines. The speedboat people with their Unlimited race boats were not only buying up and blowing up the Merlins, they also drilled holes in the engines and ran sea water through them to cool them. They ran them as high as 4,600 RPM. Stock Mustangs are redlined at 3,000 RPM. Once that was done, a Merlin could no longer be used in a plane.

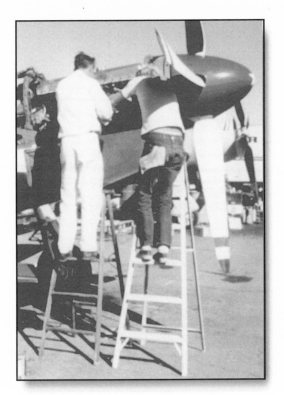

Jim Reid was walking through the pits, saw that Dick needed help to change a valve, jumped up beside him and worked all night. Amazing! (Jim is on the right.)

I recall going into the "Miss Budweiser" headquarters in the Seattle area and seeing Merlin engines on shelves on either side of a long aisle. There must have been 12 of them and I couldn't believe my eyes. That was not only a fortune in engines, even though at the time a Merlin was maybe $10,000 versus $80,000 today, but for just one vehicle, a boat, to have that many engines verged on gluttony. In air racing if you had a stock engine for flying around during the year and a race engine for Reno, you were in the super-privileged class. We bowed in all humility when those owners walked by. Today, the Unlimited boats no longer use piston engines, so Mustang owners don't have to compete with Budweiser's deep pockets for Merlin engines and parts.

My final logbook entry of my first Unlimited Race read "In the Silver Race finals which is the second 6 fastest, I took second place at 335 mph average speed for 10 laps but my cooler doors were full open due to over heating."

The next thing that I recall was flying the plane from the Reno race site back to the Long Beach–Santa Monica area, a distance of about 500 miles, over some initial mountains and then down the Owens Valley with few emergency airports. This is a scenario I would face 15 more times in my racing career, flying back home on an engine that had been abused to the max. Would it quit on takeoff? Would it get over

EMERGENCIES
The No. 2 Problem

- Prethink your options — plan for the worst
- Fly your machine
- Airspeed and altitude, two energy forms
- Safest place, inside the pylons
- Any runway is available, 26 is the worst
- Aim for halfway down the runway
- Don't turn away from a runway
- Try to communicate intentions
- Wing rock for NORDO (Gear down for Landing)
- Gear is low drag, flaps high drag
- Energy lost by flaps, prop, turns, gear, damage
- After landing 08/26, try to clear runway (excepting MLG)
- Know your bailout and EGRESS procedure
- Fly your machine

An air race site is the best place to have a problem if you're going to have one. It's sanitary, has fire engines, ambulances and experienced crews standing by. In a Mayday, the whole airport is at the alert for you. These are the Emergency Procedures given to the Unlimited pilots at Reno. I take issue with Runway 26 being the worst (landing right to left in front of the stands). For me it's the best. I've used it for two blown engines. It has a long runover at the end and the wind is usually from the west. Their caution probably comes as a result of the "Red Baron" and "Miss Candance" crashing short near the cliff, but if you follow the "Aim halfway down the runway," as I always preach, it's much better than coming in the opposite direction and going over the cliff on the other end!

the mountains? Is something wrong that did not show up on the ground test? In one case, I had left the plane at Reno because of an engine problem. I had to get back to my job in Los Angeles. My engine man, Dave Zeuschel, fixed the problem and started to fly it back to Los Angeles. We always flew back down U.S. 395 so in case we had to land in an emergency at least there would be a concrete pad below because airports were few and far between.

On this flight, Dave Zeuschel, not only a great engine man but an able P-51 pilot, saw the oil pressure start to drop. He was at the east entrance to the Yosemite National Park over the town of Lee Vining. U.S. 395 doesn't have even a half-mile of straight road there. But there was a small grass strip for airplanes. To Dave's credit, he landed on that grass strip with the oil light flashing in his face. He left the plane there and went into town. That night I got a call from the sheriff's office in the area wanting to know why I had landed there. They had checked the registration on the plane through the FAA and located me that way. Of course, I knew nothing about it. Dave was not the type of guy to turn on the red flashing lights when anything happened. He had been through too many hairy situations to have much phase him. (He was killed when thrown from a plane at an air show because he did not have his seat belt fastened, but he may have died in the crash even if it had been fastened. I like to think that, even though an unfastened seat belt in an airplane doesn't make sense, that even if it was fastened, the crash would have still been fatal.). Dave checked into a local motel, examined the engine the next day and discovered that the oil filter had been clogged with debris from my blown engine. He cleaned it out and took off from the small strip.

The Reno airport on Monday morning after an air race is a lonely place. You've hopped a ride out there after a night of festivities in Reno, the awards banquet and private parties where your friends hope you'll show up. The aluminum drink cans are the only noise as the wind blows them across the almost-deserted ramp. With only a 2-hour flight home, I didn't

In a way, I had it easier than race pilots ferrying their planes back east over the Rockies after punishing the engines in hard racing, but that thought didn't make it any easier for me. When I lifted off the race site on Monday mornings heading the 500 miles back to Los Angeles, there were mountain ranges at each end. The slight sound change of the engine got my attention very quickly if the highway below wasn't a long straight-away. Fortunately, I always made it, but one time, Dave Zeuschel flying her back after an engine change, didn't.

have to get there early as did those who had to fly back east. By the time I got there, most had already left…and there wasn't an engine man to be found. My crew had changed the spark plugs back to "ferry" plugs, run up the engine the night before and had headed home to their jobs.

I'd just stand there, look at the plane and say "Baby, are you alright? Are you going to get me home? Please do." It always did. But when my wheels touched down at Van Nuys where the post-race big exam was done and I turned off the engines and locked the canopy, I gave a sigh of relief…and maybe a feeling of achievement.

The Last Transcontinental Air Race
September 13, 1970 • Milwaukee to Reno
"Weather Rears Its Ugly Head"

As the year before, the race was the same 1,667 miles from Milwaukee to Reno. Pete Hoyt and I were now veterans in this type of cross-country air racing. We had done it once! And we learned from last year to:

1. have enough oxygen on board,
2. take a shorter route, and
3. not let the engine quit because of air in the wing-bladder tanks.

Again, Pete played a Peter Sellers' Inspector Clouseau the night before at the various pre-race gatherings while I pretended to remain aloof. I wanted to know where others planned to refuel, what their gas capacity was, what course were they planning to take or any other bits of information we might use.

Pete and I were the only 2-man team. Everyone else flew solo. The lightweight bladder tanks were my secret weapon. They allowed me to carry a passenger and not have the weight of heavy metal or fiberglass tanks. They also gave me the most gallons because as they filled, their thin rubber-like material melded into all the space available in the ammo bay. Others got only 36 gallons with their tanks. I got 43 gallons, almost 20% more.

Prior to taxiing out, I filed an IFR (instrument) flight plan with the FAA by phone so no one would hear me file it over the radio. Like others, I didn't want my route and altitude known. They would hear the altitude I had chosen for presumably the best wind conditions and where I'd refuel. I said in my flight plan that I would pick up my IFR clearance when I was over the Madison VOR about 80 miles west of Milwaukee. That would let me stay off the Center frequencies that everyone else would probably be on and be able to talk on a local FAA Flight Service Station frequency. I thought I was pretty smart to figure all that out. Pete and I felt pretty smug about ourselves—especially since we hadn't been able to glean any intelligence from the other racers on their plans. At least we had a way to keep our secrets from them. But it didn't work!

All the racers were listening in on the Ground Control frequency for taxi instructions and clearance to takeoff position. When I got to the middle of the "X" intersection of the two runways at Mitchell field and tried to turn into takeoff position (I had the best runway heading, to the southwest), the tailwheel lock jammed. I couldn't turn the nose of the plane the 90° to the right that I needed to line up down the center of the takeoff runway. A P-51 is no toy on takeoff. You better start out going straight or you'll have a tiger on your hands when the power goes on. (Later I discovered the cable had stretched so much it would not pull the pin loose.) So what to do? It was about 5 minutes before takeoff and my creeping forward with every attempt to jar it loose with hard right brake was putting me past the right turn to the centerline of the runway. Pete later said he was getting a little woozy from the tail jerking from side-to-side, felt like he was riding on the tail of an alligator—back near the tail where he was, he could feel it more.

I finally told Pete on the intercom that I was going to give it a blast of power to see if I could lift the tail off the ground enough to get the plane to turn when I hit the right brake. The worry was we'd nose over or ding the prop. On the first try, I got it turned about halfway. The next blast took it into almost-perfect position, but I got a call on the radio of "Keefe! What the hell are you doing? You almost blew me off the runway!" A meek, "Sorry about that" was all I could transmit. There was no sense in trying to give an excuse at that point. As I settled back waiting for Ground Control to tell the 4 of us to switch to the tower for our simultaneous takeoff clearance in the 4 different directions, the call came from Ground Control "North American N991 Romeo, ready to copy your clearance?" I was stunned. I was just getting over 5 minutes of trying to make a buckin' bronco get headed the right way and now this! In those days, there weren't different freqs for getting your instrument plan read to you. It was always done on Ground Control at an airport with a tower. I muttered something about getting it from the radio station FSS at Madison. Ground came back with "IFR weather 25 miles west requires you have clearance before takeoff." A few seconds of silence while my brain raced trying to figure a way out of letting everyone hear where I was going and what altitude I had picked, when sweet Judy Wagner, sitting in her E33 single engine Bonanza with most of her cockpit filled with extra

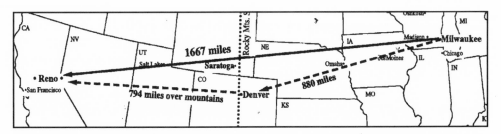

Some planes had the fuel to go nonstop. My limit at a race speed of 300 mph burning 80 gallons per hour was about 1,000 miles. In the first race in 1969, the weather was perfect. In the second race, 1970, I planned to refuel at Saratoga, Wyoming where I trout fished, and had friends there to refuel me. But weather and storms forced me to use Denver again. I barely made it against 80 mph headwinds.

gas tanks transmitted, "Come on, Howie, copy your clearance. Let us know where you're going." I heard a few other mike buttons being clicked. Our Peter Sellers' Inspector Clouseau act must have been a wee-bit transparent. I copied the clearance. The tower could not release me and, therefore, all 4 of us had to wait until I copied the clearance down as to what airway, what altitude and final destination and then read it all back so they made sure I understood it all—that's standard procedure.

Off we went, finally. I had picked 24,000 feet. Above 19,000 feet today you are on a high-altitude control phase of radar. In those days most airliners were props and flying from 20,000–25,000 feet versus today's jets at 30,000 feet and up. Today, virtually no airliners are flying in the 18,000- to 25,000-foot range. You can almost pick any altitude in that range you want and they'll give it to you. They require 1,000 feet vertical separation going in opposite directions. I tell you this because of what some of the others had done. I still shudder when I think about it how they used the system. I was naive to say the least.

Before I reached the Madison, Wisconsin radio station (VOR) some 75 miles away, I had been able to climb to 24,000 feet. M-m-m-m. With average headwinds of 50 mph I had figured I'd have only 18,000 feet altitude by Madison. I leveled off at 24,000 and set it up for a cross-country race cruise of 40" manifold pressure versus normal 36". My airspeed indicator showed I was doing 250 mph, but you are actually going 2% per thousand feet faster than it indicates because of the lighter air pressure against the sensor. So at 24,000 feet, I was really doing 48% more speed than my airspeed was showing. So I was doing 370 mph. Great. The VOR needle showed I was on course to the Madison VOR. I reset my directional gyro. Then sat back to relax. My first reporting point was to be over the Madison VOR. We didn't have DME (Distance Measuring Equipment) then to measure our speed over the ground. It was all calculated by time from one station or radio fix to another. Even center radar didn't know. We didn't have the radar transponders of today.

So I sat there—and sat there. It was solid IFR in the soup. A P-51 is not the easiest platform to have when you're flying instruments, especially in rough air. It takes all your attention just to hold altitude without an automatic pilot, which I didn't have. Drop a pencil on the floor, reach down to pick it up and at 370 mph you're lucky if you don't lose more than 500 feet. Of course, the poor person in the back seat feels like he's on a roller coaster if you drop too many things as you quickly pull back stick to get back up to your assigned altitude. In those days, radar didn't know you were yo-yoing through space. With today's transponders, which came about 8 years later, reporting your altitude directly on to their radar scopes, you might get a radio call of "Anything wrong?" or "You're below your assigned altitude" or a simple, polite "Please remain at your assigned altitude." I've heard them all!

I waited and waited for the VOR needle to get sensitive indicating I was nearing the Madison VOR. It was so firm it was as if it was glued there. I tried a few intersection checks and couldn't believe what I was getting. It showed I was doing a ground speed of only about 245 mph! Wow! That meant a headwind of 125 mph was bucking into us! No wonder I was able to climb to 24,000 feet before reaching Madison.

That's why I'm sitting up here like a dirigible going nowhere. It's all relative. If you're flying the average plane that's indicating 180 mph and you discover you're doing only 100 mph, you almost feel as if you could get out and walk. There's nothing that matches going slower than normal in a plane. You want to curse the wind. You forget the times when that same 80 mph wind was at your back and you were streaking along showing 180 on your airspeed and your ground speed was a sizzling 260 mph.

If you're flying a cross-country race westbound which means you're almost always going to be fighting the wind, there is no quid pro quo—you suffer. Period. Well, I was suffering. I called Center and asked if they had any upper air wind velocity reports recently. I had checked them a few hours before and had an average headwind from surface to 24,000 feet of 50 mph. But now, at 24,000 feet, they came back with the 120 mph forecast. I was in the damn jet stream, but we didn't know much about jet streams in 1970. All we knew was that it was strong, with winds up to 175 mph. I asked at what altitude the winds decreased. They were strong all the way down to 17,000 feet. I requested 16,000 feet. Sorry, all altitudes below 20,000 feet are occupied. I was to stand-by and maintain 24,000 feet. All my plans were starting to melt. At that rate, all I could think about was that the others were having the same headwinds, but maybe not. Maybe they elected lower altitudes. Maybe the reason I couldn't get a lower altitude with less headwind was because they were all occupied by the others. Damn!

But wait a minute. I didn't hear any of them having to copy an IFR clearance from Ground Control…and that's the only place they could get it. They couldn't be flying the same route I was without being on an instrument flight plan. Could they have gone around the bad weather instead of right into it as I had done? I keyed the mike and called center. "Are there any planes at the altitudes below me at about my same speed?" The reply was "No." Good. But where the hell were they?

After another 200 miles, the winds started to relent a bit. They now seemed to be down to only 50 mph on the nose. At that speed I could make it to Saratoga, Wyoming's Shivley Airport where I had planned a secret fuel stop. They had virtually no traffic in mid-September. The fishing season was pretty much over. They had a long runway there. It was nearly 9,000 feet long and the elevation was about 7,000 feet above sea level. A rule of thumb is that you want a runway at least as long in feet as the elevation is high in feet to compensate for the less dense air and the resultant drop in the ability of the air to give you the needed lift. So 9,000 feet long with only 7,000 feet high was a good ratio. Also I had fly-fished for trout in that area on the North Platte River in the 1950s and early '60s and had met some local pilots who would help get me a fast refueling and send us on our way again. But that was not to happen!

About 200 miles out from Saratoga, I checked the weather. It had been forecast to be clear, but now the report I got back was that the weather had closed in and the field was below visual minimums and there was no instrument approach to Saratoga. In that mountainous area around Snowy Range, minimums to me are a clear sky and 25 miles visibility, especially with a fast plane like a P-51. The decision to not attempt to go there was a no-brainer. I not only wanted an airport with an instrument approach, I wanted one that was covered by some radar facility to give me steers and help if needed.

Last year, we had refueled at Jeffco airport northwest of Denver. Maybe some of the same crew who knew how to fill my bladder tanks were still at the Phillips gas stop. But there was no way to contact them. I asked center to amend my flight plan to land at Denver's Jeffco airport even though it would take me well south of my planned route. I could have tried Laramie or Cheyenne, but I had never been there and didn't know any of the facilities. Though I had airport reference books, it seemed just too much work to take the time to make the effort to do book research and fly the plane. Too much was happening. Once the decision was made to stop at Jeffco, my mind could start focusing on other things.

First of all, I needed to file an instrument flight plan from Denver to Reno. As usual, the weather was socked in over the Rockies, especially the first part of the course. As anyone who has approached Denver in plane or car from the east knows, the Rockies rise up just past Denver like a giant wall. If you've lived in the east all your life and think you know mountains, this is an awesome sight to behold. To climb up out of Denver to clear the mountains, you almost had to go into the clouds and be on instruments—especially if you were trying to make time in an air race. Going up and around via a lower route through Salt Lake City was like quitting the race. You'd arrive way after deadline.

After I filed my flight plan with center, I got permission to leave the frequency to call Jeffco airport to contact the gas base there. Approach control was nice enough to give me their unicom freq. Sure, they'd be ready for me and sure, one of the fellows who had refueled us last year was still there. Great! Something was working out for us for a change. We had purposely limited our fluid intake before takeoff so we wouldn't need to get out of the plane at the refueling stop. We had another 700 miles left to go—about $2^{1}/_{2}$ hours at the most. I asked Pete if he was okay and got the affirmative which was a good thing. I mentioned earlier that we made sure that we had enough oxygen on board this year. No more of that sharing the meager supply by taking 5 minute turns using it as we had to do last year.

The 2,000 pounds I built into the plane's system wasn't enough last year for the two us at that high altitude. This year's solution was that Pete brought a tank for his own use. The only problem is that we really didn't address where the tank would be stored. The result was that Pete held it on his lap. It was a sight to behold. Pete with the giant green pumpkin that he could all but see around. In level flight in the air, it was one thing, but tilted back in the back seat of a tailwheel airplane, it looked like he had caught a giant green mass with both arms and was wondering what to do with it. Just staying there was a better choice than trying to get up and out of the back seat to relieve himself.

Taking off up and out of Jeffco, we had gotten a heading slightly to the left in order to have a greater distance to climb over that wall of mountains, but still to the right of towering Pike's Peak. I recall seeing another plane out of the corner of my eye before we went into the clouds. Later at Reno, its pilot came to our pit. It was a twin-engine Aero Commander. He said that Departure Control had told him we would be passing him off to his right and just hold his course. It was nice to hear him say that he looked out to his right and saw us go by him like we were shot out of a cannon. He had never seen another plane go past him that fast. We thrived on observations like that—especially when you don't come in first. We came in fourth versus sixth last year, but as I mentioned earlier, the others had figured out a different way.

I won't mention any names except to say that I was naive. I had developed and published an aviation atlas, Sky Prints. I was serving on the FAA's FIAC Group, their Flight Aviation Advisory Committee. It was made up of government and civilian members from the industry to examine and expand ways to get information to pilots in the rapidly-changing airspace system that jets were about to enter in large numbers, and that turboprop planes like the Lockheed Electra had already expanded the borders beyond prop planes in speed and altitude. To me, the flight rules were the best way to keep us all safe in the airspace. What I discovered first by innuendo and later by admission was that some of the other planes flew in the soup without an instrument clearance! Of course it could be done and perhaps even safely.

To set the stage for this, let me review some things. Planes on an IFR instrument flight plan were assigned to the cardinal altitudes, i.e., 10,000 feet, 11,000 feet, 12,000 feet. Planes flying eastbound used the odd altitudes, 11,000 feet, 13,000 feet, 15,000 feet, etc. Planes headed westbound were assigned the even altitudes of 10,000 feet, 12,000 feet, 14,000 feet, etc. This gave a 1,000-foot (2 block) vertical separation from planes flying in opposite directions on an IFR flight plan. Planes not on an IFR flight plan, planes that could be flying without any flight plan, added 500 feet to the east or west direction they were flying which gave them a 500-foot (1 block) vertical separation from the IFR planes above or below them. Now add to the fact that at that time even if the FAA's centers had your plane as a blip on their radar scopes, they

1. did not know your altitude, and

2. they did not know (nor do they know today) if you are in the clouds, above the clouds or can see the ground.

That's what some of these guys had figured out. As long as the weather was VFR (you could see the ground) where they were going and they did not have to contact an FAA radar facility, they could fly in the soup anywhere they wanted. With the altitude separations, the chance of hitting an airliner or any other plane was slim. Of course, running into each other or any other plane that might be evading the system was always a gamble, but the odds are good for you. Thank god that was the case for me in my future episode when I was lost over the Rockies! I call it my "Dumb Luck Flight."

Reno National Air Races • September 1970

"Rudder Trim Tab Explodes — I Soar into Space!"

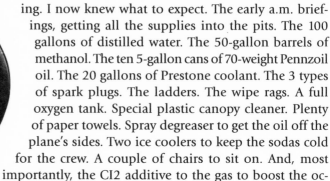

This was my sophomore year of Unlimited pylon air racing. I now knew what to expect. The early a.m. briefings, getting all the supplies into the pits. The 100 gallons of distilled water. The 50-gallon barrels of methanol. The ten 5-gallon cans of 70-weight Pennzoil oil. The 20 gallons of Prestone coolant. The 3 types of spark plugs. The ladders. The wipe rags. A full oxygen tank. Special plastic canopy cleaner. Plenty of paper towels. Spray degreaser to get the oil off the plane's sides. Two ice coolers to keep the sodas cold for the crew. A couple of chairs to sit on. And, most importantly, the CI2 additive to the gas to boost the octane rating up as high as possible. This CI2 is mean stuff. Only a pint to 10 gallons will save an engine at high boost, but it is so powerful and dangerous that to inhale its fumes or spill some on your hands could result in permanent damage. Only the top members of the crew were allowed to handle it; all others had to stand at least 10 feet away. The only place I could get it was at a Texaco plant near Long Beach, but soon there were regulations that only qualified personnel like certified engine mechanics were allowed to buy it. It was a major logistics program to get all the needed items, but had to be done if you wanted to race Unlimiteds on the fast track.

My qualifying speed went up to 376 mph. Remember, this is not the cross-country high-speed course with the gentle pylon turns they fly today. This was a true oval course with 3 pylons on each end. You made only two turns on each lap. On one end you started your turn and kept it tight until you had rounded 3 pylons, then the straight-away, and then the bottom 3 pylons were taken all in one turn. You were in a high-G turn of about 4 Gs for about 30 seconds. In 4 Gs, your 200-pound body weighs 4 times the weight of gravity, or 800 pounds pressing down in the seat. But that's not all. I found my oxygen mask being pulled down off my face, my arms pulled down off the control stick, my glasses sliding down off my face, my 5-pound helmet becoming a 20-pound rock on top of my head and my jowls deforming my mouth. And I was, at age 49, starting to feel a slight "gray-out" as the blood was being drained from my head.

I recall feeling this at age 23 when 21-year-old hard-body cadets would not "black me out," but "gray me out" with high-G pull-ups in their Immelmann demos.

To combat these high-G turns and "gray-outs," instead of a G-suit which was not all that effective, I had a Mandarin collar on my flight suit with a strong velcro-fastening overlap. As I started the race, I tightened it so it was snug. As I entered a turn, I bull-frogged my neck to the point that it stopped most of the blood draining out of my head and kept it that way until about 25 seconds later when starting to round out past the final pylon on that turn. It worked great. Try bull-frogging your own neck for 20 seconds. Without a restriction, it'll be harder to hold it, but the effect will be much the same. You can do this on the sharp upgrade of a roller-coaster with your granddaughter so you won't look glassy-eyed at the top.

In the race finals, my logbook notes translate into this: "I was holding back behind Clay Lacy (the eventual winner),

To keep from blacking out in high-G turns, I had a Mandarin-type collar on my flight suit. It could be tightened with Velcro. By bull-frogging my neck, it helped keep blood from draining from my brain.

so as to give him the feeling that his power setting there was no need to add more power. He was in the lead. But I had power in reserve. It was an 8-lap final race. Maybe I could 'sling-shot' by him and cross the finish line before he could get up to my speed. The Gold Race was on Sunday, the last race day. At the sixth lap heading down the straight-away in front of the grandstand, I made my move. I added all the power I had. The plane literally leapt forward. I started to pass Lacy just before the next turn when all of a sudden I shot skyward!" To this day, I describe it as thinking that I had gone through the speed of sound—that all my control surfaces had reversed. It was like my first high bounce off a trampoline. I couldn't figure out what was going on. Nothing made any sense. All I knew was that I was headed out into space. The race course was rapidly disappearing to the left below me. I was at least 500 feet above it. I could see the others like model plane sizes still going around below me.

I did not know it, but the rudder trim tab had broken in half. The remaining half was still attached to the trim bar but it had flipped over causing what canoeists call a "bow-rudder"—a diagonal force out against the forward flow. The natural instinct of a pilot who feels he is veering right is to add left rudder. I did. At first it was not enough. I added more. The soaring away from the race course stopped. I was even starting to go back down. But the need for left rudder pressure was more than I could sustain for more than a few seconds. When I relaxed, the plane in a 60° bank, would start to soar outward again. I was able to press down on the left rudder and then lock the toe of my shoe under a rib of the plane to maintain the heavy rudder pressure.

My fix of locking a shoe under a rib was fine for the straight-away, but in the left turns I had no more ability to add the needed extra left-rudder pressure to make the left pylon turns. Up high on the course in a left turn, my only option to get down was to roll the plane to the left nearly on its back, pull back stick and dive back on to the course. For the final two laps, I must have looked like an aerobatic plane trying

This shot is taking off to the east to join up in an echelon for the race start. Note the strong wind shown by the flag position and the lack of clouds. For me, these are ideal race conditions. Strong wind blows prop wash off the course line and no clouds means you can see shadows on the ground of nearby planes.

to get into the act. I had been in second place behind Clay Lacy but I finished in fourth place in the finals. As I pulled back on the power after the race, the need for heavy rudder pressure quickly ebbed, I still had no idea of what caused it all.

I radioed asking any plane near me to come alongside to examine my plane to see if they saw anything unusual. Lacy, an air-race veteran pulled up beside me in his purple Mustang, Race 64, and radioed "Howie, your rudder trim tab is broken. Part of it is still on there. It looks okay to land with it." That made sense. I didn't know if part of the entire tail was missing or a rudder cable had broken. It helped explain why the problem was less at slower speeds and why there was a tendency to make the plane turn in one direction at higher speeds. I could land knowing, at least, that the tail was still there! Actually at the slow speeds of approaching to land at 140 mph it wasn't very noticeable. I flew the 500 miles back to Van Nuys without any rudder trim tab. Under 200 mph, you didn't need any rudder. I was even surprised on takeoff without a rudder trim that is normally set at 6° right rudder to counteract the torque, the difference was not that great. Of course, I was aware of it and added takeoff power very slowly to keep the nose straight down the runway.

It turned out that 16 years before during WWII when metal, especially aluminum, was scarce, anything that could be made of something besides aluminum or any metal was a good substitute. The Mustang's rudder trim tabs were made out of a phenolic resin material somewhat like the fiberglass of today. The Corsair's ailerons were also made out of the stuff. One broke off a Corsair in the starting dive on to the course in Cape May, New Jersey. I saw that thing whizzing by me. It just missed my prop. There were no projections as to how long they would last. Long enough to fly out, engage the enemy and fly back to base was all that was needed. Forget the 100,000 mile warranty. There wasn't anything like "warranties" in those days. Not even on cars, much less on war planes. After mine blew apart, most Mustangs had the rudder trim tab fabricated out of metal. In spite of having to fly a weird pattern up and down for the final two laps, I came in fourth in the Gold Race. Anybody today would be happy with that finish in a fairly-standard racing Mustang.

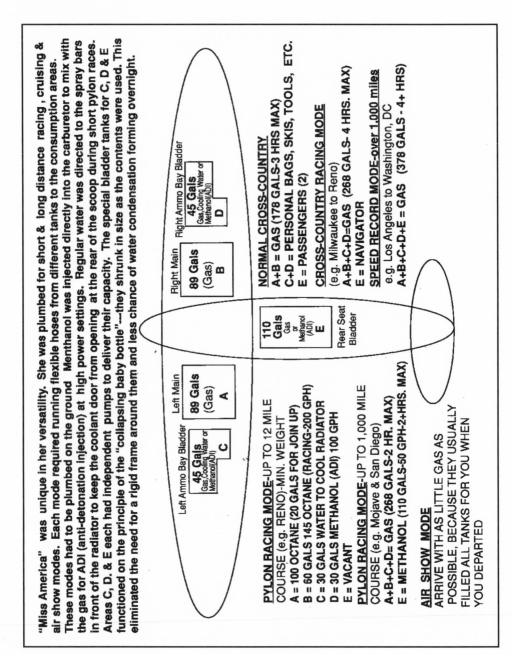

"Miss America" was unique in her versatility. She was plumbed for short & long distance racing, cruising & air show modes. Each mode required running flexible hoses from different tanks to the consumption areas. These modes had to be plumbed on the ground   Menthanol was injected directly into the carburetor to mix with the gas for ADI (anti-detonation injection) at high power settings. Regular water was directed to the spray bars in front of the radiator to keep the coolant door from opening at the rear of the scoop during short pylon races. Areas C, D. & E each had independent pumps to deliver their capacity. The special bladder tanks for C, D & E functioned on the principle of the "collapsing baby bottle"—they shrunk in size as the contents were used. This eliminated the need for a rigid frame around them and less chance of water condensation forming overnight.

Left Ammo Bay Bladder

C — 45 Gals — Gas,Cooling Water or Methanol(ADI)

Left Main

A — 89 Gals (Gas)

E — 110 Gals — Gas or Methanol (ADI)

Rear Seat Bladder

Right Main

B — 89 Gals (Gas)

Right Ammo Bay Bladder

D — 45 Gals — Gas,Cooling Water or Methanol(ADI)

PYLON RACING MODE-UP TO 12 MILE
COURSE (e.g. RENO)-MIN. WEIGHT
A = 100 OCTANE (20 GALS FOR JOIN UP)
B = 60 GALS 145 OCTANE (RACING-200 GPH)
C = 30 GALS WATER TO COOL RADIATOR
D = 30 GALS METHANOL (ADI) 100 GPH
E = VACANT

PYLON RACING MODE-UP TO 1,000 MILE
COURSE (e.g. Mojave & San Diego)
A+B+C+D= GAS (268 GALS-2 HR. MAX)
E = METHANOL (110 GALS-50 GPH-2+HRS. MAX)

AIR SHOW MODE
ARRIVE WITH AS LITTLE GAS AS
POSSIBLE, BECAUSE THEY USUALLY
FILLED ALL TANKS FOR YOU WHEN
YOU DEPARTED

NORMAL CROSS-COUNTRY
A+B = GAS (178 GALS-3 HRS MAX)
C+D = PERSONAL BAGS, SKIS, TOOLS, ETC.
E = PASSENGERS (2)

CROSS-COUNTRY RACING MODE
(e.g. Milwaukee to Reno)
A+B+C+D=GAS (268 GALS- 4 HRS. MAX)
E = NAVIGATOR
SPEED RECORD MODE-over 1,000 miles
e.g. Los Angeles to Washington, DC
A+B+C+D+E = GAS (378 GALS - 4+ HRS)

Miss America's gas tanks

Chapter 9

California 1,000 Race

Mojave, California • November 13–15, 1970
"A First in Air Racing—2$\frac{1}{2}$ Hours Around Pylons!"

This was a first in modern air racing: A 1,000-mile race around pylons. I was exhausted doing the 90 to 100 mile course at Reno after just 12 minutes of pylon racing. This race of 1,000 miles would be almost 3 hours! Its concept was taken from the Indy 500 Races. It was to be a 3- to 4-hour show for the spectators so they could watch the start, walk around for awhile and catch up again with the race's progress. None of us knew what to expect in such a long race.

Regular unlimited pylon races are started in the air in a step-up echelon formation with the pace plane in first position. With 20 planes starting the California 1000, we were staggered in groups of three to fit across the runway. I hate to think of the carnage if even one plane swerved out of control. The pilots of the planes behind could not see over their noses until they had their speed up. I vowed to be the fastest qualifier in the next race so I could be in the front row.

Of course, I wouldn't be pulling the power I would in the shorter races, but at 85" manifold pressure and 3,000 RPM versus normal cruise of 36" and 2,400 RPM, it was still a lot of power and required high-octane fuel and possible engine problems. I tossed and turned many nights just thinking about the endurance it would require. Should I have a stand-by pilot just in case it got too grueling for me? But who? All the Mustang pilots I knew who were race-qualified would be flying their own planes.

I was explaining my dilemma during a legal conference with my attorney, Victor (Vic) Baker. Vic was a member of the Condor Squadron at Van Nuys. He owned a T-6, had a lot of that Condor Squadron disciplined-flying experience and had raced in the T-6 races at Reno. He didn't have any P-51 time, so I wasn't thinking of him being my back-up pilot. But as I talked to him about my concern of trying to do the race by myself, I noticed his eyes start to glaze over and maybe a little drool come from the corner of his mouth in a half-smile. "Boy, I sure wish I could be that guy, Howie" he sighed as he slowly moved his head from side-to-side.

After I left his office I thought "Why not Vic? The T-6 was the fighter trainer that Mustang pilots flew in WWII before they had to solo the P-51. With its wide landing gear, the P-51 was actually easier to land than a T-6. It just had more systems to monitor with its water-cooling system versus the round-nose engines which were air-cooled. The race was a month away. Time enough to have Vic get some time in "Miss America." And he was a good pilot and a nice guy." When I called him with the proposition to be my back-up pilot, he almost pulled me to his office through the phone line! "Wow! Really? I'd love it!" I slept better that night.

Clay Lacy, a United Captain, had plenty of experience racing his Mustang.

I let Vic fly it as much as he wanted—even at high-power settings. He gratefully paid to top off the gas tanks after each flight, even when I rode in the back seat to suggest how to monitor the engine instruments. Putting time on the engine never concerned me during my racing years. The engines were majored normally at about 200–300 hours, but racing them as hard as I did, routine flying around was almost free. If they didn't blow up, something would happen. To get 35 hours out of one before something went sour was about what I came to expect.

After Vic was checked out, we planned our strategy. I'd fly it the first $1^1/_2$ hours and he'd take it the last part of the almost 3-hour race. If I got too tired at any time, we'd break it into shorter segments. I had to make a pit stop anyway. I could carry just enough gas for about 600 miles because the ammo bay on one side had to carry the ADI (anti-detonation injection) mix of 50% methanol and 50% distilled water. Anything over 65 inches of manifold pressure was an engine waiting to blow without ADI.

As I recall, there were 15 pylons on the course. Do the math. There are 360° on any race course that is in a circular shape. 360 divided by 15 is 24. So the average pylon turn is only 24°—that's about half of a 45° turn and about one-third as severe a G-load as the original Reno Unlimited course oval with a 60° turn at each pylon. Really a piece of cake. Even for a guy now almost 50 years

Allen Paulson, later head of Grumman Aircraft, also flew the DC-7 with Clay Lacy.

old. This turned out to be the difference. I wasn't tired. After the first 20 minutes on the course, the adrenaline rush faded. I settled into a rhythm and even the pylons were easy to find. I actually started to enjoy it. It was like organized flat-hatting.

The only gremlin in the race was a DC-7B. Okay, it was an Unlimited race as long as the planes had piston engines. John Lear had a twin-engine bomber. The DC-7B was flown by Clay Lacy, a United Captain, and Allen Paulson, who later bought Grumman Aircraft and developed the famous Gulfstream Jets. Maybe Clay's wife, sweet Lois, a United attendant, was on board serving them sodas and hors d'oeuvres. Anyway here was this gigantic, 117-foot-plus wingspan DC-7B with 4 engines churning up the course. Just as I tried to pass this behemoth, a pylon was coming up. Lacy was an experienced race pilot and didn't climb on the turns where I might sneak under him. At each pylon that long wing would go down so there was no way I could sneak under him. And I wasn't going that much faster than he was going to fly out around him. It was frustrating to say the least. And he had enough fuel on board to fly the entire race without needing to make a pit stop. In our next long-distance race, a Lockheed Constellation with a 123-foot wingspan flown by the famous Lockheed test pilot "Fish" Salmon showed up in addition to Lacy's DC-7. Pilots voted to have

Clay Lacy and Allen Paulson raced this DC-7 nonstop for the 1,000 miles around pylons. They were doing about 375 mph. Even though I was going about 390 mph, the straight-aways weren't long enough to pass them. At each pylon, that giant 117-foot wingspan went sky-high and pylon-low at the same time with 4 engines churning the air. Flying behind that air-mass was frustrating to say the least!

Herman "Fish" Salmon was a top Lockheed test pilot.

a maximum altitude on the race course of 200 feet which automatically eliminated these giants. It would have been interesting to watch them race each other, though.

As the time to make a pit stop neared and I could turn it over to Vic, I began to wish I hadn't involved him. I wondered if he'd mind if I just kept on racing. My only problem was that I had chosen to sip Gatorade, a new drink at the time, from a half-gallon Thermos jug. I had a plastic hose fitted through my oxygen mask like a long straw. Big mistake! Dehydration in the hot Mustang sitting on top of the water radiator was a major concern. After about one hour of sipping Gatorade, I can't look at even an empty bottle of Gatorade any more. I turn away watching football on TV when they show the Gatorade cups. The stuff started to taste like I was drinking straight sugar syrup. The more I took to try to quench my thirst, the thicker my mouth felt. It must be like what happens when you're dying of thirst on a raft in the ocean and you start drinking salt water. Instead of quenching your thirst, it magnifies it. When I got out of the plane I ran for the ice cooler and put as many ice cubes as I could cram into my mouth. We had cokes and soft drinks galore but no water. I grabbed the distilled water we had for the ADI mix and washed my mouth out with it then drank it to my heart's content. Never was distilled water so refreshing. I could have done a believable commercial for it at that moment.

The crew was gassing it up and adding more ADI. Vic, his wife and his young son were looking at me as I walked back to the plane. I looked at the excitement in his son's eyes as he jumped up and down saying "Dad! Dad! Are you going to fly it now?" Vic just looked at me. I looked at him. I looked at his son jumping up and down. I couldn't get the words out of "I'm really not tired, Vic, how about if I take it until I do get tired." In my heart I really wanted to finish the race...not for the glory nor for the experience,

Vic Baker said his share of the California 1,000 was his best racing memory.

but just for the fun I was having. I had never experienced that feeling before of going over 350 mph about 50 feet off the deck with a smooth-running engine for almost forever, it seemed. But in looking at his son's anticipation for his father to fly "Miss America," the words stuck in my throat. After all, I created "Miss America" to give kids some of the dreams I had as a boy with the Lindberghs and Roscoe Turners. And here was one of those kids.

I reached out my hand to shake Vic's, and said "Go for it, guy…it's fun." I think he was in the cockpit before our hands parted from our handshake. The smile on his face and his son still jumping up and down was also a new feeling for me. I barely remember 30 years later the deeper feelings of flying that day, but I fondly recall that father–son scene of Vic standing there with his son tugging at his jacket. Vic Baker did a great job and he loved doing it. We took seventh place. Several planes could carry enough fuel to go the entire distance. We weren't far behind the others who had to stop for fuel.

Sherm Cooper in his Sea Fury "Miss Merced" was able to go nonstop and took first place. In addition to a large fuel capacity, he had the advantage of a Sea Fury (a British carrier plane) flying the unusual clockwise course at Mojave. The Sea Fury's prop turns in the opposite direction of a Mustang's prop. Going around the pylons clockwise, the torque of the Sea Fury's prop almost pulls it around with little rudder drag. The P-51 not only requires more rudder to do a high-power right turn to counteract the force pulling it to the outside, but has to deal with the resultant greater drag. I like being able to introduce these technical facts to explain why I didn't come in first!

(Note: Vic Baker was killed the next year in the tragic T-6 race at Cape May, New Jersey where four T-6 pilots died in collisions on the race course, which I'll describe later. At his funeral, his wife came up to me and, nodding her head said, "Howie, Vic often said that one of the greatest privileges in his life was being able to fly 'Miss America' in that race. He spoke about it many times.")

Dumb Luck Flight • January 1, 1971
"Lost Over the Rockies—Dumb, Deaf and Blind"

That I am still alive and not a frozen mummy and "Miss America" is still in one piece on the racing circuit could have ended on this date, January 1, 1971. I still get chills when I think about what could have been the outcome of this flight. It was just simply amazing dumb luck that I did not have to parachute into the middle of the frozen Rockies with only a light sweater under my flight suit and "Miss America" splattered on the side of some unnamed mountain.

I had flown "Miss America" to Aspen, Colorado three days earlier to ski with and stay with Pete and Judy Hoyt who had a winter house there. The weather on the 700-mile flight from Los Angeles was beautiful blue skies and 50 miles of visibility all the way. In those days, there was not an approved instrument approach to the Aspen airport. Aspen Airways had petitioned the FAA and received a special waiver to fly their trained pilots into Aspen in conditions where you could not see where you were going. The use of this approach was limited to Aspen Airways pilots only in 1971. It required rapid step-downs in descent never before allowed in any instrument approach procedure at any airport in the U.S. The Aspen Airway pilots were a breed apart from other pilots by being trained in this unusual approach.

(Note: Today there is an FAA-approved instrument approach to the Aspen airport that anyone can use. To me, it's an invitation to disaster. There is no way an aircraft landing at Aspen should be allowed to come in unless they have full view of the airport and the surrounding mountains at the same time. It's too much to ask any pilot to do an approach threading his way down that valley between mountains on either side. My personal opinion is that the FAA should cancel their authorization and approval of any approach into Aspen unless the pilot can see all the terrain. To come in at night is like playing Russian roulette with a loaded pistol at your head.)

While inching up in the type of maze ski-lift operators had devised to deceive us as to how long the line really was (versus a long, single line) to get back on a chair lift up the mountain, I spotted a pylon race buddy, Burns Byrum. He had flown his Mustang in from Marengo, Iowa where he was a medical doctor. Later on, he amused us all by painting a giant Playboy bunny on his tail fin. Burns was a smiling, self-effacing, soft-spoken type of guy. He let his beautiful Mustang speak for him. To see him in a chair-lift line compared to in the race pits at Reno seemed strange. To me it was like I could be in any place or setting, but everyone else should stay in the area I met them. Only I could leap-frog from air racing to sailing to riding a bike around the marina. If I met you as an air race pilot, don't show up on the ski slopes at Aspen. You're out of place. Sadly, Burns was killed ferrying a P-51 from Central America. The story I heard was that he was over Mexico when the coolant line from the engine to the radiator below the cockpit broke, spraying boiling water, 200°+, into the cockpit. They found the plane crashed about a mile short of an airfield. Burns had the presence of mind to pop open his parachute in the cockpit and try his best to wrap himself up in it to shield his body from the deadly water spray. He probably wasn't wearing goggles. None of us did. It must have been terrifying for him.

Dr. Burns Byrum had his P-51 race plane at Aspen, too.

I wasn't getting much sleep at Aspen's 7,000-foot-plus altitude. Having grown up in the low-altitude areas of the Midwest, I hadn't learned the trick of taking a couple of aspirin the first few days at high-altitude to help slow down a pounding heart that's trying to adjust getting more oxygen into your system. The first few nights it was taking me almost two hours of lying there until sleep took over because of the sound of my heart beating so fast. It was as if I had consumed 4 cups of strong coffee before bedtime. In the P-51, of course, I have oxygen when wanted. By the time I was ready to leave on New Year's Day to get back to my job in Los Angeles for the Newspaper Advertising Bureau on Monday morning, I was pretty groggy. What I saw when I got to the airport was not nice!

As I checked out at the flight office to pay for my parking and gas, the girl said, "Oh, all the line boys want to thank you."

"For what?" I replied, thinking that they liked the sight of "Miss America" sitting on the ramp in all her glory.

"For deicing the ramp for them."

"Whaddya mean, deicing the ramp?"

"Well, your coolant has been leaking out for the past 3 days. You were parked at the uphill end of the ramp so it flowed down the entire ramp line, melting all the snow and ice in its path."

Damn, I was groggy from too little sleep. They did not have any glycol coolant (e.g., Prestone) at the field (who flew water-cooled engines any more?).

It was New Year's Day so all the stores would be closed. I wouldn't get back to work on time and my boss, located in our New York home office, would be sure to call me as they were going to lunch to see if I was on the job. Not only was Los Angeles La La Land to them, and I was a bachelor at the time living in Marina del Rey by the ocean, they did not approve of my flying a fighter plane around the country. Folks who work in New York City fly so often on business, they have a built-in fear of flying it seems. Of course, I always teasingly poked at this phobia with tales that started out with "I don't understand why the airlines use such flying-on-the-edge techniques as zooming up sharply on takeoff" (jets have to—unlike prop-plane wings that lift off the ground at a certain speed, a jet has to rotate and literally fire itself into the air) or "Those new anti-noise regulations at New York Int'l that requires the plane to raise its nose so high to gain altitude before going over houses that I fear it'll stall and drop out of the sky." I'd always end the statement with a sigh as if to say, "You poor guys having to take that risk so often."

Fortunately, even though it was a cold New Year's Day in Aspen, not only were the auto parts stores open, but they had supplies of glycol anti-freeze. We used a 50/50 mix of glycol and water, not because of the anti-freeze properties, but because glycol cooled the engine better than pure water and, as I recall, had a higher boiling point. Before heading off to buy the glycol, I wanted to start the plane and warm it up. The reason the coolant leaks out (and if you look under Mustangs at Reno after a cold night you'll probably see green color on the ground beneath the scoop) is because the aluminum pipes contract in the cold weather. If the hose clamps were tightened too tightly, the metal ends can be crimped, resulting in leakage. I wanted to heat up the coolant enough to not only expand the tubes and stop the leaking, but to have a tight system when I got back with the coolant. I looked at Burns Byrum's plane down the ramp and didn't see much coolant draining from under it. Of course, my coolant had flowed under his plane as well, so I really couldn't tell. Maybe he had more sense than I did and came out each day and ran it up to temperature for a while. Being from Iowa, he had experience with cold weather and Mustangs. I never did get the chance to ask him.

Not knowing how much had leaked out, I came back with 35 gallons of Prestone. If it didn't take it all, Pete could use the extra during the winters. It took all but 5 gallons. I didn't use distilled water because there wasn't any for sale at the auto parts store. I was so behind time as it was and I wanted to get back to Santa Monica before dark that I didn't want to take the time to canvass the supermarkets for distilled water, and certainly didn't want to put Aspen's probably rock-hard water into the P-51's important cooling pipes. Santa Monica's instrument approach was down for repairs to the VOR.

I had checked weather. It was clear 250 miles west of Aspen. But in the Aspen–Grand Junction area it was "sky partially obscured." The ceiling at Aspen was being reported at a comfortable 3,000 feet. Looking up, I could see the image of the sun through the hazy sky. I couldn't get any "tops" reports which would tell where the top of the haze stopped and the sky would be clear above that. Surely, they couldn't be too high because I could see the sun's position through the haze. Aspen did not have an instrument departure procedure. It didn't even have an instrument approach then. Okay, so what I'll do is take off, come back over the field, start climbing up over the field in a circular pattern because there were mountains all around. Climbing in a circle to 16,000 feet would get me higher than all the mountains in the area and anyway, I'd probably be in the clear by then.

I don't recall Aspen even having a tower then. Just a unicom in the flight office. I told Pete I would monitor the unicom freq and report my progress if he wanted to go inside and listen. I'd say when I got on top in the clear. As I went through 16,000 feet, I radioed that I was still in the soup, but the sun looked even brighter now. I didn't get a return radio call so I tried again, but still nothing. I had two radios. The antenna for the top radio was on the top of the plane to use when I was on the ground so it wasn't blanked by any part of the plane. The bottom radio had the antenna on the bottom to use when calling ground stations from high altitudes. I checked, and sure enough I was still using the top radio I was tuned to on the ground. The higher I climbed, the more the plane's metal surface blocked its transmissions. I was now getting too occupied flying in circles on instruments to try to activate the other radio, tune to the freq and try to contact Aspen's unicom. It wouldn't serve any purpose anyway. Pete said later that he just assumed I had flown out of range of the low-powered station.

But I was getting cold. All I had on was my flight suit over a shirt, sweater and pants. A fire-retardant flight suit out of Nomex is cold to the touch as it is. It is not designed to be warm clothing. The flight was to be so short that I did not put on my thermal underwear. All I could think of as I climbed higher and higher was getting on top into the sunshine, warming up the cockpit through the canopy. I often cursed the sun for the heat it gave off at high altitudes. Now I welcomed it as my P-51 did not have a cockpit heater. I don't think any of them did. The way you got heat was to crack the canopy back a bit. The vacuum that was created sucked the air up from the floor boards where the coolant lines were located with near-boiling water going through them. But the noise was disturbing and any papers or maps you might have loose in the cockpit would get sucked up and maybe out. Besides, the sun was getting brighter all the time.

As I went through 18,000 feet, I decided I could clear any mountain west of Aspen. The 14,000-foot-plus Pike's Peak was in the opposite direction. So I checked my compass and started on my heading of due west, 270°, until I came to the clear-forecast air. I did not have a standard "wet" compass that floated in a solution and bobbled around in rough air. When I bought the plane, it had a Magnuson compass in it which runs on electricity with the dial being remote-reading from a sensor elsewhere. The needle was on a flat compass face and was much steadier than the standard type. Furthermore, your compass card could be right next to a radio and there was no magnetic interference with its read-out. The procedure is to set your directional gyro on the course the compass shows and then fly by it rather than the jumpy compass. I recall resetting my gyro about every 5 minutes because it precesses off its setting. The compass, when stable, is your only correct reading at all times. Each time I looked at the compass, I recall complimenting myself on what a straight course I was flying. The compass needle hadn't moved. By now I was at 24,000 feet and still no clear air or warm sun. The tops were still somewhere up there. At 24,000 feet, I'd be at the same altitude as westbound airliners (I don't recall having QNE above 19,000 feet in those days), so I climbed to 24,500 feet. It would be only about 30 minutes before I'd reach the area were they were reporting clear skies. I tried to think warm thoughts.

By now I should be able to pick up a VOR station for navigation and get a heading. I switched the radio from "com" to "nav" mode and tuned it to the nearest VOR. Nothing. Zilch. Nada! Not even a crackle. I tried the other radio. Same thing. No sound or any movement on the VOR needle. I sat there trying to figure that out. Could it be that I am still too far away from any station? Then I got the idea to switch on the intercom circuit used to talk between a passenger in the back seat and myself. By clicking the mike, I could hear my own transmission. Again, nothing. My heart was pounding again. What was going on? Both radios and the com system wouldn't fail at the same time. I looked down at the circuit breaker panel at my right thigh. Nothing seemed to be popped out. Above the circuit breaker panel and down too low to read without putting your head down and turning it hard to the right side was the ammeter. It showed the electrical power output of the generator. No wonder my radio calls while climbing out of Aspen went unanswered. No wonder I couldn't get any navigation signals on the radio. And, wait a minute, the compass! The needle was so still it was like it was painted on there. I wasn't flying a super-straight course after all! The compass wasn't even working! I didn't know where I was or where I was headed. The sun above was still too straight overhead to give me an idea of where west was as it would if it were later in the day.

To say I was stunned and befuddled would be putting it mildly. It was as if I were flying around inside a giant ping-pong ball with a dim light showing through up above. All my attitude flight instruments were functioning off a vacuum-pump system. They were independent of the electrical system and seemed to be working fine. Okay, so what to do now? I suddenly started getting colder. The flush of the blood rushing through my system caused by my mounting worry did help add a little feeling of warmth in my body. The outside air temperature dial showed it was minus 60° F. I wished I hadn't looked at it. It made me colder just looking at it.

Number one on my priority list was to get into warmer air. The temperature drop is 3.5° F per thousand feet in stable air. So if I go down to 16,500 feet from 24,500, a drop of 8,000 feet, the temperature would rise 28° F, but that would mean it would still be over minus 30° F. Not knowing where I was, I could even be headed east. I could have been in a slow turn all the while I thought I was flying a straight course. Yes, I had been resetting my directional gyro every 5 minutes, but not to a live compass. I could be headed in any direction on the compass at that point. I had to make a decision. I had to make a choice of which direction to fly.

I recalled the weather was clear toward Mexico. Ah! That would be warmer air. Looking at the hazy sun above me, I convinced myself I was now headed west. Recalling the P-51 pilot telling me how he set his DG at 0° over the Ft. Lauderdale airport in a rainstorm, I set mine at 0°. Then I made a left turn until it read 270°. After rolling out, I reset the gyro to 0°. Now I would be flying south into warm air. The thought of warm air started to be the only wish I ever had in life and was consuming

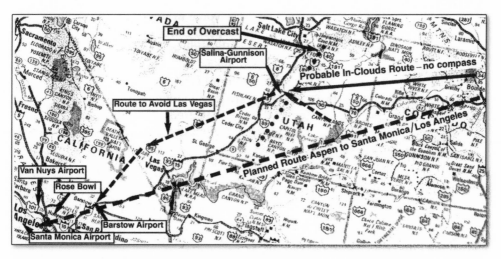

The top line above shows what I think might have been my route while I was in the "soup," but I thought I was headed straight south toward warmer air. Aspen to Los Angeles was about 800 miles. With my 1,000 miles safe range, I could have made it nonstop. I'm lucky I made it at all.

me. But having made the decision and convinced it was right, I sat back relaxed and accepted the fact that I was flying on instruments and my electrical system was totally wiped out.

Ten minutes passed. Then twenty minutes. I had about 4 hours of gas on board when I took off and I had been flying just an hour, so gas was not a worry at the point—just warm air. That's all I craved. Thirty minutes passed. I did start to notice that the sun now seemed to be more to the left of my course than directly overhead. Ummm. I started to think: winter sun to the left. The winter sun on January 1 would be low on the southern horizon and to my left if I were flying west or maybe northwest. But no. I was flying south. I was flying to warmer air. I just knew it.

In the middle of this conversation with myself, I burst out into the clearest air I ever saw! It was as if I had gone through a wall. On one side of the wall was a hazy, filmy world and on the other side was brilliant, clear air. There was no transition of clouds breaking up with partial clearing. It was just, boom! Another world! Now the sun was at my left. To the right were tall snow-capped mountains. Far below, almost exactly on the course I was flying, was a macadam highway. Alongside the highway was a river almost as straight as the highway. I checked my altimeter. I was still at 24,500 feet. I put the plane in a dive to that warmer air below. Going through 10,000 feet, it felt like someone had opened a furnace door. I leveled off at 8,500 feet.

Warmer air! Now my brain could start to function again. I could see everywhere. I could stay low in the warmer air and climb back up only if I needed to. But the straight highway below would now be my compass. It would lead to somewhere and that somewhere would have an airport and I could land at that airport and find out where I was, maybe even stay overnight, get the plane fixed and be able to fly back to Los Angeles the next day. Hey, I was warm and alive and I didn't give a damn if my boss in New York called while I wasn't at the office. If Marylinda, my secretary, didn't cover for me as she often did, I'd deal with all that later.

The highway went through a wide pass in a low mountain range and ahead I saw an airport. I headed for it. I was about 2,000 feet above it looking down and saw a the name of the airport in big letters: Salina–Gunnison. Salina–Gunnison? How could that be? Salina was in Kansas and Gunnison was in Colorado. How could they be together? Have I been flying in a time-warp? While I was flying around in this giant ping-pong ball did the earth open and Gunnison, Colorado and Salina, Kansas get pulled together? At this point, I was open to any possibility. You could have told me I was in Moscow and I would have believed you. Nothing was making any sense. I was flying toward snow-capped mountains off to my right.

I descended over the airport. A few planes were on the ground, but nothing was moving. No life anywhere. There was a town to one side of the airport and another town on the other side. I decided to come in low across the airport from the left just above the houses, flat-hat the airport, exit low over the houses on the other side. Surely the sound of a P-51 would arouse someone. I'd land, they'd come to the airport and I'd find out where I was.

I made my low passes, landed, taxied to midfield and waited. Nothing. No one came. About 200 yards away, cars were going along on the highway. I didn't dare shut the engine off because I'd never get it started again. The thought of leaving a P-51 with its parking brake on and the engine running never crossed my mind. You just didn't do that. If it got loose, it could chew up a block of homes before it stopped. I waved to the passing cars. They waved back. I stood up in the cockpit and waved to them. They still just waved back. I saw a man with a Labrador retriever working his dog in the tall grass between the airport and the highway. I got back into the cockpit, turned the plane toward him off the taxiway and swung it around just short of the tall grass, Instead of waving, I was close enough to him to swing my arm and hand in a motion asking him to come to me. He called his dog to attach a leash and came toward the plane.

I grabbed a flight planning chart. It covered the entire U.S. I held it up, pointed to it and then gave the "I don't know" shrug of the shoulders and beckoned him to come alongside and take the map. I throttled back as much as I dared. I didn't want the engine to quit. He had his dog in tow, but the dog, I feared, was not going to let him get close enough to the plane for him to get the map. I had considered just tossing it in the air and letting him pick it up off the ground behind the prop wash. But then how would I get it back? Fortunately, he approached the plane from the right wingtip where there was little prop wash. I could yell to him and he nodded back that he understood. He came in quickly, grabbed the chart from my outstretched arm and backed out. He studied it out of the prop wash. Folded and unfolded it several times. Then pointed at it, nodded his head, looked at me, and kept pointing at a spot on the chart. I motioned to fold the chart so that spot was on top. He did and worked his way with his still-wary dog back toward the cockpit. I was able to grab the chart from his up-stretched arm.

He was pointing at a spot south of Salt Lake City about a quarter of the way to Las Vegas to the south. Holy smokes! When I turned 90° to the left thinking at the time that I was flying west and was turning south toward Mexico, I was really flying north to Canada and I had turned to really fly almost due west. I'm so glad I turned. Flying into even colder air may have done me in. Now I knew where I was, but what should I do about it? The road alongside the airport showed on the WAC chart to be a major highway from Salt Lake City to Las Vegas. I'd follow it and at least get back to some sort of civilization. I went to the end of the airport, checked my mags, and roared down the runway toward the north, made a gentle turn back the other way and stayed about 2,000 feet above the highway.

I checked my gas. There was not enough left to make Santa Monica. Stopping at Las Vegas for gas was probably not a good idea. I had to have the plane refueled with the engine running. Without a battery, I couldn't restart it. I had refueled before with the engine running, but the sparks coming out of the exhaust stacks on both sides would make any sensible refueler worried. And Las Vegas was too well lighted. What you were doing could be seen everywhere. And there was the major problem that my radios weren't working. It's tough to sneak in and then out again from an airport without having radio contact with the tower, especially in a P-51 painted red, white and blue. Barstow, a nontower, large airport, was just past Las Vegas. I could make it on the fuel I had. I could fly in and out of there without any need for radio contact. Barstow it would be. I landed there and taxied up to the gas pit.

After stopping at the gas pit, a young fellow came out of the office and stood about 50 feet away from the plane. I motioned him to come to me which he did. With his head just below the cockpit he could hear me explain that I could not shut off the engine and would he please fill my tanks on the starboard side. That was all I needed. With what I had and that, I could make Santa Monica. I gave him a credit card. Without even questioning it, he pulled the hose from the bay and filled me up. When he handed me the credit card to sign, I asked him to call the local FSS (Flight Service Station) there and have them radio Santa Monica's tower saying that I'd be arriving in about 45 minutes as a NORDO (no radio) aircraft. He gave me a thumbs-up sign. I taxied back to the end of the runway and took off as it was starting to get dark. I would not have landing lights, but I knew the Santa Monica airport, how to judge altitude by the distance between the runway lights (the lower you go, the closer the lights appear to be together). But without running lights, other planes could not see me although I could see them.

I followed the string of red tail lights returning to Los Angeles from Las Vegas on Interstate 15. As soon as I was past the mountains on the right, I stayed to the right to avoid any planes flying the busy route from Los Angeles to Palm Springs. This route took me right over the Rose Bowl. It stood out like a bright jewel below me. Oh, how I wished this flight was over and I was down there watching the game. Maybe I could even make an emergency landing in all those bright lights. I'd surely be able to see what was in front of me. A reality check would be that the only way you could put a P-51 down on a 120-yard patch of lighted grass would be to go in nose first. The debris would probably spray out more than a 120 yards. Santa Monica was only about 40 miles ahead. Another 15 minutes and I'd be on the ground with "Miss America" tucked safely into her chocks alongside the hangar.

As I approached the coastal area, I could see the flickering lights below become obscured by low clouds drifting in from the ocean.

Low coastal clouds were the norm at night. They were always about 100 feet thick, 2,000 feet up and in puffs that covered about 50% of the ceiling. Fifty percent clouds was a ceiling and technically you had to make an instrument approach to go down through them. But, hey, I knew the airport. I'd just dive down through a big hole and land. No problem. I approached the airport to do an overhead flight down the runway toward the ocean, circle back and land. The over-flight would let the tower hear the Mustang's roar. It would be a courtesy to the tower to let them know I had arrived. As I looked down on my pass just south of the tower, I saw a red light flashing from the tower. With only 50% cloud cover, it was clearly visible. As I turned to go back to fly my downwind leg, the red light from the tower seemed even more frantic and authoritative. It was flashing madly on and off. The tower guy is telling me in no uncertain terms that I can't land. Should I pretend I don't see the red Aldus light and just land anyway? I could see the airport. It was about 6:00 p.m. now and dark but I could see the runway lights. But then my Navy experience must have kicked in. A strong red Aldus light aimed at you meant no-no-no-and-no in no uncertain terms!

I had better go elsewhere. Twenty-five miles north over the mountains was Van Nuys airport in the San Fernando Valley. At 2,000 feet over Santa Monica, you could see their clear lights glistening. I'd head there. But they also had a tower and I was required to call for permission to land. Van Nuys was a much busier airport than Santa Monica. Van Nuys was the busiest non-airliner airport in the U.S. at one time. Maybe it still is. I headed there. I also knew it fairly well. The longest runway was north–south on the west side of the field close to the tower. Planes landing on it used a right-hand pattern landing south which was normally in use or were cleared for straight-in approach. Without lights or radio ability, and it was now very dark, I decided my best bet was to follow another plane in closely behind them and hopefully well in front of a plane that would then be landing behind me. I flew north and east of the airport, looked at the planes in the landing pattern, noticed one rounding out on final and went toward his tail, did a hard left turn to stay right under his glide path, touched down as soon as I could and turned off at the high-speed runway turn-off. Luckily, he was apparently hangared at the south end of the field and went to the end of the runway. I taxied back to the northwest end where the FBO and parking were located.

Then came a fright that I still think about. I still wake up at night and get cold sweats when it creeps back into my thoughts. Again, understand that it was New Year's Day. Two hours before, I was over the Rockies not knowing where I was. Now I was taxiing into a warm parking bay in Los Angeles. As I rounded the turn on to the apron, the motion lights came on and flooded the entire ramp area. A lone line-boy came out, waved me forward, approached the right side and suddenly gave the cut-engine sign. That was a normal sign, but I noticed as I leisurely started to shut down the systems that he began to even more rapidly do the cut-across-his-throat sign. When the prop stopped, he urged me to quickly get out of the cockpit to see where he was pointing. I got out, slid down the wing to the ground, walked forward around the wing to see a large pool of oil on the ground under the engine. I took a Zeus fastener out of my flight suit, popped off the small piece of cowling on the right side and there it was. A brass line that transfers oil from the bottom to the top part of the engine had ruptured. Oil was pouring out. In 10 minutes time, all the oil would be gone. Without oil, the engine would dry out, heat up and seize. I called this my "Dumb Luck Flight." I still do. If it had happened a few hours earlier, that would have been the end of me and "Miss America." It really was Dumb Luck!

I was at my office at 9:00 a.m. on Monday, January 2, 1971. The phone did ring.

Here's What Happens on the Unlimited Race Course in ONE SECOND!

The Unlimiteds go flashing through the race course, engines howling, air shearing heat waves streaming. 480 mph is 8 miles-a-minute—the elite racers take about 75 seconds to make one lap on Reno's 9.1 mile race course.

If you take a souped-up P-51 racing at Reno and examine just *one second* of its flight, here's what you would find:

The Engine—The V-12 Rolls-Royce Merlin engine would have gone through 60 revolutions, each of the 48 valves slamming open and closed 30 times, the 24 spark plugs would have fired 720 times. Each piston would have traveled a linear distance 60 feet with an average speed of 40 miles per hour and the direction of each piston reverses itself every 6 inches of travel. 360 power pulses have been transmitted to the crankshaft making 360 sonic booms as the exhaust gas is expelled from the cylinders with a velocity exceeding the speed of sound!

The Accessories—The water pump impeller has spun 90 revolutions surging 4 gallons of coolant through the engine and the radiator. The oil pumps have forced 47 ounces of oil, roughly one-third of a gallon, through the engine, the oil cooler and the oil tank, scavenging the heat and lubricating the flailing machinery! The supercharger rotor completes 348 revolutions, its rim spinning at Mach 1, forcing 4.2 pounds or 44 foot-pounds of ambient air into the combustion chamber under 3 atmospheres of boost pressure. Around 9 ounces of high octane aviation gasoline fuel, 7,843 BTUs worth of energy, has been injected into the carburetor along with a mixture of 5.3 ounces of methanol/water/anti-detonation injection fluid. Over 1.65 million foot-pounds of work has been done, enough to lift a station wagon to the top of the Statute of Liberty!

The Propeller has gone through 25 complete revolutions, with each of the blade tips having arced through a distance of 884 feet at a rotational velocity of .8 Mach, 15 ounces of spray bar water has been atomized and spread across the radiator in the belly scoop to accelerate transfer of heat from the engine to the atmosphere.

The Aircraft itself has traveled 704 feet, more than two football fields, in that one second!

The Pilot's heart has taken 1.5 beats, pumping 5.4 ounces of blood through his body at a peak pressure of 4.7 of mercury over ambient pressure. The pilot happened to inspire, in that second, inhaling approximately 30 cubic inches of oxygen from the on-board system and 2.4 million (yes, a *million*) new red blood cells have been formed in the pilot's bone marrow.

An amazing sequence of events has taken place inside that tight cowling and under that visored helmet.

It's the *World's Fastest Motor Sport!*

Chapter 10

My Wings Get Clipped in May 1971
"To Race, Ya Gotta Do What Ya Gotta Do"

It was now May and not too early to start thinking about the Reno Air Races in September, a little more than 90 days away. The first P-51 flew 60 days after its plans were approved by the British, but getting even an engine tune-up on one in this day and age might take that long—and maybe cost that much. My crew chief, Dick Tomasulo, responded to my question of how I could get more speed out of it by using his hand to simulate sawing off a wingtip at its outboard rivet line. Dick and his partner in Pylon-Air, Vern Barker, were more into modifying a plane by fabrication than engine mods. Clipped wings would be fairly reasonable and they could be restored if desired.

This shot shows the clipped wings with the Hoerner tips added to deflect the airflow out instead of back and over the wing, destroying more lift.

So the wings were clipped. And it flew great. Two feet had been taken off each tip, reducing the wingspan from 37 feet to 33 feet. Hoerner tips were added to deflect the wing-tip vortices out rather than lap back over the remaining wing and reduce lift. We generally speak of it as 4 feet off the wingspan, but reducing wingspan is not the same as reducing wing area. Because the wingspan includes the width of the cockpit and the cockpit width is about 14% of the wingspan, the total width of the wings is only about 31 feet. Taking 4 feet from 31 feet means you now have only about 27 feet of your lift area left. From the P-51 Mustang's high-speed laminar-flow wing, that's a lot of wing area. But, as I said, it flew great.

As I learned a year later in setting the speed record from Los Angeles to Washington, DC with the wings clipped, I'm sure glad I had those wingtips and full ailerons on when I was lost over the Rockies at 24,500 feet. They were designed to take the Mustang up to 40,000 feet—the highest of any fighter at the time. Without them at 20,000 feet, you not only had lost almost all aileron control, but had to fly with the nose at a slightly higher attitude to keep enough lift to maintain your altitude. I didn't need that problem added on to my other ones.

At altitudes below 10,000 feet, the loss of wing and aileron control was hardly noticeable. It was so much easier, taxiing and maneuvering on the ground. I could now sneak through smaller aisles of parked planes, be able to do the all-important "S" turns while taxiing to see where I was going and to avoid chewing up the tail of another aircraft—always a problem with a tail-dragger versus a plane with a nose-wheel that lets you see over the cowl.

But I had forgotten (or perhaps I never really thought about it) that I had modified the plane, taking a P-51 out of its cherished FAA "Limited" category designation and dropping it into the restricted limbo of "Experimental" category with other warbirds and homebuilt aircraft that restricted operations. No night flying, no instrument flying, no admittance into certain congested flight zones, plus higher insurance premiums. This was purely a subjective FAA attitude. They have 3 operational categories: Standard, Limited and Experimental with operating limits for each. In the Standard category are planes that had their plans approved by the FAA before they were built— the Cessnas, Pipers and even the airliners. The Experimentals were those who could have been built without any plans from something a guy nailed together in his backyard, to a sleek racing plane with exotic blueprints. Also dumped into Experimental were all the fighters and other war planes with long histories of good performance, but because the FAA had not approved their plans before they were built, they could not be in the Standard category—they were dumped into the Experimental classification with all of its sins.

The P-51 was in the Experimental category until a White Knight came along and lifted her magically into the Limited category. His name was Dave Lindsay from Sarasota, Florida. Of all the fighters in WWII, he chose the Mustang to build from scratch in the 1960s. He named it the "Cavalier." To this day and forward to the year 3000, the Cavalier will still be the premium Mustang of Mustangs, even though it will be about 3,045 years old! He had orders from not only foreign countries whose military were probably paying for them for their generals to fly around as personal planes with the money the U.S. was giving out, but also from the sportsmen pilots in the U.S. I don't know the full story, but to sell them to be operated in the U.S. by private citizens and be in the Experimental category would not make them very saleable with their restricted use. He probably went to North American Aviation which was no longer making the Mustang, bought their plans, knocked on the FAA's door in Washington, dropped the plans on a desk and said, "Would you please approve these plans? It's a new plane that I want to manufacture." (In autos, you can build 499 cars for resale, but not until you build that 500th one are you considered a "manufacturer." But in planes, if you build even one for resale, you're a "manufacturer.") With the P-51's stellar record in the war and many years of flying as an Experimental, the FAA probably saw North American Aviation's name stamped on the plans along with the Mustang name and said, "Come back after lunch. The secretary will have the approved forms ready for you." But they also probably added, "We'll be looking forward to our test hopping it. If you give us three for our use, it will go much faster." That's what I would have said.

As a result, the Mustang's plans *per se* were approved by the FAA. Not only were the Cavaliers anointed with the Limited pedigree, all standard, stock Mustangs were elevated into that rare society—but here I had turned mine into a wayward child by clipping her wings. And don't think that I didn't hear snide remarks from the Mustang purists who felt if you even painted a Mustang in other than its squadron's colors, you were defacing a national monument. When the name "Miss America" and its colors became well known, the remarks disappeared. But at warbird gatherings I would still notice a person standing back examining her and slowly shaking his head from side to side.

About this time, an ex-military jet flown by a civilian taking off from Sacramento's Executive airport, slammed into an ice cream parlor off the end of the runway. It was a true disaster. Many were killed and many of those were children. Naturally the hue-and-cry went up about not only all airplanes, but especially ex-war and Experimental planes. I don't recall any blame being directed at Sacramento's zoning board for permitting an ice cream parlor or any business where people congregate to be operated only about 100 yards off the end of a runway.

The FAA had to react and do something. They focused on two things: Experimental aircraft and pilot qualifications. As I recall the restrictions issued by the FAA, all Experimental aircraft were severely restricted to not only daytime, non-instrument flying operations, but to be able to go only 50 miles from your home airport—anything farther required an FAA "ferry" permit, e.g., to the races at Reno, spelling out reasons, dates, times, etc. They were wartime conditions. The other was on the pilots flying the ex-warplanes. We had to be examined and approved by an FAA flight inspector to demonstrate we knew how to fly and control the experimental plane. In a way, this was reasonable—to show the FAA we could fly them. I was lucky in that the FAA inspectors had seen me race for several years at Reno, so I was, in a sense, "grandfathered in." There wasn't any way an FAA inspector would actually ride with you in a plane with a single set of flight controls to see if you were capable. They had families too.

So I got my "Letter of Authorization" that I always had to carry when flying "Miss America" to show FAA inspectors who requested it. But "Miss America"? What of her? How could she marry a Prince and be elevated back into the Limited category? Would she now be destined to be a milk-maid for the rest of her life? When I asked the FAA, they just shook their heads. "Got to go through the FAA's plans-approval program" was the constant answer. I couldn't even get a copy of North American's P-51 Mustang plans, as Dave Lindsay had done, to get her approved. She now had to wear the "Scarlet Letter E" and after the crash in Sacramento, it was definitely a capital "E." I was looking for a Prince for her to marry and I'd give the bride away.

While I was at the Cape May, New Jersey air races later that year, I saw Bob Hoover, a legendary war hero and P-51 pilot extraordinaire, who had a ground level waiver for the aerobatics he had performed before millions attended by multitudes of FAA types—and he worked for North American Aviation's Rockwell. The longer I looked at Bob, the more he looked like that Prince in shining armor, with his Mustang steed, riding up to the castle to find his damsel to marry. I would be the "yenta," the father, the dowry- provider, the whatever-it-tooker. I went over to him.

"Hello, Prince, er, I mean Bob, how are things?"

"Fine, Howie, what's up?"

"Well, you know, I clipped the wings on my Mustang. Have you had the opportunity to put a clipped-wing Mustang through its paces?"

"Not exactly."

"Would you do it in mine?"

"Sure, when?"

"How about now?" I was trying not to show my glee. I was waiting for the "I can'ts" like "My insurance won't let me. My contract with the air show prevents it. My company needs to approve it first." And so on.

His reply, "After I air-start this Unlimited race, I'll have some time. I'd be glad to then."

Man, oh, man! He was not only a Prince in shining armor. He would be nice to his future father-in-law as well.

After he test hopped it, even doing his signature "Tennessee Waltz" of one wheel to the other to check low-speed aileron control, he said "Howie, it handles fine. Really just like a stock P-51."

Okay, he likes the babe, but how do I get him to commit to her? I thought it best just to blurt it out. I didn't quite say that she was damaged goods, but I did play up the fact that this beautiful girl had been put down in a class with all those bullies like Corsairs, Sea Furies, Thunderbolts, P-40s, P-38 Lightnings and what-nots. The street-smart gang. She, with her North American heritage, didn't belong there.

"Would you give me a letter stating your opinion as a test pilot of her status?"

"Certainly. I'll dictate one when I get back to Los Angeles and mail it to you." The knot was tied! She had a lover!

When his "To Whom It May Concern" letter arrived, I quickly drove the 25 miles from Santa Monica to the Regional FAA office at Van Nuys airport. The beautifully-phrased word that flowed from their leathered faces were "Looks good enough for us. Just get the specs drawn up, ailerons balanced by an A&P (top rung aviation mechanic), have him sign off in the plane's logbook, bring the log back with the specs and we'll okay it. We'll give you an ST-137." An ST-137? Wow! That's somewhat like Dave Lindsay would be required to get from the FAA to build his Cavaliers if he made even the slightest modification. An ST-137 could cost thousands of dollars, and I mean thousands, of testing, design, FAA test hopping, etc. For maybe only 500 bucks, I'd have one. A passport back into Limited country for my darling daughter! And I could even maybe make money on the deal. Why shouldn't a father expect some profit from his daughter's success in life? Other Mustang owners who wanted to clip their wings could use my ST-137 as a model, for a price, of course. I don't recall having the nerve to charge them. I did have my morals, after all.

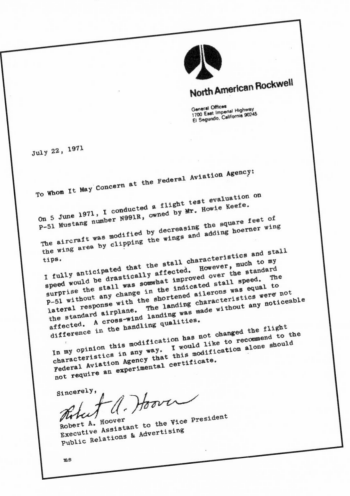

North American Rockwell

General Offices
1700 East Imperial Highway
El Segundo, California 90245

July 22, 1971

To Whom It May Concern at the Federal Aviation Agency:

On 5 June 1971, I conducted a flight test evaluation on P-51 Mustang number N991R, owned by Mr. Howie Keefe.

The aircraft was modified by decreasing the square feet of the wing area by clipping the wings and adding hoerner wing tips.

I fully anticipated that the stall characteristics and stall speed would be drastically affected. However, much to my surprise the stall was somwhat improved over the standard P-51 without any change in the indicated stall speed. The lateral response with the shortened ailerons was equal to the standard airplane. The landing characteristics were not affected. A cross-wind landing was made without any noticeable difference in the handling qualities.

In my opinion this modification has not changed the flight characteristics in any way. I would like to recommend to the Federal Aviation Agency that this modification alone should not require an experimental certificate.

Sincerely,

Robert A. Hoover
Executive Assistant to the Vice President
Public Relations & Advertising

ms

The Two-Year Nightmare Starts
"It's Even Painful to Write About It"

I don't know the best way to relate this two-year nightmare.

Of all the ongoing flight problems, this was the worst in my 12 years of racing and flying "Miss America." If I reveal the cause at the outset, it denies me being able to express my angst over each episode and will be somewhat like telling who killed the butler at the beginning of a mystery story. (Yeah, I know.) Why was I dropping out of the sky and making emergency landings from 20,000 feet up at such wide-spread airports as Winslow, Arizona and Toledo, Ohio—or lost races and time in the St. Louis area at Alton, Illinois and San Diego, California race events? I'd like you, the reader, to suffer as long and as often as I had. I want to relate every tiny detail, frustration, concern and expense that it caused me—but I'm going to spare you. No reason you should endure what I had to.

Okay, here it is. The killer, actually it was a pair of killers, was like a disease that lies dormant in your body for years, defies detection in routine tests, flares up when you least expect it, then runs and hides again when the experts are called in. It is so insidious that it imitates other organs so well that it throws you off the track and are sure you found the cure by fixing something else. It even has a name that starts with the "Dial M for Murder." It was the magnetos!—there, I said it. But don't go away.

I mentioned magnetos in my experience with the Cessna 172. But their place in an engine bears repeating to set the stage for understanding my nightmare. This is dull stuff for pilots, but the importance of the magnetos to an aircraft engine is the same as yeast is to a cake-baker. Without functioning well, things don't rise. Magnetos are part of the main difference between aircraft and car engines. They make planes safer. In a car, there is one spark plug per cylinder; in a plane there are two. Each has its own electrical system firing it. If one plug goes bad, the other does the job of firing that cylinder. A pilot always runs-up the engine to a specified minimum RPM to "check the mags," but what he is really doing is checking mainly the plugs. This mind-set of "checking the plugs" which can often fail due to carbon, getting "wet," overheating, etc., versus the magneto itself, which you don't think of as the cause unless there is a blatant discrepancy.

On the ground and during run-ups to even 2,400 RPM instead of the normal run-up of 1,800 RPM to check the mags, everything was always good. Adding to the confusion was the fact that Champion was always developing new spark plugs for us to use. No other engines on tractors, buses, etc., used them. In a sense, the Rolls Royce Merlin was a test bed. We focused on the plugs. When I was flying back from New Jersey to Chicago at about 20,000 feet just past Cleveland, the engine first got rough then started to really rattle and shake. I could have turned back to Cleveland's large Hopkins Airport and made it easily, but, damn it, I wanted someone from Champion Spark Plug to see the problem firsthand. I chose Toledo for my emergency landing.

Don Hullet was the race plane expert for Champion but he wasn't there that day. Bill Paradise, also a race-plug specialist, came out to the Toledo airport instead. He brought a new set of plugs so mine could be taken back to their lab for examination. (Later, the report was that the plugs were fine.) With new plugs in, everything would be fine, right? Wrong! All went well to Chicago, to Kansas City, to Liberal, Kansas. Over Winslow, Arizona at about 20,000 feet, WHAM!...the entire scenario started over again. Winslow airport is not only large and the base for fire-fighting tankers, but in the middle of June, it's almost vacant. It did not have a tower. It was easy to land on any runway I wanted. I descended in a tight circle over the airport so if the engine quit entirely, I could make any runway with ease. As always, in an emergency landing, halfway down any runway over 4,000 feet long is my target to land. None of this trying to put it "on the numbers" at the beginning of a runway. I've seen too many guys without power come up short.

A call to Dave Zeuschel my engine man explaining the series of events brought him out the next day from Los Angeles in his own Mustang. He now suspected the magnetos. He brought two rebuilt ones with him, installed them and we flew back to Van Nuys in formation.

After that, it happened again at the San Diego Cup races and in the race from Milwaukee to Alton, Illinois in the St. Louis area. But suddenly it was happening to others. Dr. Burns Byrum had a similar event over Iowa on a routine flight. Several other reports came in. They weren't using experimental racing-engine plugs; theirs were standard. So, the butler didn't do it! Now the mags were on the hot seat and they confessed. Here was a part of the engine that we were using with full trust that was last manufactured in 1944. Upon checking military specs, they showed a mag had a "shelf-life" of 4 years. Four years? This was 1971, 27 years later, almost seven times the 4-year shelf-life, 23 years "out-of-warranty" and it was, in a sense, the heart of the engine's power source. We were grounded by Father Time. There were no substitutes, no replacements.

Like any good engine man, Dave Zeuschel sprang into action. He found a source to make brand-new mags. Mags that would fire a jolting 5,000 volts into a spark plug. They looked beautiful, were beautiful in operation and made my life beautiful—to say nothing of Champion's relief to get off the suspect list. Mustangs flying today owe those of us who flew in 1971 a debt of gratitude. The mags could just as well have lasted 60 years and today's Mustang pilots would be dropping out of the sky!

Leo "Baron" Volkmer—A Fresh Breeze!

Baron Volkmer was one of my first trainees in T-6 racing. He had style, class and a friendly attitude. A real pleasure to be around. Always smiling, always willing. His T-6 was as neat and tasteful as his Dutch heritage. It was all white with a modest-sized emblem of the Royal Dutch Air Force on its side. With less than 2 years of T-6 racing under his belt, he was going to put on an air race. It was to be held in 1971 over Memorial Day weekend, in Alton, Illinois, just across the Mississippi River from St. Louis. The Unlimiteds would not be racing. There wasn't enough open space, but he wanted the Unlimiteds at his "show." In conjunction with EAA and Paul Poberezny, head of EAA, he arranged for a start at the same field the now defunct cross-country races started, Mitchell Field in Milwaukee. The finish line would be at the center of the airport at Alton, hopefully drawing a crowd from St. Louis. Then at Alton, he would have a new and novel idea to draw crowds and P-51s, a "P-51 Tournament."

The race itself was novel. It was just under 350 miles or about 4 times longer than the 80 plus miles of the pylon races at Reno. But no turns. Interesting. It brought a new dimension to air racing, the profile. Planning the profile of your flight, how high to climb, reach it early and fly it a while or plan to be at that altitude for a moment halfway, about 175 miles, and then make a long fast, full power dive to Alton...or stay lower all the way at high power.

Leo "Baron" Volkmer — a friendly Dutchman.

My calculations opted for the climb-then-dive profile. It made me feel good to learn later that the winner, Clay Lacy, an experienced airline captain, had also chosen this strategy, but it was of little comfort, not that I came in third, but the way it happened.

The takeoff from Milwaukee in cloudless skies on May 29, 1971 was uneventful, which means that instead of concentrating on weather, racing and navigation, only the latter two needed my attention. I can't recall and my logbook doesn't show the altitude I picked, but let's say it was 16,000 feet. Milwaukee and Alton (now also called St. Louis Regional) were about the same altitude above sea level, so that wasn't a factor. My logs do show that I planned to run at 90" manifold pressure and use water injection (ADI). I had 70 gallons of it on board, 50/50 distilled water/methanol. Then I'll get to 16,000 feet that way at about 2,000 feet per minute climb rate for 8 minutes. That would put me high about halfway to Chicago and a long dive to Alton at high power. I'd be going close to redline of over 400 mph. This was going to be fun! Going "down hill" for 45 minutes passing up everything in sight. I forget how we had FAA's permission to exceed the 288 mph (250 knots) speed limit below 10,000 feet, but all 8 of us would and did.

About halfway, my engine started running rough again. I pulled back to 60", still rough. Forty inches, still rough. At 20" it seemed to go away. But at that manifold pressure, I'd barely be flying. I remembered my experience with the Cessna 172. If I had done an in-air check of the mags, I would have discovered that I had at least some smooth power. But an in-air check, at even low power with a Merlin might cause a backfire and the carburetor would get blown and then I'd have no power. I had about 12,000 feet now and down below were interstates and a fair choice of airports in the Peoria area. I swallowed hard and switched to R (right mag) on the ignition switch. No unusual drop in RPM. Then to L and all hell broke loose! The engine shook like a bull ready to charge. Back to "R" fast! Okay, that was it. Fly it just on "R" (really the left mag)…and finish the race on just one mag—not recommended for the faint of heart, but I had altitude and I was a divorced man.

Power. That was the question now. How much power can I put into a Merlin engine with just one mag operating? I had never thought of that before. I didn't know then and I don't know the answer to this day. Some might guess, but who has tried it? My no-brainer was to not turn back on the ADI and bring the power back to normal cruise of about 30–36 inches. I made my descent shallower, but by now all my calculations were out the window. I didn't have time to work up a new set and at the same time navigate and keep a sharp eye on the engine instruments. I'd just wing it. I saw the Alton airport ahead, steepened my dive a little bit. Only one plane, Lacy's, was there on the ground. Maybe I can take second place. That's good. Just at that moment I saw a yellow Mustang zoom under me and cross the finish line 15 seconds ahead of me! Where did he come from? It was Leroy Penhall in his new P-51. He was in the race too.

When I asked Leroy after the race, where he came from? What profile he flew? His answer riled me at first and then I had to laugh at how ludicrous the entire thing was. When talking to you, Leroy had the habit of turning slightly to the side, bending his head forward and then turning it toward you, looking at you over the side of his glasses. When it seemed he didn't want to say something, his mouth area tightened a bit. That's the way it was now. "Well," he started, "I took off from Milwaukee heading directly southwest almost on course. You took off in the opposite direction and had to double-back over the airport. I don't think you saw me a little below you. You were climbing up faster. The thought ran through my mind that I would follow you. I wasn't that good at navigation yet and you had military experience plus you had published charts for pilots. I found that with my ADI on, I could stay just under and behind you. The longer I did it, the more I figured it was working for me. And then I'd dive ahead of you at the finish like Weiner did once—he had heard that rumor too. But tell me, why did you slow down so much?—and then speed up again?—and then go so much slower the rest of the way? I almost shot past you before I realized you had slowed down. I almost had my plane back to idle for a while there."

I had to laugh at how puzzled he must have been when I slowed down to do the mag check, then resume partial speed in a race while he was trying to remain back and unnoticed. Had he gone on his own at that time, he might have come in first ahead of Lacy.

Leroy Penhall was killed about 10 years later while climbing out of Mammoth Mountain airport at the end of a ski trip flying his twin-engine Duke Beechcraft. He had one of his sons and a friend's son aboard. Two items probably caused him to crash after stalling out in a nose-high turn. It was reported that a friend's plane had taken off before him and he was eager to catch up with him. There was a slight layer of frost on his wings that he did not take the time to clean off. He was taking off north and had to turn to the south to get back to Los Angeles and catch up with the other plane. To the north of Mammoth, the ground rises rapidly. It's easy to get fooled into thinking the horizon you see, of where the earth meets the sky, is the horizon. The real horizon is at the base of the mountains or even below that. This can cause a nose-high turn. Add the high altitude of nearly 8,000 feet, wings coated with frost and all the ingredients for a stall-spin are there.

The rest of the tournament had speed runs and time to climb. I got only 398 mph in the speed runs with the mag acting up again. In the time-to-climb to 1,000 feet from a standing start on the runway, I took second place (again, Lacy was first) with a time of 30 seconds to 1,087 feet, but I had clipped wings. I was happy with that performance with less lift than Lacy had. Adding full power to a Merlin engine from a standing start should not be tried by a novice. You might wind up on your back. The power of the Merlin is awesome. I think many of the accidents pilots have had in the Mustang are because they tried to emulate experienced pilots, particularly Bob Hoover, who makes it look so easy.

Cape May, New Jersey Races • June 1971
And the T-6 Tragedy!
(We Lost Four T-6 Pilots in the Worst Race Tragedy Ever)

Going to Cape May, New Jersey after the cross-country race to Alton, I took along Roger Davies as a passenger. Roger was Ormond Haydon-Baillie's crew chief. Ormond's Sea Fury could not carry passengers and my rear seat was wide open. It was an 800-mile flight of a little over $2^1/_2$ hours and I welcomed the company. Roger was always good for a few laughs. Playing tricks on someone was not beneath his British dignity. He liked to recount them holding a beer in his hand and throwing his head back as he delivered the punch line.

The airport at Cape May did not have a control tower. I wanted to fly over at about 3,000 feet high to check out what was going on. As we were circling the field, Roger tapped me on the shoulder and pointed to the ground. I looked and then gave him a shrug of my shoulders showing I didn't understand what he was pointing at. He picked up his mike on the intercom circuit and said that Ormond Haydon-Baillie was taxiing in. He'd be putting on an arrival show—Ormond even had me beat in that department. He'd be folding up his Sea Fury's wings as he was coming to a stop. That would make the last 50 yards of his entry a very "prancing one" as he loved to say. At the stop with engine off, he would push back the canopy, put on his officer's cap—he was a Royal Canadian Air Force (RCAF) pilot—hop out onto the wing with his officer's crop tucked under his left arm and survey the scene in front of him, hoping to spot a fair damsel's welcoming smile in the crowd.

Roger sometimes can't get through the story of what happened next. He'd get laughing so hard, he'd be spitting out beer. Roger told me of this progressive scene over the intercom and suggested we give Ormond a low altitude buzz job as he stood there. I, too, didn't mind a little fun now and then. Because I was so high and didn't want the scene to get away from me with delays, I pointed the nose of the plane straight down at Ormond in about a 70° angle dive—virtually straight down—and then at the last minute swooped up high. I couldn't see behind me, but Roger could. In telling the story, this is where Roger becomes unintelligible. Ormond, caught unaware, said he heard this screaming high-speed noise getting louder and louder, but he couldn't see where it was coming from. From 6 feet in the air he jumped off the plane and landed on his hands and knees. He remained on the ground on all fours watching "Miss America" disappear straight up. The timing was perfect. But knowing Ormond, some sweet, young thing probably came over and caressed him, thinking he was hurt. If one did, I'm sure he'd add the jump to his routine next time!

My sponsor, COX Models, had made this race a big promotional event among their eastern sales force and customers. It was rare to have Unlimited races in the east. There had never been any in modern times. COX had come out with their gas-powered U-control model of "Miss America." All other models had been military designs. They had never had a "personality" plane and the pilot to go along with it to greet people. The people who had recently purchased COX, Leisure Dynamic in Minneapolis, had directed COX to put some "marketing life" into their products. They wanted to expand from the hobby stores into the K-Marts with something that would catch a grandmother's eye for a gift. Ben Garrett, their savvy marketing director, approached Art Scholl, a famous aerobatic pilot, and myself to see if we'd be interested in their sponsorship. Interested? I almost couldn't let go of his hand when I shook it. Art was much more blasé. He had sponsors like Pennzoil and a lot of experience at air shows and promotions. To him, this would be a new world and fun. To me, it would help stop the drain on my pocketbook.

Bill Selzer, the affable president of COX, was there. Bill was a WWII B-17 gunner—they called the P-51 "Little Friend." Bill had red/white/blue race crew jackets with "Miss America" and COX emblems for all the customers, sales staff and even all the children that came. It was quite a sight to see: almost 30 people from large men to little girls in skirts all with "Miss A" jackets on everywhere I looked. My contribution was

Mike Foster was a human forklift! One time I heard him ask "Where do you want it?" He had a bear hug on a 50-gallon drum of methanol holding it 2 feet above the ground—it must have weighed 400 pounds! We made sure he got all the food he wanted!

getting stuck in the soft turf between the taxiways and needing a local farmer's tractor to pull me out. With no interesting pictures the first day, it ran on the front page of the local paper. The COX emblem on the side of the plane was large enough for all to see. Of course, my peers contended I had staged the entire thing. They even pointed out that they saw me directing the photographer to take a side shot so the COX emblem could be seen. I wasn't that alert. A side shot showed best the tractor doing the pulling. Besides, I had to be in the plane to ride the brakes when we got on the pavement. Even that didn't fly with them. Having a red/white/blue plane with the name "Miss America" gives others the impression you're a promoter! How could they think that?

I had complained at the Reno races that on the new race course, the start location where Bob Hoover released us was unfair to the slower planes in the heat races where your individual time placed you in successive race brackets. On the old course, we were released at the home pylon in front of the crowd. We crossed the start line within

a few seconds of each other. The clock starts when the first plane crosses the start line. But on the new long course and the overflying of the crowd by planes on the outside, the FAA stepped in and stopped that. They should have because with the planes so close together, a midair collision over the crowd would have been a disaster.

But the start line and the pace plane's release of the racers was moved to a position going away from the crowd to the farthest-away pylon. This meant that you were flying almost a full lap to get back to the home pylon where the race starts when the first plane crosses it. If there is a much faster plane in your heat, you might be 2 miles behind when he crosses the start line and the clock starts on you then, not when *you* cross the start line. It makes

This photo of Ormond Haydon-Baillie by Tegler is a classic, showing this lovable Brit at his best. He could have upstaged Roscoe Turner as a showman! (John Tegler photo)

your time slower than the same plane as yours that is in the next heat with a slower plane causing the clock to start. This could make you wind up in a lower money bracket event in the finals. It doesn't make any difference except in races where you can get bumped down by a plane that is even slower than yours. I think they still use that crazy system. The race and timing should start when the planes are released with "Gentlemen, you have a race!" not when a fast plane gets ahead of the pack and starts the clock on everyone behind him.

My wish for an even start almost got me done in! It was done right in front of the crowd alright, but within 5 seconds after the release, we had the first pylon turn. It must have been nearly a 120-degree turn like a scatter pylon to get to the course away from houses. To get the space for an Unlimited Race that requires a mile distance from any belly-up turns and people, the course had to go back out into the bay west of Cape May. That produced a weird set of circumstances in itself. The pylons in the bay were balloons tied to anchored row boats. The problem was that the anchors were not strong enough to keep the boats from the moving from the forces of wind and tide. A dense forest of tall pine went almost to the waters edge. You couldn't see the rowboats until the last minute. On one lap, the balloons would be to left of course, on the next lap to the right or close to shore. The danger was that a plane ahead might suddenly turn into you to avoid cutting a pylon. My problem came at the start.

Ormond, in his Sea Fury RAF carrier plane, and I got to the first pylon at the same time. I sucked it in for a high-G left turn. He did too, but his engine turns the opposite way from the Mustang. It tends to pull the plane to the right. In a high-G turn, the force is even greater. It pulled him up high, causing him to almost roll over

Ormond's Sea Fury dove down in front of me while I was on my side in a turn. Suddenly I was on my back at treetop level!

onto his back and dive to get back on course. Out of the corner of my eye I saw him diving down. His extra speed in the dive put him about two plane lengths ahead of me. Just as I was starting the next left turn, he had swooped down dead ahead of me. His prop wash was so violent that I suddenly was on my back before I knew what had happened. I recall looking down and seeing the trees whizzing by just below my head. It was almost as if the canopy was going to be scratched by the tree tops. Suddenly that pre-programmed thing in my brain took over and I finished the roll in the same direction it had started but slightly nose-up. The generally accepted technique at low altitudes is not to try to fight the direction of the roll. Use its momentum to keep it going on around. The natural reaction is to fight the force. But you don't know if the force has left you or if it's still there. Behind that big Centurion 18-cylinder engine of the Sea Fury, you can bet it was still there. It took me a few hours to get over that one. I told Ormond that without knowing it, he had sure gotten back at me for the buzz job I did on him.

I shake my head at Ormond's death at the U.S. Air Force Base in Mainz, Germany. He begged me to fly his Mustang in this show so he could fly his Sea Fury because the Air Force wanted the Mustang for sure. I was on my way from the Paris Air Show to "do my roots" in Ireland. On a stop-over in London, I dropped in on him. Ormond Haydon-Baillie was killed in his P-51 Mustang in the mid-'70s in Germany during preshow publicity fly-bys for TV coverage. Killed riding with him was the Glider Champion of Germany. From the minute I stepped in his house in London, he was requesting, begging, pleading with me to abort my trip to Ireland and stay the week with him. He had just gotten a Mustang from somewhere in Italy.

He drove me to Heathrow the next day. I had never driven with him. Not only was he driving on the wrong side of the road, he was looking more at me than the road while still insisting I stay and fly his Mustang to Germany while he flew his Sea Fury. We would fly formation in the show. We were in his top-down Austin–Healy. I think I just closed my eyes, feeling I'd rather die without knowing than seeing the impact coming. He dropped me off at the circle in Heathrow where Aer Lingus was but made me promise to stay at the curb until he parked and came back. I had 2 hours before my flight anyway. To him, parking his car was pulling it up on top of a narrow median strip, turning on the flashers and rushing back to me.

He sat on the curb, I sat on my bags. He had now given up trying to get me to stay. He wanted me to tell him all I knew about the Mustang. I reminded him that he had been flying his Sea Fury, a Navy carrier plane, with good control at slow speeds. That the Mustang was built for speed. Most accidents were the stall-spin type at low altitudes at slow speed. Avoid any nose-high slow speed (under 200 mph) turns. The story I heard about the crash is that he was making a low pass in front of the TV camera, pulled up in a nose-high turn to come back for another pass, stalled and spun in. What a nice guy he was. What a waste. One aviation writer opined that without H-B at the races anymore, they seemed hollow. I agree.

But a real tragedy was about to happen in front of us all at Cape May's first T-6 race. Four pilots would die within four minutes of the race start. Four factors caused it:

1. It was the first ever air-start for a T-6 race.
2. The pace-plane pilot was inexperienced at air starts.
3. It was mostly over a forested area.
4. There was a strong wind.

My home movies show the first crash. I was focused on the racers coming toward the crowd, but what I saw in my view finder so startled me, I lowered the camera in disbelief! It looked like flattened cardboard boxes were blowing off a speeding truck. It was the simultaneous break up of three planes with their pieces flying through the air. Everyone was speechless. What had happened? What could you do? It was awful!

Here's what happened. In an air start, the planes dive down in a ragged line-abreast formation. Each pilot's eyes are trained on the plane next to him. The pole-plane's eyes are trained on the pace plane. Only the pace-plane's eyes are looking where you are going. Instead of saying "Gentleman, you have a race" at a high enough altitude so that their eyes can look straight ahead on the course while still being aware of the planes around them, the pace plane swooped down almost to the ground before releasing them. What they saw ahead was a mass of trees coming at them at over 200 mph. There was no time to think. Pulling up was the only option and it had to be done quickly while entering a turn at the first pylon. A plane below Dick Minges, he not seeing Dick above him and Dick not being able to see below the large T-6 wing, pulled into a sharp left turn and slight climb. His canopy came in contact with Dick's wing, broke it off and Dick did a one-wing twirl into the ground.

The fellow whose canopy was crushed, fortunately just the back seat area, immediately pulled out of the race and landed. None of the other racers saw or knew what had happened. After another two laps had gone by, the race officials decided to stop the race because it was right over the rescue squad at the fallen plane. They lit a red smoke bomb/flare near the finish line. The wind was so strong that the smoke just strung along the ground. As the racers came around a pylon to enter the straight-away where the red smoke was, there was still forest and they were low down, they couldn't see it until they suddenly came into the opening. The lead plane, my attorney and friend, Vic Baker, immediately pulled up just as Ed Snyder, flying above and slightly to the right of him pulled over him. Vic's wing hit Ed's wing and both wings broke off. High speeds cause high-wing loads, and it doesn't take much more pressure to snap a wing off. The third plane was flying behind them, Jay Quinn, a young handsome, blond fireman from Van Nuys. He was so close behind that he had no chance to avoid the debris that filled the air. It was all over in less than 20 seconds. The best I could do was to take Ed Snyder's wife, Jere, into a nearby line office and attempt to comfort her. She was one sweet southern lady. All she could do was stare at me with wide, open eyes and mouth. I think she was in shock for a moment. She said later that she was so stunned she couldn't cry or feel anything. Twenty-five years later when she visited us in California, she was still thanking me for being there. Of the six of us in the Unlimited class scheduled to race later, only three took off. We had all been in the service and were somewhat hardened having seen our share of crashes and losing friends. The other three couldn't make it. Leroy Penhall was so struck by the event that he was throwing up on the flight line next to his plane.

The irony of it all was that in 1933 New Jersey had banned air racing in the state. A local Cape May politician had lobbied their assembly to lift the ban. It would be good publicity for the primarily tourist area at the isolated southern tip of New Jersey. A very congenial Cape May booster, Steve Cicala, almost single-handedly promoted and put on the races. He was devastated. There hasn't been a race in New Jersey since. I wonder if the ban on air racing in the state was ever lifted.

U.S. Cup Race—1,000 Miles
Brown Field San Diego, California • July 18, 1971
"Near Crash at Start—Bearcat Crashes—Fateful Finish"

This is what I vividly recall about this race from 30 years ago.

1. Almost crashing on takeoff trapped in prop wash.
2. Sherm Cooper's Sea Fury up-swoops at pylons.
3. Stench of Mike Geren's burning body.
4. Barely being able to keep flying with a fuel load.
5. The traffic jam that delayed the start.

Never had I ever, then or since, had so many experiences in one race event! It seemed like an evolving nightmare from beginning to end. I had experienced long-distance pylon racing at Mojave the year before. I was looking forward to a second race like Mojave. I knew now I could stand the $2^1/_2$ hours of flying around pylons. My hope was that this one would be in the traditional counterclockwise direction. The way the prop turns on the Mustang and all U.S. planes makes it much easier on long races to make left turns. The prop torque helps. You just lay the plane over in a 45- to 60-degree bank depending on the course to the next pylon, pull back then push forward on the stick (to keep it from climbing in the turns, a rookie turn) and then roll out with hardly any rudder pressure needed to enter or in the turn itself. It's like ski turns in fresh powder. They just happen.

Well, the course wasn't counterclockwise. It was clockwise. It would be $2^1/_2$ hours of right turns. But there were two great new rules for this race versus the one at Mojave:

1. Everyone had to make one mandatory pit stop—I think it was for a minimum of 10 or 15 minutes, I can't recall. Not only would this level the playing field of planes able to carry enough fuel to fly the 1,000 miles without stopping (e.g., Sherm Cooper's Sea Fury that had won at Mojave by being able to go nonstop) versus the majority of other planes, but it would be great theater for the crowd watching the planes taxi in, shut down, refuel, restart and taxi back out to rejoin the fray.

2. No 4-engine airliners! Indy doesn't allow buses in its 500, why should we have to fly a course clogged up by them either? "Fish" Salmon, a legendary Lockheed test pilot, showed up with a 4-engine Lockheed Constellation, the tri-tail classic, "Connie" because the rule had not been set in stone. However, the pilots voted against it, especially those of us who had raced at Mojave when the DC-7B was on the course. It might have been a great spectator sight taxiing in to the pits for the pit stop, shutting down all 4 engines, waiting the time to restart, restarting all 4 engines, then making a lumbering turn in the pits back out to the runway. In the turn, its prop wash hitting the grandstand might have blown every girl's new hairdo apart. Maybe a good show, but lousy pylon racing.

"Miss America" was hot in the qualifying times. She qualified second to Lyle Shelton's Bearcat at 374 mph, a good time in those days. I was pleased, very pleased. None of the engine problems that had been plaguing me (which turned out, as I have already divulged, to be the mags). Also, our HQ hotel where we stayed was the Hotel del Coronado, called the "Del" by those in the know. The Del is one of the 3 Grande Dames. The others are the Empress Hotel in Victoria, B.C., Canada and the Grand Hotel on Mackinac Island in upper Michigan. Some would like to include the Breakers in Palm Beach, the Banff resort-hotel in Alberta, Canada and the Fountainbleau in Quebec, but to me they lack the grace. View and glitter don't count.

Brown Field is right next to the Mexican border. As a matter of fact, if you fly a wide traffic pattern south of the field, you could be in the air space of Tijuana's tower. They're that close. Naturally, our course had to be laid out going north out of Brown Field. To the east of Brown were the wastelands and nondescript hills of the Otay area. They are plane-hostile. You don't want to even look in that direction. Pretty much the same thing to the north. To the west was friendly country. Only 10 miles away was the Pacific Ocean on a line with the Navy's famous North Island Naval Air Station. They'd love to have a P-51 make an emergency landing there—they'd adore a Bearcat, I'm sure. The stove-pipe jets lack style.

The problem. As at the St. Louis Air Races, a two-lane winding road snaking in from San Diego from the west was the only in-out road from the

Pilot Killed as Racing Plane Burns, Crashes

World War II Fighter Craft Was Flying in Contest at San Diego

Exclusive to The Times from a Staff Writer

SAN DIEGO—A World War II Navy fighter plane burst into flames during the U.S. Cup air race at Brown Field Sunday and crashed more than a mile from the grandstand, carrying its pilot to his death.

Witnesses said the aircraft, a Grumman Bearcat, first trailed smoke and then began to spout flames from its engine cowling on the 95th lap of the 1,000-mile low-altitude race.

Pilot Michael Allen Geren, 32, of Kansas City, a professional airline captain, pulled up and out of the race in which he was in fifth position and turned back for an approach on the east-west runway.

Plunges and Explodes

Officials of the American Pylon Racing Assn., which sponsors the annual race, said he was at 300 feet when he apparently lost control of the aircraft, which plunged to earth and exploded.

The air race continued despite the burning wreckage nearby.

Of 16 aircraft that began the race, only 12 were able to finish, though Geren's was the only crash of the day. Three other fliers pulled out of the contest due to mechanical difficulties.

populous San Diego area into Brown Field. Having been at St. Louis and seeing the traffic jam there, it was a no-brainer to predict there would be one at Brown. The race was to start at noon so I made it a point to be off the road at least by 9:00 a.m. on race day, Sunday. Even at that, they had the gate entrance so crawling with security measures to make sure no one would sneak in, there was a delay in getting our own cars in. They had already started to turn the 3 miles of the 2-lane entrance road into a one-way road.

At 11:00 a.m., an hour before the race was to start, I started to warm up the engine, check the ADI system, do a mag check, get the oil temperature up to the green, etc. We received word about 11:45 to taxi out to the runway and take up our takeoff positions. We would be in groups of three, staggered to the left. The pole plane, Lyle Shelton's Bearcat, would be ahead at my right. As second fastest qualifier, I'd be a plane length behind him at his left with my right wing barely outside his left wing. In position, we got the orders to shut down our engines because there was a delay. The traffic was bumper-to-bumper almost the entire 15 miles back to San Diego including the freeway off-ramp and the freeway itself. I could imagine that they had maybe only two ticket-takers at the gate, stopping each car and having to make change. The race sponsors, I think Darryl Greenamyer was in on it along with Tony LeVier, were frantic, as they should be. There were bundles of cash sitting out there. We must have waited almost an hour to start. But it was to be an almost 3-hour race, so it was somewhat like a football game. You could get in late and still see the game.

Finally the word was given to restart our engines. That was only a problem for those who needed a power cart with a generator on it that plugged into a receptacle

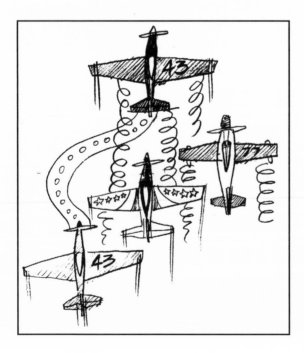

At the race start, Shelton (77), the fastest qualifier, had the pole position, I was second and Penhall (43) was third. But Shelton added wing tanks and was slow to start. Penhall whipped around me. As I staggered off with my heavier load, I thought for sure their prop wash would flatten me into the ground. It was all I could do to keep the plane upright and straight until I got clean air!

on the side of the plane to get enough starting juice. With all the air show and cross-country flying I did, I had to be able to start with my own built-in system.

What happened after the checkered flag went down to start the race is still an incident I hope I'll never have to live through again in an airplane, especially one heavily loaded with high-octane fuel and 100 gallons of highly inflammable methanol in a vinyl bladder in the cockpit behind me.

Shelton had added large wing tanks to his plane. He had qualified without them. Never before did we have a situation where a plane that qualified had its flight characteristics significantly modified when it raced. Those tanks might have been 100 gallons each, or 200 gallons total. Gas weighs 6 pounds per gallon so we are talking taking off with 1,200 pounds more weight plus the drag of the tanks. If we each had a clear takeoff runway of our own, no problem. But in a tight takeoff formation, it was a problem. A big problem, because I was the meat in the sandwich. I was trapped between Leroy Penhall's P-51, third fastest qualifier on my left and Shelton's lumbering Bearcat on my right. I have often thought of what might have happened if I had slowed my takeoff so Shelton could get out ahead and away. The only scene I come up with is the plane in the middle behind me chewing up my tail and others piling into that mess. It sure would have made the front pages and the news highlights that night.

Not that I was a nimble-footed babe myself. I had qualified, but not with the 600 pounds of methanol in the cockpit bladder tank behind me. I needed only half of what the bladders in the machine-gun bay held. But I had a lot better takeoff speed than Shelton's Bearcat had. My home movies taken by my crew show the entire thing. I take a deep breath each time I watch that race start. I sometimes think I just might crash the next time I view it.

The checkered flag went down, I powered up. I powered down, fast! Shelton was barely moving. At about 30", one-half the regular takeoff power of 60", I was going down the runway. The plane was trying to get airborne. Shelton was about 20 feet higher, but we still had wing overlap. I was literally staggering off the ground and the end of the runway was coming up. Gradually, Shelton's speed increased. I could add more power. Just at that moment Penhall, who gained speed by pulling off to the left to avoid me, cut right back in front of me to go on course and pass Shelton. My wings had been clipped. Thirty percent had been taken off my ailerons in the process. I was trapped in the prop wash of a Bearcat and a P-51 while being able to pull only low power 10 feet off the deck. I had the thought of bouncing down on the runway until the tornado I was in softened, but there wasn't much runway left and there was a pack of hounds behind me. As Penhall passed Shelton, I felt there was clear air to my left. I coaxed the plane left, keeping it stable by controlling it with the rudder until the mini-ailerons would be effective. What a relief to be able to add full power and get her up above the earth where she belonged.

In a long-distance race, loaded with extra gas and extra ADI tanks, we are all fairly close in speed. The hot shots that are designed to race only 10 to 12 minutes at the Reno races can't compete in these long-distance pylon races. No one can really zoom past another. Your flying skills come more into play. And the best place to sneak ahead of another plane is at a pylon turn. In a straight-away from pylon to pylon, no special flying ability is needed as long as you head for the next pylon. It's rare for planes of somewhat equal speed to pass another. It's not like oval-track auto racing where one might go high on the straight-away coming out of a turn and the other might go low and pass them. Yes, that could happen if racing against a rookie pilot, but rarely. Overtaking one on a pylon turn is the more probable place to move ahead.

I use the term "rookie" not for new race pilots, but for those who just don't seem to grasp the basics. They can be old-timers like Mike Loening who blew his engine doing over 400 mph and, instead of pulling up to get altitude and then glide back down, immediately dove for the nearest runway, came in downwind and had to ground loop at the end of the runway at Reno to keep from going over a steep cliff. A "rookie" to me is one who puts his gear and flaps down with a dead engine before being over the runway. To me, a "rookie" on a race course is one who zooms upward when rounding a pylon at the turn—he does not understand that when you put a wing down to make a turn at high speed the extra lift created will cause the plane to rise. What you need to do is to push forward, not pull back on the stick as you would do at normal speeds. Those of you who watch the races, note the pilots who don't understand the plane's tendency to climb.

I have struggled with what I am about to say, because it is a critique of a fellow race pilot who is now dead. Sherm Cooper was killed in a Pitts aerobatic plane that had known wing-spar damage and crashed when the wing collapsed while he was doing aerobatics. He was a successful orthodontist in Merced, California. His plane was a Sea Fury painted in the flamboyant style of yellow with the flames of Hades coming out of the engine cowl. I liked any paint scheme that didn't make a war plane look like a Bonanza. Like boats, I still think every plane should have a name. Why not? Kids would love it.

To let planes race without a name confuses the race fans. To post times using a pilot's name (who could be assigned to fly several different planes) would be like posting jockeys' name as winners instead of the name of the horse. Major sponsors want the company name in the plane name (e.g., "Miss Budweiser") in the posted results. Air racing pilots and especially air race management have been naive in not recognizing that it is the plane and not the pilot that wins a race—and the way to get major sponsors is to have their name in bright lights. Pilots should insist on it. Any good pilot flying a fast plane can win a race. In the old days, a pilot owned and flew his own plane. Today companies, museums and nonflying people own the planes. One pilot can qualify a plane owned by someone else and a second pilot can fly it in the heat race and yet a third pilot fly and win in the finals. Like a race horse with many different jockeys, only the plane should be called the winner. The pilot, like the jockey, should be a subtitle.

Back to the race course. Trying to pass Cooper's Sea Fury became my main objective. I was maybe only 5 to 10 mph faster than he was. I'd pull in just behind him on the straight-aways and get ready to pass him when he'd go into the turn low down on the course, but as soon as his wing was down, he'd zoom up over 50 feet leaving a large swath of air with the Sea Fury's heavy turbulent prop wash in trail. Even though he had gone up high, I couldn't risk going low and being turned upside-down in a steep bank by his descending prop wash and vortices (turbulence from vortices drops at the rate of 300 feet per minute, it doesn't just hang there). Flying under and behind planes like jets, you might think if you stay below you'll be safe. Not so. That's the most dangerous area. It wouldn't have been so bad if he had stayed high, but just before rolling out of the turn while still in a steep bank, he'd come shooting back down on the course. I couldn't risk being under him. He wouldn't know I was there until probably too late. My speed wasn't enough faster than his to fly wide around him. This happened pylon after pylon after pylon and was frustrating. In car races on an oval track, if one goes high on a turn, it's probably easy to cut under him by going low. Not in pylon air racing with the turbulence factor while you're banked well over on your side where you are vulnerable.

A rough-running engine started again. It took my focus away from the passing frustration to the engine. Damn! It's now about 1 hour into the 3-hour race. In another 30 minutes I had planned to make the mandatory fuel stop. If I stop now, I might have to make another stop for enough fuel to finish the race. I decided to reduce power from the 90" to 60" and turn off the water injection. It helped, but that was no way to win a race. I asked Race Control for permission to switch frequencies (you're required to stay on the Race Control frequency throughout the race) so I could tell my pit crew what the engine as doing. Dave Zeuschel came back with the reply of "Not only can I hear it when you go by, the timer says your lap speed has dropped way down. We'll be ready to change plugs when you land." Compared to the other times when I had to land at Toledo and Winslow with no one there, it was a welcome sight seeing three crewmen on either side wave me into the pit with their wrenches in hand. I like to rerun that scene several times on my home movies. It's like being wheeled into an operating room and seeing the masked surgeons and nurses with rubber gloves and hands elevated waiting to give you the fixer-upper...but without that nice spaced-out feeling from the pre-op drugs.

Dave had concluded it was the exhaust plugs that needed changing. They are the ones that get the hottest in the Merlin engine. Both sides of the lower cowl were off almost before the prop stopped. The wrenches seemed to dive on the plugs by themselves. I got out on the right wing to stretch my back and pour cold water over my very hot, bald head. Dave was taking out the exhaust plugs on that side. Once he had a broken a plug loose, no easy task when they are swollen from the heat, he impatiently twisted the additional 10 to 12 turns with his fingers, all the while uttering all the proper expressions of "damn, they're hot!...ouch! ouch!...damn, damn, damn." As each plug released, he'd toss it over his shoulder on to the ramp, where some of the younger crew from the next pit clamored after them for souvenirs. I noticed some of them dropping them quickly and snapping their fingers, then hovering over them like a bird over its prey. Dave said that he couldn't feel anything with the fingers of his right hand for over 6 months.

Back into the air and on the course again, at least that yo-yoing Sea Fury wasn't ahead of me. All was running smoothly. I was now in third place, but that was about to end. At the 15 minute mark, pulling 90" of manifold pressure, the engine started to get rough again. What the hell was wrong with those plugs? If you read the last few chapters carefully, you know, don't you? It wasn't the butler. I was lucky to finish in eighth place. As a matter of fact, I was lucky to finish at all. I returned to the prior routine of pulling back the power from 90", but this time down to 50" hoping that might help and again shutting down the water injection system to keep the engine from getting too cool. Engines need heat.

About this time, I caught a disturbing sight to my right. Mike Geren in his Bearcat had flames coming out of the exhaust stack on the right side. He was pulling to the inside of the course to presumably circle back to land. I was headed outbound on the course at the time. As I turned inbound, I could see the smoke from a crash on the base leg to the runway. It was directly below the course line—just 50 feet below where we were flying. My first over-flight was through bellowing smoke. By the time I came around again, the smoke had ebbed, but the cockpit air vent directed right at my face delivered the sickening odor of burning flesh. We were required to have oxygen masks on during a race, but that didn't seem to stifle it each time I passed over it. I tried not to inhale or breathe though my nose after passing that area.

Let me deal with Mike Geren's crash at this point. My movies show that he was probably dead before he crashed. His plane had entered a shallow right turn from which it never recovered. The Bearcat had magnesium cylinders and magnesium burns fiercely. I am convinced that the cause was that the fire had entered the cockpit through an air vent. He probably had his oxygen regulator set to "NORMAL" which meant that the air he was inhaling was part oxygen from his bottles and part air from the cockpit. The regulator determines that mix depending upon your altitude. The only other setting closes the system and all the air is from the bottles. Aircraft oxygen, by law, cannot have moisture in it as does medical oxygen. With any water content, the system might freeze up at the low temperatures at high-altitude. The problem is that in the FULL setting, it is so dry that your mouth thickens up to the point you can barely swallow. Your saliva glands can't keep up with your needs, especially when you're exerting yourself. I found myself stiffening my cheeks to get the sides of the oxygen mask to leak so I could breath more of the moisturized ambient air in the cockpit. When the flames reached the outside air intake of the oxygen regulator, which is normally mounted low at the right knee, the system exploded directly into his lungs. Bud Fountain's crash in a Bearcat was almost identical. He finished a race at Mojave. The right side exhaust stack was on the opposite side from the pits. I couldn't see if he had a stack fire. His plane started to climb, nosed over and plunged to the ground.

The end of the race had real drama too. My engine was running so rough, my log shows I had to throttle back to 28" before the roughness was tamed enough to keep flying, but I was barely flying at that low power. Adding to my dilemma was the 600 pounds of unused methanol I had behind me. Its weight was causing the center of gravity to go back so far that I had to crank in almost full forward trim on the elevator tab to keep the plane's nose from turning up. There was no drain to let me jettison the unused ADI overboard. The more gas I burned from the wings' tanks, the worse it became.

I was able to keep staggering around the course to finish the race, but I winced and held my breath each time another plane passed me and I had to deal with his prop wash too. I decided to fly the outside of the course, but as I turned down the home pylon runway in front of the crowd, I had to stay in that narrow slot. Over-flying the crowd not only disqualifies you from the race, it is sure to bring strong disciplinary action from the FAA.

At the last lap of the race, I decided not to press my luck anymore. I'd land and cross the finish line on the runway. I didn't want to take a chance at flying another lap or even pull off onto a downwind leg in a standard pattern. Then I did a dumb thing. I lowered my landing gear about 200 yards before the runway started. That added drag was too much to keep flying. I started to sink. My horror was having to land in the brush before I got to the runway. There wasn't time to retract the gear then lower it again. At that moment Gary Levitz in his P-38 radioed, "Howie! I have an engine on fire, please pull up so I can land." I keyed the mike and radioed back, "Sorry Gary, my power's gone, I'm sinking too fast. Land short behind me, I'll taxi tail-high as long as I can. Don't chew my tail off." He did, I did.

My "Never Again" Flight • August 16, 1971
"Trapped in a Winding Canyon"

It was on the way to an air show in Terrace, British Columbia, Canada about 90 miles from Kechikan, Alaska. I had flown in the air show at Abbotsford, British Columbia a few miles east of Vancouver. The Rotary Club at Terrace asked me to fly their air show the week after. My sponsor COX, was eager to have more exposure in Canada and encouraged me to go. They even approved of pretty Mary Hively, from their marketing department, to go along with me. First to Abbotsford and then on to Terrace. Tough assignment.

The Abbotsford Air Show was always a delight. Their hospitality and understanding and friendly DOT (their FAA) were a pleasure to deal with. Only Canadian customs seemed to be the stern ones in Canada. Following the show, we took off for the flight to Terrace a little over 450 miles to the north. The plan was to fly up the length of Vancouver Island, land at Port Hardy at the northern tip of Vancouver Island, gas up and head the last 150 miles to Terrace with enough fuel to fly back in case of bad weather.

The weather at Kitimat, 40 miles south of Terrace, was clear but there were no weather station reports between Port Hardy and Kitimat. The rule in Canada is that you cannot fly "on top" without being on an instrument flight plan. In the States, as long as you can see the ground where you are going, you can climb above the clouds and fly "on top" in clear air over a solid area of clouds. I decided to play ball. "When in Rome, etc." We gassed up, took off from Port Hardy and headed north along the coast. Without radio navigation aids for the route to allow an IFR flight plan, I planned to fly north along the coastline until I came to the Douglas Channel.

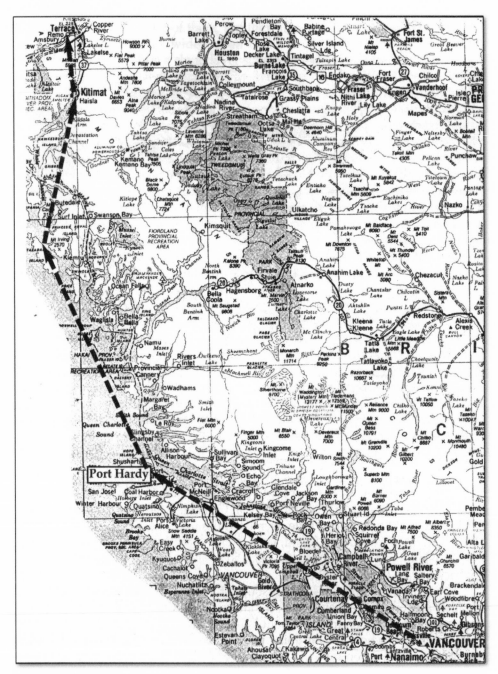

Flying 500 miles over water and the scraggly Canadian coast in a single-engine WWII fighter is not the smartest thing I've ever done, but I wanted the challenge.

The Douglas Channel went north to Kitimat. Then just 40 miles beyond Kitimat was Terrace. No problem.

Although I wish the channel had a billboard sign at the entrance, I finally located the Douglas Channel. There were a lot of channels to choose from. I poked my nose up several of them, but they all seemed to narrow too soon. The Douglas Channel was the widest in the area so I started up it. The first 10 miles were fine but then a cloud layer began to form about 2,000 feet above the mountaintops. I was flying up the river about even with the mountaintops on either side. As I went around a bend to the left, the clouds suddenly were lower than the sides of the river. In a split second all I could see was straight down. We were trapped going 250 mph and no idea of what was ahead. Another bend? A higher mountain? All I knew was what was behind me. Directly behind me. The channel was so narrow there was no room to turn around.

Flying above the clouds may be against Canadian regulations, but this was no time to worry about that. I had to get "on top." That's all there was to it. Even a steep climb on instruments straight ahead to "on-top," there might be what pilots refer to as "rock cloud"—imbedded in the cloud might be a mountain. Back was the only way to go. I told Mary over the intercom to hang on, we were going to "go up and

I was trying to obey the Canadian law of no flying on-top of clouds. Suddenly around a bend in the river, the clouds trapped me in a narrow canyon. The only way out was an Immelmann on instruments through the clouds. That was my first and last attempt to fly under the clouds in the Canadian mountains!

over." I didn't know how thick the cloud layer was. I didn't have the power of a jet fighter to stand on my tail, kick in the afterburners and shoot straight up.

I put the prop in full low pitch, pushed the throttle forward to 60" and pulled back on the stick to start a loop into the clouds. For racing, I had installed a gyro-horizon that didn't "tumble." It worked through 360°. When inverted, I would roll out, hopefully going back in the opposite direction. Between catching a glimpse in the mirror of Mary's purse floating toward the canopy top and my gyro horizon showing I was inverted, I started a roll out a la an Immelmann maneuver. Just at that moment we broke out into the clear and I was able to finish the roll seeing the horizon. I would like to think that I could have done the entire maneuver on instruments alone, but others have told me that the last part of the roll from wings vertical to level, without a lot of practice, might not have gone so well. I'll never know. I'll never, ever, ever allow myself to get trapped in a canyon again.

Leaving Terrace was the same as Aspen. There wasn't any instrument departure but the cloud tops were definitely known to be at 4,000 feet. I described to the local DOT agent at the show that I would like to climb through the clouds in a circular climbing departure pattern tuned to their low-powered NDB radio to stay oriented until I was on top of the cloud layer. I would radio back when I was on top and then be high enough to contact their radar center to request an "on top" clearance back to Vancouver. He granted my request. What authority he did it with, I don't know. He did call their radar center and told them I'd be checking in with them when I was high enough. It worked.

"Miss America" Race Preparations v   Jan. 1973

<u>CONFIDENTIAL</u>   for Crew Use Only

<u>OIL</u>--Keep level at about 10 gals. of 60W <u>non</u>-detergent...add 70W if available.

<u>FUEL</u>- Add ethyl combustion improver (CI_2) in ratio of one oz. per 10 gals. of gas.
        Best way to mix is add to gasoline in gal. can then pour in tank while being
        filled. Add only to left main fuel (115/145). Right main can be 100 oct. used
        for taxi, take off, join up BUT be sure to use left main at least 2 minutes
        before going to over 60" power. RACE in <u>Auto Rich</u>.
        Keep at least 75 gals in left main and at least 20 gals. in right.
        Fuel pressure should be set at 24(Twenty-four)PSI
           Race in AUTO RICH setting.
<u>SPARK PLUGS</u>- use 25# torque(be sure to use ground down 7/8 socket to avoid false
        torque reading because of binding on intake plugs(Top side ones).
        Use Champion 296's for race course practice, then Champion 237's for
        qualifying and racing.   296's are good to about 90" . Under no circumstances
        should the plane be flown more than 10 minutes at normal cruise with the
        237 plugs...nor idled for a long period.

<u>ADI</u> - Pump pressure should be about 29 psi + 1...Use right wing bay tank for ADI
        mixture of 50% Methanol and 50% Distilled Water. Put in about 40 gallons
        for normal race of 12 minutes or 90 miles
        Flow should be slightly higher than fuel flow on matched flow meter. The only
        way to vary it is to put in a different "pill" in the regulator which requires
        a special wide screw driver made from a chisel..the only pill we have extra
        meters in less ADI so no change antidpated.
        Induction temp at 115" MP should be about 75°C...maximum would be 90°C..if
        over that, something is wrong with ADI.
        Turn ADI pump (right side) on at setting of 45" or less.
<u>SPRAY BAR</u> -At Reno 72, the valve was 1/2 turn open and we ran out of water about
        10 minutes for a 12 min. race (but blown coolant line may have opened coolant
        doors early anyway.) Suggest 1/3 turn should do it and then must be safetied
        to prevent creep.   To test flow..fly for 5 min. and check usage....turn valve
        only 1/8th at a time as very sensitive.

<u>POWER SETTINGS</u> -3400 RPM   ...start at 105"MP and do not exceed 115"

To Connect Spray Bar connect to bare female hose at rear of front seat. Feed
        thru floor about 2' ahead of control column with hose going alongside
        left of front seat. Connect at check valve of line from left bay tank.
        Be sure tied up and clear of gear and mechanism.
To Connect ADI Flow Transmitter- separate union on -8 braided steel line, remove
        B nut caps on either side of flow meter letting pickling fluid drain out
        (if all not out, it is OK to have some go thru engine) Hook up the
        separated steel braided lines...can't make mistake because one too short.

<u>BEFORE RACE</u>
1. Install spray bar line
2. Put in 237 plugs in both exhaust & intake
3. Hook up ADI flow meter &drain mystery oil
4. Take out wing lights
5. Remove strobe light
6. Remove Collins antenna
7. Check pump pressures
8. Calibrate spray bar flow
9. Add ethyl (CI_2) to tank
10. Fill ADI
11. Remove omni antenna

<u>AFTER RACE</u>
1. Disconnect spray bar hose adremove.
2. Flush left bay tank with gas
3. Unhook flow meter and put in oil
4. Hook up wing lights.
5. Install strobe
6. Install Collins antenna
7. Install omni antenna
8. Put in 296 plugs

Chapter 11

The Reno National Air Races
September 1971
"I Blow My First Engine at 130 inches of MP! Wow!"

The rough-engine problems had been solved in early August with brand new, high-performance mags built from the ground up. All the pieces and parts were new. What a relief to have a smooth-running engine in front of you. I like thrills, but not chills. Dave Zeuschel had the engine running smoothly. The crankshaft had been taken out and balanced so well that it could have run a Swiss watch. I put a Dash 7 blower in versus the higher power drag of the Dash 9 that came with my engine. The blower case had been ground down to cut the blower fin clearance to the outer case to raise the blower's efficiency. Dull stuff to me. I understood about every other word they used to describe it to me. I had changed spark plugs and scraped the carbon dust off the distributor points in my '39 Ford way back, but that was it. What they were talking about was beyond me.

When I saw my qualifying speed of 412.63 mph, the first time I was able to go over 400 mph, it all seemed worth it. Now I was up with the big boys. I was third fastest, but the two faster were Bearcats at 420 mph for Gunther Balz and 418 mph for Darryl Greenamyer. "Miss America" was the fastest qualifier of the Mustangs. As the rule of thumb you fly 10% farther than the course measures because it is measured from the top of pylon to pylon. You could drive that distance, but you can't fly it. You have to go outside the pylons in your bank. Exactly *over* one would risk cutting a pylon and a time penalty. So my 412 mph would be that the plane really was going 412 plus 41 mph or 463 mph! That's streaking!

This was the first year of the race course change from the classic oval with 3 pylons at each end to what I call the "cross-country course" now being used. Its gentler turns spread over 9 pylons versus 6, helped all of us better our former speed times. I didn't care why I qualified over 400 mph; I had broken through that 400 mph wall. That's all that mattered. Dave Zeuschel's dimples showed even more with the wide grin on his face.

I took first in the heat race. For the first time, I had a ride in the convertible with the Race Queen the full length of the grandstands with the race announcer singing the praises of "Miss America." It was fun, but it lasted less than 5 minutes! I wanted

Mike Loening and I blew our engines in about the same place. He was about 5 plane lengths ahead of me approximately a mile away from the crowd. He dove down immediately for runway 7. He must have been going over 300 mph on final and had to ground loop to keep from going over the cliff at the end. I saw the dust swirl. Two laps later it was my turn. At over 400 mph, I climbed until it slowed to best-glide speed of 175 mph...I had climbed almost 5,000 feet. By putting the prop in high-pitch, I was able to circle high over the crowd and land halfway down the opposite way on runway 23.

*This unusual shot was taken from the home pylon area toward the crowd. It shows the scorched right side from the fire and oil. I'm about halfway down runway 23 about to touchdown. My motto: "halfway down in emergency landings is the **start** of a runway." Note that the canopy is open to get out quickly in case of a crash, and the prop is in high pitch to "feather" as much as possible for best-glide speed.*

them to make another lap or two. I enjoyed it. At least they could have slowed down a bit on the way back past the crowd.

For your 15 minutes of fame in life, you should spend a lot more time out of the limelight. Not so in the Championship Finals; I was on display again. I blew my engine! The finals were a 10-lap race around the new 9.8-mile course versus the old 8.3-mile oval. Ninety-eight miles from pylon to pylon, but with that 10% more, it was 107 miles, and then tack on that 8 extra miles from where the planes are released until they come past the Home Pylon in front of the grandstand and the total is more like a 115-mile race.

The notes appended to my log read as follows:

Engine blows on lap 7 of 10 laps at pylon 6 where Mike Loening blew his a few laps earlier, landed downwind and wiped out his plane needing to ground-loop it. I had enough speed to climb to 5,000 feet above airport before slowing down to 175 mph, the Mustang's best glide speed. Had been doing about 460 mph pulling 130 inches of manifold pressure at 3,600 RPM. Fire started on right side at the stacks, cut mixture control, applied right rudder and fire literally separated from side of plane. Able to glide easily to upwind runway for a dead stick landing. Only problem was that Greenamyer failed to pull up on the course for my mayday and I was distracted, landing directly into his low flight path.

That's the terse version, I was flush with luck. I had a new engine with all the tricky mods, a high qualifying speed, first place in the Heat Race, I was on a roll. Now would be the cherry on top. I'd push it up to give it all it had. At normal max RPM of 3,000, all you can get is about 85" of manifold pressure without turning on the high-altitude blower. But to turn that on, you would very likely blow the engine below 18,000 feet. No one ever turned on the high blower that I know of. It was too dangerous. The way to get a higher manifold pressure would be to crank in more RPM. All aircraft engines have a redline RPM. The Merlin's is 3,000 RPM. But, "they" say that an engine can safely go 10% over that which would be 3,300 RPM. 3,300 RPM would get you up to about 110" MP. You need more, so you alter the prop governor even more to allow another 300 RPM. Now you're at 3,600 RPM and you've got the awesome power of 130" of manifold pressure, double the 65" of War Emergency power a Mustang was allowed during the war to get out of a jam. If it was flown at more than 5 minutes at 65", the engine had to be torn down and rebuilt before it could fly again…and I was pulling double that! No problem, they claimed. You have a balanced crankshaft, water injection, radiator spray bars, etc.

Thirty years later a friend commented, "I'll never forget when they took the cowling off and I could see people's faces on the other side—the whole bottom of the engine was blown off." That's what I get for thinking my Merlin could handle 130 inches of manifold pressure. But, oh, what a sensation it was!

While it lasted it was something else. There was a little shaking, but you could feel the power. I had never felt anything like it before. Maybe on my first flight in the Mustang, I was aware of more power than I had ever experienced, but I had gotten used to that by now. This was at a higher level, a much higher level. I was passing up planes like they were motor scooters. It was like a video game—which didn't exist in those days—to put it in today's frame of reference. Then suddenly a sneeze, a pop and oil was streaming over my canopy. The sudden drop in power made it feel as if I had been snagged by a net.

When birds try to get away from an oncoming plane, they climb as straight up as possible. So do you when you have over 400 mph of airspeed. Climb to the max, assess the situation, then either bail out or use your altitude for a long glide. The P-51's 14-to-1 glide range meant from my almost 1 mile up at 5,000 feet AGL, I could glide, even with the clipped wings, at least 10 miles. I'd have to pull the prop back to full high pitch to reduce its drag. As I slowed, I noticed flames shooting out on the right side near the exhaust stacks. I immediately cut the fuel flow to the engine by pulling back on the fuel mixture control and adding right rudder. The flame left in a giant fireball. Following my rule of the middle part of the runway length as being the place to land, I aimed for it. Once down I knew there was a long overrun at the other end. I didn't know if the brakes had been soaked by oil while in the up position, so I didn't try to apply them until I had slowed way down. For one brake to grab and the other with a slippery oil covered disc, a wild ground loop might be the result. The overrun was fine with me.

Yes, the engine blew. The worst had happened, but damn it was great while it lasted!

California 1,000 Kilometers (620 miles)
November 14, 1971 (42 Laps Around a 14.8-Mile Pylon Course)
"Drinking Milk Can be Hazardous to Racing"

This is a race I should have won. If I didn't like milk so much, maybe I would have won. The milk jug was my undoing. I came in only 28 seconds behind the winner after a $1^1/_2$ hour race.

The race promoters wanted to again use the "1,000" catchy number, but the two "1,000 milers" we had, one at Mojave and the other at San Diego, proved tough on planes, pilots and crew—and tended to get boring for the spectators who often didn't have a clue as to what was going on. Two-and-a-half hours is a long time to watch and concentrate on anything. The thought of turning to the metric system's "kilometers" to be able to still call it a "1,000" (only 620 miles) was a bit of marketing genius. I was sure for it. It also would have a minimum-time mandatory pit stop. I liked those.

"Miss America's" engine was back in good shape after having a connecting rod break and go through the bottom case with the force of an armor-piercing cannon in the Nationals a few months ago. No way was I ever going to try to pull 130" of

manifold pressure again. Been there, done that. This was an ideal race to pull 90."
An RPM increase from the 3,000 redline to just 3,400 RPM would give me that 90."
The Unlimited boat racers turned these Merlins up as high as 4,600 RPM, about
what a car engine will do. Of course, if they blew an engine, the boat just slowed
down to a stop in the water.

The engine was running great. I had the fastest qualifying time at 407 mph. I
wasn't going to be the "meat in the sandwich" in this starting formation. No, sir. I'd
have the pole position with clear air and space ahead of me. The rest could deal with
my prop wash for a change. I had not taken any liquid drink with me at the San
Diego Race. That experience with Gatorade thickening my mouth with a bitter yet
sugar-like taste at the prior Mojave race made me leery of trying to drink anything
for nourishment in the plane during the race.

At San Diego, we had to make a pit stop anyway. I'd take a drink at that time. But
I found I still wanted something "wet" in my mouth while in the race. The oxygen
was so drying. If it was drying at San Diego's almost sea-level altitude, my oxygen
regulator would be allowing even more oxygen in the mix at Mojave's almost 3,000-
foot elevation. That would mean I'd been inhaling even drier air and my mouth
would be that much drier, too. I wanted to have the option of being able to get
something into my mouth when I wanted it during the race.

I love milk. If I had to make the choice of giving up either milk or vodka, I'd
favor the milk. To me, cold milk is the most refreshing drink in the world. In a tub-
type of Thermos jug, I could carry it on my lap and suck through that same line as
I had before through my oxygen mask. I tried it a few times with ice cubes in with
the milk. It was ideal. And with milk I'd have some nourishment too. That was it. In
these 45 minutes of high-energy, heavy-breathing flying around the pylons, my stand-
by "wet" would be milk. Today, it's nonfat milk. In 1971 we didn't think about those
things.

For a land-start, the start was pure joy. Not only was I not going to fight a mass
of turbulence buffeting me on takeoff, the air at the pylon turns would be wonder-
fully calm, if I stayed out in front that is.

A press report described the start as this:

> *"To see 16 of the world's most powerful planes lined up staggered down the run-*
> *way waiting to start the race, their snorting engines waiting to go all out, was a*
> *memorable sight. When the starter's green flag went down, Howie Keefe, in "Miss*
> *America," in the pole position as the fastest qualifier, leapt forward as if shot from*
> *a catapult. He suddenly was so far ahead, that it looked like he'd leave the entire*
> *field behind."*

Ah, yes, it was a great sensation. And I'm not too cool not to say I enjoyed it. But
often enjoyment doesn't last long. The pit stop went well. The milk was a pleasant
"wetting" agent. Its cool feeling not only gave me moisture, but it seemed to coat my
mouth and throat against the harshness and dryness of the oxygen. At the pit stop
we had to take on a mandatory 100 gallons of gasoline. The way my tanks were
configured is that the regular wing tanks each held 92 gallons of gas. The 100-gallon

bladder tank behind me was to be solely for 100 gallons of methanol. That left the two gun bay tanks of 45 gallons each to be one of three things I could quickly plumb them for, gas for the engine, methanol for the water injection or regular water for the spray bars to cool the radiators for engine coolant and oil. I had both the left and right gun bays assigned do the spray bars for radiator cooling—that would keep the door behind the belly scoop in a low-drag trail position.

When I made the pit stop to take on the 100 gallons of gas, I had not burned a 100 gallons worth from my wing tanks. The tanks overflowed with 15 gallons left to take on board. What to do? I had never been confronted with this dilemma before. I stupidly had not even considered it as a "what if" possibility. If I were allowed, I would have just pumped the 15 gallons on the ground (not a very wise safety move) and been done with it. I had to take it on board somehow. The sacrificial lamb had to be one of the 45-gallon gun bay tanks. Quick! Disconnect the least full tank from the spray bars. Open the gun bay. Someone jump up and sit on the bladder tank to force all the water out. Close off the tank outlet. Put the 15 gallons of gas in. Don't worry about the little bit of water left. Don't hook it up to the engine gas feed line. I'm not going to use it anyway. This drill took far too much time. I lost precious racing time on the course because I had simply stopped to pit too soon. I was looking at the clock and not paying attention to my gas gauges. I should have kept flying until they showed below 40 gallons in each tank so I could take on another 100 gallons.

So off I went to play catch-up. At this point, I had no idea of where I was in the race, I'd pass a plane not knowing if he was on lap 30 and I was on lap 31 or on lap 29. At this point, it was just the "go-for-it" mode. Forget where I was, just keep the power up and race. After about 30 minutes, I felt a strange cooling system on my back. The Mustang cockpit can easily get up to 110° F. This day it was cold outside. Very cold. Those in the stands were bundled up. Maybe in my cockpit that day it was only 90° F riding on top of those giant tubes carrying 200° F hot water to the radiator and "cool" 150° F water back to the engine. Any cool feeling was appreciated.

Then I thought, "Wait a minute here. I shouldn't be getting a nice cool feeling on my back. Where's it coming from?" I cocked my left arm and reached around to feel my left back side. It was wet! Soaking wet! I dropped my hand down and felt a steady wet stream coming from below behind me. My hand went lower to the stream source. It was coming from the lower left corner of the polyvinyl bladder bag filled with highly-flammable methanol mix. The bladder was suspended from two bars across the rear cockpit to give it shape. As the bladder emptied, it collapsed upward as a baby bottle would. The high-G turn forces on the suspended bladder caused the seam to part at the lower-left corner. I certainly wasn't going to light up a cigarette in the cockpit, but what if a spark got in there? When methanol burns, you don't even see the flame, you just feel the heat of its fire. Oh, great!

What to do? Land and abort the race with only about six laps left? Let's see. Maybe I can get this thing under control. I twisted my body to the left so my arm could reach the broken corner seam. It was right on the corner. I grabbed the corner angle, tightened my grip to cut off the bottom few inches and the spray stopped. I had to turn even a little more left to really secure my grip. The Thermos of milk slid off my lap to the left, resting partly on my left thigh and partly on the side of the cockpit. I may have been zooming up and down all over the course while this was going on. But now I could concentrate on racing again (as it turned out, I did cut a pylon, which I'll explain later).

I now started to feel and hear a buffeting sound. It was somewhat like you'd hear and feel in a car going 80 mph with all the windows down. I now had two radios. One was tuned to the mandatory Race Control frequency to tell you to pull up if there was a mayday on course, the other to my pit crew on the ground. I was puzzled by the buffeting feeling. I'd never felt that before. I radioed, asking them to put the binoculars on me as I went by to see if they could see anything. Maybe an elevator had come loose and was flapping in the prop wash. The radio call I got back

Frank Sanders, flying his Royal Navy Sea Fury, passed me to take first place when the milk jug fell off my lap onto the flap handle and put down my flaps.

was, "No problem, Miss America, you're looking good." Okay, so the tail was on, nothing was coming off, maybe a piece of cowling is a little loose.

I saw Frank Sanders pass me in his Sea Fury. Wait a minute. I was going slower! Something was wrong. I happened to move the milk jug back on my lap and noticed the flap control handle was in the Down position. That was it! That was the buffeting! Of course it was. That's what you feel when the flaps go down. You can even notice it when you're on an airliner. When it's coming in for a landing and you hear all that "gear noise" and then the "boomf, boomf" noise, it's the flaps slowing down the plane while at the same time providing more lift. I had been flying for maybe four laps with the flaps partially down!

(Note: The P-51 is designed so that the flap handle can be put down to the 45° position, but the flaps will go down no more than 15°. I understood this was to let a fighter pilot, being pursued by another plane, dump his flaps without any concern to look at the flap handle position, yet not have them go down so far that they would be torn off the plane at high speeds. By dumping his flaps to slow him down, the enemy plane behind would overshoot him and then he would be on its tail. Made sense to me.)

In my case, it would have been better if the flaps had gone the full 45°. I would have paid immediate attention to them and solved the problem sooner. After the race I asked Frank Sanders if he noticed my flaps were down when he passed me. His haughty reply was, "Of course I did. Did you think I was going to tell you? I thought you were show boating." That was a typical Frank Sanders remark rendered in a loud, throaty, laughing voice. But really, why should he tell me? I was his competitor.

Frank Sanders flying his Royal Navy Sea Fury.

When Frank crossed the finish line at 42 laps, the race officially ended. The radio call went out that the race was over. But I had a special call. "Keefe, you cut Pylon 6, go circle it." The rule was that if you cut a pylon (or pylons) during the race, when the race was declared over, you must go to those pylons and circle them at 200 feet above the ground and then finish the course. Your finish time was based on your race time, plus the time it took you to do one more lap circling all the pylons you cut. Even having to do that, no plane came in ahead of me; I still took second place. The leaking bladder was a problem, but the milk jug was the culprit.

It was the last long-distance pylon race ever held. If they had another one today, I'd try to figure how to get this fat, overweight, big-bellied body into a fast plane to fly it. "Just one more time" is what I guess we all want.

Introduction to the Speed Record

The famous Paris Air Show at Le Bourget Airport outside Paris is held in odd-numbered years. John Volpe, Secretary of Transportation under President Nixon, felt that the U.S. should have a show in the alternate (even) years. In addition to it being just an air show, Volpe wanted to include all forms of transportation in the U.S., from moving walkways, autos, buses to trains, boats, military, etc.

I was asked to set a speed record across the U.S. in "Miss America" on the opening day of the show. My then sponsor, COX Manufacturing, would cover the approximately $2,000 cost of gasoline, travel expenses and record fees. The U.S. branch of the FAI (Federation Aeronautique Internationale located in France) is the National Aeronautical Association located in Washington, DC. They supervise all record attempts, grant a 4-week exclusive window for your attempt, and hire an official at each end to time your start and finish. World records are between cities of 1 million or more population (less if it is the capital of a country). Other records from point-to-point are national records.

The large Dulles airport west of Washington, DC was an ideal place. It was really two airports. One half could be kept open for airline operations and the other half (west side) had wide-open areas for exhibits and demonstrations. It was called Transpo '72. Unfortunately, Nixon's troubles dominated 1973 and he resigned in 1974. Transpo '74 never happened and the idea was never picked up by future administrations. While there are major annual air shows and exhibitions like Dayton, Ohio and Oshkosh, Wisconsin EAA Show, the U.S. still does not have a national air show of its own.

A Glitch Occurs in the Record Attempt—a.k.a. Snafu

Because my attempt was requested by Secretary Volpe, the skids were greased for me all the way. Radar centers put me under their Mission Control designed to steer military planes over the U.S., FAA towers at Wichita and Dulles were alerted to give me priority handling. But as in the saying "the best laid plans of mice and men oft go astray" and Murphy's Law, a key piece was left out of the puzzle—Washington, DC's radar approach control. For those readers who are not familiar with the radar operations of the airspace system, this explanation may help to understand my dilemma. There are 3 basic radar air traffic units that handle all aircraft movements in the U.S.:

The **Tower** handles traffic in and around a given airport.

The **Approach and Departure Control** handles traffic for all the airports in the area up to about 4,000 feet and even 12,500 feet in high density regions like New York, Chicago, Los Angeles, etc.

The **ARTCC or "Centers"** cover wide multi-state areas usually above 4,000 feet.

Planes are "handed-off" from one unit to another. Before handing you off, the controller in one unit contacts the controller in the next unit with your information. When the new controller accepts you, you are told what frequency to use to contact the new controller. My glitch came on the hand-off from Center to Washington Approach Control at the end of the flight. Somehow, Washington Approach Control was left out of the loop that I was setting a record. The rule is that below 10,000 feet, no plane can exceed 250 knots (288 mph) ground speed without prior clearance.

Don Dwiggin's article says that I finished 2 miles up over the field. Here's why. Part of my plan was to start a let down at high power from 21,000-foot altitude about 150 miles west of Dulles and average over 450 mph in the dive to the finish line. When I requested to leave 21,000 feet for the descent just east of Charleston, West Virginia, Center gave me the okay and I started the dive. When I was at about 14,000 feet descending at about 1,200 feet a minute, Center handed me off to Washington Approach Control.

Their first transmission was, "Slow down! You're doing over 400 knots (460 mph)! Do not go below 10,000 feet over 250 knots (288 mph)." I tried to explain that I was setting a speed record from Los Angeles, was due to flash over the finish line at Dulles during the air show. Approach would have none of it. No way were they going to clear me below 10,000 feet at that speed. What to do? There was no way to slow the sleek Mustang down from 460 mph to 288 mph without a big wide off-course arc that would eat up valuable time. I needed to slow to 175 mph to even put down the gear to keep from tearing it off. Couldn't slow down that way. Put down flaps? The flap system on a P-51 is designed to let the fighter pilot being chased put the flap lever full down even at high speeds without any worry about the exact degree to hopefully have the other plane overshoot. The flaps will not go down over about 10° (45° is max) at high speeds. That's not going to slow it down enough either. And then there are the spectators and air show announcer waiting below for the finish. I was taking deep breaths of oxygen, hoping more oxygen to the brain would give me the best answer.

The answer came. The point was to set a record, not to put on an air show. I leveled off at 10,000 feet and kept heading for Dulles with approach control giving me radar steers (at least they did that). They had called Dulles tower and were told that an observer from the FAI (National Aeronautical Association, U.S. branch) was in the Dulles tower alongside the tower controller to clock the finish. I never did find out his name, but I am deeply indebted to him for his quick thinking.

He knew that the approach controller was in the same tower on the floor below in the windowless area where the radar screens were. He ran down the flight of stairs, located the approach controller handling me at that point and asked him to tell him when I was over the center of the field. He would stop his stopwatch then. That would be my finish line—almost two miles up! The tower kindly let me make a high-speed (288 mph max) low pass down the air show runway.

I doubt if many knew the difference. But my savvy sponsor, Ben Garrett, Marketing Director of COX, a pilot himself, asked why I made the finish going south down the runway rather than from the south to the north. Why waste the time to go around to come in the other way? Ben was a sharp guy!

(The difference between my clocked speed of 6 hours, 18 minutes, 5 seconds and the record speed of 6 hours, 20 minutes, 3.5 seconds is that city-to-city records are allowed to start/finish within a 50 mile radius of the city center but the time is adjusted as if you started/finished over the center of the cities.)

Race Against Time: Thrills of Beating the Clock!
(Reprinted from Air Racing Magazine, *Winter 1973 edition*)
By Don Dwiggins

The cold front was a sinister black wall, towering 40,000 feet skyward, ugly, laced with lightning. The moment of decision was gone. To vector left or right would consume minutes that could not be spared. Howie Keefe, World War II naval aviator and veteran racing pilot, grimaced as his red-white-and-blue Mustang bored straight ahead, knowing the terror that lay inside that wall.

Indianapolis Center had asked whether he intended to divert. His answer had been no. He was racing the clock, a deadly race against time. True airspeed 410 mph, almost seven miles a minute. He set his jaw and slammed into it, half expecting to feel the awful impact.

Race
against
time:
THRILLS OF
BEATING
THE CLOCK!

Air Racing Magazine
Winter, 1973

Quite suddenly it came, the terrifying wrenching force of the boiling internal winds that gripped his P-51 racing plane with forces utterly beyond belief. The storm gods engulfed him, wrenched the stick from his hand, and slammed his plane sideways.

Keefe grabbed the stick with both hands and did his best to level the wings to fight back against this aerial whirlpool. He grabbed the throttle, pulled back, reduced speed to 300 mph, but still the hammering went on. Windshield and wings coated with ice, temperatures freezing inside the cockpit, Keefe felt cut off from the world, alone.

In the darkening blackness of the storm cell there was no up nor down, his instruments spun wildly. All radio contact was lost, he was buried, hidden from radar contact, transponder and all.

A wild memory flashed across Keefe's mind of a similar experience during the war years, when he flew PBYs and first knew the terror of a storm, the suddenness with which it comes. And he remembered something else, trying to explain to youngsters why it is you must stick with your flight plan when things go sour.

"The idea of trying to change course is where a guy starts getting into real trouble," he'd said. "IFR rules require that if anything happens to you, they don't tell you to turn around and go back. They tell you to go on. The truth in that is more than just to let them know where you are. The truth is that it is easier and safer to continue on with what you have preplanned, than to try and recalculate things in an unholy situation."

The unholiness worsened, and Keefe had the thought that has come to so many pilots in trouble—what the heck am I doing here?

What Howard (Howie) Keefe, at 51 one of the nation's top racing pilots, was doing, was racing the clock the hard way. It's easy if you pick your day when the *weather is good and the tailwinds strong and then go, but he did not have that privilege.*

Keefe's transcontinental record attempt was tightly geared to the opening of Transpo '72 in Washington, D.C., and his responsibilities were heavy. To himself…to the Transpo people…to his sponsor, the L. M. Cox Manufacturing Company of Santa Ana, Calif., who had honored his Mustang with a gas powered model that carried the same beautiful paint job as the big "Miss America" racer he was piloting.

And Keefe well knew that pressures can kill, responsibilities grow too big. Still he bored on, fighting the wild turbulence and the hammering of hail and sleet that scoured and gouged the paint job.

If only he had been given a choice of days to fly, it would be different, but there were no options. A race against a clock on a firm schedule puts you in the hands of the gods, and you can only pray they will be kind.

Things had gone wrong from the start. Despite careful preflight-planning, it came up strong headwinds when Keefe lifted the wheels of his Mustang off from Van Nuys Airport, flashed around a climbing turn over Malibu, and zapped across the starting gate at 300 mph.

In Van Nuys Tower the NAA timer, Earl Hanson, strained to see "Miss America" high above him, his ears tuned to the loudspeaker, waiting for Los Angeles Center at Palmdale to catch his transponder blip on the radarscope. Suddenly there it was—Keefe climbing hard through 19,000 feet, going for 21,000 absolute, 22,000 feet pressure altitude on the dial.

He might have climbed over Catalina Island and hit the gate full bore at 21,000, but that would have cost him precious extra fuel. Better this way, climbing now to hit en route altitude 10 miles east of Van Nuys. In the cockpit were High Altitude Jet Route charts carefully marked with courses, headings, checkpoints. But now they were useless.

"The Center vectored me through Hector Gap then gave me zero-six-five, all the way to Wichita! Right between the jet routes, over country I'd never navigated before!"

There was a reason for this on this bright Saturday morning, May 27, 1972. It was a thing called Mission Control, a special, little-known activity the FAA invented to handle oil burners and military jet refueling operations in the stratosphere. They'd put Howie under Mission Control.

"It caught me with mixed emotions," he told me afterward. "It was fine to have them give me headings to steer through the positive airspace, but it was kind of crazy to be lost for the first time! I'd flown two transcon races, Milwaukee to Reno in 1969 and '70, flying specific check points. But no way now—they were doing the flying down there!"

As Keefe had once said, "You don't turn back if things go wrong, not if you intend to complete your mission. That's fine for VFR guys stumbling into IFR inadvertently, doing the old one-eighty. But when you get caught in the wringer, stick with your plan," he always preached.

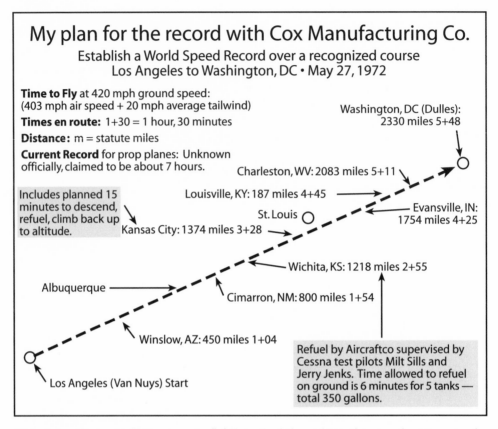

My plan for the record with Cox Manufacturing Co.
Establish a World Speed Record over a recognized course
Los Angeles to Washington, DC • May 27, 1972

Time to Fly at 420 mph ground speed:
(403 mph air speed + 20 mph average tailwind)

Times en route: 1+30 = 1 hour, 30 minutes

Distance: m = statute miles

Current Record for prop planes: Unknown
officially, claimed to be about 7 hours.

Washington, DC (Dulles):
2330 miles 5+48

Charleston, WV: 2083 miles 5+11

Louisville, KY: 187 miles 4+45

Evansville, IN:
1754 miles 4+25

St. Louis

Includes planned 15
minutes to descend,
refuel, climb back up
to altitude.

Kansas City: 1374 miles 3+28

Wichita, KS: 1218 miles 2+55

Albuquerque

Cimarron, NM: 800 miles 1+54

Winslow, AZ: 450 miles 1+04

Refuel by Aircraftco supervised by
Cessna test pilots Milt Sills and
Jerry Jenks. Time allowed to refuel
on ground is 6 minutes for 5 tanks —
total 350 gallons.

Los Angeles (Van Nuys) Start

This shows the route "Miss America" followed while making the record-setting speed run across the country.

Art Scholl (center), also sponsored by COX, flew in the air show. With kids looking on, he is discussing some stunts to show with a COX U-control demo pilot.

I'm showing where I had my canopy cut down for more streamlining for pylon racing. In the rough air of a storm, my head bumped it hard. I felt blood coming down my cheek. Whoa! Was I too high without a pressure suit? It turned out the cause was the button on the top of the cap cutting my scalp when my head banged into the canopy. I was relieved!

Howie Keefe's plan had been to establish a Federation Aeronautique Internationale-approved world record coast-to-coast from Los Angeles to Washington, making the run in under 6 hours, not counting 15 minutes for refueling on the ground, at Wichita. He had a fine crew waiting there, headed up Wayne Houge, Cessna's Service Manager who had managed his pit stops at Denver's Jeffco Airport in 1969 and '70.

"Wayne had two gas trucks, an oil truck, a fire truck and eighteen guys waiting at the end of the runway," Keefe related. "All I had to do was land toward them—the tower had the runway shut down—then take on a load and go out the way I came in."

But Howie Keefe's best-laid plans, as I said, didn't quite work out the way he had figured them, starting with the weather. There were these two big highs up above the Mason-Dixon Line, churning the wind around clockwise, and a couple of lows, over Atlanta and Dallas, sucking in winds counterclockwise.

The result: "It would'a been fine for an East-to-West record run," said Howie, "but there I was with 18-knot headwinds blowing right in my face, all the way!"

Keefe had made a careful study of jet stream patterns, how they swing further south in late fall, in midwinter, in the spring. In colder weather the cores lie at about 28,000 to 34,000 feet, and the outer layers move still lower, to about 18,000 feet. But Howie did not program the flight to get up into the swift-flowing river of westerly air, because he'd clipped four feet from his wingspan, and to fly above 22,000 to 23,000 feet pressure altitude would mean flying at a too-high angle of attack and hence a loss of cruise speed.

There was another consideration—his big 1,670 hp Rolls Royce Merlin engine has no blower, it was an interim engine his crew chief, Dave Zeuchel, had rebuilt for use as a pylon race engine that didn't need one. "Dave was afraid I'd blow the engine all to hell," said Howie.

That had actually happened at Reno '71, and already had raced the replacement engine at the California 1,000 for 1 hour 40 minutes, pulling 90 inches manifold pressure, and here he was flying six hours at 48 inches, which figured out to be ten percent above METO (Maximum Except Takeoff) Power.

"All I could possibly get at 21,000 feet was 48.5 inches," he explained, "because at that altitude my best performance was at 2,800 rpm, I needed that extra 100 rpm over the METO 2,700 rpm to drive the supercharger faster. In pylon flying you can go right up to 65 inches, but only for a short time without water-injection."

Streaking eastward on a heading of 065, Keefe thought back to the splendid days of the old Bendix Race when guys like Paul Mantz and Joe De Bona and Stan Reavor flew wet-wing Mustangs, loaded with gallons of fuel chilled with dry ice to get the most into the wings.

In the back seat, he'd installed a 97-gallon tank, which, with the wing mains and fuel bladders in the gun and ammo bays, gave him gallons absolute, with 340 usable. That was cutting it fine, with consumption 100 gallons per hour at race speed. He could have pulled back and burned far less, but there was that clock!

Howie Keefe felt like singing, the clear sky at 21,000 feet was that beautiful across Arizona and New Mexico and the Continental Divide and over the great prairie country. No problems, except the headwinds that were taking their toll eating up precious fuel.

Things turned sour over Garden City, Kansas when "Miss America" was confronted with the first of two cold fronts that lay in his path to Transpo '72.

The Cessna Citation group arranged a refuel stop in Wichita. Two gas trucks, one for each side, pumped in nearly 300 gallons in less than 6 minutes. There was also an oil truck and a fire truck on hand. The only glitch was a balky gas cap that took almost a minute to solve. They even had the tuna-fish sandwich I requested—a bad choice by me! Not easy to eat with an oxygen mask on!

He'd flown the Mustang IFR for three hours at a stretch in the earlier transcons and well knew the trickiness of a Mustang, if you let go to reach down for a dropped pencil—there you are going downhill in a spiral dive at 3,000 feet a minute!"

Radar reports advised him the front was just passing Wichita, but there would be minutes of IFR flying through the stratocumulus that lay behind it, a sort of warm front overrunning the cold front. No sweat, but breaking out over mid-Kansas, on a hand-off from the Center to Approach Control, that feeling of being absolutely lost struck again—Howie had never flown into Wichita before and all was strange.

Besides, there was the problem of boring into a control zone where you were limited to 250 knots below 10,000 feet, and Howie had speed to burn. He'd trued out at 408 mph and was making good 392 ground speed into the headwinds, and he had all the help in the world from airline jocks who were pulling for him—one American Airlines captain gave him the computer winds all the way up as he crossed Arizona.

Breaking out at 8,000 feet over Wichita, Howie knew he could never land on the assigned runway without a slowing turn—the Mustang is that clean. So around he went, lined up, touched down and rolled to the waiting pit crew. Six minutes later his tanks were topped off, but another two minutes went down the drain when a balky gas cap wouldn't fit.

There was still a chance to set a world record, though, despite the pair of ugly fronts towering across his flight path to the east. Climbing out of Wichita, the Mustang snarled its way into the first one, wallowing heavily with its full tanks. A coating of rime ice enclosed Keefe as in a tiny cocoon, and trying to stuff down a tuna sandwich under his oxygen mask and juggle a carton of milk proved almost too much.

Finally he broke into the clear at cruise altitude and again breathed easier. But not for long—200 miles ahead stretched the second front, bigger of the two, its gigantic towering cells reaching from Indianapolis south past Louisville. Keefe, at this point, felt a cold chill and realized he had been sweating hard.

"It suddenly dawned on me what a race against time means on a cross-country flight," he told me soberly afterward. "Center asked whether I wanted to fly around the front, but that was out if I didn't want to blow the race. It was simply a huge wall going straight up, laced with lightning.

"Radar advised me it was bad in there, very active cells reaching up to 35,000 feet, but to divert would not be to fly the hypotenuse route. I wasn't sure of my position as the Jet Route charts only show the protected VORs, and I wished I had along a Sky Prints chart, a thing I invented, because it gives more stations to tune in on to find out where you are.

"I tried to be casual, and asked Indianapolis Center how the Indy was going—it was real eerie, sitting there unable to do anything, trying to think of something else. They told me Mark Donahue had won the race, that it was all over, and it was then I asked myself, "What am I doing here?"

"I hit the wall at 410 mph and buried the plane inside the cold front and things went wild, tearing the stick out of my hand, threatening to wrest away all control. I called radar, but they had lost me completely inside the cell. I remembered, you instinctively think you're in trouble a lot longer than you actually are, and suddenly I was through it.

"Down below was Louisville and in the distance I could almost see Africa. It was downhill from there on, but I couldn't trade off as much altitude for speed as I wanted, because now I had to cross Washington–Dulles at 10,000 feet. I figured my rate of descent at 850 fpm for the revised profile, flying 460 mph true on 48 inches, and all of a sudden it was all over. "Down there at Transpo '72 there must have been a hundred thousand people looking up, but I was two miles high, just a blip on the radar scope."

Keefe averaged 362.35 mph over the 2298.07-mile course and his elapsed time was a world point-to-point record—6 hours, 18 minutes, 5 seconds. It was exciting and tiring, but looking back, he reflects: "It was really great—I felt like I had the entire United States aviation industry rooting for me!"

At Washington, DC after the cross-country record flight, Henry Haffke a model builder from New Jersey, entertained me and the crowd by flying his 5-foot-wingspan (about one-eighth scale) model of "Miss America." Gear and flapse went up and down. From 50 yards away it looked like a real P-51. It was an amazing sight to watch take off, fly and land to the applause of the crowd.

Of Statistical Interest

Sponsor: COX Manufacturing. Santa Ana, California, manufacturers of gas engine powered models.

Plane: "Miss America" P-51 Mustang (Air Force fighter, esp. WWII)

Modifications:

- Armor and equipment of about 3,000 pounds removed to reduce weight to 8,000 pounds (4 tons)—engine alone weighs 2,000 pounds (1 ton) and prop about 600 pounds.

- Wings clipped for a total of 4 feet (about 15% of wing area) for pylon racing. P-51 wing area designed to fly at 40,000 feet. Now max. controllable altitude about 25,000 feet.

- Merlin Rolls-Royce engine, normally develops over 1,600 hp, now over 2,000 hp.

Pilot: Howie Keefe, owner, an Unlimited Air Race pilot

Occasion: Opening Day of Transpo '72 at Washington, DC Dulles Airport scheduled for May 27–June 4, 1972 and sponsored by the U.S.

Conditions: "Miss America" does not have an automatic pilot. It must be hand-controlled at all times. If the route requires more than 2 consecutive hours of flight solely on instruments, it will be moved to the next day. The P-51 is not a stable instrument flying platform. Trying to pick up a dropped pencil you could easily lose 1,000 feet at high-speeds and max, throttle settings. Plus, as a solo pilot, you need to do all the navigation and math work while flying the plane.

Fuel: About 700 gallons of high-octane fuel will be used. During takeoff and climb 180 gph will be burned, 100 gph in level flight which is about 50% higher than normal cruise.

Power: Engine max. for sustained flight (METO Power—Maximum Except Takeoff) will be exceeded by a safe margin of about 10%.

Concerns:

- Malfunction of oxygen at high altitude.
- Engine failure due to sustained strain.
- Loss of communication with radar units.
- Gas tank ruptures due to load shifts in turbulent air at high speeds
- Aircraft structure failure in rough weather at high speeds.

August 1972 — My "Canadian Crisis"

If there ever was a month that I could expunge from my flying experiences, it would be the month of August 1972. And the scene would be Canada. It wasn't the fault of Canada, it's just that is where the problem with the engine chose to take place. And, like with the mags, I'm going to tell you at the start who/what the villain was.

It doesn't have a name as such, but it could be called EVB-6. It was the rearmost exhaust valve on the left side. It would hang up, stick or whatever you want to call it. The result was even worse than the mag results. It would let you stick your neck out making it feel like everything was fine, like about to lift-off the runway with no room ahead to abort the landing and stop, then it would show its ugly head. Pop, bang, shudder, cough so badly you had to pull back on the power and hope you wouldn't be bringing the top of a pine tree back with you as you limped around to land.

Most of this happened at the Prince George airport in British Columbia, Canada over 400 miles due north of Seattle. There was a tower at the airport and at one point it announced to me that I had broken the yearly record for emergency landings there in just 5 day's time. It was something like 10 declared emergencies. All this was happening when I was scheduled to be at the Abbotsford Airshow outside of Vancouver about 300 miles to the south. I wanted desperately to get there for the show.

Each morning I'd check out of the hotel at Prince George with all my gear, load up the plane, run it up for a high-RPM mag check, get tower clearance for taxi and takeoff, barrel down the runway and just at liftoff it was bang-bang-snort-bang. Oh no! Another emergency landing. Fortunately, the airport was on a high ridge and the town was in the river valley below it. With what little power I had, I was able to make a gentle left turn just above the tree tops and then lower the nose into the valley to pick up enough speed to slowly climb back up for a short base leg back to the airport. I had several places on the river bank picked out to land in case I couldn't get back up to the airport's altitude.

After 3 days of this I had to get help. I called my secretary, Marla, back in Los Angeles. I asked her to contact Randy Scoville of my crew to get a new additive I had tested and ship it up to me. When the airline found out what was in it, they wouldn't allow it to be sent. She called and told me. I then asked her to contact Randy and have him bring it up. Buy him a ticket and put it on my credit card. Randy arrived the next day at the airport looking like he'd been shanghaied.

"That secretary of yours!" he exclaimed.

"I was just talking to her on the phone and the next thing I knew I was on a plane to Seattle. As I was changing for a plane to Vancouver, I thought about just going back to LA, but then I'd have to face her. I thought it best to keep going." Yes, Marla was Miss "Super-Efficiency" and she loved challenges. She never backed down from any assignment.

Randy was staggering around. It was evening. He'd been up all night transferring from plane to plane to plane to get there. He wouldn't even let me talk about it until he got some sleep. In my hotel room there was a single bed and a big king-size waterbed. I told him to take his choice. Without a word, he flopped fully clothed onto the waterbed. The force of his flop caused the bed to undulate. On his back with his eyes opening wider as each wave went under him, he struggled to get off the bed, then said "Help me off, Howie, I'm getting seasick." Once standing, he lurched for the single bed and didn't wake up until 8 a.m. the next morning, still fully clothed.

At breakfast, I gave him the run down of all that had happened. New mags were on, plugs always seemed fine, what the heck could it be? Probably ignition wiring, was his quick assessment. At the airport, he began checking the ignition wiring. Upside down with his feet straight up out of the cockpit and his head under the dash, he was trying to find the culprit—he had concluded it was a wire shorting out somewhere that would cut off one magneto at random times. Randy was a good engine man. Ten years later, he was Champion Spark Plugs top race expert for not only planes, but boats and cars too. Search and test as he might, he couldn't find a specific flaw, but redid some of the ignition wiring. I was to test hop it again. I asked him if he wanted to ride in the back seat to hear it. "No, thanks, I'll do all the hearing I need from here on the ground."

Same thing. Just at lift off and around for another emergency landing. He was stumped. He had to get back to Los Angeles but he'd make a phone call to friends on the Pay 'N' Pak Unlimited boat race crew in Seattle. He did. Two of them flew up for one day in a borrowed company plane bringing along new mags, which they changed with my almost-new ones. No change. Same problem. They left. Now what? My crew gave up. A top boat-racing crew gave up. Leave the plane here? What good would that do? If experts couldn't solve the problem, it would mean dismantling the plane and shipping it home or take out the engine and replace it with a new one. That would all cost more

Navigating the 500 miles between Abbotsford and Prince George was easy—just follow the Fraser River gorge. But with no airports along the way (there's now one at Lilloette), any strange engine sound gets your heart pumping faster. Fortunately, Pierre's fix was perfect.

money than I really could afford. This was the end of the line. No races at Reno next month.

The line boy who had been gassing me up came up as I was dejectedly leaning on the wing. "A mechanic in that hangar behind the tower thinks he knows what's wrong," he offered with his head slightly bowed. He was aware of what I had gone through the last 5 days. I immediately went to the hangar. I hadn't noticed it was back there. A 50ish French-Canadian with black, wavy hair was sitting outside in an old captain's chair eating a sandwich. I introduced myself.

"I know who you are. I've been watching you the last few days trying to kill yourself and crash that beautiful Mustang. Nobody could figure out the problem, eh? (Ay, as Canadians pronounce it.) Sounds to me like you've got a valve sticking."

I was incredulous at his casual manner! "But, but why didn't you come and say something to me? Do you have experience with the Rolls-Royce Merlin engine?"

I listened with joy as he told me that he worked on the Mustang while in the Royal Canadian Air Force during the Korean War. He had worked on all parts of the plane. He didn't come forward with his opinion because I had "all these experts coming up from the States." His name was Pierre Fallon. He said, "Wait until it's dark tonight. We'll tie down the tail and run it up to the 45" of manifold pressure where you say it starts and see what we can see." I couldn't wait. I went back to the hotel to eat dinner. I could barely get it down. Might this be it? He certainly seemed to know what he was talking about. But his laid-back way? His shop looked like someone who just tinkered with things. Tools and parts all over the place.

I got to the airport a half hour before sunset. In the high-north country in August, the sun doesn't set until after 10 p.m. I thought it wasn't ever going to get dark that night. We talked about where to tie down the tail. Any anchoring place I saw didn't look right to me. What if the cable broke? At 45" MP, the Mustang would be airborne or quickly headed for the nearest obstacle. I suggested we try it first with my holding the brakes. The tower closed at 11 p.m. so there would be no authority controlling traffic after they secured for the night. Planes would just advise with blind calls on the unicom frequency where they were taxiing, coming in to land or taking off, so other planes would know what was going on. I'd monitor the freq and announce my intentions of "running up at the start of Runway 22."

Pierre followed me out in his small truck and parked it off the runway on my left side about 100 feet away. I headed straight down the runway, turned on the landing light in case I started to roll so I could keep straight until I could stop. Then I slowly added power with my shoe toes full on the brakes and the stick as far back as I could pull it to keep the tail down. I had done this up to 36" before and it was quite an experience with the plane shaking like an enraged bull trying to break loose. 30", 36", 38" then 40". I was getting ready for a fast break down the runway. Ready to immediately pull back throttle at the first sign of forward movement. The engine was running smoothly. 42", 44". Bang! Pop! Bang-Bang! I saw a flame streak by the cockpit on the left as if there were a large dragon spewing fire at me. I pulled off the power and all seemed suddenly to be much quieter, except for my heart which was racing at top speed.

Pierre came into view of the landing light's arc in front and to the left, motioning to pull way back on the power. I did. He came alongside the cockpit, holding his wavy hair that was being blown even though the engine was at idle.

"I saw it! I saw it! That's it!" he exclaimed, "I saw the fire stream! But I couldn't tell which stack it was coming from. Do it again and I'll shine my flashlight on the stacks."

Powering up a second time wasn't that scary. I'd done it and it worked. At 44", it happened again. The dragon sure had a powerful fire stream. Even though I was expecting it, I flinched when it happened. Pierre's flashlight beam went up and down then in circles. I went back to idle. He came alongside and said to taxi it back to his hangar area. After getting out he said "Just as I thought, a valve is hanging up. The exhaust valve on cylinder B6 is sticking."

It was now close to midnight, but I was wide awake. So was Pierre. In his office with cold Cokes in hand, he told me the problem. When that cylinder fired, the exhaust valve opened, but wouldn't close all the way. The next time the cylinder was due to fire, the valve was still open and the firing combustion that should be pushing the cylinder down with all valves closed was instead coming out of the stack as a flame of fire. "But," he said, "I don't have any engine manuals to guide me in getting to that valve."

I barely slept that night. I called Randy, waking him up at 6:30 a.m. with the news. Could he come back up here with some manuals? Pierre has the tools. He couldn't. Then would he give me the phone number for the Pay 'N' Pak boat crew?

Pierre had a long phone line installed so he could tuck the phone under his chin while talking to the Pay N' Pak boat crew in Seattle. The crew gave him step-by-step instructions on replacing a Merlin engine exhaust valve. Only Miss America's tail would fit into his hangar.

He would. At 8:00 a.m. sharp I called them in Seattle. No, they couldn't come back up, but they'd be glad to guide Pierre through the steps on the phone and read him the specs from the manual. I skipped breakfast and hurried out to Pierre's hangar. He called the Pay 'N' Pak crew, spent about half an hour on the phone writing down the steps needed to get to the exhaust valve. When it got to the tricky part of taking off the cam shaft that made all 24 valves in that 12 cylinder engine go up and down in perfect sequence, they'd talk him through it on the phone.

Pierre went into action. The plane wouldn't fit in his hangar because it was too tall. But he pushed it back in as far as he could. It just covered the canopy area. The nose and prop stuck out looking as if it had crashed through the back and was coming out the front. He had the top cowling off and two tall wooden step ladders placed on either side. As I looked at the scene, I felt that wonderful sensation of hope after a long, negative siege. Then a telephone truck pulled up outside the hangar. The driver got out and greeted Pierre by his first name. They motioned to his office then to the plane. I went over. Pierre wanted a long phone line to the top of the engine. Not only were there no cordless phones in 1972, there weren't any Radio Shack-type stores in the area that sold long extension lines. This was to be a true "jury-rig" operation. And it worked.

With the phone tucked between his ear and shrugged-up right shoulder, he asked the questions and they gave the answers. The critical point was taking off the almost four-foot-long cam shaft wired in place so it could be put back at the same degree of rotation so the valves would open and close properly. Pierre was able to release the valve keepers and extract the exhaust valve. He held it in both hands, examining it like a bank teller might examine a $1,000 bill. He began nodding his head and came down the ladder toward me.

"Here it is and here's the problem. When someone ground this valve, it was held on the stem with strong pliers or vise-grips. You can see the marks on the stem. They trapped carbon. When hot, they expand. The valve spring wasn't strong enough to force the valve down."

"Can you fix it?" I asked.

"Should have a new valve and valve spring, but I don't have any. Best I can do is to grind the stem as smooth as I can and hope it holds. They're filled with salt to help dissipate the heat. Want to try it?"

Of course I did. At this point my hopes were high. That night back out on the runway, it went up to 45" and was smooth all the way up and down. Pierre had a bottle in his drawer. We finished it. He didn't take credit cards, just gave me a bill and said, "Send me a check in Canadian funds." He was a trusting man.

The next day the tower cleared me for takeoff. Pierre was at the edge of the runway. I waved a "thank you" to him as I added power. Off it went. Perfect. I asked the tower if I could turn back for a low pass. The answer came back, "Certainly you can, we like to see that thing flying for a change." I came back as fast and as low as I could. Right at Pierre's hangar I pulled the nose up into a departing slow roll. In the States, the FAA may not have been so approving of those antics within the boundaries of an active airport, but I think everyone on the ground understood my elation.

Chapter 12

The Racing Saga Continues
1972 National Air Races • Reno, Nevada

This was my fourth National Air Race. By now I was getting used to all the time and preparation it took to get an Unlimited race plane in the air. I was even getting used to all the problems. As a matter of fact, I was getting used to problems as being a way of life in Unlimited air racing—sort of like raising children. By the third bout with diseases like measles, mumps and whooping cough, you just accept problems as part of raising children. I had my part in raising four.

When another problem showed up it was just that—another problem. But by the fifth time in air racing and all the problems I'd had, I felt I had paid my dues. I deserved to have problemless races from now on.

But that isn't the way it works.

Here are the entries from my logbook for the 1972 National Championships, my fourth appearance:

...Changed to a longer Bearcat prop. Qualified at 387 mph/3,400 RPM, but plane seemed not to be developing full power.

...Oil pan gasket blew in heat race, but came in third so got in finals

...In FINALS, coolant line blew on second to last lap—pulled back power, came in third with 398 mph average speed.

...New Bearcat prop on, but plane seemed to hit slush over 400 mph. Later discovery was that the large Bearcat prop needed lower gears to reduce the RPMs. The Mustang's regular higher .42 gears (42% of engine RPM) had the prop turning too fast. At 400 mph, it was like an air brake and the tips were probably going through the speed of sound (cavitating). A slower turning prop was needed, so I had one made—the next explosion was a lulu!

Well, at least there is another fix, another idea to try, surely there's nothing else that can go wrong with the plane itself. A new event has entered the race circuit. I won't have to wait a year before the Reno races in September to try new prop gears. The "First Miami National Air Races" will be January 17–19, 1973 at the New Tamiami Airport.

Can't wait!

This year was highlighted by a visit to the airport by "Miss America 1972" who inscribed her picture "from one Miss America to another... Laurie Lea Schaefer, Miss America 1972."

"Another Blow-Up—and Dead Stick Landing"
Miami National Air Races • January 17 – 19, 1973
New Tamiami Airport (Now Kendall–Miami Airport)

This was to get back to wonderful, flat Florida to go pylon air racing—and in the middle of winter what could be nicer? Dave Zeuschel had the "boat people" up in Seattle make me new prop gears, .38 (38%).

To review the entire RPM (revolutions per minute) thing so the significance of the next incident will be clearer and make more sense to the reader, the original Merlin gears were .47, i.e., the prop turned at 47% of engine speed. In Piper Cubs and other "non-geared" engines, the prop turns at the same RPM the engine does. But RPM is power. The higher the RPM, the higher the power. Today's small 4-cylinder cars develop their power by having the engine turn faster than larger cars. An 8-cylinder larger car carrying 4 people might do 2,500 RPM at 70 mph, but a small 4-cylinder car with 4 people would do 4,600 RPM, the engine turning nearly twice as fast to carry 4 people. At those high RPMs, it's important to change oil at least every 3,000 miles—the more often the better. But cars have relatively small flywheels to absorb the torque power; planes have propellers. Props are an airfoil. The longer the prop, the faster the tip ends go through the air at the same RPM as at the hub. When the tips go so fast that they exceed the speed of sound (about 750 mph), the tips actually slow the plane down by "cavitating." They almost suck air the opposite way. So for me to put on the longer Bearcat prop, I had to make it go slower but still feed it with high RPM for power. As I mentioned, the original Merlin gears turned the prop at 47% of engine RPM (.47 gears). To get even more RPM and more power from the Merlin with a longer prop, I think, Rolls-Royce tested and developed the .42 gears for the Merlin. The lower the gear ratio, the thinner, and therefore weaker, the gear vanes. Mine were to be the "boat" (Unlimiteds) type gears.

With a Bearcat prop and new .38 gears, I'd sure as hell give those Bearcats a race for their money, even with their 3,250 hp engines versus the 2,800 hp stock!

Christa and I left the Los Angeles area on a clear, sun-filled day for Miami. I was so confident of a trouble-free race that I packed our skis in the wing bay. The long ammo area was the perfect length to carry both pairs of skis as well as boots and poles. We'd stop off at Aspen on the way back for a few days of skiing. To accommodate all our baggage for swimming, racing and skiing, I took out the rear seat, put everything in soft parachute-type bags that I stuffed in the rear compartment. This gave Christa a bean-bag, rather comfortable looking, I thought, lounge chair. She, however, said she preferred the regular padded, bucket rear seat. But she managed.

Up in the clear air I climbed to 17,500 feet, an eastbound VFR (non-instrument altitude), to see what the large Bearcat prop did at high altitude. I could have gone over the 18,500 feet westbound altitude, but higher than 18,500 feet, I would have to be on an instrument flight plan being tracked by radar with my transponder on. I could see over 200 miles. I wanted the freedom to go down and up in altitude without having to get the permission an IFR flight would require. I wanted to check the prop's performance at different altitudes. It had to be good. Good? It was phenomenal! That big prop took large bites out of the cold air up there. You could just feel it belonged up there. With my airspeed showing 250 mph, at that altitude I was really doing about 340 mph allowing for the less dense air. My DME showed a ground speed of 415 mph! That's really moving. Of course, it meant that I had a tailwind of about 75 mph, not unusual going east, but to me it was the prop. I didn't want to think tailwind. I needed the confidence booster that this prop was doing it all by itself and would eat those Bearcats alive on the race course!

I stopped at Albuquerque to refuel and then headed for Jackson, Mississippi. What I am about to tell you must be held in the strictest of confidence. It'll be just between you and me. Okay? You'll never repeat it another living soul. As a matter of fact, maybe you could just tear this page out of the book so no one else can read it. It will destroy my "I'm never wrong, I can't afford to be" mantra. Okay, here it is.

Back up to 17,500 feet, the air was still clear and I could see at least 200 miles. I decided to shut down all my navigation radios including the radar transponder. I wanted to really enjoy this speed—this freedom from worry. Not to be tethered to radar, VOR signals, ADF directions—nothing. Just fly as if I were in my sailboat where I can go anywhere, no questions asked. I could see the Mississippi River in the distance, maybe 100 miles ahead. I started my slow descent to get the maximum out of every drop of gasoline.

At 10,000 feet, I switched back on all the radios and transponder and DME, but didn't bother to tune in a VOR radio navigation station. I could see everything. Why bother to have navigation aids? After all, I was coming back far enough into the real world by even deigning to make a radio call. I could see Jackson, Mississippi right ahead on the Mississippi River. I called Jackson approach control and announced that I was about 25 miles out for landing. Approach called back saying they didn't have any targets in that area. (In those days, we had only Mode A transponders, not like

from *Sports Illustrated* 10/2/72

wouldn't be here. But who likes normal human beings?"

Partly as a result of Duty's proficiency and partly as a result of meticulous planning by Chief Judge Stan Brown and his staff of hyperenergetic businessmen, the Reno races rang up eight consecutive years without a fatality or injury. "We've had our Maydays," Duty said, "but—knock wood—we've brought 'em all back alive every year." But this year he didn't knock wood hard enough.

The first heat of the Unlimited races brought a baleful omen. Howie Keefe, in his *Miss America*, began a routine pass over the top of Lyle Shelton, a DC-8 pilot from Cypress, Calif. flying a beautiful purple-and-white F8F Bearcat, *The Phast Phoenix*. Just as Keefe's red-white-and-blue Mustang lapped onto the Bearcat at something over 400 mph, Shelton began to climb into him; the result was a near collision that had the crowd gasping. "Oh, they missed by two, three feet," Jerry Duty said, his eyes blazing with anger. "It adds spice to the races, but it's the kind of spice we can do without." At a meeting later, Duty reminded all the pilots at the top of his lungs: "Don't move into any space you haven't cleared or you'll do your racing someplace else." The message was received.

continued

the Mode C of today that tells radar our altitude and speed and a special "squawk" that identifies us from other planes). No target? What's wrong here? They asked me to make some identifying turns, so I turned left for one minute then back right one minute. They came back, "We have you as a target about 10 miles west of Vicksburg." "Vicksburg?" I thought. "How could it be? That's Jackson right ahead."

At that moment, Christa leaned forward from her bean-bag, baggage ensemble, tapped me on the shoulder, held a Ramada Inn road atlas at my right shoulder and pointed sternly to Vicksburg on the road map and then moved her finger forward to Jackson to the east. My gosh! Vicksburg! A quick glance at my chart showed it had just a 4,000-foot runway (today's charts show it at 5,000 feet). I wanted at least 5,000 feet, especially at a strange airport. In putting on the longer Bearcat prop, my crew had pumped the oleo struts on the landing gear up to full height, but even then I had to make a low tail landing to keep the prop from possibly hitting the ground. With the nose up high, the runway was almost fully blocked out by it. You might need a long ground run after touching down. At an airport you knew, you could judge how soon the runway end was coming by familiar buildings whizzing by.

Approach told me I was about 50 miles from Jackson. My gas was low. I probably could make it, but I had already used up all my glide altitude thinking Vicksburg was Jackson. I was kicking myself. Hell, I'd driven across the Mississippi on the bridge into Vicksburg some years ago. I'd never even been to Jackson. How ever did I get the notion that Jackson was on the Mississippi River? Just another dumb Yankee's misconception of the South. And Christa. She loved to follow road maps. It was a perfect clear day for it. In the average plane, you're usually lower and can see the ground. It's boring riding in the back seat of a Mustang, up high for 3 hours, without anything to do, especially when you're flying in or above the clouds and can't see the ground. It's rare to be in air that clear. If I was going to dope off, I'm sure thankful it was on a clear day so that Christa could follow a road map. Of course, if it hadn't been so clear, I'd have been attending to my Ps and Qs, as my mother would say, and been doing radio navigation instead of visual.

So my choices were to try to stretch the gas to Jackson, 75 miles away, or attempt a landing at Vicksburg. I was now low enough so that I could see a golf course at the

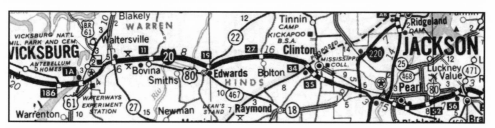

For some reason, I had it fixed in my mind that Jackson, Mississippi was on the Mississippi River, when in reality it was Vicksburg. I decided not to try to go the extra 75 miles to Jackson—running out of gas is the worst thing a pilot can do and I wasn't going to try to stretch it just because it was my plan to land at Jackson. I'd take my chances with the smaller airport at Vicksburg.

south end of the airport with minor tree growth. That meant I could make a long, low approach to the runway. With that, only a 4,000-foot-long runway wasn't too bad. I called on their unicom frequency to get wind direction and velocity and to broadcast my intentions to land from the south. I didn't want anyone pulling out on the runway when my nose was up so I couldn't see them. I made this clear on my unicom transmission. It's best to not try to be airline-pilot cool in such conditions. When coming into an airport in a P-51 Mustang, you know from your own pre-owner days that P-51 pilots are looked up to. I did. There's a strong temptation to play that larger-than-life "Roger, that" role in your radio transmissions but my MO at a strange airport always did and always will include the phrase "This is my first time here (even if it wasn't), I'd like all the help and advice you can give me." It's amazing what that will do for you, no matter what you're flying.

So I set up a pattern to land to the north, with an approach over the golf course. One hundred yards before the runway, I was hanging it on the prop like a carrier approach. Instead of holding the stick back in that configuration, you have slight forward pressure ahead and to the right to help counteract the torque. This leaves your rudders free to pick up a low wing. I was low, carrying a fair amount of power and a Mustang has a distinctive, loud sound. I could see golfers moving quickly out of my path. Boy, if I screw this landing up, I'm really going to be pissed off at myself for being so stupid in the first place. The 4,000 feet proved to be plenty with that low approach. To top it off, I took off and left my Chevron gas charge card behind at the FBO! Okay, so you've promised you won't relate any of this to a soul. Not even to me, if we meet.

At the races, I qualified in the number 2 spot at 376 mph, pretty good in the denser altitude at nearly sea level versus the 5,000-foot elevation at Reno and nearly 3,000 feet at Mojave. Also, it was the much tighter oval 6-pylon course than Reno's high-speed "cross-country" pylon course. I was happy. It meant that my actual speed was about 10% faster, in the area of 410 mph. I'll take that. I pulled only 95" doing it. Wait until I open it up to the "safe" limit of 115". Those Bearcats will think a V2 rocket is in the race with them. That will make them shrink and shudder. Just because those big Bearcat bullies are taller and beefier than "Miss A" in the pits (I try to never pit next to one), I'll no longer be flying in their prop wash, they'll be staggering around in mine! Just they wait. They're not going to kick sand in my face anymore (if you're under 50, you won't get the full meaning of that last assertion).

So the races begin. It's just a heat race to determine pole positions. I didn't need to be on the pole. It would be an air start. I could hang back and take an easy third place. Not show my colors yet. But I couldn't do that. I'd been suckin' hind parts too long. This was my fifth race against those bullies. I'd make 'em pay today, tomorrow and every race into the distant future. The patsy had grown into a real man. The start was routine. I was in the third pole position and rounded the first pylon set of 3 in third place. Stayed in third the next set of 3 with a constant bank turn around the 3, then down the straightaway in front of the crowd. Ahead were 2 Bearcats. I wasn't gaining on them nor were they pulling away from me. Another 3 pylons. Nothing changed. Rounding out of the turn to the right of the grandstand headed down the straightaway, I couldn't resist it anymore.

From a mild 90" of manifold pressure, I upped the RPM to 3,400. They told me that with my lower-power drain Dash 7 Merlin blower, I could go to 115" and it would be like 125" of manifold pressure. If that power was just sitting there for me to use and my super-tricked-up engine, to paraphrase Dave my engine guy "115 MP would be like it was running at cruise" (again, let's remember folks, that max with water injection during the war was 73 MP and then for only 5 minutes, over that you had to tear the engine down). With utter confidence and not one, but two Bearcats to mow down ahead of me, I'd pull abreast at the turn and then on the straightaway in front of the crowd, I'd leave them in my dust. As I look back, maybe I was a wee bit cocky, but someone had to challenge the schoolyard bullies. And where best to show them up? Right in front of all the girls rolling their hoops.

I rolled out of the turn, pulled ahead of the lead Bearcat, leveled my wings, took aim at the next set of 3 pylons and WHAM, BANG! ZSSSSSOOOOM! I frantically scanned the instrument cluster for some indication of what had happened. It felt like I had hit an air wall. My speed was slowing dramatically. The RPM gauge had gone from 3,400 to almost its peg at 5,000. Five thousand RPM! Holy smokes! And

2 Pilots Escape Injury In Race Emergencies

By DON BEDWELL
Herald Aviation Writer

Two front-running competition pilots narrowly escaped injury in aerial emergencies during Saturday's action in the Great Miami Air Race.

The two Unlimited Division leaders were knocked out of contention by mechanical troubles on the next-to-last laps of their cup races.

Both hope to be back in action for today's finals of the six-day meet at Tamiami Airport.

HOWIE KEEFE, a Los Angeles advertising executive, made a hurried landing billowing smoke after his P51 fighter "Miss America" blew an engine in one race. Keefe said his greatest concern was that scalding oil from the damaged engine would blow into his eyes.

Another P51 pilot, Dr. Chris Cummins of Riverside, Calif., declared an emergency while leading in an earlier race.

After a throttle linkage broke, Cummins found his modified fighter coasting along without power with six competitors bearing down on him at nearly 500 miles an hour.

"Suddenly it got real quiet out there," the radiologist said of his power loss. "I immediately declared 'mayday' and pulled up to get out of the traffic."

BOTH PILOTS safely dead-sticked in for landings as fire and rescue units roared into position alongside the runway and an emergency helicopter warmed up nearby to hurry casualties to a hospital.

Keefe's misfortune gave his race to Grumman Bearcat pilot Lyle Shelton, last year's national point champion and leading money winner.

Cummins' race was captured by Lloyd Hamilton of Santa Rosa, Calif., piloting a British Hawker Sea Fury.

Saturday's day of racing brought out a crowd variously estimated at 25,000 to 35,000.

SPONSORS, who hope to raise funds for a Miami aviation museum, predict a larger turnout for today's showdown event.

"We've got the weather, we've got the press with us and we've got the planes," said Jay Van Vechten, a race organizer. "We'll just have to see how the public turns out today."

Finals and consolation races are scheduled today in the Unlimited, Formula One or "midget" division, T6 trainer and sport biplane divisions.

Wing-walking, precision flying, parachuting and other aviation-oriented activities will be repeated for today's air race crowd.

The airport is at SW 137th Avenue and 120th Street.

Escaping injury was not my concern—it was the injury to the engine and to my plans to show-up those "bully-Bearcats" that really hurt!

I was slowing down. What the hell happened? But my speed was dropping so fast, there was no time to think. I had to get this baby down in one piece. There were two east/west runways, one to the south in front of the grandstand where all the emergency equipment was and one about a half mile north. I had never landed on the north one. I had no "markers" to tell me how close I might be coming to the end of the runway.

The best choice was to use the south side runway. I decided to make a teardrop approach to it rather than risk getting too far away. The approach end was almost under me and I was headed away from it. I turned about 30° left, tried to gain altitude, but my airspeed had already dropped from over 400 mph to just over 200 mph and I hadn't climbed at all! *Let me explain to you, the reader, what I didn't know, so that you can have a bird's-eye view to better appreciate what was happening—the prop gears had sheared, the prop went into a free-wheeling, low (flat) pitch. That big, flat Bearcat prop made it like pushing a barn door in front of me.* I pulled the prop control full back to put it into the less-air-resistant high pitch—not like feathering a prop, but as close to it as you can get with a prop that doesn't feather. No change. In the 210° turn back to the runway, I used mostly rudder. I didn't want to increase drag with anymore back stick elevator pressure than I needed to make the turn. I watched the airspeed. As fast as the airspeed was dropping, if it went below 150 mph when I rolled out, I was in trouble. The runway was still over a football field away and I was sinking fast. I could not understand why the long-gliding Mustang that was "clean" (i.e., gear and flaps up) was losing speed as if they were down. Don't touch the flaps or even the gear. Landing on the runway gear up was better than gear down in the brush even 10 yards short of the runway.

I was about 10 feet over the end of the runway. I dumped the gear. I kept the flaps up so I'd have more rudder control. Flaps disturb the air going back over the rudder. Then the oil that covered the windshield became a problem. I knew it was there, but high in the approach, you're looking mostly off to the side, not over the nose. As you are about to land, you look straight down the cowl line on top of the engine and use your side vision through the windshield to stay straight ahead on your landing. I couldn't see through the windshield. By side vision, I got near the ground, raised the nose, then was compelled to see ahead where I was going. Instinctively, I put my head outside the cockpit to look ahead. A stream of oil immediately hit me in the face and coated my glasses. I couldn't see anything now. With my left hand I pulled off my glasses. I could see again. In the movies I have, at this point the plane's right wing starts to dip, the plane starts to turn right, balloons, then settles back down and goes straight. As I slowed down to about 60 mph with all wheels on the deck, I started gentle "S" turns to see where the end of the runway was coming up. I saw two tow bars forming an "X" and decided to go over them rather than risk a ground loop with one brake oil-covered and the other grabbing. The way they say a runway is closed is to paint an "X" on it. The runway on the north side was open when there wasn't racing, but the south one was closed. They figured putting tow-bars there would be the same as painting an "X" because it was temporary. They sure made a rattle when I went over them. After that, they painted a big "X" using white-wash hoping those Miami rainstorms wouldn't wash it away. I got out, wiped the oil off the part of the cowl that had COX, my sponsor's name, printed on it because there were sure to be pictures, and let the crew be aboard while towed back in front of the crowd into the pit area. The crew deserved some display. I rode back in the fire truck. Besides, they got their clothes oily from the cockpit. Mine already were.

It was futile to attempt to fix the engine to get ready for the races. Even using the full resources of all the other teams on the ramp back at Reno, repairing an engine that had been run up to 5,000 RPM with rods that had probably been stretched, was not realistic. Putting in a new engine, yes. But I didn't have a new engine. This is the engine I was going to race until I retired some 30 years later.

The prop gears had sheared. But how? Why? Dave Zeuschel checked with the Seattle "boat" people that had cut them. They were puzzled to hear they had sheared. They claimed, "Those gears were good until 2,500 horsepower and you're running them in the Merlin's 1,600 hp engine to maybe only 1,800 horsepower."

Dave did the math. At 3,400 RPM and 115" MP, my "transport" engine Merlin with Dash 7 gears was right at 2,500 horsepower. Warranty voided. Plus, a $20,000 engine was mostly scrap. I felt funny with Christa in the Miami International Airport carrying our skis mixed in with all the returning Caribbean cruise passengers with their suntans, floppy hats and large straw baskets. I did spot another couple carrying skis. I tried to blend in with them. When I queried them, they said, "Of course, a lot of people in Miami go to the Rockies to ski, just like you people from Los Angeles." How come that still doesn't make any sense to me?

Dejection and Rebirth • 1973–'74

Reno National Air Races 1973
"A Wet Ignition System Doesn't Hack It"

After getting a new engine following the near disaster in Miami, I took it to Reno to race the 1973 Nationals. A real dud. Couldn't get the new engine up to any power at all. This was getting discouraging. To me, the real down side was not that things happened with the temperamental Mustang and finely-machined Merlin engine, but that no one seemed to know what was happening at the time. It was having to deal with this seemingly constant series of unknowns that was getting to me. The prop gears exploding in Miami was certainly not an unknown. Those things I could handle. The two years of dropping out of the sky with bad mags, and the agony of the mystery of the sticking valve in

Bleacher-type seats were at the races, but many bought "pit passes" and watched the races from the pit area. Those who insured the races usually restricted the pit passes to those 18 years or older.

Canada had developed in me a depressed attitude of "What the hell." Then along came another one.

At the Reno 1973 races with a new engine, I could not get over 82" MP. What in the hell is going on here? A new engine and no one knows why it's running rough? Why can't I get it over 82 inches? No answers. I dropped way down to ninth in qualifying. Of course, more Unlimiteds were now racing and they were getting faster. My 384-mph qualifying speed would have been pretty good a few years before. In spite of it all, I was able to grab third place in a heat race that got me into the FINALS (now called the Gold Race). I was in the sixth pole spot and with a rough-running engine was lucky to finish the race, and even luckier to get a fifth place because the fast planes were starting to blow engines. If you were able to finish a race, you could almost start counting on moving up a place. At least one plane ahead of you on the pole would probably blow an engine.

After the races were over, it was discovered that my problems were coming from a shorted-out spark plug harness which had water in it. Now I saw the reason so my frustrations eased. Back at Van Nuys someone had okay'd the mobile engine-wash service to clean my engine. They used a high-pressure, steam-cleaning system. They were used to cleaning regular engines and knew the areas, like the magnetos, to avoid shooting with their powerful steam spray. They didn't understand the places to avoid shooting high-pressure in a Merlin. They didn't know a harness line carrying a high-voltage charge to the spark plugs from a flexible oil-feed line may also have collected a little oil. Clean was their objective, especially if they were going to have their work judged on what they had done to a racing Mustang. Racing at high voltage and power, water caused shorts. Naturally, the engine would be rough. Okay, so problem solved, but my interest was waning in this atmosphere of high-speed, high-cost, mystery-problem plagued world.

I parked the plane off in the boonies and started to find other interests such as sailboat racing in my newly acquired Coronado 25. We had an active racing-around-the-buoys group in Marina del Rey. And I had found a crewman, Jim Wood, who loved to race too. For the Wednesday night "Beer Can" races, he'd have the boat ready and trimmed at 5:30 for a 6 p.m. start. I could just make it from the office, change clothes and out we'd go. We got pretty good at it.

Skip and His Crew to the Rescue

I wasn't missing the plane. My crew chief, Skip Higginbotham, seemed to have some time on his hands. From him I learned that there is a species of man in the world who likes to do things without any thought of compensation, using their brains and their hands and their backs. They have a vision of making mechanical things better. This was a foreign concept to me because I understood marketing. Working on a new

Skip Higginbotham (right) was a "hands-on" crew chief. Along with Ron Gullett (left), he quarterbacked a volunteer overhaul of "Miss America" by working nights and weekends.

consumer product or advertising program could keep me up until the wee hours of the morning and then, with only a few hours sleep, get up and start working on it again. Not so with engines and complicated systems, at which Skip was a master. He was a specialist at Lockheed, had helped build and race cars and seemed to love all facets of motor sports. I always thought all those types lived in the southeastern U.S. and spoke with a twangy, southern drawl.

We still joke about it today. Skip found a hangar on his own initiative, kidnapped "Miss America" (which wasn't hard because no one was guarding her) and sequestered her from not only view, but from me. It was his "Don't worry, driver, let me take care of this" attitude, that let me walk away in peace and forget about the old girl. Somehow, I still don't know how, he recruited 4 other nonpaid guys to help him do the work, including Ron Fleming, Russ Gullett and Bill Statler. Skip was obviously not only handy with his brains and hands, but also with management and leadership skills. This was beyond what Tom Sawyer had pulled on Huckleberry Finn to get

In keeping with the "Miss America" image, crew and friends always had race crew jackets to wear in the pits. In this photo are (standing) Sue Keefe (son Tom's wife), Pete Hoyt, Mary Hively (COX), son Don Keefe, me, daughter Dorrie, Jim Reid, Bill Yoak, Bob Garrett (COX), Joyce Pitts, (kneeling) Ben Garrett (COX), Bob Willen, Bill Miller, Bill Pitts, my son Tom Keefe.

him to white-wash the fence. Skip was a real leader for over 8 months! A few asides from Skip's notes during his TLC period with "Miss America," whom he called the "Lady," are:

"In an attempt to keep costs down, I solicited and found free hangar space on Van Nuys airport to do the overhaul on the Lady. It was a large, empty hangar. A perfect place for what I wanted and off the beaten path so we could work in privacy. One day, we all showed up and there was a padlock on the door! All our gear, tools and the Lady were being held hostage due to an unknown litigation by the owner. I tracked the owner down to a place 70 miles south in Orange County, brought along pictures and models of the Lady to show them she was no ordinary Lady. I was able to swap these for 2 months hangar rent so we could finish the overhaul. What he got are now collector's items—if he still has them, he got good rent for those two months.

"We finished a complete overhaul of the electrical system, no small feat in a P-51, the cooling system with new aluminum pipes, all engine systems and a host of other items. After Howie test-hopped it, he said it was better than perfect, it was fantastic! That, along with a compliment from the respected engine man, Dave Zeuschel, gave me a lift I'll always remember!"

After this facelift by Skip and his gang, my spirits had risen once again. I was eager to take her "out-on-the-town."

```
Howie Keefe----13376 Beach Ave., Venice, CA. 90272 (213) 822-1996
        President, Pro-Plates--Airport Approach Charts
  * * * * * Howie Keefe  and "Miss America",Unlimited Class Race Plane * * * * *
Type: P-51 Mustang(Highly Modified) | Fuel: 100 octane cruise, 130/145 racing.
Value:$150,000                       | Consumption:  Cruise- 65 gal per hr
Top Speed:510 mph  Landing Speed: 110mph |           Racing- 300 gph(200 gals gas plus
Cruise:300 mph @ 10,000'             |                        100 gals methanol)
       350 mph @ 20,000'             | Originally Built: 1943
Race Speeds: Up to 450 mph around    | Special Modifications:
            pylons-40' above ground. |   Clipped Wings-(4 ft removed) Hoerner tips added
Engine: Rolls Royce Merlin V-12(12 clyn) | Canopy specially blown to streamline
       1800 hp(2500 while racing)    |   Can carry two passengers(or 125 extra gals)
Engine Cost: $25,000                 |   Engine:Balanced crankshaft,shimmed blowers,
Gas Capacity: 190 gals normal(special|       special timing, special piston rings,
  tanks can increase to 400 gals)    |       extra ring at top(Headland type),Water
Minimum Runway Length: 4,000'(possible|       injected(ADI)
  to 3,500' with clear approach)     |   Gun Bays in Wings used for special tanks
Power Settings:                      | Maneuvering Speeds: (Clipped wings add about 10%
  Take-Off:61"MP/3000 RPM            |                    to normal Mustang minimums)
  Climb: 46"/2700 RPM                |   Stall: 105 mph
  Max. Cruise: 46"/2700 RPM          |   Climb: 175 mph
  War Emergency Power: 65"(5 minutes) |   Cruise:250 mph(plus 2% per thousand feet)
  Race Power:*110"/3600 RPM (15 minutes) |  Land: 110 mph
  *Race settings are 70% over Red Line |   Red Line: 510 mph
  often causing engines to "blow".   | Maximum Range: 2,000 miles
Paint Scheme: Designed to be seen top & bottom going around pylons(by Gene Clay, Chief
                                                Designer, North American)
```

Shown above are data for the various phases of "Miss America's" operations.

Chapter 13

Another Wild, Wild August 1974!
This Time Coast-to-Coast

I t seemed that when flying "Miss America," the year was divided into two seasons: August and September. August was the height of the air show season and September was the National Air Races at Reno. Other times were random and incidental. This year was no exception, but I wanted to make this August, August of 1974, especially full of activity. August was named after Augustus Caesar, a leader of the Roman Empire. The adjective, august, means majestic dignity and grandeur. This August was going to be all of that.

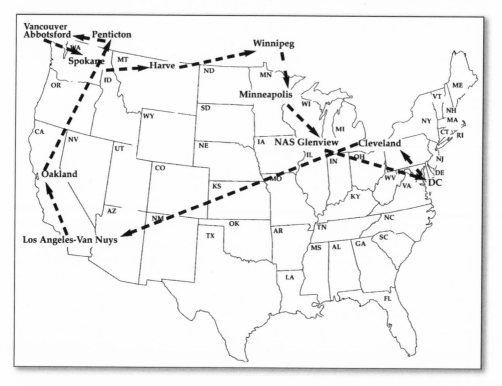

My memories are still fresh of the footloose month of air shows across Canada and the United States.

I had been fired from my job as the Southern California Regional Manager of the arm of the newspaper industry's Bureau of Advertising, but was getting a nice 6-month separation package. I was going to use that time to not have to worry about flying back from an air show in Denver, over the Rockies on a Sunday night, to be back at work on Monday morning. This "air show August" I was going to do air shows coast-to-coast. I'd become a "carnie," a traveling carnival showman.

I lined up air shows in Seattle and Spokane (the year of the World's Fair), Abbotsford, Penticton and Winnipeg (their 100th year), Canada, COX's home office brass in Minneapolis, Glenview Naval Air Station north of Chicago, the Cleveland Lakefront Air Show and a meeting with the FAA in Washington, DC. I loved the thought of "hitting the road," of accommodations and cars arranged for you at each stop. Just show up and enjoy. This was the life. Later on I could find another job and go back to the real world, but not now.

August 2, 1974

I headed north from Los Angeles for Oakland. My former counterpart in San Francisco, John Temple-Raston, had a son who loved P-51s. I stopped to see him and on the way had three weird experiences:

1. the VOR needle didn't seem to track right;
2. Christa, in the back seat, couldn't get her ears unplugged in a fast dive; and
3. you don't ever want to land a P-51 into a setting sun. All these 3 things combined to make me about an hour late.

I decided not to file an instrument flight plan. It was mostly broken to scattered clouds and clear at Oakland. I'd just go "on top" of the clouds. With the VOR tuned to a station en route to Oakland, the first puzzle was that I suddenly found myself over Santa Maria, well west of my course. I shrugged off the anomaly and followed the coast to the Oakland area, not bothering to navigate by radio. Oakland now had a broken layer of clouds over it. I called Oakland Radar Approach Control, became a known "target" for traffic advisory from them, found a big hole in the clouds, put the nose down and dove for it from about 10,000 feet. Just as I went through the hole into the clear air, Christa was pounding on my back. Her face showed pain. She pointed vigorously to her ears. I realized what had happened. I had not prepared her for a sudden descent. I had not warned her to clear her ears and keep them clear in the dive. If you don't do that, the pressure builds up to the point that you can't clear them—and the pain is excruciating! My only choice for her was to immediately climb back up to altitude and lower pressure. I pulled back on the stick and zoomed almost straight up through the cloud layer. If someone had seen me, they might have thought that I was doing a loop starting down through the clouds, had gone up and would be coming back down again. We had gone down from 10,000 feet. It required me to go up to 11,000 feet before she indicated relief and a nodding smile. I descended slower this time. She was holding her nose and blowing all the way down.

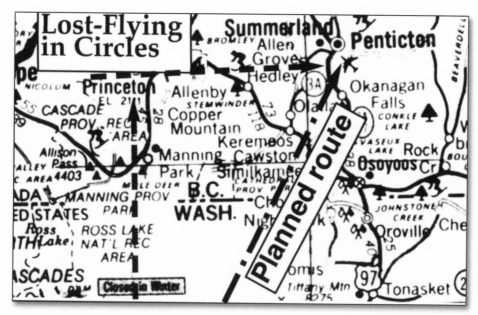

Before I spotted, by chance, the Princeton VOR station's white/orange building, I was ready to land on a road before fuel ran out. This map doesn't show the sharp drop in elevation into the Penticton area.

Under the clouds again, the sun was setting on the horizon which was clear. It was a marine cloud layer that ended at the shore. I was cleared to land, made the standard approach to the long runway on the west side, touched down, throttled back and suddenly I couldn't see! With the giant prop at idle and having to look through it at the sun at the level of the runway, the strobe effect was dramatic! I had never experienced that before and will never let myself get into that situation again. I was getting totally disoriented. Fortunately, I had a long runway and power to add. Just a little increase in the RPM and the strobe effect abated. But that little increase was more than I could handle and taxi; besides, when I pulled back the power again, the dazzling strobe would return. My subconscious was shouting at me to "Go around! Take off. You'll be safe up in the air!" I did.

I explained to the tower what happened. Received an "I understand. Cleared for another landing." But I wasn't going to try that again. I'd fly around until after sunset if I had to. The wind was only about 5 mph. With that long runway, I asked for and received permission to make a downwind, *down-sun* landing. When I got to the terminal, John and his son were there. As we talked, he said his son almost went crazy when I took off again. He had been waiting for over an hour and now you weren't going to stop at all, you were going away. He was doing flip-flops and pounding the arm of the leather couch in the lobby. I understood. I was a kid once, too.

August 3, 1974

We headed north to the Penticton Air Show, about 50 miles north of the U.S./Canadian border, with a stop for gas at Redmond, Oregon. This was all new country to me. The leg from Redmond to Penticton, Canada was about 450 miles long with few visual checkpoints or radio navigation aids, especially at the end. It was one of those "shoot and aim" DR (dead reckoning) flights, but with the comfort of one radio navigation station at the other end, 50 miles west of Penticton, the Princeton VOR station. What happened "at the other end" still sends chills through me to this day.

There was nothing, absolutely nothing to use as a strong checkpoint on the ground or in the air. The rivers and forests below all looked the same. And, of course, there wouldn't be a large "Welcome to Canada" billboard in the woods or a long line on the ground showing where the border was. Being over country like that, I might as well have been out over the Pacific Ocean. Over the ocean might have been even better. I wouldn't have spent so much time and energy trying to identify which river that was below and the "but wait, no town should be there" false identifications. I had tuned into the Princeton VOR and the needle on the VOR was starting to get twitchy. Ah, fine, I thought and settled back. Just fly to the VOR, head due east 50 miles and you'll be over Penticton. A snap.

The closer I got to the VOR, instead of the VOR needle settling down to give me a solid course to the VOR, it would be solid for a minute then suddenly jump to the left 30°, then back to the right 30° to right of course, then stay on course. Watching these weird dances of the VOR needle, I began thinking I must be over an undiscovered uranium-ore deposit. What else could cause this? I bored straight ahead at 300 mph at 11,500 feet. The mountains ahead were up to 8,000 feet and rising. Three thousand feet up is not very high. Suddenly the VOR needle swung radically to the right and the VOR switched from TO to FROM. Had I passed over the VOR without seeing it? Impossible. A VOR is a very distinctive orange and white structure that looks like an ice cream cone stuck upside down in a cake. You can't miss them, especially in the green wilderness I was over. Just plowing on ahead no longer seemed the wise thing to do. My gas was starting to get low. I had maybe one-half hour left and I didn't know where the hell I was. No towns below, no roads, no rivers, nothing. What to do? Where to go?

One thing I knew was that I didn't have the time to stumble around in this wilderness.

I picked up the mike and called Vancouver's Radar Center that was located about 150 miles to the west, but they had remote stations closer than that. I asked if they had a target near the Princeton VOR. They didn't. I was only 3,500 feet above the ground so they probably couldn't pick me up on their scopes. I now had only about 20 minutes worth of gas left, but there was nothing I had passed over 20 minutes (100 plus miles) back where I could land, and there certainly wasn't anything below me for even an emergency landing. I had to at least know where I was. Vancouver Radar said that if I was at least 15,000 feet near Princeton VOR, they could pick me up. But climbing would take gas. Which way to head when climbing? I had been able to contact their radar from where I was, so I decided to climb to 15,000 feet in a circular pattern. At least I could talk to them. At about 14,000 feet, they called out "Radar contact. We see you circling. You're 15 miles west of the Princeton VOR and about 65 miles west of the Penticton airport." If there had been a grotto up there, I might have parked the plane and gone in to kneel down. I wasn't religious, but at that moment, I could have been.

I headed due east on my compass, pulled back on the throttle to conserve fuel and went into a long, low power glide. At 250 mph, I'd cover the 65 miles to Penticton in about 15 minutes. My 20 minutes of gas at regular cruise power would last at least another 25 minutes at this low power. Even though I seemed to be home safe, my heart was beating fast. I barely breathed. Christa, riding trustingly in the back, didn't have a clue as to what had happened nor what was happening. Below me, plain as day, I saw the Princeton VOR, looking bright and white/orange as a VOR should look. The needle was still doing its idiot dance and twitch, but I no longer cared at that moment. In an instant, the high mountains suddenly ended. The almost 9,000-foot-high mountains dropped 8,000 feet into the valley below. It was as if I were suddenly suspended in air! Never can I recall such a sudden change in height. And what a welcome sight! Way down below was an airport on the edge of a lake. I could cut off the engine and easily glide down to it from that altitude. I almost started chortling at my new-found comfort. Approaching over the lake, the wheels screeched as they touched down. It was like sinking into a warm bath. Penticton was like a Shangri-La. It was Peach Festival time there. Peaches in Canada? This valley area is unique. If only it were near civilization or had a major train route through it, it would be a prime tourist destination. I must go back there some time.

August 5, 1974

On the way to the famous Abbotsford Air Show, just east of Vancouver, I decided to take a day/night side trip to the quaint city of Victoria, British Columbia. Like Christchurch, New Zealand, Victoria is frozen in a time capsule even earlier than Christchurch's 1930s era. Let's call Victoria, at the southern tip of Vancouver Island about 25 miles west of the modern city of Vancouver, a true Victorian-era city. The homes are gracious Victorian, the famous Empress Hotel emits quiet style and class. Its Tiger Bar has a sense of Rudyard Kipling and Teddy Roosevelt sitting in a corner booth discussing a far-off world.

The harbor looks as if it is waiting for a 5-masted ship under full sail to arrive, furl its sails and glide in. Near the harbor, the brown, subdued, rather modest capitol building of the Province of British Columbia welcomes one to come see its vivid, story-telling stained-glass windows. Alongside the harbor are dainty, hanging flower baskets. Cannons would be present at other British ports, but British Columbia was settled by the Scots. They didn't have the Germanic heritage of Britain where the Prince of Wales' motto to this day is in German *"Ich diene auch"* (I also serve) and the monarchy's German name, House of Hanover, was changed to House of Windsor in an attempt to shed its Germanic roots. As an Irishman and a Celt, like the Scots who were crushed under boot of Britain's Prussian culture, I like to point out these things. Germany wasn't even a nation until 1871, seven years after the end of our civil war! The current British monarchy trace their roots back to Germanic rulers, not Scot or Irish Celts, part of whom they still rule today. In Victoria, you get a true sense of the gentile part of the Scots who settled British Columbia. My wife's maiden name is Fraser. She is a relative of Simon Fraser for whom the University in Vancouver is named, as well as the long Fraser River that flows from the innards of British Columbia to the south, then west to the sea past Vancouver. A highlight of my life was meeting the head of the Fraser clan, Lord Lovat (Simon Fraser) in 1993 near Inverness, in the Scottish Highlands. He was a member of the House of Lords and strongly stated to me that President Reagan was the man who deserved to be the President of the United States. Fraser stood a straight, strong 6-foot-plus tall. He was head of the fearless British Commandos during World War II. They could be compared to our dauntless Navy SEALs of today. He was most gracious to my wife, Midge, and to me. You don't see his type around much anymore.

August 6, 1974

Back to the 20th century and the Abbotsford Air Show just west of Vancouver. Unless you've flown in this air show, it's hard to explain the warm, receptive attitude of those who run it. It's the largest attended air show in North America. Admission was

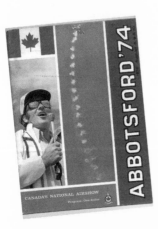

charged by the car—$5 per car then. Grandma and all the kids came. As one person observed, "The only thing to watch up in this country is a log-rolling match twice a year. We're starved for watching activities." The management has every reason to be aloof and dogmatic, but they are the opposite. They welcome you as if you are doing them the greatest favor in the world for just coming to be in their show.

My strange VOR readings were solved at Abbotsford. A friendly avionics chap from the Seattle area happened to stop by. I told him about the erratic antics of the VOR needle, how it stabilized and then jumped back and forth. He squeezed himself up through the small opening near the tail of the plane. In a few minutes he emerged with the answer. The communication radio had been hooked up to the VOR antenna and the VOR had been hooked up to the communication antenna. That explained everything. That's why while heading for Oakland, I wound up over Santa Maria, 50 miles off course. That's why I couldn't find the Princeton VOR. Once again the mysteries had been solved. But that didn't soften the yet another deposit of frustration in my memory bank—and this one could have meant an emergency landing in hostile terrain.

Anyone who has any chance to be in the northwest in mid-August, I encourage you to be in the Abbotsford show. You can even just fly in at the last minute if you have a Mustang or any WWI or WWII plane. They'd love to have you, but at the last minute they may not have a car and free lodging available. Like the Oshkosh Air Show in Wisconsin, there's no pay, but you'll get all the high-octane gas your plane can drink (pssst!—arrive with empty tanks). A word of caution: A gallon there is an Imperial gallon. Don't do like I did and say, "put 40 gallons in the ammo bay tank." That tank held 42 U.S. gallons but only 38 Imperial gallons. It overflowed and I had a highly inflammable pool of gas below my plane. I didn't dare try to start it for fear a spark would make me a cinder ball. A few years later at the Abbotsford Show, I brought the entire show to a stop with my masterful demonstration of a gear-up landing. Stay tuned.

To Fly at the Spokane World's Fair
August 12, 1974

This was an appearance I had dreamed up myself and sold to the World's Fair show management. I was "Miss America." I would light up their fair. Just how I would do this, I didn't have the faintest idea. Fly in and bust balloons over the fair grounds? Buzz the fairgrounds every half hour on the half hour? Arrange "Miss America" as an exhibit?

When I got there and contacted the PR people, I felt dumb. They welcomed me, gave me a car and a hard-to-find hotel room during the height of the fair and then said, "What will you do?" I asked if they had any other planes, especially those doing aerobatics near or over the fairgrounds? They hadn't. Therefore, I knew the FAA hadn't even surveyed the area for waivers to get permission to bust the minimums of no lower than 1,000 feet over a populated area, providing you can glide to an open area in case your engine quits. I now seemed knowledgeable. I could speak with that authority called out from the top of a mountain that is reserved for all pilots.

"I will give you the maximum performance over the fair that the FAA will allow," I offered. The reply came back as "okay," but it sounded more to me like, "Oh! You wonderful person! You are going to give us a maximum show! Our publicity department will love it!"

My "show" amounted to two acts each of my 2 days there.

Act I—Show a P-51-lover in their PR department all the instruments and parts of a P-51.

Act II—Take Act I up as a passenger while I made 4 circles around the fair, explaining the near and dangerous (to me, from the FAA) proximity to the fairgrounds we were flying—and then, of course, on the way back to the airport, a few high-G turns of the "gee whiz" type they could describe in vivid detail back at the office about how they "weighed 600 pounds for 15 seconds" and how "my cheeks went below my chin line." The PR department cut me a small check for gas and expenses. It was under a thousand dollars.

Spokane to Winnipeg Air Show
August 15, 1974

I had seen the name Harve, Montana on charts and bulletins the FAA sent us to update our charts. It was one of those crazy things, but I always wanted to visit Harve. The name intrigued me, so I planned a stop there for gas—and got a surprise. About

20 miles out I called for their wind direction and velocity on the unicom. No reply. I called again 10 miles out. Still no reply. I circled the field, noted the windsock showing a light wind from the west and made the normal left-hand pattern approach. On the downwind leg, I saw across the field to my left a group of people. I reasoned they must be having a BBQ or something and had not heard my radio calls.

As I was coming in "dirty" (i.e., gear and full flap down) on final to a long 5,200-foot runway, all of a sudden the air in front of me was filled with seagulls! There must have been over a 100 of them flying in all directions. Seagulls are nearly as big as chickens. They can do a lot of damage to a plane and propeller doing about 125 mph. I recall hitting a pigeon in a Cessna 310 while taking off from Glenview Naval Air Station. It hit the right leading edge at the outboard seam and not only left a deep impression, but popped about a dozen rivets a foot back on the wing. I was amazed at the damage one pigeon could do. I also recalled seeing the pigeon climbing like crazy, straight up. We were climbing and I was sure we'd miss it, but splat! It climbed right into our path.

Now, seeing a mass of seagulls ahead, birds bigger than pigeons, in the middle of Montana less than 50 miles south of the Canadian border and almost a thousand miles from the ocean took me by surprise—and with a dirty plane on my hands. They had risen from a small lake near the approach end of the runway. Two things were certain. I wasn't going to fly through them and I wasn't going to try to out-climb them. I lowered the nose, veered right and headed for the lake they had left, retracting the flaps and pulling up the landing gear as I picked up speed. I was headed directly for the airport building and the group of people. About 50 yards before reaching them, I had enough speed to turn away to the left and climb in clear, birdless air. Whew!

I decided the wind was light enough to make a downwind landing at the other end of the runway away from the lake. As I taxied in, an energetic lady in a patterned house-dress motioned me to a parking place. When I shut the engine down, about 10 smiling people gathered around the plane. The house-dress rushed up and exclaimed, "Thank you, that was great!"

"What was great?" I asked, puzzled.

"The little show you put on for us. I am here on duty at the airport. When I heard you calling in saying you were 20 miles out and you were the P-51 "Miss America" stopping for gas, I called some people to come out to see your plane. It was nice of you to put on that show for us." Show? A near miss of seagulls 1,000 miles from the ocean? A crowd to watch me land? No one on the radio? If they were having a swim-suit beauty contest, it might have fit right in! The house-dress gassed me up and was still waving as I climbed out with the lake at my back on the leg to Winnipeg, Canada.

Winnipeg's 100th Anniversary
August 1974

It's fun to be featured in an event that has some historical meaning and pride to a community. Everyone seems "up" and wants to make the best of it—there's no "next year"—this year is it. Winnipeg's founding year was in 1874—100 years ago— and they were out to celebrate it all. A highlight of the summer events was their first major air show. I was lucky it was in the month and year I was taking my sabbatical from the details of earning an honest living. Also, after 3 airshow events within 3 weeks, I was beginning to feel the release from a 9 to 5 job—of stepping across that line that runs between business and entertainment, between a suit and a costume, between the reserved world and the carnival world. I was becoming a "carnie" and I liked it.

Wing-walkers said "hi" to me as if I were one of the gang. At the morning local breakfasts, they pulled up chairs for us to join them. They talked about the weather forecast for the day. What would the wind do to the parachute jumpers' routine? Would the clouds be high enough for the loop-de-loops of the aerobatic teams? Was the runway wide enough for formation takeoffs? Would we need to start to the airport early in case of traffic jams? Would someone be going out later to bring the wives in time for the show? And, of course, the wives were wondering "How's the shopping in this area?"

Yes, I had entered a new world. At first I felt strange, as if I were eavesdropping on their world. We had known each other at the air races where there was always some sort of air show going on along with the races, but they were the "performers" and we were the "racers"—they could exist without us and we could exist without

The Red Devils flew in eye-popping tight formation. This takes practice, trust and a keen flying ability.

them. They were year-round "air professionals," we were a ragged collection of conceited pilots, oil-soaked mechanics and ding-a-ling groupies. They'd see us maybe once a year. Hello, good-bye.

At first, I found myself being condescending like a church-marm talking to a visiting missionary group. "You must have a tough life...I bet you miss not being home more...What's it like having to eat out all the time? Don't you miss a good home-cooked meal?" Finally, I was able to properly interpret the looks those remarks generated. The looks conveyed the replies of, "If this is a tough life, I'd hate to be in the straight-jacket world you're from...Eat meals at home? Have to do all that shopping and preparing? Be eating in the same place all the time?...Get a life, buddy— I'm happy as hell!"

And so I became "happy as hell." But they didn't have a 4-ton plane with a 1-ton, fire-breathing, finicky monster to feed and care for. They could stand on the ground to put oil in their engines. If they needed parts and hoses, they could probably get

The Red Devils were the only 3-plane aerobatic group I had ever seen. Shown are (L–R) Gene Soucy (flying a wing-walker today), Tom Poberezny (now President of EAA), and Charlie Hillard (killed at a show). It was fun being on the air show circuit with these pros.

them from the local airport-supply store or from an auto shop in town. If they needed a mechanic, the airport mechanic had probably worked on their type of engine many times. Those who used smoke-oil or fireworks in their routines could carry enough supplies with them. Their engines needed only 8 to 12 spark plugs, not the 24 I had to change. But I was fitting into their routine and the mentality of "tomorrow's the last day of this show, a couple of days of R and R and then the next one." I liked it. I liked to look forward to and especially liked being looked-forward-to with a warm reception at the next show.

Unlike most of the performing planes, any P-51 Mustang is widely photographed on the ground and people are eager to see inside the cockpit. "Miss America" was no exception. The name, the exciting items about her in the air show program and, most importantly, the air show announcer keeping the crowd alert with the "Now, have your cameras ready for this rare shot even spectators at the races don't see (view of top)…Guard your children's ears at this high-speed pass…You'll probably never be this close to watch something going nearly 400 miles an hour."

My 8-minute act was limited to a demonstration of an air-racer in action. The other planes did aerobatics with even more "Wow! Look at that!" than I could. I wanted to have my own niche of promoting and educating what an Unlimited Air Racer is but not horn-in on the "daredevils-of-the-air" acts of my new buddies. Yet,

Ed Schnepf and his B-25 "Executive Suite" from Van Nuys, was also a Warbird-type from Van Nuys at the Winnipeg Centennial show.

someone I might alienate at shows were local area pilots with a P-51 or other type of warbird who wanted to be in the show with me flying formation with them in front of the crowd. Bob Hoover said he has faced this many times, too. It's a local hotshot, probably with no military training, whose skills you don't know and whose prop could rip you to pieces in a moment of distraction. I could get away with the "Golly, I'd like to, but I don't feel I'm a good enough pilot to do that," but Bob Hoover couldn't get away with inferring he wasn't good enough—he could do it flying upside down and everyone knew it. I think his out might have been, "I'd love to but my company's insurance won't permit it."

We all cringed upon hearing that a local pilot was going to do his air-show act. For many, it was their last act. We called it "airshow-itis"—instead of stopping a spin 500 feet up, they'd go to 300 feet and not recover. Instead of pulling out of a loop 200 feet up, they went down to 100 feet and didn't make it. "Airshow-itis" is not limited to novice pilots. The airport at Orly, France where the famous Paris Air Show is held in odd-numbered years is littered with the debris of high-time test pilots doing simple loops or slow speed fly-bys of military aircraft and exceeding the limits of recovery trying to get that one last ounce out of a low-level maneuver. If you attend an air show and it's announced that a local pilot is going to be the next act, get out the prayer beads.

With the announcer in full, eloquent voice (I hoped), I did fly-bys for in-air camera shots of "Miss America" in five sequences:

1. a 150-mph slow-speed pass for a side view down the show line,
2. a knife-edge return pass showing the bottom design of the plane,
3. a knife-edge pass showing the top design,
4. a "down and dirty" pass with full flaps and gear down, and finally,

5. a 350-plus mph high-speed pass with a pylon turn around the windsock or other object about three-quarters down the runway show line, followed by an abrupt pull-up, almost straight up, then lay it nearly on its back, hoping I'd get the press person riding the show with me on the ground before they threw up. Heading back toward the field, I'd slow down and do a wheel landing, the type that's best in a crosswind—air show runways and grandstand lines are set— they don't always match wind direction—and besides, very few people, including the average pilot, appreciate the difficult timing of a 3-point landing of tailwheel and mains touching down at the same time. A wheel landing looks better, too.

My greatest satisfaction after the show was seeing a kid sitting in the cockpit with his face beaming while his mom or dad took his picture. I know that kid still has that picture and he might even be retired now. I never had "Miss America" cordoned off unless the crew needed to work on the plane. Kids were always welcomed, even solicited to sit in the cockpit and have their pictures taken. Yes, I was sponsored by a company appealing to youngsters, but my personal agenda was to let kids see and experience something they could aspire to on their own. My fellow race pilots would say to me, "Howie, that's your life you're fooling with there, how can you let those kids in there touching everything?" My answer was "What can they do? Break the stick? With all the systems shut down, nothing can happen." At least a thousand kids sat in "Miss America's" cockpit. Nothing ever happened, except the glee they left behind.

The airport at Winnipeg was not their major airport. It was the much smaller St. Andrews on the outskirts of town where airline flights would not be interrupted. But the runway was only 2,850 feet long, about 5 blocks. No problem for the other show aircraft, but my minimum desires were at least 4,000 feet with my clipped, fast wings. Yes, I could land in even 2,500 feet, but each landing took special concentration with the thought of making an immediate go-around if I sensed even the slightest variation of wind speed, landing too long or needing to drop down faster and pick up too much speed. St. Andrews had the advantage of a wide-open approach and I took every advantage of it. It was a wheat field about a mile wide.

I'd make a power-on approach, referred to in aviation as a "short-field" landing. Drop down low. Keep the plane barely above stalling speed with enough power. Nose slightly high. Drag it across the ground. Over the runway, chop the throttle and literally drop in on three points hoping one wheel wouldn't hit first and careen you off to one side, then get ready to immediately power-up for takeoff in case you misjudged. Sure, any good pilot can do it, but like carrying a tray of filled-to-the-brim soup bowls, you'd rather not. Art Scholl, a fellow show pilot already in the air waiting to do his act when mine was finished said, "Howie, you should see behind you while you're coming in to land. You were so low, the wheat was parting from your prop wash—from above, it looked like you were taxiing through it!" You do what you gotta do.

On to Minneapolis
August 19, 1974

Anybody who lives or has lived in Minneapolis will tell you it can get hot. Those who have never been there in the summer are amazed that it can get so hot—and humid—so far up north. Humidity I can understand because it is in the "Land of Lakes," but to even need air-conditioning seems unusual. Well, mid-August is that time of year. I wasn't doing an air show. It was worse. I was scheduled to give rides to the people of Leisure Dynamics, the company that recently bought my sponsor, COX models. Some lucky P-51 pilots have air-conditioning in their planes, maybe a bar as well. I didn't. The temperature in the cockpit of a P-51 can easily get to 100° F. Add in humidity, and your flight suit looks like you just got out of a steam bath.

Of course, the passengers could show up in shorts, light, short-sleeve shirts and sandals, but the race pilot had to look like a race pilot, not someone ready to tee-off on the first hole. It would destroy the entire image, especially the image the sales force wanted to see if they wanted to relate to the buyer at K-Mart what their model of "Miss America" represented—and show them a picture of them with the pilot and the plane itself. Nothing is hotter than the black asphalt on an airport. I've seen the tires of heavy planes sink 3 inches into the stuff on a hot day. I learned not to stand on it longer than a few minutes. Find a shady spot and talk there.

But later, at the steak dinner at a fine air-conditioned restaurant overlooking Lake Wayzata and a few vodkas-on-the-rocks with the officers and sales force telling me how much they enjoyed it (not just their kids who were at home), the day became just another one. I was happy!

When leaving the next day, we'd be flying south to the Chicago area at 21,000 feet on an instrument flight plan to get over some weather. At 20,000 feet up, the temperature would be about 70 degrees colder than the surface. That meant only 15° above zero. Christa was always uncomfortable in the cold when she couldn't move around. I wasn't much better, but I could at least stomp my feet on the floor boards. She was splayed out on that bean-bag arrangement in the back and could just wiggle her fingers with her oxygen mask on. When Skip and his cohorts redid the innards of the plane, Skip recalled me complaining about how hot it was in the cockpit, especially in those long races. What I forgot to add was "thank goodness, however, for those radiator pipes under the cockpit. Without them, I'd freeze at high altitudes." So when Skip had the pipes covered with high-quality insulation, my high-altitude radiator had disappeared! Man, was it cold up there!

The people in the flight office were surprised to see us unpacking and bringing in our thermal underwear to put on. Once I had it on in 85° humid weather, my only thought was to climb as quickly as I could into the refreshing colder air above.

These ads were fun to see how COX tied in the real "Miss America" with its U-controlled model.

With founder COX at the Reno races. He developed the .049 gas engine used in his U-Controlled and other airplane models.

COX Model and COX Catalog ad featured the "Miss America" model in its catalog.

Naval Air Station at Glenview, Illinois
August 20, 1974

If you've never been piped aboard a Navy ship, you have something to look forward to. For a moment, no matter how brief a moment, you're a star. Until this day, I never had the pleasure. The air Navy didn't have ships to pipe you aboard and even if they did, at my low rank, I'd probably be the one doing the piping.

My initial inkling of arriving in splendor was the response to my first radio call to the Navy control tower at NAS Glenview. When you are on an instrument flight plan, you don't need to know any frequencies or facilities to call. The radar facility controlling you, unbeknownst to you, calls the next facility to handle you to find out if they can accept your flight and control you from that point on. Then they tell you to call that next facility on such-and-such a frequency and end with "have a good day." When you call on the next frequency, they are expecting you.

I picked up the mike and said "Navy Glenview tower, this is North American P-51 Niner-Niner-One Romeo (991R) for landing instructions."

The reply came back "Welcome Captain Howie Keefe and 'Miss America,' this is Captain Paul Merchant, Commanding Officer of NAS Glenview. You're cleared straight-in to land on Runway 18. After landing, taxi to the base of the tower." I was speechless! The C.O. was running the tower? He called me Captain? I had the retired rank of a Navy Lieutenant, same as a Captain in the Air Force, but in the Navy, a Captain is close to God (like a full Colonel.) He runs the ship.

Prior to starting my month of being a hedonistic air-jockey, I sent a letter addressed simply to the Commanding Officer, NAS Glenview, Glenview, Illinois stating who I was and that I wanted to stop in the Chicago area with "Miss America" because many family members were in the vicinity of the Glenview NAS. Before, I had always stopped at the Pal-Waukee Airport, due west of Winnetka where I used to live. I thought I'd just try to see if I could sneak into Glenview. Pete Hoyt used to be amazed at my gall. When he'd asked how I thought I could go shoot landings at NAS Glenview in his Cessna 310 to practice on their "meatball" (an aircraft-carrier landing aid), I'd answer with, "Because I'm an Official U.S. Taxpayer." He'd snort with laughter each time I'd say it and often said, "Keefe (he rarely called me Howie), tell Joe here why you're able to land at Glenview" and then Pete would put the back of his hand up to his mouth to stifle his laugh until I said it in all seriousness. Pete loved to hear me say it.

When a response to my letter came back with, "I invite you to stop over at NAS Glenview. Please advise what facilities you would like," signed "Capt. Paul Merchant, Commanding Officer." I replied that I'd like to park the plane there for a few days and stay in a nearby motel. Well, a little chutzpa was paying off. After all, what did I have to lose by asking?

After the initial call and Captain Merchant's reply, the regular tower-control operator took over, reaffirmed my landing clearance and guided me in to taxi to the base of the tower. On the way in, I noticed the top of the water tower was painted in a red/white/blue stripped color scheme. I thought that looked nice. But when I approached the base of the tower, it started to feel like a dream. There was a red carpet from the apron in to the building. A line mech wearing large earguards was wig-wagging me to the place to stop and cut my engine. On each side of the red carpet were two seaman in white uniforms standing nearly at attention. When the engine stopped, they dove under the plane to put chocks on each wheel, then stood back to help Christa and me down. At that moment, an officer with scrambled eggs on his hat and a smile on his face, rushed down the carpet toward the plane, saluted me and stuck out his hand. Were they in the middle of shooting a movie here and had mistaken me for someone else?

Every time I replay the scene in my mind, like now, I try to rewind it to play it again and say to myself, "This is all for me," so I can relive it. Normally, I'm not shy, but this was different from anything I had ever experienced. Much different. Captain Merchant (Captain now, but Paul the next day) was a smiling, enthusiastic host. He

This shot of "Miss America" flying past "her tower," as Capt. Merchant wrote on the picture, was the cover of the Bi-Centennial 1976 phone book for the base.

had been a "River Rat" in the Vietnam War—a Navy carrier-based jet fighter pilot who routinely flew up the heavily fortified Red River in Vietnam engaging the MIGs in combat. Not a good way to make a living.

He called me Captain Keefe, introduced me as Captain Keefe to his staff and had us registered at the Officer's quarters as "Captain Keefe and guest." When I tried to point out that I had a temporary rank as a $2^1/_2$ striper Lt. Commander when I was Aide-to-the-CO and might be called Commander, I never had been a 4-striper Captain. His official reply was, "This is my base, you're a retired Navy pilot and you will be accorded a Captain's privileges on my base. By the way, did you notice I had the water tower painted in Miss America's honor?" This was getting to be too much. He departed with, "We're having dinner at my house on the base (I'd never been in a C.O.'s house on a base before). My car will pick you both up at 1900 hours (7 p.m.). See you then."

The fantasy continued into the night. I never wanted it to end. We were in what was known as the "Admiral's House" when I was based there in the late 1940s. It was a white, charming, rambling clapboard house just off the golf course. Capt. Merchant was a bachelor and took care of all the activities with the help of two male servants. His other guests intrigued Christa and me. Carol Cichon was a flight attendant and a private pilot herself. Her escort, Dan Macintyre, was an American Airlines captain, a Navy captain, Squadron Commander of the fighter squadron at Glenview,

Capt. Paul Merchant, Commanding Officer of NAS Glenview and a Navy fighter pilot in the Vietnam war, was a gracious and enthusiastic host.

Capt. Dan Macintyre, both a Navy and American Airlines captain and a former Blue Angel, felt "Miss America" glided like a jet with power off.

a former Blue Angel, also a "River Rat" with the distinction of being the fifth Navy pilot to shoot down a MIG-17 with his carrier-based F4 Phantom in the Vietnam War. I may be entitled to wear Navy wings, but among these guys, I would barely be qualified to warm up their planes.

As the evening wore on with statements like "Having your plane here is unique. It's a morale builder versus the boredom of the daily routine. I'm even putting on an on-base rodeo for the men and their families. You can have all the gas you want— we spill more in one day than your plane can take. Our men are itching to get their hands on it. They don't see P-51s in the Navy. What can they do short of an engine overhaul?" What was this? Christmas in August? I tossed up a test balloon with, "Well, the brakes on a P-51 are a problem. It operated mainly off grass fields that slowed it down naturally. The brakes of the Army Air Corps' P-63 King Cobra's are larger and fit the P-51. Bill Ross, a friend who used to be a student of mine in the Navy, has some. But they are out at DuPage County airport about 20 miles from here."

The next day a Navy plane inbound from Detroit was diverted to DuPage to pick up the brakes and bring them to Glenview. "Gives them a chance to make another landing—see another airport—expands their training skills" was Paul's succinct reasoning. (Yes, it was Paul now, after all we were brother Captains). His reasoning had a grain of truth and that certainly was okay with me, an Official U.S. Taxpayer. My plane was jacked up, wheels removed, new large brakes installed, wheels reassembled, gear cycled up/down a few times and she was ready to go.

The night before I had mildly stunned Paul and Dan by offering to let them fly "Miss America." They were there at the hangar to supervise the work and examine the plane. These guys were carrier-qualified fighter pilots, currently flying with military flight physicals. The P-51 is probably the easiest plane to land on a long runway that I have ever flown. Its wide gear gives it baby-carriage stability. All I requested is that they make their first landing on the main gear only, not to try a tailwheel-first carrier landing all Navy pilots are trained to do. They each took her up, first Paul then Dan, and both loved it.

In his own words, Dan relates:

"Though I had flown several stock P-51s many years ago loaned to me by gracious local pilots when touring as a Blue Angel, seeing Miss America on the base now, with her clipped wings and powerful race engine, I wanted to fly her in the worst way, but you just don't go up and ask to fly such a gem, especially to a stranger. Well, at the end of the evening, Howie was easy to get to know and was no longer a stranger, but I still didn't want to ask. Then in a very casual way he offered us the chance to fly 'Miss America' the next day. Howie was a no-nonsense guy who knew flying, knew his plane and showed that certain reserve and positiveness you find in good, experienced pilots. He was a pilot who honored the skills of other trained pilots—certainly not a fussy, worrywart. He told me about the plane's systems, its particular traits. After only 10 minutes I was in the air with Carol in a jury-rigged back seat. Loops, slow rolls, barrel rolls and Immelmanns were smooth

and natural. When I pulled back on the power, the plane was so sleek with its clipped wings and streamlined canopy, it felt more like a jet in that it barely slowed down. It had been a long time since I had flown a propeller-driven aircraft. It was a flashback to feel engine and prop torque trying to pull the plane off course—to feel the immediate forward response of a prop versus the slower initial power of a jet engine. In short, it gave me a long forgotten, wonderful flight experience."

The second day, I had my family and friends come out to the base to visit and gave them rides in "Miss America." Traffic on a weekday was minor. I could taxi out and take off with ease—and of course, Captain Keefe received top priority from the tower controllers. No doubt it was the morale booster Paul had mentioned for them too, to see a brightly painted, toy racing plane take off and land mixed in with all those gray/white Navy planes.

To Washington, DC and a Surprise!
August 25, 1974

I hated to leave Paul, Dan and NAS Glenview's hospitality, but I had a plan to get to Washington to see the FAA on how they revised IFR approach plates, and then fly the Cleveland Air Show over Labor Day weekend. As always, the weather in the midwest and east in August is hot and humid. But the route to Washington, DC was mostly clear with some scattered clouds. To save time, I decided to go VFR and not file an instrument flight plan. In those days, I could go up to the cool air at 18,500 feet without needing to file a flight plan. Besides, if filing an IFR flight plan en route was needed, you could do it with any center. So off we went, nonstop for the 600 miles (2^1/$_2$ hours) to Washington, DC.

About an hour out of DCA (250 miles), I checked weather again. The cloud cover that was scattered at 3,000 feet had now closed up to "broken at 2,500 feet." Broken means that more than 50% of the sky is covered by clouds. Whether it's 51% with a lot of holes or 90% covered with few holes, it's still "broken" and you're not legal going through it unless you are on an instrument flight plan. And who is dumb enough to attempt to evade the rules in one of the most crowded air spaces in the world, the "Golden Triangle" of Chicago, New York and Washington, especially in the Washington area, home of the FAA? Not me.

I contacted the radar center, asked for an instrument flight plan to Washington National (now Reagan). They told me to descend from my 18,500 altitude to 13,000. I nosed over, pulled back slightly on the power and began my descent. Going through 15,000 feet they called me to slow down because I was passing up the airliners. I explained that my racing engine needed to carry power—if I reduced power any more, it would be below the ambient air pressure and my engine could quit. "Okay then, turn 20° left to a course of 090°." A quick look at my charts showed that I'd be heading for Philadelphia instead of Washington. Their answer was, "We have to route you around traffic inbound to Washington—you're going faster than they are." Naturally,

I smirked at that. I was top dog at a Navy base and now airliners were eating my dust. Maybe a Presidential escort would be at the airport to meet me! If only that gradeschool bully could see me now!

Soon, Center told me to turn to One-Three-Zero (130°) and to contact Washington Approach Control on 124.7. I was now going to get a lower altitude and my next control would be the tower at the airport for my landing clearance. They told me to descend from 4,000 feet to 2,500 feet. It was getting hotter and more humid and I was on solid instruments in and out of haze and low clouds. I didn't dare take my eyes off my artificial horizon for even one second to look outside to see if I could see anything. A P-51, as I explained earlier, can't be trusted to go in the same direction or to stay at the same altitude without having complete attention paid to it. My eyes were glued to the instruments. I had no idea of where I was or where I was heading. All I knew was that I was at 2,500 feet altitude and flying 130° (southeast). I could have been over the Sahara Desert for all I knew. I was being controlled 100 percent by a radar operator probably a 100 miles from where I was, but I was his baby at that moment.

Then the call came to turn immediately to 180° (directly south) and descend to 1,000 feet. As I turned sharply to the right, I saw the Washington Monument below off my right wingtip. It was as if I were making a pylon turn around it. As I leveled the wings, the flashing strobe approach lights of the airport were directly ahead. They looked like a crazed torch-bearer running up and down a long track. Here I was on a final approach to the runway at Washington (Reagan) Int'l without any gear or flaps down! No way could I land straight ahead with the 175 miles of minimum-maneuvering speed I was carrying. I could see the Eastern Airlines planes lined up nose-to-tail; there must have been at least 15 of them, waiting for takeoff clearance. If I declared a "missed approach," they might send me down to some place in Georgia to circle for an hour until they could release all the planes waiting to take off. Obviously, they had been held up while I was doing my thing of circling around the normal flight pattern and then busting into the chow line. No way was I going to give up my place in line.

I called the tower stating I was doing "an overhead 360 approach." Dead silence, then a meek "okay." (*A "360 overhead" is a military fighter-plane approach, often in formation, that comes over the field, pitches up at midfield and then circles back to land.*) Not only is this not a normal approach at an airport with airline traffic, but the rules at Washington National and LaGuardia were that no fighter planes could land at either airport. A few years back, a South American general in a P-38 collided with an airliner over Washington. The South American military had our WWII fighters for the private use of their brass who loved to fly into New York and Washington, but they could barely understand instructions in English. To not discriminate, all fighters were banned. I knew it, but why not try? I told Christa on the intercom to "suck it in, we're going to pull Gs." At midfield, I started a sharp right turn, dumped the gear, held a tight circle around to the runway heading, put down full flaps and landed. During my roll-out, a blind transmission came over the radio, obviously from one of the airliners waiting to take off: "I thought fighter planes weren't allowed to land

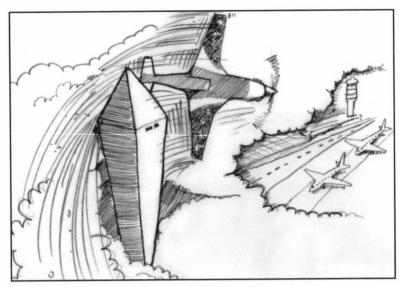

I was still flying with my head in the cockpit on instruments when approach control said "Turn right to 180 degrees." In the turn, I saw the top of the Washington Monument in my right-side vision. It was like being on a race course and the monument was a pylon! I must have been just missing the Prohibited Air Space over the White House. Then I saw the Eastern Airliners nose-to-tail waiting to take off.

here." I picked up the mike and said, "This isn't a fighter, it's a toy racing plane." Then another blind transmission came of "Don't worry, that guy's just jealous." That was followed by many rapid clicks of mikes, same thing as many applauding.

Meeting With the FAA

In flying to many different airports for air shows and races, the problem plagued me, as it did many private pilots, of getting and keeping up-to-date charts. Not only was this important to have for your own use, but it was a major FAA requirement that you have up-to-date information in your cockpit. Fine for the airlines who went out and back the next day, but a private pilot away for a week or more did not have access to updated charts. I was determined to find out what might be done to solve the problem for me and others. In the Navy we had the MANS system (Military Aviation Notification System). We got new approach plate books every 8 weeks, and every 4 weeks in between we had a text document saying what changes, if any, had been made to an approach. It was easy. It was simple. The next year I introduced a service called "Pro-Plates," which has expanded into today's "Air Chart System." It had its beginnings that August in Washington, DC.

The Air Chart System I developed after visiting the FAA grew from an update system for approach plates (Pro-Plates in 1975) to a full IFR and VFR system today. Not shown is the approach plate update service designed to update both NOS and Jeppessen approach plate procedures. (For more information and prices: 1-800-338-7220 or www.airchart.com on the Web.)

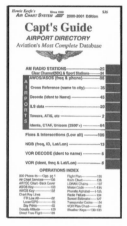

*The **Capt's Guide** is the largest printed data base of nav and airport data ranging from airport and nav IDs to the lat/long of over 10,000 fix-intersections. All the flight data a pilot might need for cross-country flight.*

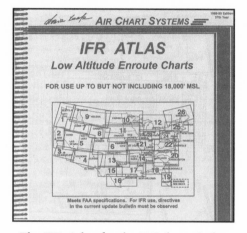

*The **IFR Atlas** for the U.S. has spiral-bound reproductions of their NOS Low Altitude charts and Area Charts. It is updated on the FAA's 28-day cycle.*

*The **VFR Atlas** is spiral-bound and contains both the famous SKY PRINTS charts with direct VOR routes and aviation's only charts devoted exclusively to GPS Navigation. Updated on the FAA's 28-day cycle.*

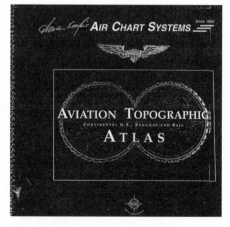

*The **Aviation Topographic Atlas** is aviation's only spiral-bound collection of all U.S. WAC charts plus Sectional chart portions for the more than 140 B & C spaces. Updated on the FAA's 28-day cycle.*

Cleveland Air Show
Labor Day Weekend 1974

If you have a chance to be in the Cleveland area when the air show at Burke Lakefront Airport is held, it's worth flying in or watching. The lakefront is an ideal setting, even better than Chicago's lakefront because it has a large spectator area and a grassy rise along the show runway.

All airplane racers know Cleveland was the major birthplace of modern-day air racing. For me to race a T-6 there, even though the Cleveland Air Races in the late 1940s were held at the Hopkins airport, it was a little like being at Kitty Hawk where the Wright Brothers stood. Cleveland is a small enough big town so that everyone seems to know everyone else who has anything to do with getting something done.

The press is very aviation-oriented. Charles "Chuck" Tracy of the Cleveland *Plain Dealer* is the Dean of Aviation writers. I first met him in the early 1970s and he is still going strong in the year 2001. He's the reason the people of Cleveland get the straight scoop on aviation disasters as well as aviation progress.

The only sad item I associate with Cleveland's Air Show is that a few years back, in 1992 I think, I was talking to Art Scholl at the Reno Air Races. Art was performing there.

Before going to Reno, I had been going through my various collections and came across a 1972 Cleveland Air Show program and noted that the only ones in that show that were still alive were Bob Hoover, Art and myself. The others had been killed flying. I named them: Mary Gaffney, aerobatics; Bevo Howard, aerobatics (hit a tree in an air show at Greenville, North Carolina); Scotty McCrea, glider aerobatics (wing came off in show at Rio de Janeiro); Hal Krier and Skip Volk, killed practicing aerobatics. Tragically, the very next day Art was killed. He was filming a scene to be used in the movie "Top Gun." It called for a shot of spinning through a cloud layer. To get the shot, he had to mount the camera on the top of his wing and then do an inverted flat spin so his plane would not show in the film. Art entered the thin marine cloud layer, which was now probably lower than he thought, he was heard to make

Cleveland's Burke Lake Front airport next to the stadium offered grand views of air shows and air races. It was far away from the busy Hopkins airport where air racing flourished before the 1949 tragedy stopped Unlimited air racing until Bill Stead restarted it in Reno in 1964.

Bud Groom, a friend and a WWII P-51 pilot who still carries a bullet near his spine, introduced me to others in the Wheel Chair Pilots Association. They had their own planes with controls modified to fit their condition. I attended many of their Fly-Ins. A very upbeat bunch of guys. It was easy to remove Miss America's canopy so they could be helped in and out of the back seat for a ride in Miss America. This photo was taken at their Fly-In at the California City Airport about 150 miles north of Los Angeles.

a radio call of "I'm in trouble—I'm in *real* trouble!" He and his plane are entombed in water over a mile deep in the ocean north of San Diego about 5 miles offshore. They were all great pilots, really tops in their field at their time. None of this happened at any of Cleveland's wonderful air shows. Someday, I'm going back.

Busted Prop — Very, Very Lucky!

On every flight since I left Los Angeles for my August coast-to-coast air show tour, I was puzzled by a strange feeling of vibration at low-RPM settings. I noted it especially at high altitudes where the blade angle takes its biggest bite out of the air. Usually this is the most relaxed mode on the prop and the engine. Like being in cruise-control mode on a level interstate going 70 mph with an 8-cylinder engine in front of you, there's no strain on any part of the car. It's built to do that with ease. Ditto a 12-cylinder, Rolls-Royce Merlin engine and that hefty Bearcat prop.

When calling back to report the engine progress to my crew chief, Skip, I'd mentioned this as being the only strange thing that seemed to be happening. When I felt it, I'd increase the RPM a bit and it would go away. Strange. My real reason for sending timely reports back to Skip was that after I got back to LA just after Labor Day, the Reno air races were less than 2 weeks away. Skip had to work fast. Also, if anything needed more brain power, Skip had the great support at Lockheed of Pete Law and Bruce Boland, the whiz kids. And one of the purposes of my trip was to put time on the engine and get the rings to seat. Skip wanted over 50 hours and I came back with about 55 hours. You cover a lot of ground in 55 hours in a P-51 averaging 250 mph— almost 15,000 miles, with a major part of it air-show flying.

When I landed back at Van Nuys, Skip and his loyal gang were there to greet us. They apologized for the wrong hook-up of the antenna cables—a radio man had done it. Not many people are familiar with the innards of a P-51, especially a highly-modified one like "Miss America." As the prop stopped, Skip went around to the front, casually hit the down blade with the side of his fist and jumped back at the

This photo was taken by a Navy photographer as Capt. Dan Macintyre took off from Glenview Naval Air Station. It shows the one blade (at 5 o'clock) lagging because it had an internal separation of the Aero Products steel propeller that was built like a pea pod with a hollow interior. Had it broken, the vibration would probably tear off the engine before I could stop it, especially at take-off power.

rattling sound it made. He pulled the prop through and repeated the hit with the other 3 blades. All solid. Another hit on the first one and the rattle was still there. He carefully examined the front and back. No cracks, no external signs of anything different.

An unusual blade construction—it was an Aero Products prop. Instead of being solid aluminum from hub to tip, the blades were made of steel. Probably to save weight to match the aluminum blades' weight. To maintain the same center of gravity for the plane, the blades were hollow like a pea pod. For strength, a welded spine ran the length of the blade, then ended in a flower-like curve to each side of the tip. This was the same prop I had used at the Miami races when the prop gears failed. I doubt that this type of prop design had ever been pushed to 20% over its maximum RPM and had 2,500 horsepower fed into it.

So, another mystery solved. Like a car or a 10-speed bike, the faster you go, the larger the cog that drives the car or bike. There's no actual gearshift in a plane. In a plane, the process that functions like a gearshift is the angle of attack of the propeller blade that you can vary with your propeller control. The faster you go, the greater the blade angle. It's flattest to the direction the prop is turning, like a paddle at its greatest flex point. Had I tolerated the vibration for any length of time, the blade, with its support broken, could have snapped in the middle. The nose of the plane would have started making wild arcs in the sky.

No one I have asked can tell me if I would have lost control before I had time to shut the engine down, or even if shutting down the engine would have given me a controllable plane. I know one thing: this type of emergency was not programmed into my mental data bank to act on without thinking. I would have spent a precious few seconds after a "What the hell is going on?" before collecting my wits about me. The worst part about this is that it would not show on engine run-ups on the ground when the propeller has only a small angle of attack. Jack Norris, a fellow QB who is writing a book on propellers, gave me an interesting statistic. In one revolution of my prop, the plane travels over 35 feet through the air, and that prop is turning over 1,000 times per minute. That is one big bite of air for each revolution!

When I told Capt. Dan Macintyre back in Chicago about the prop problem the plane had when he flew it, he looked through some of the photos the Navy photographer had taken and given to him. In one head-on shot, there it was. One blade on the prop looked like it was made of rubber. At first glance it just looked like the distortion of a high-speed object being still-photographed. Now we know it wasn't. The camera was seeing what was actually happening. So much for the "photographic explanation" of distortion from the prop speed.

Reno National Air Races
September 13–15, 1974
Parade of Planes Through Streets of Reno — A Blast!
My First Pylon Cut — Ouch!

The Reno Air Race committee had put planes, mostly the smaller ones like Formula One and bi-planes, on exhibit in the main part of downtown. This year they wanted to have a true parade through the city. We landed at the main Reno airport, were each hooked up to a tug and started a two-mile-long parade toward a reviewing stand just south of the city.

The parade streets were blocked off to traffic, but the two main north–south bridges across the Truckee River were too important to the city's lifelines to have them blocked off. As it turned out, that was a blessing for me.

I had never seen, nor had anyone else, a parade of Unlimited Class Race planes being towed through the streets of any city. It was quite a sight. There was to be a contest and an award for the best-in-show. This appealed to me. With a red/white/blue plane and colorful COX uniforms and jackets, we'd be a favorite. My plans were to come to a halt in front of the reviewing stand, have the crew do a line-abreast

facing the reviewers, come to attention, do a smart salute to the judges on my command and then I would raise my boy scout bugle to my lips and play a sharp rendition of the lively tune "First Call." Here's what happened:

I called a halt to the tow operator, the crew quickly assembled between the rear of the left wing and the tail; they "dressed right" smartly, I called out "Attention, crew salute!" They snapped to attention, gave a smart salute, I put the bugle to my lips, pursed my lips for the tune, gave an initial note and all that came out was "blubrbbberedmph." No tone, no note, nothing! Thinking my lips were cold, I licked them madly and tried again. They described the sound that came out as a new-born calf looking for its mother. At least my thinking was quick enough to give the command "Two—forward march!" to end the salute

and get on with the parade. The COX people who were photographing it said it looked great in print, but added, "Thank God it wasn't in sound!" There weren't camcorders in those days, just 8mm silent movies (thankfully).

After the parade, it took us nearly two hours to get "Miss America" back to the airport. Of course, no one really thought through what would happen after the parade was over and the roads were open again. Well, what happened was that we were all stranded on the side streets. No problem for the small bi-planes and Formula Ones (the T-6s weren't in the parade—they were too big with 42-foot wingspans). The carrier-based planes merely folded their wings up and were easily towed down the side streets. We Mustangs were almost left to die there! Where were the cheering crowds? Where was the wide-open Virginia Avenue we came up on? No crowds. No wide-open streets. I couldn't believe it. For a while, I thought about just having it towed into a parking lot and then hopefully have a police escort let me take it back down Virginia Avenue the next morning. But what if they wouldn't do it? I was land-locked and would miss the races the next day. The only way out seemed to be to try to negotiate the narrow streets with cars parked on either side.

So we started out. As we were towed into each block, cars had no choice but to back up when they came face to face with props rising 14 feet into the air. But to avoid damaging our wingtips, we had to do a careful zig-zag, slow tow with the wingtip on one side over the hood of a parked car, then make a zig to clear the other wingtip, then a zag to clear the other and so on down each block for over a mile. That was the last parade they ever had and certainly the last one that I would ever commit to without the return route open, too.

The Next Day—The Races and I Dope Off!

When I was growing up, the 4-minute mile run was considered elusive—mere mortal man would probably never be able to run that fast. But it was broken. For me, the elusive mark was the qualifying speed of 400 mph. I'd gotten near in the 390-mph range, but just couldn't seem to get over that 400-mph mark on the Reno race course. But September 11, 1974 was my day—even though my personal Friday the 13th was about to come up.

Using 100" of manifold pressure and needing 3,400 RPM (400 RPM over redline) to get up to 100" MP, I rejoiced when they posted my qualifying speed on the qual board at a whopping (for me) 407.31 mph! To make it even better, I did it with the coolant door wide open because the engine was not only overheating, but cylinder B3 was oiling on the exhaust side. As usual, some things had to be a bit off the mark. But having finally busted the 400-mph mark after 5 years of trying at Reno, this, the sixth year, paid off.

But now, it was Friday the 13th and the first heat race. With my 400+ mph qual speed, I had the pole position and was determined to milk it for every advantage I could get. I'd be flying in clean air, especially at Pylon 4 which is the first one we hit after being released by Bob Hoover with "Gentlemen, you have a race." Being in the pole position has the advantage of being right on the wing of the pace plane knowing that you're not jumping the start line, but it also has a psychological advantage of not having the distraction of having to look at all the other planes as they bob up and down in formation like fans doing the wave at a sporting event. You're also not concerned with someone skidding to their right into you while all are concentrating on the plane to the left to stay in formation. Then, there's always the chance that some jockey will try to slingshot the start line by laying back and try to come up on power early, to time the pace plane's release. In doing so, they may suddenly appear zooming under or over you because the formation is, of necessity, a loose one. It's not only alarming, but takes away your concentration at a critical time while trying to give a final check of your engine, pump and fuel-flow instruments. In the pole position, you're in the cat-bird seat.

Upon release, I went up to full power and was so euphoric at being the first one at the pylon that I almost forgot to begin my turn! That is one advantage of being back-in-the-pack. You see the pylon by noting those in front making their turn around it. You see the "rhythm" of the race ahead of you. You don't have to think. Just get there and do the same thing you see the others doing. It turns out that this was my undoing in this race.

I was so far ahead by the end of lap 4 and it was so easy to fly the pylons without the turbulence of other planes' prop wash and wing vortices (which are severe as they pull heavy Gs around the pylons), that I pulled back on the power and decided to go as low as allowed (25 feet above the ground but not below pylon height). It was delightful. Like legal flat-hatting. Didn't even have to worry about bird strikes,

This is how the pylons look on the race course. The drum pylon that I cut was like this, but hidden from view by a hill as you rounded the pylon before it.

because by now any birds in the area that might be spooked were long gone and jack rabbits couldn't jump that high. I didn't have to think about flying a "level course," which put me at ground level at the far pylon, but then 200 feet above the crowd line at the home pylon, which is 200 feet lower (above sea level) to avoid losing speed in climbs. It was all "just fly it, baby"…and I was enjoying it.

After the race, I enjoyed my first ride before the crowd in the winner's convertible with the pretty race queen. I could get used to that! But then reality hit! The word came in that I didn't win after all. I had cut pylon 6, not once but twice! I went out on the course the next day to try to figure out what had happened and sure enough, I didn't "cut" the pylon, I missed it entirely! In going lower on the course than I had ever gone with reduced power, pylon 6 was then hidden behind a hill. When I rolled out after pylon 5, pylon 7 was the only one visible on the horizon and I headed for it. I was so far off course that the judges at pylon 6 didn't even know I had cut the pylon—it was a judge at pylon 7 who began to wonder how I could be coming from another angle compared to the other racers. One of the problems with having such a recognizable plane as "Miss America" was that the pylon judges were sure to know if they had or had not seen it go by. They were used to planes not showing up the next time around because of engine blow-ups, etc., but when one down-course pylon judge radios an up-course pylon judge and asks "Did you see Miss America go by" and gets a "No," they knew I had taken a different route! This, of course, is the problem that the first plane has—they have to find the pylon for the pack behind them. That used to be easy on the old traditional oval track, but on this cross-country type of course with 9 pylons, instead of only 3 in a tight pattern at each end of the oval, finding the pylons became an added problem.

Well, at least I got the ride in the winner's convertible in front of the grandstands. They couldn't take that away from me. Hell, I'd cut across the course again just for that ride with the race queen in the convertible in front of the crowd! I often wondered if you could cut across the course and enter a pylon as if you had come from the prior one. Marathon runners had tried that trick, too.

The race turned out well. I won the Silver race with an 8-lap speed average of 385 mph. With the rule of thumb that you are going 10% faster than your clocked time because you're flying outside the pylons, that would mean an average speed of 385 + 38.5 = 423.5 mph. I'll take that in basically a stock P-51 with a few mods.

California Air Races Mojave, California
October 10–13, 1974

"Miss America" was really humming. I recall this race as a reward from the race gods for all the afflictions I endured in the past 6 years of racing. I qualified at 396 mph, took it easy in the heat races and came in a respectable third place in the finals.

Again, we had the drag races—a crowd-pleasing event. Two snorting, high-powered Unlimited race planes side-by-side at the start line on the runway in front of the crowd. The starter gave the sign to rev up the engines, then dropped the flag and we were off! It sure gave me an adrenaline rush. The trick was to be the first to get to the first pylon. Once there, you could start a tight turn around it in clear air while the plane behind was almost certain to get some of your prop wash and wing-tip vortices. This not only would slow him down a bit, but also probably cause him to go higher seeking clearer air. Once he went high, causing him to lose even more ground, you were pretty sure of victory in the one-lap race. At only one lap, the race wasn't long enough to make up even a 2-plane-length gap if the lead plane flew a tight course around the next end of the 3-pylon oval. I heard many comments from spectators that these drag races were the highlight of the races for them. By contrast to an 8-lap race with racers strung out over almost a full lap, the announcer was the one who had to keep the crowd informed of what was going on and who was leading by what. In the drag races, the screams of the crowd almost drowned out the announcer's voice because it was clear who was winning and how close the other plane was behind the leader. You didn't need an announcer to hold your attention at that spectacle—and it was a lot gentler on our engines than a grueling 8- to 10-lap race at high-power settings. I often wondered why the drag race format has never been repeated at the Reno National Air Races where the crowd would really get into it.

Most importantly after this race, I flew it home at night with no concerns, parked it, and locked it up without needing a laundry list of repairs. It doesn't get much better than that when racing P-51 Mustangs!

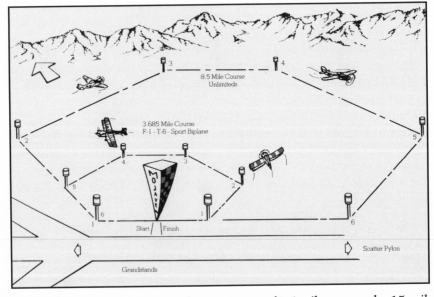

The Unlimited short-distance-pylon race course (8.5 miles versus the 15-mile-long distance) at the California Nationals at Mojave, California was the only clockwise short course we raced. Sea Furys, with their props pulling the plane to the right, had an advantage at high-power settings—less rudder. The smaller oval was really too small for the T-6s, but okay for the others.

Chapter 14

Jammed Gear–A Flight to Remember!
Orange County (now John Wayne) Airport
Almost Foamed • June 6, 1975

This was to be one of those days every P-51 pilot likes—give rides to people who are looking forward to it and getting free gas to boot, with the cool breeze off the Pacific Ocean refreshing you between hops. It doesn't get much better, especially when your passengers are the sales force and management of your sponsor. Orange County Airport, Santa Ana, California was in COX's backyard. It was easy to meet and greet their brass there.

After I had made a few hops with the usual demonstration of what a high-G turn felt like, a rapid turn from one direction to the other, I then asked if they wanted more. In most cases asking them the question was really not necessary. I could look in my rear-view mirror and see the expression and coloring on their faces. If there was a green tinge to their faces, it was simply my statement of "Going back now. All through. Be on the ground in 3 minutes." A half-smile would come over their faces while heads nodded up and down. Once in awhile I'd have one of those give-me-all-you've-got passengers. Never would I attempt any aerobatics with the casual passenger, but I was sure tempted sometimes, in the pilot's vernacular, to "wring them out" until they cried "uncle."

On this clear, cool June day, I got an unusual request from the tower controller during one of the rides I was giving. Over the radio came the question of "Would you mind making several low passes close to the tower so I can record the sound of your engine?" Would I mind? Doing routine landings and takeoffs at a major airport and being asked to buzz the tower. Those are the easy requests—yeah, privileges—you get now and then. He added the explanation of "I am head of the Packard Motor Car Association. We are having our convention in Seattle in a few weeks and I want to play a tape for them of the Packard-built Merlin engine." (One of the amazing mights of America was the ready conversion of manufacturing plants to the making of wartime machinery during WWII—it was a might grossly under-estimated by Japan and the Axis powers. Packard, the maker of a top-quality luxury car with its distinctive ledge on either side of the hood that any school boy could recognize at a glance, was licensed by Rolls-Royce to make its top performing high-altitude Merlin engine in the U.S. Every Mustang made had a Packard-built Merlin engine. And, of course, a Mustang engine is one of the most beautiful harmonics one can hear coming from the sky.)

This special ride of buzzing the tower was a delight to the passenger I had, especially when I explained the reason. Also, those on the ground who were watching each flight enjoyed seeing "their toy model" performing such antics. After the first passenger told them what was going on, their sales manager said his staff sensed a new dimension had been added to their product. The famous COX .049 gas-powered engine turning 25,000 RPM and sounding more like a mad hornet in your ear was hardly the soothing sound of a P-51 Merlin, but their engine was an engine too.

It was after all the rides were given to the COX people that my show really started! In 1975 the only airline that flew there was Air California. Maybe just 10 flights a day. Not nearly as busy a hub as it is today, serving a large southern California coastal area. After the COX people had departed, I was enjoying a coke at the FBO before getting my free gas fill-up. An Air California baggage cart stopped at my plane and a young man hopped out, walked around the plane once and then came to where I was sitting.

"Are you selling rides? If so, I'd sure like to buy one. How much are they?" My legal explanation would be that I'm not allowed to sell rides. That even though I hold an FAA Commercial license and could be paid for flying, the plane is in the FAA's Limited Category, which means it cannot carry passengers or cargo for hire.

"Oh, nuts. I've been watching you. I'm a licensed parachute-packer and just love the P-51." He had just said a magic phrase, "licensed parachute-packer." Suddenly, to me, this was no average airline baggage handler, he was a rare species—a species that the FAA stated I must interface with every 90 days if I were doing any turns over a 60-degree bank. Anything over 60° was considered "aerobatic" and that required "all occupants to have a parachute with a certification that it had been packed within the last 90 days." While I couldn't sell rides, the terse limitation "not for hire" didn't say I couldn't give rides "as a favor."

Getting a parachute repacked every 90 days bugged me. As mentioned, the law used to be every 60 days. That rule was established by the CAA in the olden days when 'chutes were made of cotton. They could get moldy in damp hangars and if

The area where I had the stuck gear at John Wayne (Orange County) Airport was in a highly-populated area. Today there are many airline flights in and out. Thankfully, there weren't many then.

moisture and humidity affected them, they could stick together and not release when opened. But that was then. Chutes now are made of lightweight nylon, virtually impervious to sticking, mold and even accidental ripping. So the FAA extended the time to 90 days. Big deal. But the size of our "lobby" was small. Parachute jumpers were licensed repackers themselves.

Nobody did "barnstorming" anymore—selling rides in an open cockpit out of hayfields. The open cockpit had long ago been replaced by planes with cabins.

To get your parachute repacked commercially requires the company to hang the chute for a period of time. This requires a temperature-controlled environment with a ceiling of at least 25 feet. This allows the parachute to be hung by its apex so the folds are loose before being repacked. It is time-consuming as well as costly. It meant a delivery and then a pick-up trip later to a far-away location. At the air races, it was one of the inspections the FAA Inspector in charge required of us and our equipment.

"Can you repack my chute for me and certify it if I give you a ride?" I queried.

"I can do a field repack and if it's in good shape, I can certify it. It'll take about a half hour and I can do it back at the hangar."

"Go for it, I'll wait here." I had the time. I'd wait and put on my fill-up of free gas on my sponsor's signed gas slip they left behind. That's what sponsors are for, isn't it?

He was back in under half an hour. There was his signature, the date and his FAA license number on the little certification card carried in a pocket on every legal chute. Now I was really legal, but it was just a formality. I had no intentions of doing any aerobatics. I used to teach them. Had all I really wanted. Besides I was no longer a youth; I was 54 years old. If cadets could gray-me-out when I was 24, thirty years later might be the same.

He climbed in, strapped up and off we went. By now the tower controller and I were old buddies, even though we'd never met. He had his audio tape recording of the Packard Merlin. After half an hour of the usual stuff, I made a short final approach to save taxiing too far. Instead of the standard base leg and then a 90° left turn to final, I made a carrier approach of a rounded pattern to save time. I put the gear handle in the down position about halfway through the turn. When I leveled the wings to land, the landing gear still showed a red light. It had not turned green, indicating the gear was down. I added power, milked the flaps up a bit and called my buddy in the tower.

"Can you check to see if my gear is down? I'll do a fly-by."

His quick response was, "I was about to call you. The right wheel appears to be down, but the left one is only halfway down. I noticed it as you were coming in. I had the glasses on you."

"Going around," I broadcast and added takeoff power. On the downwind leg, I pulled up the gear handle to recycle it and waited for the "thump" felt when the gear locks up in place. Nothing. The light was still a brilliant red, not like the soft red when the gear has been up for a while in cruise mode. I told the tower I was going to leave the traffic pattern, go out over the ocean to see if I can force it down with some high-G turns. A P-51 is not a plane like a T-6 that you do snap rolls in for sudden high-G loads to try to force the gear down. Its elevator is too short for positive recovery. I wouldn't try one even at 10,000 feet, so that was out.

My options were dives with sudden pull-ups, high-G load turns and constant attempts at gear handle up/down positions during those maneuvers. I then tried dumping the 70 pounds of hydraulic pressure my gauge showed I had, which was normal. You always dump the hydraulic pressure before getting out of the plane in case someone touches the gear handle and it folds up while being towed. My passenger was enjoying it all, but I sure wasn't. In all my civil and military flying, I had not only never had this problem, but also didn't know anyone who had. The left gear was locked down at a 45° angle the way the tower explained it and the gear door was about 60° versus the straight down it should be. The maximum gear-down speed in a P-51 is 170 mph. I certainly didn't want exceed that speed and have bent parts to deal with as well.

Now my air show started. I asked and received permission from the tower to fly down the runway, bouncing up and down off the right wheel. You need to have the left wing down a bit and be careful not to plow up the runway with your prop (I managed to do that a few months later—read on). With almost 6,000 feet of runway, I was able to make 4 or 5 good bounces to put a sharp G load on the gear. Still a brilliant red gear light and a "It's still not down" radio call as I climbed up at the end

The tower gave me free use of the runway. I tried bouncing on the runway to get the stuck left gear to come down. No luck. The answer turned out to be negative Gs.

of the runway. What now? Suddenly I realized that Frank Tallman's "Tallmantz Aviation" was located on the field. Frank was a good friend, an ex-Navy pilot, a partner with Paul Mantz serving the movie industry with old planes and skillful flying. Paul was killed flying the hybrid plane built in the "Flight of the Phoenix." In the final scene the plane disappears over the sand hill. The engine quit and he crashed in the desert. Both Paul and the stuntman were killed. Frank Tallman's two great appearances to me were his flying in the "Great Waldo Pepper" movie doing the flying as Robert Redford, and his feat in "It's a Mad, Mad, Mad, Mad World" of flying a twin-Beech through a billboard that has a heavy iron frame around it "so it would stay in place and not be dragged by me and foul up the plane." Say what? How about a gust of wind tossing you off course and that heavy metal frame taking a wing off? "Oh, I made sure there were no gusts that day." "Yeah, but still..." was the only reply I could come up with.

I asked my tower buddy if he could call Frank at his place and see if he had any ideas I could try. The call came back that Frank wasn't there but that someone else would talk to me. He'll go to a plane with a radio and call you on 122.9 (the freq anyone can use talking plane-to-plane). They gave me permission to leave the tower frequency, but still stay in their control area. Just go up to 3,000 feet and circle overhead "in case you need to make an emergency landing."

Tom Mooney and Wayne Burtt, Tallmantz's top mechanics, said they didn't know of any fix, but to standby while they called the P-51 experts out at Chino airport about 50 miles east. Chino was really Mustang HQ in southern California. After reviewing all that I already tried, someone suggested reaching down on the left side and breaking the hydraulic line. Even if I had the strength, the thought of 70 pounds

Frank Tallman was also an ex-Navy pilot. He flew many movie stunts including flying through the billboard in "It's a Mad, Mad World" and flew as "Waldo Pepper" in that movie with Robert Redford. His people at Tallmantz Aviation tried to figure out how to get my stuck gear down.

of pressure of hydraulic fluid flashing into the cockpit didn't seem appealing. I thanked them for their help and tuned back to the tower.

I asked the tower if there was a chance they could foam the last 500 feet of the runway. I could land on one wheel, hold up the right wing and then let it drop in the foamed area for my sure-to-come ground loop. I'd be tying up their long runway that the airline used, but to standby while they called the base fire department.

About this time my passenger called on the intercom in a very meek and apologetic voice saying that an Air California flight he was supposed to handle was due to land in 15 minutes. I looked at my gas gauge. We had been up about an hour now and had maybe 20 minutes of gas left. I said we'd be down in 15 minutes one way or the other, unless I could get air-to-air refueling (not funny). Did he maybe want to try out his own parachute? I could go up, turn the plane upside-down and with an abrupt nose-up, he'd shoot out as if shot out of a cannon—I was babbling small talk and not very funny, but it took my mind off the situation.

Then I thought, "Hey! Wait a minute. What had I just said to him? Nose up? Negative Gs? In over an hour with all the experts, no one had suggested negative Gs. Why hadn't I thought of it? Do the opposite! It was worth a try. I called the tower saying I was going back up to 3,000 feet to try something while awaiting their response on the foam. At 3,000 feet, I warned him that there would be the sensation of his stomach trying to come out of his mouth, that he'd be weightless for a few seconds. I'd be pulling the nose up, then suddenly pushing the stick forward, his body and all his organs would want to keep going up. Fasten his seat belt as tightly as he could to keep from knocking his head on the canopy. Was he ready? He nodded yes.

From level flight doing 160 mph to stay under the 170 mph gear-down max speed, I eased the stick back and the nose started up. When I felt the G-pressure holding me down in my seat, I shoved the stick forward and could feel the negative-Gs leading to weightlessness. At that moment the gear light went from red-to-green-to-red-to a steady green. I could feel that wonderful thud saying the gear had reached its max down position! At that moment, it was as if I had come out of a nightmare! Everything that had happened before, didn't really happen. It was all a part of my imagination, my subconscious. I was back into the real world again!

The fire trucks were headed for the end of the field to survey the situation, the tower said. Later, my passenger wrote that he was late and got fired, but it was an hour's ride he'd never forget. Neither will I. I flew home gear-down all the way. The diagnosis was that one of the gear door arms was out of adjustment—more gear to come.

California National Air Races
Mojave, California • June 20, 1975

Unlimited air racing was on a roll! We had not only another air-race each year besides Reno, but we now were having two California Air Races between the September Renos.

One last October and now one in June before the next September Reno. This was getting to be heady stuff indeed—3 major Unlimited air races in a 9-month period! As I look back at that era, it was something like hearing swing music in the late '30s—it was so good that you felt no music will ever replace it (and, in a way, nothing has). On top of it, my Merlin engine was going strong, souped up to the max and still a plane I could fly across country.

The thing about Mojave, in the high-desert country 100 miles north of Los Angeles just west of the famous Edwards Air Force Base, the space shuttle's alternate recovery field, is the wind. The trade-off is enduring higher winds in the more mild June period vs. risking bone-chilling temperatures in the fall but maybe, just maybe, lighter winds (no guarantee). As a P-51 race pilot, I rather liked the cooler temperatures because the P-51's cockpit at high-power could easily reach over 100° F with the 200° + water flowing just under the cockpit from the engine to the radiator scoop below the seat and then back to the engine at maybe still 180°.

The higher winds were a violent enemy to the smaller Formula One and Bi-plane races. Even at Reno, their races had to be scheduled before the strong, gusty afternoon winds came up. But for the heavy 8,000 pounds and up Unlimiteds, the winds weren't a "go-no-go" condition. As a matter of fact, when I wasn't the fastest plane in a race and especially if I had to fly behind those air-churning Bearcats and Sea Furys, the higher winds were my friend. They blew the churned air off the race course and either inside or outside the pylon air-space depending upon which way the wind was blowing. Of course, when the crew had the cowling off, the wind was their enemy trying to stabilize the step ladders and the keep the cowling pieces from being blown around and getting their finely-waxed paint job scuffed. They always preferred working in the calmer morning periods.

This race required them to work in the dark, lonely evening and for an all-night session! When it came my turn to qualify, I was perhaps too overconfident on the ability of the engine to keep sustaining the high-power settings as it had the last two races with no problems—two Unlimited races at high power on the same engine with no problems was already a stretch beyond the norm. A P-51 Merlin engine, cared for with lots of TLC and flown well inside the redlines, will last maybe 400 hours of flying versus 2,000 hours on a regular plane before needing overhaul. My reality was that if the engine lasted 40 hours of racing and personal flying, that was pretty good. As a matter of fact, the way I looked at it was that any hours I flew it outside of racing was really "free engine time." The more hours between racing cost me only gas because with two races on an engine, its life was that of an 80-year-old man, uninsurable.

Wanting to get a pole position in at least one heat race (second fastest qualifier would give me that because the fastest would be in Heat 1A and I'd be in Heat 1B), I went up to 90" MP and needed to bust the 3,000 RPM redline by just 200 RPM to get 90" (usually a prop can go 10% over redline without any real concern) in my qualifying run which was the average of two laps versus the normal one lap. Then it happened! About midway through the second lap two cylinders fell apart, B4 and B5 (why does it always seem to be the left bank that gives the trouble?—some say it's the swirl of the fuel going down the intake manifold that favors the right bank). I had to immediately back off on power. While the engine seemed to be trying to tear itself apart, I coasted to a downwind landing to save whatever I could. At nearly $30,000 each, I didn't have a spare racing engine, I didn't even have a large racing truck like the deep-pocket boys had.

But what I did have was a small but dedicated crew led by Skip Higginbotham that included Bill Pitts of Miami, a Delta Airline captain and a top mechanic; and my son, Don. We hangared the plane and set about assessing the damage. Seven hours later, about 10 p.m., they arrived at the conclusion that it could be fixed and sent me home to get some sleep. When I arrived at the airport at 9 a.m., where they were still working away without any sleep and with only the leftover cold pizzas I brought in the night before. Qualifying times ended at noon. When I looked at all the engine parts lying around the hangar, I felt there was no way they'd have it back together in time to qualify. They suggested that I go check out the other times. In short, let them work in peace. My pacing around the hangar was distracting them. I obliged.

At 10:30 when I came back, there it was outside the hangar, running! I couldn't believe my eyes. Not only was it running, but the knowledgeable Dave Zeuschel, who built the engine, was in the cockpit with a smile on his face. They explained to me that Dave said it had to be run for at least an hour to seat the pistons before I could take it out on the course and run it at race power. With Skip and Bill both nodding "Yes, that has to be done," I felt like I was getting the "must-do" advice of surgeons who had just finished their operation. My watch told me that it was now only an hour before quals ended. At least, could I just take it up and do the required two laps just to be sure to qualify, even at a slow speed? That certainly was not an option to them. I heard undertones of "Keefe, we know you'll probably go out there and get the feeling of needing more than just cruise power and 'blewee', we'd have a sick engine on our hands again."

At 11:30, they shut the engine down, motioned me to get in and take her out on the course. I called race control to tell them I was coming out. All others had finished qualifying at least two hours earlier. As I taxied out, the call came not to go onto the takeoff runway and to "stand-by for further instructions." What had happened is that the pylon judges from the Unlimited pylon-course pylons had been told to take their positions on the shorter T-6 course leaving several pylons on the Unlimited course without judges under them. The pylon coordinator had reasoned that all the Unlimiteds that were going to qualify were already done. "Miss America" was being run-up behind a row of hangars out of view. They thought my engine was still in pieces on the hangar floor. Someone had looked in on the scene at about 9:30 a.m. and had judged that there was no way it would be ready to qualify by the noon deadline.

Then I had a stroke of luck. The race committee decided that I was in place and ready to qualify before the noon deadline. They decided to let my speed on the one lap be considered my qualifying time for the event. So I squeaked in with the qualifying time of only 355 mph which gave me the fifth-fastest qualifying time…not good, but at least I was in the race and those three guys could see the fruits of their all-night labors. The other race crews knew the feat they had accomplished and gave them high-fives all around for it. Of course, it was through the generosity of the other race crews that my group was able to round up the needed parts and even loan them tools that the other crews didn't need at night. This is the unspoken rule among the race crews—to share and share alike. Their loyalty is to the planes and they foster

Christa rode rear seat in "Miss America" back and forth across the U.S. and Canada for many years. But if any woman said to her "you're so lucky" her answer was always, "Give me your plane ticket and you can ride back in my place." She dreaded hearing the tower say "Will you give us a buzz job before landing"? She knew this meant a high-G, up-and-over turn at the end of the runway.

that loyalty for even the crews of a competitor's plane. It's an honor for them to help each other out in a pinch.

I didn't record in my logbook what place I took in the race, but it does note being beaten by Bob Love in the drag race. Bob was flying a stock Mustang without water injection. That meant he would not exceed the redline of 60" manifold pressure which we routinely used on takeoff for about 30 seconds until above about 500 feet, and then throttle back to METO power (Maximum Except Takeoff) of 48" which could be used for longer periods. On the other hand, I had water injection and planned to go up to 90".

We both took off at the same pace, but then he cut in tight on the first pylon while I was still attempting to adjust my manifold pressure to reach 90", inching up on the RPM to get it to 90" (about 85" is all you can get with the RPM at the 3,000 RPM redline). In that split second, he had taken advantage of my flying a little wide on the course. Bob was a P-51 fighter-pilot in the Korean War and was known as an excellent pilot. He never flew really hot stuff in the races, so his name never surfaced in the winner circle, but he sure knew how to fly—and from behind, I witnessed it! He flew so tightly around the pylons that there was less than 20 feet between his plane and the course line—and of course, he didn't sweep upward on the turns like most rookies do, until they learn that at those speeds, when you put a wing down, lift is added that requires the use forward-stick around the initial part of the turn instead of the usual back-stick after the turn is established.

Bob beat me by about 3 plane lengths in the one-lap race of about 90 seconds. My crew tried to console me with the fact that it's easier for one lap to use just takeoff power. At slower speeds it's easier to fly the pylons tighter. But, what I saw was more than that. It made me wonder if my clipped wing-tips lost some lift to keep me tight around the pylons in an almost-90° bank. Was I mushing out? I never really resolved that point with myself in my 12 years of Unlimited air racing. All I knew is that the P-51 with its wings clipped was easier to settle down on a landing with a lot less float and is much easier to taxi around in tight places. And clipped wings are fast.

Comedy of Errors
All Scenes: Abbotsford, BC, Canada Air Show • August 1975
Prologue

It was now 60 days after my "jammed-gear air show" at Orange County Airport. Even though I had flown in the California Nationals at Mojave since that time without any gear problems, the experience was still fresh in my mind. Now for the enjoyable Abbotsford Air Show 30 miles inland from Vancouver, British Columbia. On the way up, we stopped at the picturesque airport of Sun River, Oregon. Arriving late in the day, the setting sun made the winding river look like it was flowing silver in the dark green setting. One of the drawbacks of flying is that you can't pull off to the side of the road to absorb such a sight, but the flip side of that is on the highway, you don't see panoramas so pleasant.

The entire area was so serene and bucolic that we lingered longer than we should have with our gracious host, John Heath. A late start made us arrive at the Abbotsford airport when everyone was in Vancouver at the annual pre-show banquet. The weather was starting to get a late-afternoon marine overcast that drifted in from the ocean area. By the time I reached the airport, the tops were 2,000 feet and the ceiling had dropped to 800 feet broken with about 40% cloud cover. You could see just enough of the ground to tempt you to dive through one of the holes in the clouds. But I had been here before. There were low mountain ridges on two sides of the airport area.

I made contact with the Abbotsford Control tower and they verified that the field was officially in IFR condition. I could see the green and white tower beacon rotating beneath the spotty cloud layer. When that light is rotating in daylight hours, it means the field is officially in IFR (instrument) conditions. They broadcast that they had no traffic and would accommodate me in any way they could. As I mentioned earlier, the aviation people in Canada, and particularly at Abbotsford during air show time, are super-cooperative. But technically, I would be in violation of Canadian rules if the cloud cover got thicker than 50% and moved into the classification of an "overcast" ceiling. The trend seemed to be going that way.

The airport had one of the easiest approach "blind landing" systems to use, the ILS approach (instrument landing system). The ILS requires a fairly common instrument found in most advanced planes. It has "needles" that act like crosshairs in a gun sight. The vertical needle shows if you are left or right of the course, and the horizontal needle shows if you are above or below the glide path into the airport. It guides you down a large sewer-pipe tunnel of space to the start of the airport's runway. Using this approach was a bit more of a hassle than just diving through a hole in the clouds. I had to file a mini-flight plan which I could do with the tower because I was already in their airspace and in contact with them. Then I had to tune in and identify the ILS frequency listening to its dot-dash code, tune in on another radio set to its LOM (outer marker) freq, follow an ADF needle to it and turn down the ILS path. When you're not already set up for it ahead of time, just dropping through a hole in the clouds is a lot easier, but is not a lot safer.

Abbotsford is only 40 miles north of the U.S. border. It's the go-to airport when Vancouver is socked in. In mid-August each year, it's the largest air show crowd in North America....and they are enthusiastic!

Comedy of Errors: Act I
"Gear Lights are Out"

At the outer marker, I turned left to establish myself on the glide path. I put the gear handle down and 30° of flaps. By now my eyes were glued on the ILS head with glances at the vertical speed indicator, the airspeed and altimeter. I looked down at the gear up/down lights. Nothing. They weren't lit at all! Not even the red was on. At that moment I broke down below the cloud cover with the runway in sight directly ahead. "What the hell is going on now with the unlit gear lights?" I aborted the landing. Climbed back up as high as I could without going into the clouds and told the tower my dilemma. I asked if I could veer right toward them to see if they could check my gear position. "They seem down to us—we've had two people with binoculars checking as you flew by," was their comforting reply. At least they were not jammed with one gear halfway down.

But I was still gun-shy. I asked if there was a mechanic on the ground who might check them by looking directly up to see if they were both absolutely straight. No one was around. All operations were secured. Everyone was at the dinner in Vancouver. Now the idea of talking to someone again as I had done with the Tallmantz crew at Orange County came to mind. The tower said they'd be glad to call someone. I replied "Would you please try to get Bob Hoover at the banquet? If anybody can figure this out, he can." They knew Bob Hoover, of course. He was a star of their show with his aerobatic routine in his P-51 Mustang "Ol' Yeller." I could see it parked below on the ramp. Meanwhile, I began to circle the field just under the cloud layer while waiting for any advice Bob might have. It wasn't like the one down, one up I had before where I could test the gear by banging one down on the runway. If they weren't locked down, the prop might hit the runway or they'd collapse at the slightest upward bounce.

I retracted the gear while circling, waited awhile, noted the hydraulic pressure that operated the gear at a solid 70 pounds, then put the gear handle down again, saw the hydraulic needle swing counterclockwise to 40 pounds showing the pressure that was being used.

Then I heard the "thud" that the gear had dropped in place, and the pressure rose to 70 pounds again. Everything was normal but the gear lights were still dark. I pressed them again to test. No response. Still no word from Bob—the tower said he still had not answered the phone. Why hadn't Bob replied? Answer in the Postmortem.

Comedy of Errors: Act II
"Cutting Off the Engine"

Now my gas was low. I had to make a decision. These are types of decisions you don't like to make if it's your own plane. There was no real physical danger ahead, but a strong danger of wallet drain. The logistics of getting it flyable again in a foreign country had not yet entered my mind—that would come later.

I set up for the landing with all the cautions racing through my mind. Be sure the ignition is off when you touch down. Get ready on the brakes for a violent swerve if one of the gears collapses. Try to stop the prop when one of the 4 blades is straight down so only one blade will be damaged. Get the flaps up quickly if I feel it sinking so they won't be damaged. Have all the runway ahead I might need, land short.

Doing about 110 mph, I nosed down for the landing. I'd cut all power before landing. Then I almost "bought the farm"! I stupidly cut off all power while I was still 50 yards short of the runway. I had never experienced 5 tons of airplane with clipped wings and full flaps suddenly deprived of all power at low altitude…and with the prop in low (flat) pitch acting like a giant air-brake. Thankfully, one of my pre-programmed reactions took place at the moment. Instead of trying to raise the nose to stretch my glide and maybe stall in, I dove for the pine-tree forest off the end of the runway to pick up speed. It was just enough. My wheels touched down not more than two feet into the runway. I felt stupid, as I should feel stupid, in cutting all power before I was even over the runway. Another lesson learned. The plane rolled to a stop. The gear was okay. I restarted and taxied to the tie-down area, giving a "thanks much for your help" call to the tower.

Comedy of Errors: Act III
"Shock Therapy Didn't Take"

The weather with a low marine layer still hung over the airport. The mountain range to the northeast was still shrouded in the low-hanging clouds. Because of the low ceiling, the Thunderbirds had to wait for the marine layer to burn off in order to have enough altitude for their performance. The other aerobatic acts, like Bob Hoover and Art Scholl, could do most of their routine under the 800-foot ceiling. When those acts were used up, the air show director, John McGowan, asked me if I could gather the Warbirds together to do the "Warbird Act" fly-by. I'd lead them out from the ramp area, then pull off into the grass by the side of the runway and act as their launch and flight coordinator on the Air Show frequency.

I launched the slower planes like the WWII carrier-based F4F "Wildcats" up to the faster F4U "Corsairs" circling the field close-in and the faster planes, like the P-51s and Spitfires, in a wider circle. This would give the crowd something to watch on the take off and in view in the circle, plus the two passes each plane would make down the runway with the announcer, Glenn Mathews, keeping the crowd's attention over the loud speakers with his professional repertoire of glowing facts about each plane and its pilot. After all were launched, I looked at the gear light panel one more time. Still no lights. More as a matter of habit, I pressed the green gear-down-locked light to test it. Whoa! I got a shock from my boom mike to my lips that was an immediate eye-opener!

"What was that all about?" I wondered. Clue: Earlier I had been using the mike in my oxygen mask, now I had the boom mike that had a carbon mike. Can the reader figure out what was happening? It's explained in the Postmortem. Read on. With all the others gone, I had to get in the air so as not to hold up the show. I pulled out of position in the tall grass onto the runway and took off to join the wider circle. When I was in position at the outside making a counterclockwise circle of the field,

I called for the planes on the inner circle to start making their fly-bys down the show runway.

I told them after their first fly-by to join back up in the circle under the overcast, then the planes in the outer-circle would follow the same routine. I was the last one from the outer circle, then called for the inner circle to do a second fly-by "down and dirty" (gear and flaps down) for pictures at slower speeds showing all the guts of each plane. I was playing for time, hoping the overcast would start to break up so the Thunderbirds could do their act. Finally, the sky was clear in some areas, so I radioed for the planes to break out from their circle and get in a position to land. Watch the plane ahead of them and give it at least 50% of the length of the runway ahead as an interval. So the Thunderbirds could get started in front of the crowd, Air Show control requested we land (recover) on the long runway far out from the north–south show runway that went on an angle to the southwest.

Comedy of Errors: Act IV
"Trying to Land Behind Slow Stuff"

As it developed, I was the first in position to land from the faster-plane circle. I was following an F4F "Wildcat," an earlier Navy carrier plane that required the pilot to crank down the landing gear by hand. I thought I had let him get far enough ahead, but on final, it looked like he was just hanging there in the air ahead of me. I was closing rapidly. I even recall considering going out around him. The plane ahead of him was already off the runway. No, that wouldn't be too smart. He might dump his flaps and pick up more speed. The "Go around" alert in my subconscious called out again. I pulled off to his left and paralleled the runway. At the end of the runway, Bob Love in his P-51 was just passing. He was the last plane in the fast group. Instead of stringing out behind him, I joined up on his right wing, after letting him know what I was a doing. We'd make a formation landing together. Bob Love was an ex-Korean War fighter pilot. He knew his flying. I'd feel comfortable flying formation with him anytime. We were at the end of the fast-plane circle, the last ones to land.

The weather had cleared at the end of the runway, but the mountains off the approach end of the runway were still obscured. Bob was no stranger to slow and low flying. He made a low-level turn on base and rolled out on final with me and my clipped wings "hanging-on-the-prop" to keep from over-running him and to stay in formation. I had as a passenger a commercially-rated Canadian pilot, Paul Murray, son of Bill Murray, one of the air-show officials.

I looked at my gear lights, recalled that they weren't functioning, that I had put the gear down on my previous attempt at landing behind the F4F to slow my plane down. My total attention was on Bob's plane for a formation touch-down. I was sure Bob, knowing I was on his wing would keep up his speed after touchdown to give me room. I probably could have squeaked by him on that wide runway.

Comedy of Errors: Act V
"The Phantom Horn"

Over the runway, I was carrying a fair amount of power to keep near stall with my nose high to stay behind Bob. When I saw his wheels touch, I eased back on the throttle and heard this strange horn blaring away. In my mind, it was a stall warning horn—a low-altitude stall in a P-51 is the last thing you want to have to deal with. I added power, the horn stopped and I let the plane settle slowly down to the runway with power on as you do in a short-field landing.

"Oh, no!" I thought, as I felt a severe vibration. "I've got a flat tire! I must have taxied over a broken coke bottle in that high grass while waiting for them to take off—No, it's not that, the gear is collapsing! My god!—Whoa! This is something else! The prop has stopped!—I'm on the ground and I'm going down the runway at over 100 miles per hour—I can see everything ahead, it was as if the P-51 had been converted from a tailwheel plane into a nosewheel plane in which you can see everything ahead. On either side of the cockpit, a thick band of sparks is flowing up and then down in a long arch—I've never seen a fireworks display like it!—I feel I still have rudder-control at now maybe 80 mph—I'll turn off at the high-speed taxiway to clear the runway.

Comedy of Errors: Act VI
"The Wrong Turn"

As the 45° right turn to enter the high-speed runway turn-off like an exit ramp of the freeway (an "easy-off" as the Brits say) approached, I added right rudder. It wasn't turning too well, so I added more right rudder. Still not enough. Well, anyway, I'd clear the runway as I was headed for the crotch—the open area between the two runways. At least I'd be clear of the runway. I'd just glide off into the grass area. When I hit that area, the plane came to an abrupt stop and the air was filled with flying debris. They said that from the grandstand it looked like a mini-A bomb had gone off with the dust cloud forming over the plane. I remember sitting there and feeling pebbles, dust, grass and other debris falling down from the sky on top of me in the open cockpit. For a moment I longed to return to that wonderful ride down the runway with the plume of sparks on either side. It had been one helluva-ride. I wanted to buy a ticket for another ride like that!

As the dust settled and the air cleared, I was looking through the windshield at a strange sculpture. It was my prop, bent and twisted in the shape of a blooming flower. It was pretty, not ugly as in a wreck. I looked back at my passenger. He had a look of wonderment on his face. He said later that he'd enjoyed it, too. It was just that he was wondering what was happening during it all—as if I knew what had happened! Before I knew it fire trucks, ambulances, official cars, police cars, police motorcycles and an assortment of photographers had surrounded the plane. I stepped from the wing to the ground in the shortest step I had ever taken off the wing. It felt

I had this photo printed on T-shirts which were worn at the Reno National Air Races the following month. It took out some of the sting I was bound to get from my fellow race pilots.

strange. Except for the splayed-out prop, I couldn't see any other damage. It seemed it would cost a lot less than the $20,000 no-fun experience of blowing an engine compared to the multi-colored spark filled ride I just had.

Aside: If I had stayed on the runway, the damage would have been limited mainly to the prop. The plane was riding on the air scoop. As it was, the pre-Cambrian rocks caused extensive damage to the scoop, the flaps and wing rivets stressed by the down-flaps riding over the rocks. The $10,000 repair bill took some of the fun away from that great ride.

Postmortem

Now the time for you sleuths to take a shot at guessing what caused each event. **Question:** What caused the gear lights to go out? **Answer:** The ground strap between the instrument panel and the plane's chassis had broken.

Question: Why didn't Bob Hoover call back when they said they had contacted him? **Answer:** He got the message second-hand, not from the person who answered the phone and it didn't tell him where the phone was. From a pay phone, Bob called the tower number repeatedly for nearly half-an-hour, then gave up. It was busy every time. The tower had left their phone off the hook waiting for Bob to come to the phone.

Question: Why did I get a shock on the lips when I pressed the gear test light? **Answer:** With the ground strap broken, I became the ground when I touched the gear light.

Question: Why did I get a shock on the lips with the boom mike and not with the mike in my oxygen mask? **Answer:** I was told that the boom mike was a carbon mike that conducted electricity. My body became the ground. The current passed through my body and my lips were the closest thing to the carbon mike, so it sparked from my lips to the mike. (I can still feel it! I'll never kiss a brass doorknob in winter. If you want a thrill, try it.)

Question: Why didn't I get a shock when I tested the gear lights with my oxygen mask on? **Answer:** Coming into Abbotsford from high altitude en route, I still had my oxygen mask on. During the show I had converted from the oxygen mask mike to the cooler boom mike. The mike in an oxygen mask is a non-conductive type to avoid a spark that would cause an explosion in the oxygen system under just those circumstances. From that time on, I never tucked my boom mike under my oxygen mask to save the trouble of changing the leads on the mike jacks. A spark that strong in an oxygen-in-use environment surely would have caused a flash explosion in my face and lungs.

Question: Why didn't I make sure the gear was down the second time I was landing? **Answer:** Psychologists call it "psychological set"—you are certain something is what it isn't. In Maine, they have determined that it is the veteran deer hunter with at least 5 years of hunting that is most apt to shoot a person mistaken for a deer. Rarely is it a novice. The veteran has seen a deer behind a tree, rustling the low bushes and it got away. He's looking for a repeat of that view. I was convinced I had put my gear down the first time. I had put the gear down according to movies shown to me later, but I had the automatic reaction of retracting the gear when I added power to go around. Coming in to land in a low, tight formation, I automatically checked the gear lights and the "psychological set" took over when my total concentration was to try to keep from chewing up Bob's wing—the light don't work, I recall putting the gear down and that was that.

Question: What was that horn sound? **Answer:** It was the gear-up warning horn. It's a standing joke among pilots that a person who lands with his gear-up says "the sound of that gear-warning horn was so loud, it distracted me during my landing." Improbable as it sounds, after 6 years and many hours of flying the P-51, I had not

I have this picture hanging in my art area. It is like a flower bursting into bloom. If you have lemons, what do you do? Make lemonade, of course. My gear-up landing was a giant lemon!

only never heard the gear-warning horn, I never thought to check to see if I had one or what it sounded like. When teaching people flying in their planes, I had heard the stall-warning horn many times entering a practice stall. Another "psychological set." I didn't even have a stall-warning system in the plane! When the horn quit when I added power and airspeed, it furthered my misunderstanding of what was happening. But, boy, what a ride it was!

Question: What caused the sparks? Aren't props made of aluminum that doesn't spark? **Answer:** As mentioned earlier, I had an Aero Products prop that was made of steel. Its pea-pod construction gave the feeling of being in a car going through the car wash and having the felt panels hitting the side of the car. The softness of the steel splitting and slowing the engine rotation down more gently is what probably saved me from an expensive gear-shearing, crankcase twisting sudden stop a solid blade would have caused. In other words, the prop blades sacrificed their lives for me and my wallet.

An afterthought: I had mentioned how accommodating the Canadian DOT (FAA) and other Canadian officials are, but I excluded the Canadian Customs. They are tigers. They are accommodating for you to fly in to the Abbotsford Air Show and camp under your wing as thousands do, but if you need a plane part sent in you better have the old, bad part in your hand.

I had to have my spare Bearcat prop sent up. Naively, I went to the Vancouver Airport to pick it up at Western Airline's (now Delta) freight terminal. No way was I going to get it without paying a heavy-duty tax. I tried to explain that it was a replacement part (no duty due), but they would have none of it. Bring them the old part or pay the duty. I explained that the old parts had been cut up and given away as souvenirs to local people I knew—that there was no way I could get them all back together. Then I recalled that one piece of the prop had been given to the Abbotsford Flying Club at the airport. I had signed it and it was permanently attached to a wall in their club house. Still not believing me, they sent a customs inspector with me the 30+ miles to the airport to see the prop piece. Luckily there were club members on hand who had a part in cutting it up to give as souvenirs. They explained that it was an accident and then one had the bright idea of taking him to the hangar where the plane was being repaired to see for himself the plane without a prop sitting forlornly in the hangar awaiting repairs.

When he signed the release papers, he still didn't look convinced! They're tough.

1975 Reno National Air Races

"A Grand Arrival, then Pushing a Barn Door"

I landed with the gear up on August 9 and on September 9, I had to be at the air-race site at Reno. I had been in every Unlimited Race in the country since 1969 and didn't want to break my consecutive string of pylon races.

In the amazingly short time of 4 weeks, "Miss America" was ready to fly, but if I wanted to make the Reno Air Races, in which I was already entered, I had to get to Reno on Tuesday. Wednesday was the last qualifying day. The crew needed time to convert all the systems over from cruise to race. Steve Myers, working almost alone in a hangar at Abbotsford, put it all together. A fellow race pilot, Mike Smith in Kansas, took on the difficult job of restoring the badly damaged air scoop. I learned that it had "compound curves," a term new to me in metal. It couldn't just be put on a sawhorse and pounded out. Mike solved the problem. Steve Myers checked the engine to make sure it didn't have any twisted parts from the prop stoppage. It didn't and the prop gears weren't damaged either. I don't think I ever would have gotten away with that if the prop had been solid metal.

I made a short test hop around the field, landed, filed my ADCUS (Advise Customs) flight plan to Bellingham, Washington, just across the border to clear U.S. Customs and I was off to the races. From Bellingham, I flew the roughly 700 miles direct to Reno and must confess at this late date, that I broke a few FAA flight rules on the way, but I did it with caution and safety. If you have ever flown the route east of the Cascade Range, over Richmond, Pendleton, down to Reno, you know it can be full of air bumps and rough weather. I could make 600 miles easily on my two main tanks, but 700 miles was stretching it, especially if I had to go around weather. I put 45 gallons of gas in one of the gun-bay tanks. That would give me about another 150 miles.

At Bellingham, Washington, checking the weather to Reno was like reading the minute-by-minute scores of two basketball games at the same time—the weather changed almost every 50 miles from low clouds to thunderstorms to heavy rain to light rain to clear and then back to the previous sequence. I didn't feel good about going down the calmer coastal route that would require me being in the clouds all the way. I hadn't flown on instruments in a month and wasn't that sure of the plane's reborn condition to be "in-the-soup" with it. In case of an emergency, the only way to get into an airport would be to make a landing at perhaps minimum visibility. I chose the smorgasbord weather on the lee side of the Cascade mountain range. But I had to do it VFR, without an instrument flight plan because the airways required high altitudes and I wasn't that sure of my oxygen supply.

Hopping from Bellingham east into the valley was easy. Then starting down the valley, while the visibility was very good, I could see dark clouds, light clouds, lightning flashes over here, then over at the other side. To cover my bets, I asked radar Center if they could give me their "flight following" service of watching me on radar to both give me position reports and let me know if they see any other traffic near me. The other advantage was that if worse came to worse, and I did have to go on an instrument flight plan because I couldn't see the terrain, I'd already be in contact with the Center and could transition from a VFR Flight Plan to an IFR Flight Plan seamlessly. Radar doesn't know if you can see the ground or not, or whether you are going through a cloud knowing you'll soon come out in the clear in less than a minute. In that minute, though, you aren't very legal, but being in radar contact you at least know there's not another plane in that cloud.

It was a rock 'n' roll journey all the way. I was glad I didn't have a passenger along to worry about getting queasy or having to explain why I just went down to only 500 feet to avoid a cloud or climb sharply to go through the thin part of one up higher then suddenly nose over with a tummy-thrilling negative-G maneuver to avoid another. It's easy to handle it when you're doing the flying yourself. You know when you're going to pull up, where it'll stop and why. Even I, who my wife claims has a "cast-iron stomach," would get woozy if someone else were doing the flying. I was glad I was alone.

It was getting late. It looked like I'd get to Reno about 1830 hrs. (6:30 p.m.). Maybe an hour of daylight left. Hoped the crew would be there with my rental car and a pit-spot area already established. As I neared Reno, there was this phenomenon of 5 or 6 individual storms going on over a 50-mile wide stage about 5 to 10 miles apart. If there

Those attending the air races from Japan seemed to focus on "Miss America." The women bought neck scarves and the men bought hats and jackets with "Miss America" emblems. This cute emblem was a sew-on patch that was given to me. I value it to this day.

were music, each would have its own Wagnerian chorus. It was like sitting in my sailboat off the coast of Los Angeles on a Fourth of July evening, watching the individual firework displays in communities up and down the coast.

Finally Reno's radio station came in strong, but I really didn't need it, I could see the town's brilliant lights 50 miles away and I knew the airport was about 10 miles north. I called on Stead Field's unicom. They told me all race conditions had been secured and that Race Control had reopened the field for non-race aircraft until tomorrow's qualifying times. Just as I was rounding the pattern to land, one of these pyrotechnic displays in the area started slamming lightning into the ground about 2 miles away and also cloud-to-cloud lightning on a grand scale. Visibility was clear. On final, the lightning lit up the field like a giant sunburst.

No other planes were moving. As I taxied in, Pete Hoyt and Skip came out on the ramp and motioned me down a line of planes. There it was. My pit area. Just as I liked it, at the end of the row along the walkway the spectators used. I felt a little euphoric having gotten there at the last minute after all the logistics over the last 30 days with getting the prop and repairs to this hairline finish. Pete Hoyt always was expecting me to do something unusual, perhaps even on the dramatic side. Looking down at his smiling face as the prop stopped, I stood up in the cockpit, turned around to face the line of thunderstorms behind me, pointed at them and called out, "Okay, scene over! Kill the lightning! Turn off the thunder! Wipe off the clouds!" Pete doubled over in laughter. He had been rewarded for the three hours he had been out there waiting for the arrival while wondering "if." I saw the writer from *FLYING* Magazine in the group. He apparently had seen my little act. He used it in his write up of the Reno races a few issues later. That it had gotten into print, made it an even greater event for Pete. This book is dedicated to him. I miss that guy. We sure had fun on the ground and in the air together.

The only spare prop I had was a Bearcat prop. But the prop gears in the engine were the .42 (make it turn at only 42% of the engine RPM). The longer Bearcat prop

This decal, to apply to a toolbox, was awarded to every member of any race crew who helped us.

was happy with that gear ratio as long as the engine RPM did not exceed its max redline of 3,000 RPM. Over that, the tips of the longer Bearcat prop became like a stubborn mule. They'd not only refuse to do their job of pulling the plane through the air, they'd actually try to stop it. They were going through the speed of sound, cavitating and setting their own limit on how fast the plane could go. The more power I added, the more the plane felt like it was "pushing a barn door" through the air—like it was flying through slush.

The best I could do in qualifying was only 370 mph. I barely made the Silver Race, the second fastest group. The planes were getting faster every year. They were passing up my souped up "Miss America," but it didn't hurt. I had the wrong prop gear ratio and was glad that I even got there in time to race at all after that Comedy of Errors in Canada.

The Joe Bflstk Cloud Over Mojave • June 1976

Most of you are probably too young to recall the Li'l Abner comic strip where this character of doom-and-gloom walked around with a dark rain cloud directly over his head. When he walked by a happy scene, the next panel would show some disaster had struck it. That was how I was beginning to see the California Air Races at Mojave.

They were held a convenient 75 miles away from my base at Van Nuys, but Mojave's races were a setting of constant problems. The 1976 races were no different.

It was mid-June 1976. The Reno races were ancient history—they were 9 months ago. Now things would be different. My logbook notes summarize the 1976 California National Air Races at Mojave, California 100 miles north of Los Angeles as follows:

"Having a big problem of backfiring. Later determined to be a stuck intake valve due to a keeper ring on the valve breaking. I had the engine stop 4 times in the air due to backfiring. Was able to air-start each time, but each time thought I had a dead-stick landing on my hands. Was able to limp around the qualifying course in spite of it, but made only a qualifying time of 246 mph, not even normal cruise speed!

"Low qual time put me in slowest group, the Medallion race (formerly Bronze Race). Pulled off course on Lap #2 when coolant temp gauge went into red area. If gauge correct, had to shut down engine within 10 seconds to prevent it from freezing up. Discovered gauge was faulty. Able to get into finals of the Silver race, but prop seal broke and covered windshield with oil. Couldn't see pylons until alongside. Was following other plane. Came in second, but cut a pylon. Low and fast on the desert floor not being able to see ahead is not a healthy way to live!

Back to the Abbotsford Air Show in Canada • August 1976

My show-stopping act in 1975 of landing with my gear up and the friendships I made in Canada as a result, made me want to go back up there again. Also, I heard they had a presentation for me and I can't resist getting something ever since I got

my first badge as a Cub scout when I was 8 years old. It was quite a presentation.

An artistic model builder used one of the Revell kits of my plane, the 1:32nd scale size, to show a 3-D version of "Miss America" resting after the gear-up landing the year before. The modeler was afraid I would take offense at it, but the staff finally convinced him to make the presentation at the banquet. It was an amazing model of the entire scene on a dark wood foundation about 15" x 15". It had the grass, the pebbles on the wing, the rocks beneath the plane and the prop sculpted to resemble its blooming flower shape. It was a museum piece.

The engraved plaque on it said "Awarded to Howie Keefe for the most outstanding, show stopping act at Abbotsford's 1975 Air Show." After the presentation, the cries of "Speech! Speech!" filled the air. In my "Thank You," I promised I would do it again if someone would lend me a P-51. My only caveat was that the plane had to have a steel prop so that fireworks display would again accompany me down the runway on that once-in-a-lifetime ride—and perhaps a raffle to ride along with me would cover all the expenses—and the next time, I'd stay on the runway rather than try a turn-off at the high-speed exit—in that way the costs of repair would be reduced. Nothing ever came of my offer. Strange, they said it was a good act.

Patches photographed from my flight suit.
Sponsors were great in keeping me supplied.

Chapter 15

Dead Stick IFR Landing from 20,000 Feet!

A t Abbotsford, I had sprung a leak in the coolant tank just in front of the cockpit. The 3 "musts" to run a Merlin engine are 1) Gasoline, 2) oil and 3) engine water coolant. Without #1, the engine stops, but that's all that happens. The engine is still good. Without #2, oil, the engine will eventually grind to a halt as the bearings and oiled parts wear down. The engine will be soup. Without #3, water, you have about 10 seconds to shut down the engine before parts overheat, cylinders and rings expand and the engine freezes. Really not as bad on the engine as #2, but bad enough so the plane will not stay in the air. That was my dilemma. The RCAF unit at Abbotsford had welded a crack in the coolant tank for me. We pressure-tested it and all seemed fine. On the way back from Abbotsford, things happened.

I'd been having back treatments at the Veteran's Hospital in Los Angeles. It was still hurting after jumping off the wing on to the concrete ramp after the crew had pumped up the struts to max height to accommodate the Bearcat prop's longer length— and I wasn't getting any younger. At 55, I was feeling bumps and bruises at a higher decibel level. A physical therapist at the VA, Jack Peterson was gung-ho on wanting to ride in a P-51. I jokingly said if he brought the ultrasound machine that he'd been treating me with, he could ride with me to Abbotsford and back. His supervisor overheard my offer. He mentioned to Jack that they had an older stand-by machine he could take—and we made the deal.

Jack guarded that ultrasound machine like it was a new-born baby. He wouldn't trust it in the below-freezing temps in the gun-bay baggage, so he carried it on his lap while we were in-flight. It was kind of funny to see him in the back seat with his oxygen mask on and this machine in his lap. It was a scene you might have seen in an old movie about a mad inventor. It sure felt good to start and finish the day with his treatments.

At 20,000 feet over the Sacramento area, I was on an instrument flight plan in the sunny, clear sky headed for Los Angeles when suddenly the windshield was covered with water. No question about it, the coolant tank had blown a leak again. Before when it happened, I was only 1,000 feet over an airport. Now at 20,000 feet, there were three layers of clouds with about 4,000 feet of clear air between each layer. The problem was that the bottom layer went down to 900 feet above the ground. I had no choice. If I lost all the coolant, the engine freeze-up would certainly come in a matter of seconds. I pulled back on the power and put the mixture on full rich to keep the engine as cool as I could while telling Center my problem. They responded quickly that I was clear to take any altitude I needed to reach Sacramento Executive airport about 20 miles ahead. In the mirror, I could see Jack's eyes getting a little wider. Through the earphones, he was able to hear everything that had been said— and he certainly could see the steady stream hitting the windshield. He wrapped his arms a little tighter around his precious ultrasound machine.

I decided to cut the engine. I didn't want to dive down from 20,000 feet, especially going through the cloud layers in a dive on instruments. They each were about 3,000–4,000 feet thick. I chose to do a part dive, part normal descent. Dive in between layers where the air was clear, then level off and circle down on instruments through the cloud layers. Center had me in solid radar contact and was giving me traffic priority in the two cases that arose of another plane in the area in possible conflict with my dive–circle pattern. At 4,000 feet, center handed me off to Sacramento's approach control. They had been fully advised of my intent and took no time to jump in.

"November-nine-nine-one-Romeo turn right to zero-four-five degrees and de- scend to 2,000 feet. Altimeter setting is two-nine-nine-one. Ceiling 900 and ragged, visibility 4 miles. Sacramento Executive tower is keeping runway two-zero open for you. We'll set you up for final to runway two-zero."

That sure sounded good to me, but I didn't know anything about runway two- zero. "How long is runway two-zero?" I asked. "Fifty-five hundred feet" was their reply. A little over a mile long, I thought I should be able to handle that dead-stick- ing it in with no power and mentioned my confidence to Jack over the intercom. He seemed to be managing a sick smile, while nodding his head and looking out the side into nothing but clouds.

"Nine-one Romeo, turn right to two-zero-zero degrees, descend to 800 feet until you have the runway in sight." I reset the directional gyro, started the turn, put down just 20 degrees of flap, then quickly retracted the flaps as the sink rate went up to 700 feet per minute down; too fast.

Almost before I knew it, we broke out of the clouds with the runway dead ahead. I put the gear down when I knew I was over the runway and landed without flaps, rolled as far as I could to try to clear the runway, but stopped about 200 feet short of the turn off at the runway end. I started the engine, taxied clear of the runway and shut it down again. A fire engine was standing by at the cross runway. It followed me down the runway. Soon a tug came out and towed us to a mechanic's hangar.

I got out. Jack carefully lifted his "baby" over the back of my seat, laid it gently on my seat, pulled himself up and stepped out. After an inspection of the crack in the tank and, to my surprise, a large amount of coolant still in it, the mechanic held out little hope of being able to repair it to withstand the low outside pressures at 20,000 feet and the normal pressure maintained inside the coolant system. Then I learned something that if I ever knew before, I had forgotten. The water pump will keep circulating water even if it isn't under pressure. If you have a radiator leak in your car, just keep the pressure cap off until you can reach a place to get the leak fixed. Without pressure, the water might not leak at all.

The mechanic felt that I could make it to Van Nuys okay. Just stay on the route of a lot of airports and watch the water temp closely. If it started to rise, I'd still have time to get down. The weather was clearing to the south and I noticed coming in that I broke out of the clouds at about 1,100', sooner than I had planned. While I was talking to the mechanic and deliberating the possibility of going on with the pressure cap released, I had noticed Jack climb up on the wing, cradle the instrument in his arms and slide down the wing on the other side. I didn't think much about it at the time.

About that time a fellow walked up and was listening to the mechanic and me discussing the matter. Any P-51 usually draws a few spectators, especially one with the canopy pulled back. You get the "can I have a look inside" requests all the time. My answer was always, "Certainly, please don't touch anything." The person looked, got down and came over to listen some more. He introduced himself as a Western Airlines pilot. Knowing an airline pilot had a lot of training in a plane's systems, I asked his take on being able to fly without the coolant system being pressurized. He felt it would be okay, too. So I looked around for Jack. He was nowhere to be found. I asked the airline pilot if he had seen him and he said he had gone into an office

across the ramp. He went along to show me where. Just as we neared the door a young girl came out with a piece of paper in her hand and held it out to me. "I guess this is for you. Are you Howie Keefe?"

The note was signed by Jack, "Howie, you know more than I do about flying, but what I've been through has scared me. I'm catching an airline flight home. Will you bring my bag to the

Sacramento Executive Airport. Ice cream Parlor. 5500' long runway. Jack "escaped" when parked here. Was able to stop here. Fire trucks were waiting here.

Every pilot flying high-powered military planes in the early '70s was aware of the disaster of a civilian former jet fighter taking off from Sacramento Executive and crashing into an ice cream parlor off the end of the runway. It caused the FAA to restrict operations—I was "grandfathered-in" but new pilots had to demonstrate extra ability. On my dead-stick landing over the ice cream parlor, I was determined to give it a wide berth and land well down the runway.

VA when you come next week? Thanks for the experience." I showed it to the airline pilot and shrugged my shoulders. He immediately offered to ride with me...he'd love it...he'd give me any help he could...he could catch a free flight back on Western (now Delta).

He reintroduced himself with his name as John Harrison. I thought to myself that I could sure use a guy with some tech knowledge if anything else happened. My car was at Van Nuys airport and I'd be driving to where I lived in Marina del Rey which was near LA Int'l. I could easily drop him off there.

Within 20 minutes we were gassed up and on our way. He had reminded me that a little bit of oil or coolant on a windshield or on the ground always looks like a lot more than it is. Thank you, daddy, for those comforting thoughts. I'll sleep better now. I did.

John had checked the weather with me and suggested we could go toward Santa Barbara and then come in along the coast and hop over the mountains to Van Nuys at Santa Monica. On that route, there were numerous airports along the way in case we needed to set down. He made good sense.

Past Santa Barbara and then Camarillo airport, it looked clear enough over the mountains to head straight for Van Nuys. The water temp was holding in the green—why not? To hedge my bet, I flew along the mountain crest between the valley and the Pacific Ocean until Van Nuys was the closest place to land. We made it, no problem. Thank you for the moral support John Harrison, wherever you are. I know you liked your first P-51 ride. I did, too.

My Seventh Year in the Reno Nationals • 1976

The next month now is September, and September means the National Air Races at Reno, Nevada. By the time you're 7 years old, you are supposed to have learned

something. In some religions and cultures, a 7-year-old boy has a ceremony that indicates he has reached the age of reason and responsibility. Ditto with racing Unlimiteds at Reno. By the time you've raced in the Unlimiteds at Reno for 7 years, you are expected to know which of two routes you will take—one route is that you'll be able to fly your plane on Monday after the races with some confidence that you can make it all the way home. The other route is that you are going to go "balls out" and are prepared to have your plane left in Reno as long as it may take to put in a new engine so you can fly it home at a later date—probably after

arranging for a second mortgage on your house to pay for the repairs.

I chose the first route and placed third in the finals—best I had ever done! It worked this way. I waited until late Wednesday, the last day of qualifying, to make my qualifying run. The Unlimited quals started at 3 p.m. and the race course was secured at 4:30 p.m.—no qualifying for a position after that time for the 4 days of racing that started the next day. Today they have 24 qualifying places, 8 per race; then we had only 18 planes, 6 per race. I haven't applied my strategy to today's, but it should work out about the same. Plan to go at 4 p.m. when the winds and thermals die down for smoother air. Also, the pylons are a little easier to see because they'll cast a shadow at that time of day.

After 7 years, I knew about the manifold setting I needed for each 10 mph of speed. After checking all the qual speeds to that point, I picked a speed that would surely get me into the races. This year at 4 p.m. on Wednesday, it was anything over 340 mph, a comfortable speed to obtain. It would take only 80" of manifold pressure. Yes, a fair amount over the 65" MP of War Emergency power a fighter pilot was allowed to use to escape a nasty situation, 73" with water injection, but a conservative power setting in Unlimited racing. Prior to making your qual lap, you do one lap of the course and check your time. Anything under 1 minute, 30 seconds would get me in. As it turned out, not enough planes qualified to even fill the field and the successive races added more to the mortality so that the Gold Race finals on Sunday had a strange mix of stock and highly modified planes.

John Tegler, in his book on the Reno Air Races titled "Gentlemen, You Have a Race!" described it this way:

> *The Unlimited Championship Race for 1976 was probably one of the strangest races ever flown in this class. To begin with most of the race was flown under the yellow caution flag with half the field either not finishing or being disqualified. It became to be known as The Parade of the Stocks and the Wounded. It was an all Mustang affair.*
>
> *John Crocker, in "Sumthun' Else" took the lead right off the bat with Don Whittington, in "Precious Metal" in hot pursuit. At this point, Mac McClain, in RB-51 moved into second...followed by Clay Klabo in "Iron Mistress" (renamed "Fat Cat"), Lefty Gardner in "Thunderbird," Jimmy Leeward in "Miss Florida," Howie Keefe in "Miss America" and Darryl Greenamyer in the "Flying Undertaker." Precious Metal pulled up and out when his engine threw a rod and blew two jugs...RB-51 pulled out as the custom blower gears blew again...Fat Cat pulled out with the V-drive leaking oil and excessive oil on the windshield. Sumthin' Else was flying high around the pylons with oil leaking on his windshield and, as a result, cut the deadline over the crowd and was disqualified.*
>
> *The finish was, Lefty Gardner in "Thunderbird" First; Darryl Greenamyer in "Flying Undertaker" Second; Howie Keefe in "Miss America" Third (he blew off an exhaust stack which made his engine sound like the "Wreck of the Hesperus" so he pulled back to minimum power just to finish) and in Fourth was Jimmy Leeward in "Miss Florida." Many walked away shaking their heads, but that's the way it goes in high performance racing.*

It's a sound I had never heard before. It might be good orientation for an Unlimited Mustang Racer to fly at high power with an exhaust stack off to be prepared for the staccato sound. It sure gets your attention fast inside the cockpit. It broke off at the pylon my daughter, Dorrie, was stationed at. She saw "something fly off" and heard the sound change. John Tegler, in his book "Gentlemen, You Have a Race," described it as sounding like the Wreck of the Hespersis. I might have finished better if I had not pulled back from race power, but as the saying goes, there are no "old, bold pilots."

On top of it, I flew home the next day with a coveted Gold Finals Trophy and a great-running engine. When the stack blew off in the race, I was rounding Pylon #5 where my daughter, Dorrie, happened to be watching the races. It was her first time at a pylon where the planes come by 50 feet overhead. She saw a part of "Miss America" fly off and the engine suddenly made a snorting sound. The pylon judges wisely would not let her run out into the race course to get the part so someone could warn me what it was. The strange part to me in the cockpit was that the more I throttled back, the louder the sound became. This "reverse reply" had me confused. "Why would something get louder when the power is reduced?" When I landed and discovered that the exhaust stack had broken off entirely, the answer was clear. At high engine speed the "pop-pops" were a blur, at low speeds they were more pronounced, so much so I heard the race director was thinking about asking me to land to avoid any possible emergency near the crowd. They couldn't tell what the problem was either.

15 Minutes of Fame Over Omaha • August 1977

Being originally from the Chicago area, I had always wanted to fly in the famous Chicago Lakefront Air Show. Dan Macintyre was helping to run it this year so he shoe-horned me in. His friend, Carol Cichon, an American Airlines attendant and pilot herself, wanted to make the cross-country trip in a P-51 from Los Angeles to Chicago. It could be done in about 8 hours of flying with 2 stops for gas using just the main tanks of 180 gallons. We hoped to take off about 9 a.m., but the intercom wouldn't work. A radio man checked it out but couldn't find the problem. We decided to launch anyway. The farthest east I could safely get because of weather was Salt Lake City, so I decided on the northern route.

Coming in to Salt Lake City, I was at 17,500 feet but the cloud bank went up to about 19,000 feet in between where we were and Salt Lake City. I was on a VFR flight-following status with Salt Lake Center tracking me. Over 18,500 feet I'd be required to be on an instrument flight plan. The distance up and over the clouds was only about 50 miles—I'd cover that in 10 minutes time, so it seemed to me reasonable to ask permission to go to 19,500 feet without the need to file an IFR flight plan. The radar controller would hear nothing of that plan. Either I stay in VFR conditions below 18,500 feet, or file an IFR flight plan. All this time, I was approaching the clouds and climbing slightly. At 18,200 feet, he warned me that my altitude was approaching 18,500 feet, but since I wasn't being controlled by him on an IFR flight plan, as long as I was below 18,500 feet, he could not tell me the altitude I had to fly. I was as ticked-off at his "you must" attitude as I was at his "by-the-book" attitude. There are times when you cut a little slack. As it was, I'd have to add crowding to the air lanes by turning around to take the time to get an IFR clearance filed. The way he was acting, he might even make me call a Flight Service Station on the ground and file a clearance through them and then wait 20 minutes for the clearance to go through the computers to get to him.

I was inching higher all the time. My belly was in the top of the cloud cover. He didn't know where the clouds were. If I hadn't told him, he wouldn't even know there were clouds there at all. I could just have stayed at 17,500 feet, flown through the cloud bank on instruments and come out on the other side. He never would have known. All he knew about me from my own radar transponder's signals was where I was and my altitude was a readout on his radar screen. He had me in radar contact

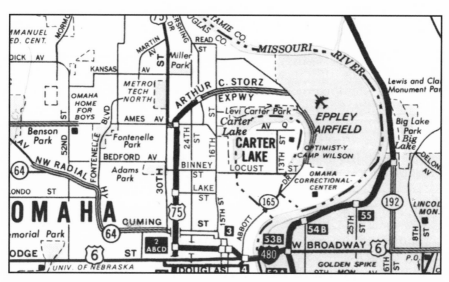

Eppley Airfield at Omaha is a no-brainer to find on a clear day. It's right at the curve of the Missouri River with nothing around it. Des Moines may have been closer, but Eppley was so easy to find, I chose it and was glad I did.

so he could alert me to any other planes in the area. Flying through the stuff was not a safety risk in any way.

Suddenly the radio crackled with "Mustang nine-one Romeo, turn your transponder back on immediately!" I checked it. It was on. I hadn't touched it. I advised that I would "ident" in which you press a button that sends a stronger signal that lights up my image on his radar screen with the assigned code. No reply.

> *Dear Reader: Let me tell you ahead of time what had happened. No sense in having you read a few more pages of this event and others and then require you to have to think, "Oh, now I see why thus and thus happened." I had to do the "thus and thus" back tracking—no sense in making you do it, too. My electric generator had failed and my battery was supplying all the power for the radios, transponder, etc., without being recharged. You who understand avionics, perhaps know why the transponder would go off with the radio still getting enough juice to operate. But that was the condition.*

By this time, I had climbed to just over 19,000 feet, was over the clouds and the Salt Lake City valley below was clear. I told Carol to keep her ears clear and went down rapidly. I called Salt Lake Tower for landing hoping against hope that Center had not called them to put me under arrest. Not a word. I had dodged another bullet. Don't misunderstand me. I have great respect for the FAA tower, approach and center controllers and the system under which they operate, but like any outfit, there's the hard-ball guy, and I got him—only one I have encountered in 60 years of flying!

We tried to find a motel in Salt Lake, but they were booked solid. Forest fires were raging in the northwest in August of 1977. At all motels we tried, the fire fighters were camped on the front and side lawns. At the Holiday Inn, I, in my flight suit and Carol in hers, were standing at the check-in counter at about 8 p.m. hoping there would be a cancellation so we could at least get a shower. Two "suits" came in for their reservations. They each had a room reserved. I asked if there was any way I could pay for both their rooms and we'd have one for just that night? Their offer was even better. "Both our rooms are already paid for on the company credit card and anybody dressed in outfits like that must need to get some sleep. You can have one of our rooms." The angels were good to me that night.

We had to get to Chicago the next day, Thursday. It was the last day of a full dress rehearsal for the air show on Saturday and Sunday. Friday was to be a ground-briefing for all events in the show. An earlier departure from Salt Lake City with both wing and main tanks filled, assured we'd get to Chicago with no need to stop for gas. So off we went. It was CAVU (Ceiling and Visibility Unlimited) all the way to Chicago. Then I noticed the VOR nav needle was a little lazy. We were at 17,500 feet, an eastbound VFR altitude with a great tailwind pushing us along. As a test, I called a ground FSS station. No answer. Well, sometimes they're busy putting out the weather sequences at :15 and :45 after the hour. I could see 100 miles ahead easily. No need to talk to anyone. Just get the hell to Chicago for the practice session on Thursday. Then I finally, duh, looked at my ammeter. It was pegged at zero. My battery was dead again like it had been out of Aspen 6 years earlier. Why in the hell don't I make the effort to look at that ampmeter? It's hard to see low, at my right hip on that panel. Until something seems wrong, I never did check it.

Then it happened! About halfway between Omaha and Des Moines, the engine started shaking and rattling like it was going to come apart. It got our attention in an instant. She had been dozing off in the smooth, clear air. What to do? No radio. An engine trying to tear itself apart. Over 3 miles above the earth. Going on is not an option. Getting down in one piece is the only option. Des Moines was closer, but I wasn't too familiar with the airport or the Des Moines area. All I knew about Des Moines was that during WWII, the WAACs (Women's Army Auxiliary Corp) trained there and it was reported they wore GI olive panties. They were seen hanging on a clothes line behind their dorms. None of us Navy types were ready for that. We never went there.

I opted to turn back to Omaha. Its airport was easy to spot at the bend of the river northeast of Omaha with its long concrete runways easily identified in the green setting of the area. I had to shut the engine down to save it for any possible use later and dove for the airport, Eppley Field. I made an attempt to call their tower, knowing there would be no answer. My only option was the get the attention of the tower and get a green light to land there amid their fairly busy airline traffic. It worked. I dove at the tower, missing it by a scant 200 feet on the airport side. I must have been doing over 400 mph when I went by and then pulled up in a sharp climbing left turn to look back over my shoulder at the tower. There it was! A "Steady Green Light" shining out of the tower window meaning I had permission to land, even though I didn't have radio contact with the tower.

I dropped the gear and flaps because I was already high over the start of the runway and swooped in for a dead-stick landing about midfield. My roll out took me just off the runway. Three fire engines were there immediately and surrounded the plane. I didn't care if I was being arrested. We were down in one piece. I tried to restart the engine and it took hold, but there was still that disturbing vibration. I was guided with a lead car to an area in back of the tower between a row of hangars. I could hear the echo of the vibration bouncing around this hangar courtyard. As I taxied toward the end, I saw a mechanic come out of a door and follow alongside before I shut it down. When I got out and helped Carol out, he said "Sounds like a fouled exhaust plug." I was amazed at such an instant opinion. Most of the time with a WWII Merlin engine you get "Gosh, what kind of an engine is that?" This old-timer had worked on the Merlin many years ago. He spotted the problem in an instant. But the way he figured out which plug it was is an old mechanic's technique, but it was new to me.

He said to wait until the engine cooled down. He took a crayon and made a mark on each exhaust stack. Told me to restart the engine, check the mags, keep it running on the bad mag awhile while he put his hand behind each exhaust stack. He did this with the precision of a surgeon going from one to the other. Then told me to cut the engine to come and look. The crayon marks were melted on all but the B-6 cylinder (farthest forward on the left side). It meant that cylinder was not firing.

And when a spark plug misses on a cylinder at the front of the engine, its effect is much greater than one at the rear. Far forward it's like the whip on the tip of a stick. One at the rear, near the cockpit is almost devoid of such vibrations. 9 years with the Mustang and I'm still learning about this beautiful but complicated type of woman.

The local TV Channel 5 News Team was around the plane asking for interviews. One of the tower control operators came up to me and introduced himself. After thanking him for their quick response, I asked what they thought when I buzzed their tower. This question and their reply was on the Channel 5 News at 6:00, 9:00, and 11:00 p.m.).

He replied, "Approach control notified us that a fast-moving object was approaching from the northeast. With the glasses, we saw this white disk coming toward us getting bigger and bigger with the sun shining on it. We had a sense that it was unusual and when you went by the tower and then pulled up, it was pretty clear you weren't hot-dogging it—that you were trying to tell us something…and with no engine sound, it was obvious it was an emergency. We alerted the airport emergency units, the TV people picked that up on their scanners and were on their way here before you even landed."

Our story aired on TV news only about 5 minutes each broadcast. I thought they could have at least made a longer story out of it. After all, how many times does a P-51 Mustang drop out of the sky onto their airport? Probably never before. Well, 3 news programs times 5 minutes equals 15 minutes of fame. That's all a person is supposed to have in a lifetime anyway.

At the time, Omni Aviation Insurance Company was my sponsor. With Mike Eisenstadt at the helm, they were hands-on sponsors—the only kind to have when you're cascading around the country and may need supplies quickly. The next morning a new generator was at the FBO and being installed when we arrived there. I had a supply of spark plugs. Any Mustang pilot is sure to have a supply in his travel kit—local FBOs don't carry them—they're not even sold by Champion, they're given to racers.

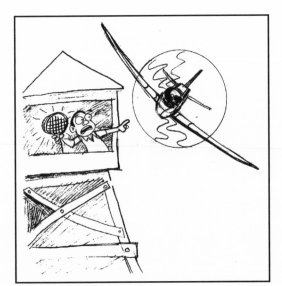

Omaha tower said that when they looked up, all they saw was a white sun-lit disk headed straight for them and getting larger by the second.

A Thrill at Chicago!

It was now Friday, the briefing day for pilots and all other Chicago Lakefront Air Show participants. Before departing Omaha, I was able to contact Dan Macintyre at show headquarters in Chicago to get instructions. He said he had taken on the responsibility to personally brief me—just to get there by 1 p.m. to do some practice runs, to land at Chicago's lakefront airport, Meigs Field. He'd meet us there, brief me, get Carol into town and watch me do my "show."

For those who know Chicago, the show line extended along the Outer Drive north from Navy Pier to short of the Oak Street Beach and the Drake Hotel. All acts were restricted to that area. It was a large enough area for the aerobatic acts but a little tight for the Blue Angels and for the show they wanted me to do. I was to circle over Belmont Harbor about 3 miles north along the shore, then exactly at 1 p.m. to open the show and appear at Air Show Center going full speed headed south. I worked on the timing. It was about a 30 second trip from Belmont Harbor to Air Show Center. At that point, what else I did to show the plane was pretty much up to me. I had 5 minutes to do it and get out of there for the next act.

The routine I settled on was a thriller for me—and, I was told, a thriller for those in the lakefront tower near Navy Pier. To keep the plane near the show center with a speed of about 400 mph to dissipate, an abrupt climb was the only solution. The residential tower was a good landmark. I climbed straight up its side with my belly

facing it. At the top, I pulled back in a half-Immelmann half-air show turn that finished over the dome at the end of Navy Pier, then leveled off about 50 feet over the water, put down gear and flaps and headed straight for the north end of the show line, turned hard left about 100 yards short of Outer Drive, headed down the show line and climbed to exit heading south to Meigs Field where Art Scholl with his Chipmunk and I were based.

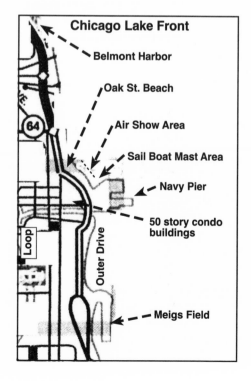

Chicago Lake Front

Belmont Harbor

Oak St. Beach

Air Show Area

Sail Boat Mast Area

Navy Pier

50 story condo buildings

Loop

Outer Drive

Meigs Field

My assignment was to hold over Belmont Harbor, be at Stage Center exactly at 1:00 p.m. going over 400 mph, then re-enter at Stage Center from the lake north of Navy Pier.

I never wanted those practice runs to end. Dan had to almost shoot me down with radio calls of "That'll do Howie! Put her in the hangar!" He knew I was having fun. In a way, I think he was a little jealous. In his years of flying as a Blue Angel, his act was so disciplined every second that there was no room for the free flying antics I could do. And he could do them a helluv-a-lot better than I could. But the next day had a surprise:

I took off from Meigs Field at 12:30 p.m. Its 3,900-foot runway is as close to a carrier-landing and takeoff that I know of anywhere in the U.S. Departing to the south, the runway ends at the water's edge. You can look back over your left shoulder to see the land disappear with just water in view. Coming in from the south—the best way to approach because you can drag it in without high obstructions—you can hang it on the prop and cut power over the "deck." In a tailwheel plane with the tail down, you can't see down the runway—just the ground whizzing by on your side. If there is too much downwind, crosswind—common at lakefront airports—and you need to land to the south with an approach over the Alder Planetarium, trees are there requiring a breathtaking drop with a "go around" mentality rather than go off the end of the runway into the water—at least it's fresh water.

Circling Belmont Harbor, I had as a passenger, Barbara Moles, my friend, Tom Moles', wife. The night before at Su Casa, Tom's twenty-something son and friends were considering my offer to ride the show with me. When none of them stepped forward, Barbara, a young 40, threw her gauntlet on the table amidst the beer mugs and declared she would. They all thought she was joking—so did I. I had explained the high-G pull-up, the tummy-floating, the nose-over to avoid speed build-up over the dome at the end of the pier. Just explaining it, I saw a few of them turn a little green—they were city-boys in suits. Sure enough, the next day, Barbara was at Meigs Field ready to go. When I dropped her off at their condo near the lake front, I saw that she was a little wobbly walking toward the lobby. At the door she gave a half-hearted wave good-bye. That night she said, while she'd never do it again, it was a most memorable part of her life.

What was the most memorable part of my life on that flight was the surprise I got after pulling out of the half-loop over the dome at Navy Pier and leveling off at about 50 feet over the water for the leg back toward the Outer Drive. During the trials the day before, the water was clear of boats. Suddenly, I was headed for a field of tall sailboat masts between where I was and where I was headed. Before I could climb over the first batch of ships that traditionally come there to watch the show (no one told me about them), I had to weave back and forth through the tallest ones. Barbara said this whip-sawing back and forth is what really did her in. It almost did me in, too!

Chapter 16

The Last Four Years of Racing
Would You, the Reader, Want Them?

I f you can spend age 56 to 60 racing a P-51 Mustang, you've got it made. If you can spend those years racing a P-51 Mustang and still have a few bucks left over to retire, you've really got it made. But the problem is that you never know ahead of time, it's only a "look back" over those years. Take a look with me at my last 7 races with "Miss America." Would you like to have them?

Reno National Championship Air Races • 1977

Qualified in eighth position at 371 mph. Races had again been formatted into moving up via heat races. Decided to save engine and not push hard in quals because easier to be in slower speed heats and move up that way. In fast plane heats, you took a time penalty when a fast plane crossed the start line far ahead of you and your time started then. A crazy system, but you had to play their game.

I moved up easily from the slow planes to the mid-range speed heat. Now the goal was to post a high enough speed to get into the finals. In the race, a keeper ring broke on exhaust valve in B3 cylinder (left bank third cylinder). The result was the most dramatic I had ever had racing. The valve dropped into the cylinder and set up a howl and vibration beyond description. In addition, with no exhaust valve, the flames shot out the left side like the engine had turned into a blowtorch. No chance to think. Shut the engine down by pulling back on the mixture control to starve it of fuel and stop the threatening tongue of flame. Had about 400 mph of airspeed as a cushion to pull up high and dead-stick it in easily.

Bob Hoover had a new set of heads and banks at Dave Zeuschel's engine shop in the Los Angeles area. Ted Thomas and Mike Eisenstadt arranged to buy them from Bob and had them flown up to Reno that evening. Jim Quinlan and his crew, aided

*This ticket is a coveted souvenir by any youngster lucky
enough to go to the National Air Races at Reno, Nevada.*

by engine expert Mike Nixon, fixed the engine with a new piston and valves. On a
test flight the next day, the engine quit on takeoff. Fortunately I was using Stead's
long 8,000-foot Runway 32 that had a long over-run at the end. I used it all. An
intake valve was out of adjustment. The result was that the back-fire an open intake
valve caused blew out the carburetor. End of takeoff. End of race.

35th Class Reunion at Hamilton College

Clinton, New York • October, 14, 1977

When I was in college, anyone who came back for a class reunion past their 25th
seemed part of ancient history. To go back for my 35th with a P-51 Mustang parked
at the nearby Utica, New York airport was my attempt to dispel this old-geezer notion. If it didn't in the fraternity house, it certainly did at the half-time ceremonies

of the on-campus Homecoming football
game with Bowdoin. I swooped down
over the field and pulled up doing a slow
roll before leaving. The announcer notified the crowd with "That's a fellow returning for his 35th reunion." There, I
showed 'em geezer stuff.

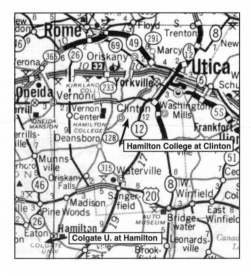

*Colgate was at Hamilton, New York, but
Hamilton was at Clinton.
Both had the beauty of fall foliage.*

Golf gloves on both hands were the best to grab the stick during a race (both hands were needed in the turbulent air) and deal with the heat and hand moisture without becoming slippery.

It was a joy to have a multi-crew all based with the Air National Guard at Van Nuys. (L to R) Jim Quinlan, Crew Chief. Ben Roberts, Don Reese, Brian Schooley, and Harry Quinlan.

In the Clouds With Smoke
Richmond, Virginia • October 18, 1977

On the way to the AOPA Convention in Miami from my class reunion near Utica, New York, Christa and I stopped at Richmond, Virginia for fuel. It was solid overcast from 800 feet on up to 15,000 feet. On taking off, we entered the clouds at just about the 800-foot point for a climb to our assigned altitude of 16,000 feet. That would be a thousand feet over the tops of the clouds in clear and warmer air. At 2,500 feet, I smelled smoke, even with the oxygen mask on. I should say that at that low altitude, the oxygen regulator was mixing mostly cockpit air with just a little oxygen, so thankfully I had been able to smell the smoke. I immediately asked for an emergency clearance back to Richmond's airport requesting steers from Richmond Approach control. They put me on a heading and altitude step down right on the approach to their long Runway 34. On the ground, I shut down the engine; again the fire trucks escorted me down a runway. My starter had stuck in the "ON" position. The smoke I smelled was it trying to burn itself up by overheating. I was able to get a rebuilt one locally. Quite a surprise.

Los Angeles to Reading Air Show • June 1978

In those days, the Reading (Pennsylvania) Air Show was the premier corporate aviation event in the U.S. It was the opposite of the Bi-Annual Paris Air Show held in odd-numbered years. I wanted to make this one because there would not be another until 1980. All the major aviation manufacturers and avionics had pavilion tents, showed their latest models and put on demonstrations. Even the Blue Angels were there along with other major acts such as Bob Hoover and Art Scholl. I was scheduled for a cameo appearance in the show, but mainly I wanted to test sales for my new IFR approach plate service, Pro-Plates, at our booth in the giant exhibit tent.

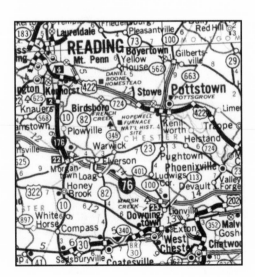

On the way there with June Allan (now Mikrut) who could get a visit from her parents in nearby New Jersey, I had to go over a 17,000-foot-high cold front between Nashville and Reading. I had only one working radio that had to be in either Communication Mode or in Navigation Mode. Back 15 years ago in 1963, that wasn't considered a go/no-go condition for IFR, but in this modern age it was considered an "emergency only" state. I couldn't file IFR to go through the front. The Reading area on the other side was all clear in the cold front's aftermath. The intercom wasn't working. June still has the notes I passed back to her. She'd tap me on the shoulder with questions written on a piece of paper like, "What are we doing so high?" "Why is the windshield covered with ice? I can't see out, can you?" With the clipped wings and short ailerons at that altitude barely effective, I scribbled answers, but not long ones.

Dayton Air Show • July 1978

At this point, my air show appearances were hooked in with booths to sell my IFR approach plate service which was showing promising acceptance in its unorthodox format. Up to this time, approach plate services like Jeppessen and the government's NOS plates, required you to keep them updated by opening a weekly packet and replace the new with the old in a ring binder.

Being gone from my mailing address for weeks at a time, I couldn't keep them updated—and it was tiresome to keep doing it for the full U.S. It was estimated that it took 200 hours a year just to keep the U.S. updated. While I was in the Navy Air Reserves, we had the MANS system (Military Aviation NOTAM Service). It gave us a set of plates and then, instead of getting new charts at mid-cycle, we'd get a listing of the changes to pencil in what we needed. My idea was to do this change notification for a year and then toss away the charts and start over. It worked quite well, especially among those pilots who had used it in the military. The pilot using the Jeppesen "replace-the-pages" system wasn't ready for it until they had been flying for at least 5 years and began to understand the way the changes occurred and how minor most were.

The Dayton Air Show was half-flying and half-selling, but the event I recall today with humor and satisfaction is my encounter with a Blue Angel named Jack Ekl, now a Southwest Airlines Captain and air show pilot of the Budweiser small BD Jet. His daughter is also an excellent air show aerobatic pilot. I had met Jack as a 19-year old who loved to be around airports. I had a standard line to all boys of that age who said they'd love to be able to have a P-51 Mustang. My instructions always were, "Son, join the Navy Air Corps, stay away from the admiral's daughters and when you retire, they give you one of these things." Being delivered while in my white flying suit with Navy wings on it, some would cock their heads, look at me quizzically and utter, "Really?" I knew they'd become Navy pilots.

Jack Ekl walked up to me in his Blue Angel flight suit, saluted and said "Commander, you probably don't remember me, but a few years back I met you at an airport when I was still in school and told you I'd love to have a P-51. Well, I'm retiring in a few more years and I haven't even looked at an admiral's daughter!" I knew immediately that we had met when he uttered that statement. He was probably one of the ones who replied "Really?"

The real Paul Harvey "And now for the rest-of-the-story…" is that Jack called me when "Miss America" was up for sale by the Santa Monica Museum of Flying. A friend of his, Dr. Brent Hisey, was interested in buying her and wanted my input on

To HOWIE —
THANKS FOR THE ADVICE,
13 YEARS AGO, THAT GOT
ME HERE. THE BEST ALWAYS
TO YOU & MISS AMERICA !!

Jack Ekl
BLUE Angel
#5
1981

My reply to young men who said they would love to have a P-51 was "Join the Navy Air Corps, stay away from the Admiral's daughter, and when you retire, they'll give you a P-51." I said this to Jack Ekl when he was 19 and now he was a Blue Angel!

the plane's value. Hisey bought "Miss America" and I am sure that Retired Navy pilot, Jack Ekl, has "his" P-51 Mustang. I don't want to know if he has ever flown it. I don't want to know. I want to think he does so my little story can end on a "that's-the-rest-of-the-story" note.

Oshkosh Air Show • August 1978

This is an air show every air show pilot likes to be accepted to fly in. No pay, just gas, but the prestige to perform in front of not only a top-notch air show staff of pilots themselves, but also the gigantic number of pilots in attendance who appreciate good flying, was a rare once-a-year opportunity. There was no way I wanted to do an aerobatic routine with the likes of Bob Hoover there. My act was to have the announcer describe "Miss America" what I was doing and me do my demo of air racing and the turns, etc. I was the only one with that theme. It was something I could handle and an audience that would appreciate it. My logbook shows that during the show I had passengers ride along with me like Sam Huntington, Chief Pilot for United Airlines and even Percy Wood, the head of United. Then rides to Sharon Jobst, wife of Vern

If you have a chance to fly the Oshkosh Air Show grab it! You'll be among the top pilots of that era and this is the type of seasoned Air Show directors you'll have. (L–R) Oshkosh 1981: Sam Huntington, Chief Pilot, UAL; Vern Jobst, Capt. UAL, Air Boss; Deke Holman, Capt. UAL; me; Starr Thompson, Capt. Flying Tigers; Jim Brady, 2001 Air Boss. (kneeling) Mark Erickson, Pre-Show Fly-Over Chief, and Bernie Faust.

Jobst, Air Boss and UAL Capt.; Deke Holman UAL Capt.; and Charlie Shuck, FAA. Starr Thompson, a Retired Flying Tiger Captain still on the Oshkosh Air Show Staff today, has been a friend for 23 years since meeting him at Oshkosh. But Starr wouldn't ride with me!

Disaster at Salt Lake City • August 13, 1978

I can still see it today. A wall of paper cups, coke cans, leaves and brown grass coming across the airport at Salt Lake City. I had stopped off for an oxygen refill on my way to the Abbotsford Air Show near Vancouver, Canada. While the line boy was filling the oxygen at the oxygen valve at the left rear of the plane, I was monitoring him so he wouldn't fill it too fast. If they turn up the pressure, the valve heats up and makes it look like your 2,000 pound tank is full when it has only 1,600 pounds in it when it cools. I wanted a full fill—not only because you pay for a "fill," no matter how much, but it had to last to get to Abbotsford and then back to Los Angeles.

I was on the General Aviation (east) side of the airport at the south end of one of their two long north/south runways. The plane was headed south. He was squatting down metering the oxygen flow. The plane blocked his view toward the other side of the airport. The runways are about 200 yards apart. I was standing up with my arm resting on the fuselage. Suddenly out of the corner of my eye I saw this wall of debris coming across the field. I exclaimed, "What the hell is this coming?" He jumped up, took one look and sped off with "Gotta tie 'em down." He headed for a group of corporate twins in front of the FBO.

The wall of swirling debris kept coming, kept coming. It was coming right for me and "Miss America." The oxygen hose was still hooked up and filling. I leaned over and shut off the valve at the tank then laid on the left part of the tail with all my weight. The wall hit, the tail and I were lifted about 6 feet into the air and blown sideways toward the oxygen cart. My left elevator came crashing down on the oxygen cart and I was thrown backwards over it and landed on my coccyx tailbone. I couldn't move. I thought I had been paralyzed. I just lay there looking painfully at the oxygen valve stick up through the bent left elevator.

I never found out what they call that phenomenon at Salt Lake. It wasn't a twister, it wasn't just a strong wind, it was like a wind–wave. It was powerful! The P-51 tail section weighs 600 pounds and my 200 pounds made its total weight 800 pounds. I spent the night in a hospital in Salt Lake City where they assured me I was just bruised, but poor "Miss America" was more than cosmetically damaged, she was "spoiled goods." Clay Lacy let them take the left elevator off his purple P-51 and have it flown up to me. I'd miss the Abbotsford Air Show, but at least I could fly home even while hobbling around. "Miss America" with a purple left elevator looked like she was trying to "accessorize" herself, as the fair sex calls it.

While getting an oxygen fill, I asked the line crew what the wall of debris was coming at us. He ran to tether some planes, I flopped my 200 pounds down on the plane's tail. The wind force lifted me backward through the air and deposited the tail on the oxygen bottles, ripping through the port elevator. Thankfully, the tail weighs 600 pounds which kept it from being upended.

Reno National Air Races • September 1978

Qualified seventh fastest at 383 mph and took a fourth in the Gold Cup Race finals on Sunday. Am now thoroughly convinced that the only way to race is to not exceed 95 inches of manifold pressure. Let the other guys with deeper pockets risk the blow-ups for the glory. For me air racing is racing, outwitting those on the course, not blowing up engines in the hopes you'll finish first. I want to finish, period. During the races John Crocker in Somethun' Else and Clay Klabo in Iron Mistress, blew their engines. That's two places I'd move up. Then Cliff Cummings in "Miss Candace" engine detonated and he blew up.

In the finals, Crocker with his engine repaired cut the deadline again this year and was disqualified. He must not be able to see very well out of that tiny bubble he has for a go-fast canopy. In an airplane, 50 feet off the deck at over 400 mph, I sure want to see where I'm going because you get there pretty fast. His cut made me move up another notch in the finals. The results were #1– Red Baron (Steve Hinton), #2–Precious Metal (Don Whittington), #3–Cruittendon (John Putnam), #4–Miss America (Howie Keefe), #5– GeGeII (Scott Smith), #6–Baby Gorilla (Lloyd Hamilton).

Iron Mistress (pictured), *Clay Klabo—Miss Candace, Doc Cummings—Somethin' Else, John Crocker blew. This time, three of my veteran race buddies blew their engines in the Unlimited Finals. You don't like to win that way, but I'd "been there, done that."*

California National Air Races
Mojave • October 1978

In October, the strong winds at Mojave start to calm down, but no ladies in Mojave wear flowing skirts at any time of the year because they can't see where they're going with a skirt up over their heads. Mojave is wind, and wind is Mojave. The great thing about the Mojave Air Races, just 100 miles north of Los Angeles, was that I could invite my friends up for a day of air racing without having to deal with the Reno problems of trying to find a place to stay and transportation. They could drive up and back in the same day on wide open highways.

In this race, as at Reno a month earlier, I vowed to never exceed 95 inches of manifold pressure, which was still 30% higher than WWII fighter pilots were allowed to push the Mustang, but seemed to be a safe power limit with today's TLCed engines. Without exceeding the 95 inches, I was able to get third place in the finals, first place in the crowd-exciting drag races and still be able to fly home without any problems.

Miami Air Races • Homestead, Florida • February 1979
"Oh No! Not Again!"

Even if you're from California, it's nice to feel the warm, moist air of Florida in February. I had a coolant leak in the right bank, so I stopped at Pensacola enroute to Miami. They gave it a treatment of epoxy and I took off. At 20,000 feet over the Tampa–St. Petersburg area, the tell-tale drips started to form on the windshield. I opted to land at St. Pete. Tampa was strictly airline stuff. They put a screw in the hole with heat-resistant glue on it in the hole. It held, so on we went to Homestead, Florida, site of the air races.

After racing at Reno and Mojave with the mountains and up-and-down terrain on the race course, it was great to be in flat Florida, come off a pylon and the next one was dead ahead, not obscured by a rise in the ground. The problem here was the new Champion "platinum" plugs. We had never raced them before. To my crew chief, Bill Pitts, they were new stuff. I didn't want to experiment with them, but he put them in anyway. In the race before the finals, I came in second. After each race, I had made it a priority of running up the engine and checking both mags before shutting the engine down, just to

make sure all plugs were doing well. I had not done it after this race. The airport at Homestead had just one runway and one taxi-way back to the pit area. To run your engine up, you might blast another plane in the tight confines of pit and taxi areas.

The next day for the finals, I fired up, pulled off to the side to check the mags and got quite a surprise. The left mag was not only low, it started snorting, almost backfiring. A backfire in an engine with a carburetor is not what you want, it can destroy the carburetor and you've lost your fuel supply. I shut it down. The new Champion plugs were junk! They were platinum with very thin wires. It was later discovered that the spark wires had weld cracks on the inside where they could not be seen. I no longer wanted to be a test bed for new gasoline, sparks plugs, oil or any other new products. Just let me race in peace!

California Air Races • Mojave • May 1979
"The Crack in the Dike"

Charlie Beck

Both "Miss America" and I were hurting in this race. My problem was that the FAA would not let me in the actual races because I had not been examined for a Second Class Physical since the operation to repair a lung that had collapsed due to a bleb—spontaneous pneumothorax, the meds call it. I could fly, but for Unlimited racing they require a valid Commercial license. I enlisted the aid of Charlie Beck, who had owned and raced a P-51 named "Candy Man"—a delight to all the kids, even to us when his pretty wife, Pat, came around giving us candy canes. Charlie had flown the "Jug" (P-47 "Thunderbolt") in WWII and was a long-time member of Dick Sykes' disciplined "Condor Squadron" of AT-6 Search and Rescue units of the Civil Air Patrol.

Poor Charlie Beck. He had 7 race starts and 6 Maydays! I'm sure he set some sort of a record for the number of Maydays in one race event. Each time Charlie got halfway down "Thunder Alley"—the point from which the start plane releases the formation to the first pylon—his windshield was saturated with coolant. The spray of near boiling water and glycol was relentless until he pulled back on the power. Each time he came in, Jim Quinlan and his crew would give it a check over for loose hoses, fittings and what not. All they saw was heavy liquid residue on the left side of the engine. After Charlie's sixth start and the fact that the flow stopped at standard power settings, the verdict was that it was the main gasket between the engine banks and block that was letting loose under high power.

Unfortunately for my pocket book, it wasn't the gasket. It was a fissure in the cylinder bank that was opening up under high pressure. The banks had been eaten away from the inside out by the coolant. The best glycol (Prestone, etc.) distilled water mix for the Merlin engine is 50/50. The glycol is used because it dissipates the heat better than water and has a higher boiling point than water. If you use either too much glycol (over 70%) or too little (under 30%), it raises hell with the insides of a Merlin's sandcast structure. It's like firing a stream of acid under high pressure against the raw side of an iron casting. There's no repair if they are used for racing. The banks are junk. So back to the piggy bank for a new set of banks plus the cost of installation—about a $20,000 overhaul at the time. So you think getting your Mercedes repaired is expensive? Wait until you taxi your P-51 into the local service bay. When they see you coming, they know there'll be a Christmas bonus this year!

Reno National Air Races • September 1979
"Comfortable at 95 inches"

There was no way I was going to try to best the souped-up planes that were entering the race circuit these days. The strategy had now turned to "wait-'em-out"—in other

words, move up in position by letting the others try to get the maximum out of an engine. I'd been there, done that. Of course, what was happening is that some lucky race pilots were flying someone else's plane. If it breaks, it's someone else's problem. I would have loved to be able to go balls-out under those circumstances. There was hardly any personal risk in pushing the engine to the max.

The race course and the airport area at a race site is probably one of the most sterile and sanitary places you can fly a plane at any power—and certainly at high power. You have the entire airport at your disposal if you have a Mayday and a blown engine. Plus, you have a factor of high speed (over 400 mph) that allows you to pull up to about

a mile (5,000 feet plus) before you slow down to best glide speed (about 175 mph in the Mustang). Then you have a chance to catch your breath, look over the situation and decide if you're going to dead-stick it in or bail out. I've never seen anyone bail out, but it's an option. I

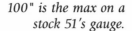

Although greatly enlarged, this photo of my MP gauge's scale to 150" can be seen.

100" is the max on a stock 51's gauge.

heard a pilot didn't survive a low-level bail-out from a Corsair on fire at a race near Phoenix in the 1990s.

On the ground, fire trucks and ambulances are standing by, ready to pounce once you've come to a stop, hopefully in one piece. Now if you're talking structural failure, that's an entirely different world. If a wing or tail section comes off, there are no soft bumpers or tires to hit. You've pretty much flown your last race. But only the most exotic hybrids of trying to mix and match wings, engines and basic structures are prone to breaking apart. Those steeds you might want to pass up.

In the qualifying, we had 24 slots available. I promised myself I wouldn't go over 95" MP, no matter what. I'd sit in the stands and watch if it took more than that. As it turned out, I used only 87" MP and qualified in the eighth position at a fairly fast 388 mph. Now life was getting more predictable. I liked it this way. I even discovered that an exhaust plug had fouled during qualifying. It was in the A6 position, at the rear of the engine where you don't feel too much. At the front of that long engine, the shaking of a fouled plug gets your attention pretty fast.

After qualifying and flying the Thursday heat race, it was time for me to repay Charlie Beck for his patience and disappointment 3 months earlier at the California Nationals when he had to abort racing during 6 starting attempts. I offered and he eagerly accepted the offer to fly "Miss America" in the Friday quarter-finals and the Saturday semi-finals. It was a pleasure to watch such a fine "stick" as Charlie take her around the pylons. As a matter of fact, watching "Miss America" from the pits was somehow better than flying her in the race. No concerns, no heat, no dry mouth.

Now 85" MP was my max. With it, I was able to take second place in the Silver Race Finals on Sunday and bank a check for $7,000 which were my highest winnings ever. The purses had started to rise, but even first place didn't pay the expenses. But the luxury of confidence in being able to go out to the field on Monday morning to fly it 700 miles over rugged terrain back to Van Nuys was a wonderful feeling. I couldn't recall having it feel so nice in a long time.

Reno National Air Races • September 1980

"The Final Act"

I read about a pitcher in the major leagues who had reached his goal of pitching in 4 decades. In the summer of 1980, he had accomplished his feat. He threw just a few

pitches to be on record as playing. Wish I could recall his name. After reading that, the idea occurred to me that this might be a good way and excuse to get in one more race. If I raced in 1980, I would have raced in the 1960s, '70s and '80s. Yes, I know the purists claimed that the new century did not start until 2001, that 2000 was the last year of the 1900s. Well, as far as I was concerned, 1980 was part of the '80s and the start of the '80s decade. It worked for me, especially since I promised my kids (all over 21) that I'd quit when I was 60, the age at which an airline pilot has to retire. They were wondering if I would ever grow up. So was I. I had to make a stab at it. The following April, I would turn 60.

There were no races between the '80 Nationals and April '81. Even though I felt great, could still pass an FAA Commercial pilot's physical, air racing was in that gray area between private flying and being a test pilot—and after seeing old test pilots try to hang on to their jobs at Northrup, North American and other majors only to kill themselves at air show exhibitions and on test flights to seemingly satisfy their egos, my mission was completed. It was to develop "Miss America" as a symbol with which youth could identify, as I did in my youth with Gar Woods' racing boat, "Miss America." This had to be my Final Act.

I qualified at 352 mph to just get in under the wire for the Silver Race at position #14. That's all I wanted. Just to be in the second fastest group, exactly where I was

Even today, 21 years later, when I go through the air race gates, I still get butterflies in my stomach. Just hearing the planes warm up and whine at high power on the race course makes me think that engine-shattering sound might come at any time.

In a hurry to button-up, a primer line on a cylinder was left open. The starter noticed flames coming from the cowling (I couldn't see them) and signaled me to shut down. After removing the small panel that allowed oxygen to enter, the explosion blasted him far back on the tarmac while still holding the panel. Luckily, he was okay, as was Miss A. (Cartoon by Wendell Dowling)

It sure felt good in "Miss America's" cockpit, but the time had come to give up my toys.

when I started Unlimited air racing 12 years earlier. With that accomplished, I again asked Charlie Beck to do the good job he had done last year in flying the heat races, and he did well again at the lower power settings. But when I took over for the Finals, true to the form of my first race of torching a valve, this, my last race, convinced me that there will always be some little gremlin lurking in the shadows of the pylons, just waiting to hitch a ride as I whizzed by. After all, they were having glitches trying to put man into space with minor problems like switches not working. Why should a guy trying to boost a Merlin over WWII War Emergency Power of 65" (73" wet) at 80" to 90", escape the gremlins?

This was to be my final race and it was going great. The engine sounded strong. After rolling out of every pylon turn, the prop seemed to dig in and pull the plane forward to get back up to full race speed. It was almost like the plane was alive and going to give me a great, last ride. Then at one of the pylons, a gremlin leapt on board and turned on the red generator warning light. I had never seen it before. If you recall my past problems of not noticing the amp gauge, I was determined to never let that happen again, so I had a warning light installed to indicate the generator had gone off-line. And it picks my last race to turn in its warning!

It happened on the fifth lap of an 8-lap race. I did another lap wondering what to do. In that 90 seconds, I tried reasoning with myself. "In 3 minutes the race will be over. Surely the battery will last 3 minutes to keep the ADI water-injection pump

My daughter, Dorrie, and Christa were able "Pit Moms," an asset to any crew.

UNITED STATES OF AMERICA
Department of Transportation
Federal Aviation Administration

MEDICAL CERTIFICATE SECOND **CLASS**

This certifies that *(Full name and address):*

HOWARD MANSFIELD KEEFE
6357 IRENA AVE
CAMARILLO CA 93012

Date of Birth	Height	Weight	Hair	Eyes	Sex
4-24-21	70	201	GRAY	HZL	M

has met the medical standards prescribed in part 67, Federal Aviation Regulations, for this class of Medical Certificate.

NOT VALID FOR ANY CLASS AFTER MAY 31, 2001.
MUST WEAR CORRECTIVE LENSES.
SECOND–CLASS LIMITED TO AIR RACING AND EXHIBITION; FULL THIRD–CLASS PRIVILEGES.

Date of Examination	Examiner's Designation No.
5-5-2000	09865-1

Signature

Typed Name
W.S. SILBERMAN, D.O. 00029-8

AIRMAN'S SIGNATURE

FAA Form 8500-9 (3-99) Supersedes Previous Edition   NSN: 0052-00-670-7002

*You **can** get a Medical after a heart attack. This is mine at age 80!*

The checkered flag is the end of the race and this was the last one I'd see on the race course.

going—but…but what if it didn't? I could monitor the pressure gauge and pull back on the power the second I saw it drop—but…but what if I didn't catch it? At those power settings of 85" the engine could sneeze, detonate and that would be it for yet another engine. No, I didn't want it to end that way." I was in second place. I pulled back on the power to 60" MP. The plane seemed to ache at the fact that I was giving up. Seeing 4 planes pass in the last two laps before crossing the finish line in sixth place was a little tough at the time.

But did I bother with the what ifs? Yes, I did. What if I had not had that warning light installed? I never would have known the generator strap broke from vibration of high-power settings. I would have finished the race at high-power in at least second place. But would it have made any difference in the big picture? No. Would a blown engine have made a difference? Yes, about $40,000 worth! I got over it fast.

Thanks for sharing my experiences with me. It was fun having you along.

THE END

Epilogue

I finally decided to sell "Miss America." It had taken me a year after my last race to accept the fact that someone else would have to continue her racing legacy. I took "Miss America" to the 1981 National Air Races at Reno to hopefully find someone who would keep racing her and keep her as "Miss America." Often a new owner wants to change the plane into his own image. I got both of my wishes in the new owners, Ron and Jeannette Smyth of Edmonds, Washington.

Ron lost his sight a few years before in an accident when a caustic soda valve aboard a merchant ship broke and scalded him. Before that, he had been a pilot and had attended the races at Reno. He loved them so much, he was still attending the air races to hear the sounds of the high-powered planes.

As I tell the story, after Sandy Sanders, the race announcer, mentioned over the loud speaker that "Miss America" was for sale for $195,000, Ron said he turned to his wife, Jeannette, and exclaimed "The announcer said the plane is for sale. He now should say was for sale. Let's buy it. I traded my sight for money and I've always wanted a P-51 Mustang. To have 'Miss America' is like icing on the cake. I used to sit in her each year. Howie let people do that. I think I remember where all the instruments and switches are."

Ron dispatched his friend, Howard Raefield, a Flying Tiger Captain, to find me. Howard mentioned Ron's desire and his condition. But I wasn't prepared for the duo that came up to me. In my youth, there was a pair of romantic movie stars by the name of Nelson Eddy and Jeannette McDonald. He played a handsome Royal Canadian Mountie and she the beautiful leading lady. And here they were standing before me! Ron was tall and muscular and Jeannette even had that leading lady's name and was just as beautiful—in her heart she was gorgeous—she didn't try to talk Ron out of it, but she did wonder what the future would hold for them.

Ron asked me if I'd continue racing it for him and understood when I explained that I had given up racing, but I would do air shows for him. It did my heart good to see him standing beside the plane at an air show with his red and white guide cane, hear a youngster say, "Oh, there's 'Miss America'" and Ron call out, "Would you like to sit in her cockpit, young man? A crew member will help you up." A big smile would come across Ron's face as he heard the youngster's excited comments.

Then, to top it off, Ron had 8x10 photos he'd sign and hand to the very pleased youngster.

Ron and I flew air shows in Canada and in the U.S. Having been a pilot himself, he handled the radio communications with the tower and ground control. "Miss America" became a true family show with his two handsome sons, Harold and Eric and mirror-like mother-daughter beauties, Jeannette and Victoria, around the plane at shows and races. AT-6 race pilot and United Captain, Bud Granley, did a magnificent job of racing her for them.

I had paid $25,000 for "Miss America" in 1969. When I sold it 12 years later in 1981 for $195,000, my accountant said I just about broke even with all the blown engines and expenses. I think Ron and Jeannette did a little better eight years later at $500,000 to Garson Fields and Giff Foley's Hanover Aviation of 3 Dartmouth grads. Then Dave Price's Santa Monica Museum of Flying took her over, kept up her racing record, made it into a rare dual control P-51 to teach others to fly it. Dr. Brent Hisey of Oklahoma City then acquired her and still today, she's thrilling kids of all ages at air shows and air races. It's nice to know "Miss A" is still "out there."

The History of the Plane that became "Miss America"

The name "Miss America" is fitting with all the bases she had! Perhaps you flew her in her earlier years.

Pre-1945 history was lost when remanufactured by North American at Los Angeles in early 1945. Placard indicated remanufacture April 1944.

Serial Number 44-74536 P-51D
June 1945—372nd Fighter Group • Esler Field, LA • Continental Air Forces
September 1945—372nd Fighter Group • Alexandria Field, LA • Continental Air Forces
November 1945—4160th Base Unit, Hobbs, NM
June 1947—4121st Base Unit, Kelly Field, TX
September 1947—126th Fighter Squadron, SE • Mitchell Field, Milwaukee, WI
January 1951—128th Fighter Wing • Air National Guard • Milwaukee, WI
March 1951—169th Fighter Squadron SE • Air National Guard • Peoria, IL
August 1951—133rd Fighter Wing • Air Defense Command • St. Paul, MN
March 1952—109th Fighter Interceptor Squadron • (ADC) • St. Paul, MN
December 1952—18th Fighter Interceptor Squadron • (ADC) • Minneapolis, MN
August 1953—2465th Air Force Reserve Combat Center • (ADC) • Minneapolis, MN
November 1953—117th Fighter–Bomber Squadron • Air National Guard • Philadelphia, PA
October 1954—112th Fighter–Bomber Squadron • Air National Guard • Akron, OH
August 1955—112th Fighter–Interceptor Squadron • Air National Guard • Akron, OH
August 1956—Sacramento Air Material Command • McClellan AFB, CA
February 1958—Dropped from USAF inventory by sale.

Post-Military Owners

January 1958—Alvin Parker, Odessa, TX • FAA Registered #N5452V
December 1960—Donald Singleton, Santa Monica, CA
January 1961—DONCA Films, Los Angeles, CA
March 1965—David G. Allender, Jr. • Race #19 at Lancaster, California.
   Raced under the name "Allender Mustang."
August 1967—Robert Cleaves, raced (?) as "Wayfayer's Club Lady"
May 1969—Howie Keefe, named and raced as "Miss America"
June 1982—Ron and Jeannette Smyth, Edmonds, WA
May 1989—Hanover Aero—(Foley, Fields, Moss) Nashua, NH
Circa 1992—Santa Monica Museum of Flying (made dual controlled)
Circa 1996—Brent Hisey, Oklahoma City, OK

Jeannette and Ron Smyth, Owners

Dave Price, Pilot

Brent Hisey,
Race Pilot, Owner

Robert Heale, Pilot

Bud Granley, Pilot

Ralph Twombly, Pilot

Joann Osterud,
Air Show Pilot

Chuck Hall, Pilot

Charlie Beck, Pilot

Alan Preston,
Pilot

Bruce Lockwood,
Pilot

Owners L–R:
Giff Foley, Mike Moss, Garson Fields

"Miss America's" Race Records 1969–1981

Note: "Miss America's" speeds are followed by the winner's in parenthesis (xxx)

Harold's Club Transcontinental Trophy Dash • Sept. 1969 Sixth Place 6:30, 275 mph (313)

National Air Races • Sept. 1969 • Reno Qual. 10th, 340 mph (415) Heat 1: 333 mph (352). Silver: Second, 336 (344). Bronze: Fourth, 315 (319)

Harold's Club Trancontinental Trophy Dash • Sept. 1970 • Milwaukee–Reno Fourth 6:33, 255 (284)

National Air Races • Sept. 1970 • Reno • Qual. 3rd: 377 (380). Heat 1: Third, 357 (369). Gold: Fourth, 372 (387)

California 1,000 (1,000 Mile Pylon Race) • Nov. 1970 Mojave, CA. Qual. #11: 291 (348). Final: 7th, 59 laps (66 laps nonstop 2:52)

P-51 Tournament • May 1971 • Alton, IL Cross-Country Race • Milwaukee to Alton • 309 miles 5th place 56 minutes (52), 30 second climb; #3: 1,050' (1,373'). Speed over a mile, #3, 397 (419)

Cape May, New Jersey Air Races • June 1971 Qual. #2: 349 (362), Heat 2A: #2 338 (340). Heat 2B: #3 330(332). Finals #5-322 (360)

U.S. Cup Race • July 1971 • San Diego, CA 1,000 mile pylon race • 8th Place: 72 of 100 laps (100/100 went nonstop)

National Air Races • Sept. 1971 Reno Qual. #3: 413 (420). Heat 1: #1 399 mph. Gold: #6 (blew engine)

California 1,000 • Nov. 1971 • Mojave, CA 1,000 km (622 miles) pylon race 2nd Place: 328, 1:48 (342). Flaps came down.

National Championship Races • Sept. 1972 Qual. #5: 386 (411). Heat 1 #3: 388 (403). Gold #3: 399 (416 new record)

Miami Air Race • Jan. 1973 • Tamiami, FL Qual. #3 at 375 (384). Heat 1: Blew engine's prop gears

National Air Races • Sept. 1973 • Reno Qual. #8 382 (427-record). Heat 2 #3: 385 (411). Gold #5: 359 (428 new record)

California National Air Races • Oct. 1973 • Mojave, CA Qual. 6th 351 (391). Drag Race 1 lap, #2 243 (247). Heat Race #4: 366 (377). Silver #3 293 (332). Finals #3: 364 (397)

National Air Races • Sept. 1974 • Reno Qual. #4: 407 (432 new record). Heat #4: 346 (cut pylon). Silver #1: 385 mph

California National Air Races • Oct. 1974 • Mojave, CA Qual. #2: 396 (414). Heat Race #5: 294 (315). Finals #3: 370 (382)

California National Air Races • June 1975 • Mojave, CA Qual #11: 355 (418). Silver Race #5: 343 (374)

National Air Races • Sept. 1975 • Reno Qual. #12 at 370 (435 new record). Silver Race #6: 342 (387)

California National Air Races • June 1976 • Mojave, CA Qual. #11: 246 (416). Drag Race 1 lap #6: 190 (232). Silver Race #6 (Cut Pylon)

National Air Races • Sept. 1976 • Reno Qual #7: 353 (439 new record). Gold Race: 316, blew exhaust stack (380)

National Air Races • Sept. 1977 • Reno Qual. #8: 371 (402). Silver Race: Blew engine, dead stick in)

National Air Races • Sept. 1978 • Reno Qual. #7: 383 (427).
Heat Race #4: 369 (407). Gold Race #4: 375 (415)
California National Air Races • Oct. 1978 • Mojave, CA Qual. #5: 348 (408).
Speed Sprint 1 #4: 328 (353). Drag Race #3: 256 (348). Silver #5: 332 (361).
Sprint 2 #4: 335(362). Gold Final #3: 340 (371)
International Air Races • Feb. 1979 • Homestead, FL (Engine detonating—bad
plugs) Qual. 15th at only 70″MP 306 (395) Silver Race: did not start—plug wires
broke on new experimental Champion platinums
California National Air Races • June 1979 • Mojave, CA (recuperating from lung
operation—Charlie Beck flew race) Qual. 360 (405). Sprint Races 6th: 343
(392). Bal of Races: DNF (fissures opening in block at high power)
National Air Races • Sept. 1979 • Reno Qual. #8: 388 (447 new record).
Gold Heat #4: 352 (392). Silver Heat #2: 379 (380). Silver Final #2: 368 (371)
National Air Races • Sept. 1980 • Reno • Qual. #14: 353 (422). Silver Heat 1 #6:
350 (381). Silver Heat 2 #5: 346 (378), Silver Finals #6: 326 (364)
National Air Races • Sept. 1981 • Reno with Charlie Beck Qual. #10: 371 (450 new
record). Silver Heat: DNF—engine overheat. Bronze Heat #2: 370 (378).
Silver Final #4: 351 (369)

Appendix

Grace and Style at a Canadian Airport
—Anonymous

Several pilot friends sent me this account by a 12-year-old boy at a Canadian airport in 1967. After reading it many times (I was a boy once), including on the Internet, it finally dawned on me that the Mustang pilot must have been **Bob Love** *(gray, wavy air, old leather jacket) from San Jose, CA. Bob raced with us many times. He was an Ace in the Korean War, 6 kills, flying F-86s. In the chapter on landing gear up at an Abbotsford Air Show, I note that I was flying on Bob's wing at the time. Bob Love passed away from a heart attack while sitting on a couch in his hangar. It was a fitting tribute that this great pilot and his P-51 were together at the end.*

It was noon on a Sunday as I recall, the day a Mustang P-51 was to take to the air. They said it had flown in during the night from some U.S. airport, the pilot was tired. I marveled at the size of the plane dwarfing the Pipers and Canucks tied down near her, it was much larger than in the movies. She glistened in the sun like a bulwark of security from days gone by.

The pilot arrived by cab, paid the driver and then stepped into the flight lounge. He was an older man, his wavy hair was grey and tossed…looked like it might have been combed, say, around the turn of the century. His bomber jacket was checked, creased, and worn, it smelled old and genuine. Old Glory was prominently sewn to its shoulders. He projected a quiet air of proficiency and pride devoid of arrogance.

He filed a quick flight plan to Montreal (Expo–67, Air Show) then walked across the tarmac. After taking several minutes to perform his walk-around check, the pilot returned to the flight lounge to ask if anyone would be available to stand by with fire extinguishers while he "flashed the old bird up…just to be safe."

Though only 12 at the time, I was allowed to stand by with an extinguisher after brief instruction on its use: "If you see a fire, point then pull this lever!" I later became a firefighter, but that's another story.

The air around the exhaust manifolds shimmered like a mirror from fuel fumes as the huge prop started to rotate. One manifold, then another, and yet another barked—I stepped back with the others. In moments the Packard-built Merlin engine came to life with a thunderous roar, blue flames knifed from her manifolds. I looked at the others' faces, there was no concern. I lowered the bell of my extinguisher. One of the guys signaled to walk back to the lounge, we did.

Several minutes later we could hear the pilot doing his preflight run-up. He'd taxied to the end of runway 19, out of sight. All went quiet for several seconds, we raced from the lounge to the second story deck to see if we could catch a glimpse of the P-51 as she started down the runway; we could not. There we stood, eyes fixed to a spot halfway down 19. Then a roar ripped across the field, much louder than before, like a furious hell spawn set loose—something mighty this way was coming.

"Listen to that thing," said the controller.

In seconds, the Mustang burst into our line of sight. Its tail was already off and it was moving faster than anything I'd ever seen by that point on 19. Two-thirds the way down 19 the Mustang was airborne with her gear going up. The prop tips were supersonic; we clasped our ears as the Mustang climbed hellish fast into the circuit to be eaten up by the dog-day haze.

We stood for a few moments in stunned silence trying to digest what we'd just seen. The radio controller rushed by me to the radio. "Kingston radio calling Mustang?" He looked back to us as he waited for an acknowledgment. The radio crackled, "Kingston radio, go ahead."

"Roger Mustang. Kingston radio would like to advise the circuit is clear for a low level pass."

I stood in shock because the controller had, more or less, just asked the pilot to return for an impromptu air show! The controller looked at us. "What?" he asked. "I can't let that guy go without asking...I couldn't forgive myself!"

The radio crackled once again, "Kingston radio, do I have permission for a low-level pass, east to west, across the field?"

"Roger Mustang, the circuit is clear for an east to west pass."

"Roger, Kingston radio, we're coming out of 3,000 feet, stand by."

We rushed back onto the second-story deck, eyes fixed toward the eastern haze. The sound was subtle at first, a high-pitched whine, a muffled screech, a distant scream. Moments later the P-51 burst through the haze...her airframe straining against positive Gs and gravity, wing tips spilling contrails of condensed air, prop-tips again supersonic as the burnished bird blasted across the eastern margin of the field shredding and tearing the air. At about 400 mph and 150 yards from where we stood, she passed with an old American pilot saluting...imagine...a salute. I felt like laughing, I felt like crying. She glistened, she screamed, the building shook, my heart pounded...then the old pilot pulled her up...and rolled, and rolled, and rolled out of sight into the broken clouds and indelibly into my memory.

I've never wanted to be an American more than on that day. It was a time when many nations in the world looked to America as their big brother, a steady and even-handed beacon of security who navigated difficult political water with grace and style; not unlike the pilot who'd just flown into my memory. He was proud, not arrogant, humble, not a braggart, old and honest projecting an aura of America at its best. That America will return one day, I know it will. Until that time, I'll just send off a story; call it a reciprocal salute, to the old American pilot who wove a memory for a young Canadian that's stayed a lifetime.

An Aviation Hero

*A friend, Dr. Robert Cornwell, recently sent me a copy of this **1939 edition of Popular Aviation Magazine**. I was in college at the time, but I can't imagine I did not see it back then—I would have bought and saved it for sure! Even though air racing myself was not even in my imagination, **Roscoe Turner** always was and always will be one of my aviation heroes. The thing that separated him from the other racers at the time like Wittman and Doolittle was that he wore a uniform of riding pants, puttees and a jacket with wings on it plus that jaunty mustache! But now I read that my "Iron-Man hero" had the same pre-race jitters I have had. Also, he did things I did like pull pieces of tape off the panel to count the laps, have sweaty hands (I laced leather thongs around my stick so my hand would not slip off) and worry about his engine breaking down. But he's still my hero!*

—H.K.

Following are some of Roscoe Turner's quotes from *Popular Aviation Magazine*, September 1939.

Comes the fateful morning of the race. A pilot's meeting at noon. Beefs, arguments, threats. "Roscoe," I tell myself, "you've got to come through or you're ruined!" It is 10 minutes before the start. I have just gotten the signal. My ship is ready. The constant-speed propeller is revving slowly. 10 minutes to go. Perspiration soaks me. My hand sweats on the stick. I start watching the instruments I'll use. Cylinder head temperature, Oil temperature, Tachometer, Oil pressure, Supercharger gauge, Fuel pressure. I glance at my chronometer. The hands lie still. It has stopped… No, it runs. Nine minutes. Eight minutes. Seven minutes. Down to one minute. Damn it! I can't control my feet! My leg muscles are making them jump up and down on the pedals. They are my feet—but they are doing things without me telling them what to do. I swear. I swear as those legs keep jittering, as the clock stops, as I think of my debts as I look ahead, fly the course in my mind. Ships to each side of me. I will not be flying my ship alone. I will be flying with nine other stinging, snorting, streaking little hornets. I will fly them because I never know what the other fellow is going to do. And at 345 mph, things happen so fast. Supposing I conk? Supposing I disintegrate? Where on the course will I be? Hell! This can't go on. The flash! The muscles in my legs stop jumping. I am cold and steady, and measuring everything that surrounds the world of my small cockpit in which I am buried so deeply. I slap the throttle wide. The ship sweeps ahead, shooting across the field, faster, faster. At 100 she seems alive, aware of her controls. At 125, she lifts. As she leaves the ground, she jumps ahead like a bullet. The motor revs up. The ship will fly to pieces. I have used low pitch for full ground power. Now with the drag of the wheels on the ground at an end, the motor revs up to 2,800–2,900. I must stop that. I pull the pitch down too low—2,000. I push it up to where I want it—2,600. Trees are wishing by beneath me. All beneath me is a streak. My mind is working like clockwork now. The strips of adhesive are on the dash to be pulled off one by one as I streak past the grandstands onto the course at 300. Nothing matters but those nine other ships, my own speed, my instruments, the landmarks, the ground, the pylons, whether my ship will stay together. Paramount is my motor. It must not suffer. It must not be overworked. My instruments will tell me. I fly slowly at first. That is, a little under 345. With this load of gas, too much speed is apt to tear the wings off. You can't pull up for a bail-out with your wing gone! Racing is an odd thing, I think. If I was up here alone, trying to get speed out of No. 29, I'd listen to

"The race is won. I'm shaking like a leaf. But I hide it with a forced smile..."

that motor and it would scare the pants off me. Here I am fanning out a motor like it's never been fanned before. If Ortman, Wittman and the other boys were not grinding along with me, building up the thrill of competition—the self pride of "I can do better than they can"—I'd throttle back, glide into the field and call it a day. But no, I stiffen my neck for another pylon.

Roscoe Turner was human after all! But he is still my hero.

Roscoe Turner poses with old No. 25 and his newer No. 29. The former is an old Wedell-Williams racer.

Glossary for Non-Pilots

ADF............................. Automatic Direction Finder

DME .... Distance Measuring Equipment

FBO............................ Fixed-Base Operator (for gas, etc.)

mags .... magneto (fires spark plugs)

MP .... manifold pressure (power to prop)

QB.............................. Quiet Birdmen (pilot group)

transponder .... sends radar signal

VOR or Omni............ navigation signal

"Miss America"— Aviation's Goodwill Ambassador
by Larry W. Bledsoe
Originally printed in Private Pilot magazine, February 1999

Miss America, perennial participant in the Reno Air Races nearly every year since 1969, is an air-racing icon. This popular, red-white-and-blue P-51 is everyone's favorite, and she has never disappointed her fans, first with Howie Keefe at the controls and now with Brent Hisey.

What hasn't been said or written about *Miss America*, one of the most famous P-51 Mustangs on the airshow and air-race circuits today? That was the question I asked myself when I started to write this article.

Since her military duties ended, *Miss America* has been raced and flown at airshows by several owners and pilots. She set a world speed record in 1969 by flying 2,289 miles from Los Angeles to Washington, D.C., in six hours and 21 minutes. In 1974, she won the Unlimited Silver Championship at Reno. In 1994, piloted by Alan Preston, she won the Unlimited Gold Championship at Reno with a speed of 425 mph. In 1996, Brent Hisey won the Unlimited Bronze Championship by a mere .28 second— the closest Reno Air Race in years. In 1998, *Miss America* again carried Hisey to victory, this time winning the Unlimited Silver Championship race.

Goodwill Mission

Miss America has a way of touching people's lives in a memorable way. She has been a goodwill ambassador to countless thousands of youngsters for generations. When Howie Keefe was not racing her in the 1970s, he toured airshows and told his crew to let the kids sit in the cockpit and have their pictures taken. Some of those youngsters are today's military and airline pilots.

Brent "Doc" Hisey, present owner of *Miss America*, and his Air Racing Team are continuing that tradition. Hisey dreamed of being a fighter pilot but was turned down by the Air Force for less-than-perfect eyesight. Now, he is a neurosurgeon and a flight surgeon for the Air Force Reserves.

Hisey found *Miss America* retired to a museum; there, she reached out and touched him with her magic. *Miss America* fulfilled his dream of owning and flying a Mustang, and he has been racing her at the Reno Air Races since 1995.

Promotional Efforts

Miss America is arguably the best-known P-51 in the world, thanks to her air-racing fame and the ways she has been promoted over the years. For example, *Miss America*, with Howie Keefe at the controls, won the Reno Unlimited Silver Championship in 1974 and also took third place in the Mojave Gold Race that year.

The model-maker, Cox, was one of *Miss America*'s sponsors. The company produced a gas hand-controlled flying model of her that was a phenomenal success and is now a collector's item. In addition, the Revell Model Company twice produced plastic kits of *Miss America*. A high-quality, collectible diecast model of *Miss America* recently hit the market, as well.

Is it possible for an inanimate object to have a soul? If so, *Miss America* has one. She started out as just another wartime production Mustang; that is, P-51D-30-NA, Mustang serial number 44-74536, built by North American and delivered to the USAAF in 1945.

She did her duty and proudly flew for the United States Air Force and then for the Air National Guard for 11 years. She was stationed at air bases in Louisiana, New Mexico, Texas, Minnesota and Ohio before being sent to the Sacramento Air Material Area at McClellan AFB in August 1956, where she was set aside after years of faithful service to await an ignominious end in a scrap heap.

Different Owners, Different Paint Schemes

As fate would have it, a Texan named Parker came along in February 1958 and purchased *Miss America* for $3,700. Two years later, on December 10, 1960, Donald Singleton handed Parker a cashier's check for $6,000 and became the owner of N5452V. Thus, she was saved by a generous soul and given an opportunity to race. That she did, time and time again, showing the world the true thoroughbred she is.

Don Singleton owned the Mustang but in June 1962, it was registered in the name of Donca Films, Inc., possibly about the time Singleton and actor Carlos Thompson named the Mustang *Lili*, after the actor's wife, Lili Palmer.

Ron Singleton, Don's brother, was one of the first to be touched by *Miss America*'s magic, because he is her most devoted fan. Ron has followed the plane's career over the years and has compiled a complete history of *Miss America* from day one. He was kind enough to share some of his information with me.

Singleton sold the Mustang to David Allender Jr., a PSA pilot, in 1965. Allender raced her that year with race number 19, under the name *Miss San Diego*, and then as *Wayfarers Club Lady* the next year.

Between 1960 and 1969, *Miss America* sported five different paint schemes. Don Singleton stripped the plane to bare metal and added a lightning bolt from the spinner to the canopy. Later, N5452V was painted olive-drab with a light-blue rudder. Next, she was painted all white from nose to tail. Still later, a red stripe was added from nose to tail.

Robert Cleaves and Gene Clay bought the plane in 1966 and changed the "N" number to N991RC. Sometime after that, Cleaves asked Gene Roddenberry (creator of *Star Trek*) to come up with a unique paint scheme. They chose the one that *Miss America* sports today from the submitted designs. Vern Barker, mechanic for several racing planes, did the actual painting.

Howie Keefe, a former U.S. Navy pilot, transferred to Los Angeles as a newspaper executive in 1965. One day, he noticed an SNJ (AT-6) for sale in the *Los Angeles Times* for only $2,000 and bought it. He started flying it to airshows and took it to Reno to watch the air races. The next year, he competed in the T-6 races and was hooked on racing.

Early in 1969, Keefe saw a red-white-and-blue P-51 Mustang sitting in a hangar and asked if it was for sale. The asking price was $25,000—a high price for the time. He bought the plane and promptly named her *Miss America*. With the encouragement of friends, he began making plans to fly in the 1969 Unlimited Air Race at Reno. He changed her race number to 11 and dropped the "C" from the "N" number to make it N991R. The rest, as some would say, is history.

What else can be said about *Miss America*? She is one of a kind, and thanks to the sharing spirit of her owners, I'll always remember her. So will many others.

Index

Boldface page numbers refer to images.